The US Navy and the War in Europe

Among the joys of operating in the North Atlantic was the occasional layer of snow on the flight deck and aircraft, as seen on Ranger *(CV4) at Argentia, April 1943. Four Avengers can be seen nearest the camera, then four Dauntlesses, eight Wildcats and then eleven more Dauntlesses. (NARA)*

The US Navy
and the War in Europe

Robert C. Stern

Seaforth
PUBLISHING

This is dedicated to my lovely, ever-patient wife, Beth, who, once again, put up with my obsessive concentration on events that took place 60-odd years ago, before either of us was born.

First published in Great Britain in 2012 by Seaforth Publishing
An imprint of Pen & Sword Books Ltd
47 Church Street, Barnsley
S Yorkshire S70 2AS

www.seaforthpublishing.com
Email info@seaforthpublishing.com

British Library Cataloguing in Publication Data
A CIP data record for this book is available from the British Library

ISBN 978-1-84832-082-6

Typeset and designed by Palindrome
Printed and bound in Great Britain by the MPG Books Group

Contents

Acknowledgements

A book like this cannot be written without assistance from a great many people. This work is no exception. Many people have helped in ways small and large whose contributions I failed to note. To them I offer my sincerest apologies and gratitude. Those whose help I made the effort to record are listed here:

Captain Jerry Mason, USN (Ret), who created and maintains the U-boat Archive website, both for that site, which is an invaluable resource for anyone interested in the Second World War in the Atlantic, and for his generosity in answering my questions,

Vincent O'Hara, and through him, his friend Enrico Cernuschi, for their help clearing up what happened on dark nights in August 1944 off the southern coast of France and for an advance copy of his article on the Naval Battle of Casablanca,

Richard Worth, for reading over some parts of this book and for supplying much vital information, especially the Mordal account of the Naval Battle of Casablanca,

Dave McComb, who runs the Destroyer History Foundation and its indispensable website, www.destroyerhistory.org,

Rick E. Davis, who helped with photo identification and generally useful information,

Kevin McKernon, for sharing his resources and his firm conviction that *Corry* (DD463) was sunk by German gunfire on 6 June 1944 and not by mining,

Michael Mohl, for permission to use photographs found at the NavSource Naval History site (www.navsource.org), most of which are USN photographs, but some are from private sources, and

More anonymously, but no less importantly, I wish to thank the staffs at the US National Archives, College Park, MD, and the British National Archives, Kew, Richmond, Surrey.

The help of all these fine people was invaluable, but, as always, any mistakes of omission or commission are mine alone.

Photo Credits

Almost all the photographs used in this book were copied by the author from the several imagery sources at the US National Archives. Most are from the US Navy's Second World War photography collections: Record Group (RG) 80, the Bureau of Aeronautics (BuAer) collection, and RG 19, the Bureau of Ships (BuShips) collection. Some were appended to action reports found in the Modern Military Records section, also at the National Archives and Records Administration (NARA) facility in College Park, MD.

The other primary source is the Naval History & Heritage Command (NHHC – formerly the Naval Historical Center), the US Navy's repository of all Second World War photography not at NARA.

The few photos that are not from NARA or NHHC are credited as appropriate. If a photo has no credit, it simply means I failed to record or have lost the record of the source of the photo. I apologize to any who are thus unacknowledged by my sometimes poor record-keeping.

Introduction

When 1918 had drawn to a close, the world may have finally seemed well ordered from the perspective of the victorious Allies, but there were already dangerous currents at work that would see Europe engulfed in war again in barely 20 years. Unfortunately for the European Allies, the forces available to meet the threat of a resurgent and rearmed Germany, backed by Fascist Italy, were in no way comparable to those they had wielded in 1914, much less 1918. Russia was no longer an ally; indeed, it signed a non-aggression pact with Nazi Germany a week before the new war began. France was still suffering physically and psychologically from the bloodletting required to win in 1918. Great Britain no longer possessed the dominant navy it had in 1918 and its army or air forces, even when combined with the French, could not match the size or equipment of the German *Wehrmacht*.

By the summer of 1918, with the crucial addition of America's fresh armies, the Allies finally had the strength to win the land war in France. The US contribution to winning the naval war against Germany was far less decisive.[*] The unrestricted U-boat campaign that began in February 1917 took a terrible toll of the shipping on which Great Britain depended, but the Royal Navy was able to prevail in 1918 with little help from the Americans. When war broke out again in 1939, the Royal Navy was far less prepared to meet the challenge, in particular lacking the escort ships needed to defeat a U-boat campaign that was for all intents unrestricted from the first day of the war. There would be no immediate help from the Americans, who appeared content to let the Europeans sort out their petty squabbles.

War, by its very nature, spawns mythology, whether in victory or defeat. These myths come in many forms, all the way from the 'stab in the back' story believed by right-wing groups in Germany after the First World War to the firm belief by US Isolationists of the 1920s and 1930s that US involvement in that war had been a costly and unnecessary mistake. Polling numbers revealed the strength of this belief among Americans. (In 1937, when Europe appeared poised on the

---

[*] Smith, *World War I at Sea.*

brink of another war, a Gallup Poll found that 94 per cent favored staying out of a foreign war over acting to prevent it.[*] Most Americans consistently described themselves as being opposed to involvement in a war in Europe, but at the same time a solid majority felt that the US should be aiding Great Britain in every way short of war, even if that meant putting US sailors in harm's way.)

All that changed dramatically on 7 December 1941. As the sun rose on a still peaceful Sunday morning, the vast majority of Americans had no idea that in a few brief hours, Isolationist or not, they would be at war. When war came to Pearl Harbor just before 8.00 a.m. local time, it was already lunchtime or later where most Americans lived. Famously, the news interrupted a radio broadcast of a professional football game in New York City at 2.26 p.m. EST.[†] In England, the news came after dinner as Prime Minister Winston S. Churchill was at Chequers, the British Prime Ministers' country retreat north-west of London. With him was a pair of frequent guests, the American Ambassador John Gilbert 'Gil' Winant and the 'expediter' for American Lend-Lease aid, W. Averell Harriman. The three were at the dining-room table, presumably enjoying a post-prandial cigar, with the 9.00 p.m. radio news in the background.[‡] After going through some communiqués about the fighting in Russia and in Libya, the newsreader added, almost in passing, that there was breaking news of Japanese attacks on British shipping in the East Indies and on naval vessels at Pearl Harbor. Initially, there was some confusion among the listeners at Chequers as to whether the announcer had said Pearl Harbor or Pearl River, the waterway that connects Canton (Guangzhou) to Hong Kong, but this was quickly cleared up and Churchill put through a phone call to the American President, Franklin Delano Roosevelt (FDR). The President cleared up any doubt: 'It's quite true. They've attacked us at Pearl Harbor. We are all in the same boat now.'

The average American reacted to the news of the Pearl Harbor attack with a mixture of sorrow, shock and anger. Even FDR, well informed by naval intelligence that the Japanese were moving troops and warships on a massive scale in the Pacific, was shocked at where and how they had attacked, and especially at how serious the damage had been.[§] The reaction at Chequers was described as having 'been delivered from a long pain'.[¶] Less diplomatic observers stated that Churchill and Winant 'sort of danced around the room'. Years after the event, Churchill's description cannot hide the satisfaction of the moment:

> No American will think it wrong of me if I proclaim that to have the United States at our side was to me the greatest joy . . . at this very moment I knew

---

[*]   Sage, *Background to World War II.*

[†]   Widner, *The Bombing of Pearl Harbor.*

[‡]   Churchill, *The Second World War: The Grand Alliance*, pp. 604–7; Olson, *Citizens of London*, pp. 142–4.

[§]   For Roosevelt's reaction to the news of the Pearl Harbor attack, cf. Olson, *loc. cit.*, p. 145.

[¶]   Churchill, *The Second World War: The Grand Alliance*, p. 605.

the United States was in the war, up to the neck and in to the death. So we had won after all! . . . How long the war would last or in what fashion it would end, no man could tell, nor did I at this moment care . . . Hitler's fate was sealed. Mussolini's fate was sealed. As for the Japanese, they would be ground to powder.[*]

Yet another myth was spawned that day, that the US had been a country at peace and only after Pearl Harbor became involved in the Second World War. One of the primary purposes of this book is to address this persistent misconception, to tell the story of US naval operations in the European theater, not just from when the US officially joined the war, but from their very beginning. Unbeknownst to all but a few Americans at the time (and since), US involvement in the war had been going on for more than two years prior to that fateful Sunday morning.

Even if the effort expended by the Americans to win the naval war against the European Axis seems small compared to the lavish investment of men and materiel poured into the Pacific, it was not for lack of commitment to the fight. Even before the US was officially in the war, the American President had met face-to-face with his British counterpart and, before that, the military staffs of the two nations held a series of meetings beginning in January 1941 to co-ordinate strategies. The most important, most basic, decision to result from these talks was the commitment by the US to pursue the defeat of Germany first, even if, as expected, the Japanese attacked in the Pacific. It says a great deal about the determination of the Americans to maintain their commitments, that this pledge was not forgotten in the emotional aftermath of the Pearl Harbor attack.

— —

A major theme of this book will be the interplay between the strong personalities running the European war. Unlike the campaign in the Pacific, the war in the waters around Europe was one that required co-operation with an equal partner. At the beginning, at least, that relationship was far from smooth, with the British believing that the experience they had gained, and the price they had paid to gain it, demanded more respect than the upstart Yankees seemed prepared to give. That relationship changed as the tide of war changed, but remained one based on co-operation between people who did not always like or trust each other.

At the top were Churchill and FDR. The unique make-up of the British Prime Minister, who simply would not allow Great Britain to fail, and the American President, who saw beyond the narrow horizons of so many of his countrymen, set the tone for the relationship. Both men had earlier in their careers been in leading positions in their respective navies – Churchill as First Lord of the

---

[*] Ibid, p. 607.

Introduction

Admiralty and FDR as Assistant Secretary of the Navy. They shared a world-view that included understanding the critical importance of sea control to the outcome of the war. Both were experienced politically and unquestionably committed to the survival of Western-style democracy in the face of an all-out assault.

Despite these two strong personalities having much in common, their relationship was not always easy. This was in part due to very different personal styles. Churchill was at root an aristocrat, a man who could endure more than a decade in the political wilderness between the wars because he never doubted himself. When he became Prime Minister on 10 May 1940, he created and took the position of Minister of Defence, making him the direct superior of the three service ministers, allowing him to control Great Britain's military activities to an unprecedented extent.* It is safe to say that very little of the strategic and even tactical direction of the war did not pass before Churchill's eyes.

Roosevelt was, in many ways, as aristocratic as Churchill, coming from the political and economic elite in American society, but successfully recast himself as a populist who was able to ride a wave of lower- and middle-class support to four successive Presidential victories. To a much greater extent than Churchill, he turned the day-to-day direction of the war over to his main military commanders – Admiral Ernest J. King and General George C. Marshall.

The personality of Admiral King, FDR's naval chief, will also play a large part in this story. He was promoted to the rank of full admiral in February 1941 and, on 30 December 1941 took over as Commander-in-Chief, US Fleet (CINCUS). Less than three months later, he also took the position of Chief of Naval Operations (CNO), thus holding the highest administrative and operational billets in the US Navy at the same time.† King had a notoriously prickly personality. A famous quote, generally attributed to his daughter, is that, 'He is the most even-tempered man in the Navy. He is always in a rage.'‡ He is often described as being an Anglophobe, but his actions in a position which put a premium on co-operation with the Royal Navy seem to contradict such a claim. The question of how much the US Navy could have and should have learned from Royal Navy experience is one of the themes of the following pages.

This book, then, is an attempt to tell the story of the US Navy's involvement

---

* The service ministers in His Majesty's Government were the Secretary of State for War, the Secretary of State for Air and the First Lord of the Admiralty. That last office was distinct from the position of First Sea Lord of the Admiralty which was the highest military posting in the RN, equivalent at the time to the USN's Chief of Naval Operations (CNO).
† The post of CINCUS was abolished at the end of the war, leaving the current US naval structure, with the post of CNO being the highest military command in the Navy.
‡ Gannon, Operation DRUMBEAT, pp. 169, 171. Winton, ULTRA at Sea, p. 66, gives an almost identical quote to describe Sir Dudley Pound. Another famous King quote is his purported statement when appointed CINCUS, that, 'When they get in trouble, they send for the sons-of-bitches.' When asked later if he had ever said that, he replied that he had not, but would have if he had thought of it.

in the war in Europe against Germany, Italy and their allies. It was a war almost entirely without the big, set-piece battles that characterized the war in the Pacific. It should not, however, be concluded that because this war lacked headline-grabbing engagements, that it lacked events of interest and moments of high drama. From the little-known series of pre-war 'incidents' that marked the steady progress of the US towards active belligerency, to the long drawn-out battle to control the Atlantic, and finally to the massive invasion armadas that carried and supplied the armies that ultimately destroyed the Axis, the US Navy's involvement will be recounted here through description of those moments of action, without forgetting the crucial part played by those who sailed day after day under leaden skies across an unforgiving sea. It was fought with only a small percentage of the big, new ships being built in such numbers by American shipyards. Rather, it was mainly fought by men in older and smaller ships, in generally less benign conditions than in the Pacific. But, the men who fought it had no less at stake than their counterparts halfway around the world.

Note on nomenclature and units

This war was fought primarily by Allies who spoke the same language, but could not agree on how to spell such basic words as 'defense' and 'armor'. I have used the American spelling of such words throughout except when quoting a British source. US warships almost always kept local time, unlike German U-boats, for example, that kept Central European Time (CET) regardless of location. In reporting the time and date of events in this book, I use local time whenever possible. When mentioning a warship for the first time, I give its official designator in parentheses. For US warships, that is its hull number; for Royal Navy ships, the pennant number; for U-boats, I give the last name of its commander, by which it was often referenced in Kriegsmarine communications (e.g. *U123* would be addressed as *U-Hardegen*). Place names are those that would have been used by an educated English-speaker in the 1940s. Where those differ from the current name or spelling of a place, I give that current version when first mentioned.

Distances over water are given in feet (12 in = 304.8 mm, abbreviated 'ft'), yards (3 ft = /0.9144m, abbreviated 'yd', 'yds') and nautical miles (2,025.37 yd = 1.853 km, abbreviated 'nm'). Distances over land are given in statute miles (1,760 yd = /1.609 km). These are the units used by American seamen in the 1940s and remain in use in America and, to a lesser extent, Great Britain. Gun calibers are given in the system used by the nation to which a ship belonged.

List of Abbreviations

The abbreviations used in this book are those used by US military personnel of the era, unless noted otherwise.

AA	Anti-Aircraft
AD	Armored Division
ASW	Anti-Submarine Warfare
ATS	Army Transport Service
BDE	British Destroyer Escort
CAP	Combat Air Patrol
CIC	Combat Information Center (American); Commander-in-Chief (British)
CINC	Commander-in-Chief (American)
CINCUS	Commander-in-Chief, US Fleet
CNO	Chief of Naval Operations
CO	Commanding Officer
CTF	Commander, TF
CTG	Commander, TG
CTU	Commander, TU
EG	Escort Group (British)
ESF	Eastern Sea Frontier
FG	USAAF Fighter Group
FS	USAAF Fighter Squadron
GC&CS	Government Code & Cypher School – British signals intelligence unit based at Bletchley Park
ID	Infantry Division
LI	*Leitender Ingenieur* (German) – Engineering Officer on a U-boat
OOD	Officer of the Deck
PC	173-foot Patrol Craft
PG	USAAC/F Pursuit Group
PS	USAAC/F Pursuit Squadron
RCT	Regimental Combat Team
RN	Royal Navy
SC	110-foot Submarine Chaser
TF	Task Force
TG	Task Group – sub-unit of a TF
TU	Task Unit – sub-unit of a TG
USAAC	US Army Air Corps
USAAF	US Army Air Force (after 9 March 1942)
USN	US Navy
VB	Bomber Aircraft
VF	Fighter Aircraft
XO	Executive Officer

1

A 'Queer Idea of Neutrality'
September 1939–November 1940*

In the almost exactly 20 years that elapsed between the Treaty of Versailles, with its fervent hopes for future tranquility, and the outbreak of the Second World War, there had in fact been very little peace. In the immediate aftermath of Versailles, small wars had been fought almost continuously, mainly in the unsettled regions of the former Hapsburg and Russian Empires arbitrarily divided into independent states. But in the main this brief interval between major wars saw the rise of single-party states with highly centralized governments. A common feature of all these states was a strong nationalistic ideology to bind the population, often by identifying political, economic or racial enemies, internal or external, which would require unity to defeat – hence the rise in the early 1920s of Stalinist Russia and Fascist Italy. Though diametrically opposed in economic philosophies, both established dictatorships that served as a model for a second wave of national-socialist states that combined nationalism, sometimes associated with religion, and a form of state-socialism that gave the government, as a proxy for the working class, ultimate control (but not necessarily ownership) of production. The most famous of these national-socialist states was Nazi Germany, which came into existence in 1933. In that same year, the Estado Novo under Salazar was set up in Portugal and a year later, Dollfuß took leadership of Austria at the head of a Fascist (but anti-Nazi) state. In 1936, in another step in what appeared to be an unstoppable movement, the Nationalist uprising in Spain very nearly toppled the elected Republican government. The incomplete success of the Nationalists' initial coup led to a lengthy and bloody civil war that lasted into 1939. In the face of blatant intervention by Germany, Italy and Soviet Russia, the remaining Allied democracies in Europe, now reduced to Great Britain and France, protested loudly, but did nothing. Encouraged by this inaction, Hitler progressively renounced the restrictions imposed by the

---

* Cressman, *The Official Chronology*, p. 353, note 13. The quotation is attributed to RAN Captain H. B. Farncomb, commanding HMAS *Perth* (D29), which was being shadowed by US heavy cruiser *Vincennes* (CA44) on 14 December 1939. Farncomb reportedly commented: 'Queer idea of neutrality these Americans have!'

Versailles Treaty and occupied, in rapid succession, Austria (March 1938), the Sudetenland (September 1938) and Bohemia, Moravia and the Memel Strip (March 1939). When, in the late summer of 1939, he turned to Poland, which, like Czechoslovakia, was dubiously protected by Anglo-French 'guarantees', he undoubtedly expected the Allies to back down again. When they did not, general war returned to Europe.

This long series of crises and disasters was watched mainly with incredulity on the other side of the Atlantic. President Woodrow Wilson had proposed a League of Nations to mediate conflicts and his ideas had been largely incorporated into the Versailles Treaty, but the US Senate had refused to ratify the treaty. More to the taste of the Americans was the Kellogg–Briand Pact of 1928, which prohibited the use of war as state policy except in self-defense, but included no means to sanction signatories who violated its provisions. It was a grand statement of principles with no attached obligations, which suited the spirit of Americans at the time.

It is against this background that news of the outbreak of war between Great Britain, France and Germany came to America on 3 September 1939. The first reaction by the United States came the next day, when CNO, Admiral Harold R. 'Betty' Stark, issued orders to the Commander, Atlantic Squadron, Rear-Admiral Alfred W. Johnson, to institute an air and sea patrol in an area bounded in the north by the latitude of Boston, MA, and in the east by the 65th meridian, running as far south as the US Virgin Islands. The boundary then swung east and south around the Windward and Leeward Islands to include Trinidad. Almost the entire eastern seaboard of the US and the entire Caribbean and Gulf of Mexico were to be included in the patrol zone.

The Atlantic Squadron had been formed in September 1938 at the specific request of the President. Prior to this, the only organized US naval forces in the Atlantic were a division of old battleships – the youngest of which was *Texas* (BB35) launched in 1912 – and three divisions of only slightly younger destroyers. This was known as the Training Detachment, and, as its name implied, was not in any manner a fighting command. Most of the US Navy's assets were organized into the Scouting Force and Battle Force, both based on the West Coast.

The new Atlantic Squadron initially comprised 14 ships separate from the Training Detachment: two divisions of brand-new *Brooklyn*-class light cruisers and seven equally new destroyers. This force probably never acted as a coherent entity. Its ships were in some cases so new that they had yet to take their shakedown cruise.[*]

In another nod towards the crisis building in Europe, the Navy's annual Fleet Problem (a fleet-wide training exercise designed around a possible wartime scenario) was in February 1939 held in the Atlantic for the first time since 1931.[†]

---

[*] Abbazia, *Mr. Roosevelt's Navy*, pp. 30–1.

[†] Ibid., pp. 33–50.

At the end of this exercise, the plan had been for the entire fleet to remain in the Atlantic for the opening of the New York World's Fair at the end of April, but renewed Japanese aggression in China caused most of the Pacific-based ships to return before then. When they departed, they took the two divisions of light cruisers and their destroyers with them, but, at FDR's insistence, left behind the aircraft carrier *Ranger* (CV4), a division of five heavy cruisers and a mixed division of four new destroyers – two big *Somers*-class leaders and two smaller *Benham*-class destroyers – leaving the Atlantic Squadron stronger than before.

Another important legacy of this exercise was the realization that the US needed bases in the West Indies if it intended to defend the Caribbean and the Gulf of Mexico. The only US naval bases in the region were Guantanamo Bay, Cuba, and San Juan, Puerto Rico, and both were merely fueling stations with little in the way of repair facilities. Vice-Admiral Adolphus 'Dolly' Andrews in his post-exercise report stated specifically that these two bases needed to be developed rapidly and others identified. In particular, bases at Bermuda and Trinidad, both British possessions, were recommended.

The final lesson drawn from Fleet Problem XX was the realization that there could never be too many destroyers available for the long list of tasks thrown their way. By the beginning of September 1939, orders had gone out to recondition and recommission 36 mothballed flush-deckers. They were supposed to be ready the first week in October, but shortages of equipment and crews meant that some of this first batch would not join the fleet until mid-December.[*]

These were destroyers that had been mass-produced during and immediately after the First World War. Three classes totaling 273 ships had been laid down, almost all of them completed after the Armistice, some as late as 1921. They earned the name flush-deckers because, instead of the raised forecastle which had characterized earlier American destroyers, they had an unbroken weather deck.[†] This gave them more freeboard amidships and was supposed to make them drier and more stable. With a variety of different machinery arrangements, they varied greatly in endurance. By 1939, 102 of them had either been lost in accidents – in one spectacular event, in September 1923, seven were lost running aground in fog near Santa Barbara, CA – or stricken. Many of the remainder were surplus to the peacetime needs of the US Navy, and had been mothballed, meaning they were laid up and sealed as well as possible against corrosion.[‡]

At the end of September 1939, Rear-Admiral Johnson was replaced in

---

[*] Ibid., pp. 64–5.

[†] They were also sometimes called 'four-pipers', because almost all of them were built with four funnels.

[‡] For purposes of this narrative, any US Navy destroyer built after construction of destroyers began again in 1932, with the laying down of *Farragut* (DD348), is described as new to distinguish it from the older flush-deckers. US destroyer development progressed rapidly, through eight intervening designs between the *Farragut*s and the *Benson* and *Gleaves* classes being built in 1939.

Not yet officially part of the US Navy, the Coast Guard cutter Campbell *(WPG32) was deployed as part of the Grand Banks Patrol in October 1939. She still wears the peacetime livery of white hull and superstructure, tan funnel with a black band at the top. (USCG)*

command of Atlantic Squadron by Rear-Admiral Hayne Ellis. The force Ellis took over had four old battleships, *Ranger*, five heavy cruisers and ten divisions of destroyers. One division comprised the four new destroyers that came from the Pacific for the Fleet Problem; all of the rest were flush-deckers.

Anyone looking seriously at the state of the American military at the beginning of September 1939 had to conclude that the United States was thoroughly unprepared to fight a war of the scale and intensity that had begun in Europe. The US Army had fallen to 175,000 men, almost none of them in motorized units. (To put that number in perspective, the army with which Poland met the German invasion in 1939 was more than five times as large.) The US Navy was in no better shape. The force level report for the end of June 1939 showed 394 ships. Excluding submarines, mine warfare ships, patrol vessels and auxiliaries, the US Navy totaled 178 warships, with most of that total based on the West Coast.[*]

The first assets of the Neutrality Patrol were deployed on 14 September. By this time the patrol had been extended to the north; the division of new destroyers was assigned to patrol between Halifax, Nova Scotia and Placentia Bay, Newfoundland, the so-called Grand Banks Patrol. The experience of these ships, among the newest and best destroyers in the fleet, proved a cautionary tale. The weather south of Newfoundland is generally stormy, particularly with the approach of winter, and the smaller pair of destroyers, *Benham* (DD397) and *Ellet* (DD398), both suffered badly, with cracks appearing in their shell plating

---

[*]   *U.S. Navy Active Ship Force Levels, 1917–Present* (www.history.navy.mil).

Patrol aircraft, such as this Catalina, were used extensively to enforce the Neutrality Patrol. These are PBY-5As, a model that went into production late in 1941, and carry early war markings including the red-and-white rudder stripes and the large nose roundel, which aircraft assigned to the Neutrality Patrol were ordered to carry in March 1940. The presence of ASV radar antennas under the wings confirms that this image was made in 1942, but not too late in the year, as the display of rudder stripes and the red center of the roundel was discontinued in May. (NARA)

and numerous minor equipment failures. The larger destroyer leaders, *Davis* (DD395) and *Jouett* (DD396), survived the rough seas in much better shape.[*] Until a sufficient number of new, large destroyers could be deployed, the Navy turned to the US Coast Guard, which had a recently built seven-ship class of large cutters that were designed to survive just this kind of weather. Several of the Secretary-class cutters were assigned to the Grand Banks Patrol, starting with *Campbell* (WPG32) on 2 October 1939.[†]

On 5 September, President Roosevelt declared US neutrality in regard to the European conflict, as required by the Neutrality Act of 1937. The most important section of the law was Section 1 (a), which read:

> Whenever the President shall find that there exists a state of war between, or among, two foreign states the President shall proclaim such fact, and, it shall thereafter be unlawful to export, or attempt to export, or cause to be exported arms, ammunition or implements of war found any place in the United States to any belligerent state named in such proclamation . . .[‡]

---

[*]   Abbazia, *Mr. Roosevelt's Navy*, p. 66. These facts were not lost on the designers working on the next-generation of US destroyers, the *Fletcher* class that emerged 300 t larger than the *Somers*-class leaders.

[†]   *Cutters, Craft & Coast Guard-manned Army & Navy Vessels* (www.uscg.mil).

[‡]   Sect. 1 (a), Neutrality Act of 1937.

On 9 October 1939, the German 'pocket-battleship' Deutschland stopped the American steamer City of Flint, inspected her papers and seized the ship because she was supposedly carrying contraband to Great Britain. This began a month-long odyssey for the Hog Islander, which led her to Norway, Russia, Norway again and finally back to the US. (NHHS)

As if that was not sweeping enough, the act allowed the President to extend the embargo beyond war materials and added penalties for the use of any American vessel to carry any prohibited materials to a belligerent state.[*] The net effect of these provisions was to establish an absolute embargo on the sale of arms to the European belligerents and to discourage (though not yet prohibit) US-flag ships from trading in any way with those states.[†]

At the same time, FDR announced the existence of the Neutrality Zone ordered by Admiral Stark, and stated that hostile operations within the zone would be considered by the United States to be an 'unfriendly act'. Admiral Stark ordered all vessels involved in the Neutrality Patrol to report the position of any belligerent warships, but to do so in code and only when no longer in contact with the warship in question. Patrol aircraft were ordered to identify any suspicious vessels by name, nationality, estimated tonnage, color and markings, and, if possible, to photograph the vessel, but to make no report by radio, reporting contacts only on return to base.[‡] This was to avoid even the appearance of aiding one side or the other.

It did not take long for incidents to occur that would put that resolve to the test. At first, the Americans had more complaints against the British than any of the other combatants, because the Royal Navy's effective control of the waters around Europe allowed the British to rapidly round up all German

---

[*] Sect. 2 (a) and Sect. 6, Neutrality Act of 1937.

[†] Bailey and Ryan, *Hitler vs. Roosevelt*, pp. 33–4.

[‡] Scarborough, *The Neutrality Patrol*, p. 19.

At the end of the cruise that featured the capture of City of Flint *and the sinking of two other ships,* Deutschland *returned safely to Germany, much to the relief of the Germans. Her sister* Admiral Graf Spee *had not survived a concurrent commerce-raiding voyage. To prevent the propaganda coup that would result from the sinking of a vessel named after Germany, her name was officially changed to* Lützow *on 15 November. (NARA)*

shipping, netting the occasional neutral in the process. On 5 September, the US-registered *Black Osprey*, headed for neutral Rotterdam, was ordered into Weymouth for contraband inspection, but was later released. On 7 September, the passenger liner *Santa Paula* was stopped by a Royal Navy cruiser near Curaçao and required to assert there were no German passengers aboard before being allowed to proceed. Incidents like this initially strained Anglo-American relations, but they decreased as US trade with Europe rapidly declined.

On the other hand, tensions with the Germans started very slowly, but mounted steadily. The first serious incident began on 9 October when the German 'pocket battleship' *Deutschland* stopped the Hog Islander *City of Flint* in the North Atlantic en route from New York to the UK with a cargo of tractors, grain and fruit.* She was stopped and her manifest examined by the German raider. Her cargo was declared to be contraband and the ship was seized and taken as a prize of war, her crew imprisoned on board. She put in

---

* Bailey and Ryan, *Hitler vs. Roosevelt*, pp. 59–63. 'Hog Islanders' were cargo/transport ships built to standard designs for the US Shipping Board, a government agency established in 1916. A shipyard was established at Hog Island, PA, hence the name given to the ships built there. None were completed before the war ended, but most of the ships originally ordered were launched, 122 hulls by early 1921, and they served as the backbone of the US merchant marine in the interwar years.

at Tromsø, Norway on 20 October, seeking provisions and navigational charts. The Norwegians, still neutral, provided only food and water, giving them 24 hours to leave. Escorted out of Norwegian waters the next day, the ship headed north to Murmansk, where she put in on the 23rd, seeking entry to repair storm damage. The Russians were put in an awkward spot by this, because, while safe haven to repair a damaged ship is a well-recognized right of seafarers, it does not apply to combatants, and *City of Flint*, as a prize of war, was a combatant by every normal definition. The Russians waffled, initially interning the German prize crew, but, at the same time, refusing to release the original crew. Finally, the Russians resolved the problem by returning the ship to the prize crew and ordering them to leave. On 3 November, attempting to slip through the Royal Navy blockade by hugging the Norwegian coast, she was eventually detected and entered Haugesund rather than risk capture. At Haugesund, she was boarded by a party from the Norwegian minelayer *Olav Tryggvason*, the American crew was released and the ship returned to their control. Their German captors were interned, though presumably were freed when Norway fell to the Germans the following May. *City of Flint* proceeded to Bergen, where her cargo was unloaded. On 14 November, she left there in ballast for the US.

One side-effect of this incident was an increase in the re-registration of US-owned merchant ships under other 'flags of convenience', most notably in Panama. The trend toward registering US-owned ships in other countries had gotten started before the war as a ploy to get around the higher tax rates and labor costs associated with US-flag ships. As expected, the US government discouraged this, as it reduced tax revenues. However, the realization that US registration offered no protection against seizure caused a change of heart not only among shipowners, but also at the highest levels of the government.

—‒—

Roosevelt knew he could not openly challenge the nation's strict neutrality, but he nevertheless wanted trade to resume between the US and Europe, which, given the reality of the Allied blockade, meant between the US and her former Allies – Great Britain and France. In fact, it is clear from a number of FDR's actions from the beginning of the European war, that he, personally, was never neutral. On 11 September he initiated a correspondence with Winston Churchill that would allow the two men a unique avenue of direct and often candid communication. Over the course of several hundred letters over nearly six years, the two developed a close relationship that was sometimes mistaken for friendship. However, neither man was ever able to forget that he represented a major nation with war aims and post-war expectations that may have been parallel but were by no means identical.

Roosevelt's first letter to Churchill, who was again appointed First Lord of the Admiralty on 3 September 1939, was certainly friendly enough.

It is because you and I occupied similar positions in the World War that I want you to know how glad I am that you are back again at the Admiralty . . . What I want you and the Prime Minister to know is that I shall at all times welcome it if you will keep me in touch personally with anything you want me to know about . . .[*]

The intimate tone of this letter is unusual. It is not standard protocol for the head of one nation to make such an offer of personal communication to someone in the government of another nation, unless he is the head of that nation or is a close personal friend. Churchill was neither.

In fact, the two men, while not total strangers, had only met once before. Their recollections of that meeting differed greatly (and characteristically). Roosevelt had been on a fact-finding mission to London in July 1918. He was a still-athletic 36-year-old that some considered ill-equipped by intellect or temperament for the post he then occupied: Assistant Secretary of the US Navy.[†] On the night of 29 July he attended a ceremonial dinner at Gray's Inn also attended by Churchill. According to Churchill, he had been struck by Roosevelt's 'magnificent presence in all his youth and strength'.[‡] FDR, on the other hand, remembered being brushed aside by Churchill, who, as usual, dominated the evening's conversation. Years later, Roosevelt remembered the perceived snub quite clearly, while Churchill had to be reminded that he had previously met the President. Despite his low opinion of Churchill's earlier behavior, Roosevelt knew his record of opposition to appeasement and saw in him a man who shared his uncompromising hatred of Fascism.[§]

Roosevelt's bias in favor of the Allied side was evident in many of the decisions made in the early months of the European war. On 21 September, he sent a message to Congress formally asking that the arms embargo provisions of the Neutrality Act be altered to allow belligerents to purchase armament in the United States, as long as they paid for them in advance and carried them on their own ships, a policy that became known as 'Cash and Carry'. With that change, the Neutrality Act of 1939 passed Congress on 4 November. While seemingly even-handed, the simple fact was that only the Allies were able to avail themselves of this relaxation of the embargo.

In a similar vein, on 9 October, Roosevelt ordered the Neutrality Patrol

---

[*]   *Map Room File*, 11 Sept 39, FDR->WSC, unnumbered.

[†]   Olson, *Citizens of London*, pp. 9–10.

[‡]   Churchill, *The Second World War: The Gathering Storm*, p. 440. Roosevelt was not struck by the disease that paralyzed his legs until 1921. Diagnosed at the time as poliomyelitis, it is now considered more likely to have been Guillain-Barré Syndrome, an autoimmune disorder of the peripheral nervous system.

[§]   Olson, *loc. cit.*, pp. 29–36. There is no question that Churchill thought the relationship more intimate than FDR did, and was personally hurt when Roosevelt distanced himself after 1942.

9

The liner Columbus *was briefly the flagship of the German merchant fleet during the 1920s, but was soon supplanted by newer passenger ships. By the late 1930s, she had been relegated to cruising the Caribbean during the winter months. She was caught on such a cruise at the outbreak of war. Trapped in a Mexican port, she made an attempt to escape back to Germany starting on 14 December. Trailed by US Navy warships, she scuttled herself rather than be captured when a Royal Navy warship approached five days later. (BAK)*

strengthened, even if that meant transferring ships from the Pacific. Also, he ordered that henceforth contacts made by ships or aircraft of the US Neutrality Patrol were to radioed immediately and in plain language. Because such plain language reporting would be in English, these changes obviously favored British merchant shipping, which could change course away from a contact, and the Royal Navy, which could send warships toward the contact.[*]

The active involvement of the US Navy in the European war began in December 1939, with the pursuit and eventual sinking of the German passenger liner *Columbus*. When she entered service with Norddeutscher Lloyd in 1924, she was the largest and fastest German ocean liner in an age when national prestige was measured in part by the speed and luxury of a nation's transatlantic steamers. *Columbus* was soon surpassed and by 1939 was used mainly as a cruise liner in the Caribbean. She was on such a cruise when the outbreak of war caught her at Barbados. After a failed attempt to fill her fuel bunkers at Curaçao, where she had been shadowed by the light cruiser HMS *Orion* (85), she headed for Havana. After dropping off her passengers, she headed across

---

[*]   Petrie, *American Neutrality*, p. 71.

The heavy cruiser Vincennes *(CA44), shown in her pre-war livery of overall light gray, was dispatched in late May 1940 to retrieve the French and Belgian gold reserves, which were in danger of falling into German hands. An estimated 200 tons was loaded at Casablanca on 9 June and carried to safe keeping at the Federal Reserve Bank in New York. (NARA)*

the Gulf to Veracruz, Mexico. *Columbus* was soon joined there by the small freighter *Arauca*.

Well aware of the location of the two valuable prizes, the Royal Navy had several warships, most notable the Australian light cruiser HMAS *Perth* (D29), patrolling the Gulf of Mexico. The US Navy, true to its official position of neutrality, closely shadowed the Royal Navy warships with a force comprising the heavy cruiser *Vincennes* (CA44) and two destroyers, while, at the same time, maintaining a close watch on Veracruz. There things stood for more than three months. Although ordered to return to Germany at the end of October, *Columbus*'s captain and crew knew the likely outcome of such an attempt, and took their time preparing the ship.

The Germans developed a plan to trick the covering forces. When both ships were ready for sea on 14 December, *Arauca* left port first, heading north-eastward into the Gulf in the hope that the Americans would follow. Several hours later, *Columbus* sailed, but the destroyers *Benham* and *Lang* (DD399) had not taken the bait, and they were waiting for the liner when she appeared. The Americans in no way interfered with *Columbus*, but they trailed her closely, regularly broadcasting her position. This steady trail of the liner by US Navy destroyers continued for five days as she made her way through the Florida Strait and out into the Atlantic. In the meanwhile, several more American destroyers searched for and eventually located *Arauca* as she made her way more slowly along the same track. On 19 December with *Tuscaloosa* (CA37) shadowing *Columbus* despite the fact that she was now well outside the Pan-American Security Zone, the destroyer HMS *Hyperion* (H97) closed the liner and ordered her to stop. Rather than be captured, the crew of *Columbus* started fires, set off scuttling charges and efficiently abandoned ship, leaving the liner burning fiercely. The

576 survivors, including nine women, were rescued by *Tuscaloosa*; only two of the crew were unaccounted for.[*]

Arauca, if anything, had a more interesting time of it. She was intercepted off Miami, FL, by HMS *Orion*, which fired a shot across her bow in an attempt to force her to heave to. However, *Arauca* was already in US territorial waters and, shepherded by the destroyer *Philip* (DD76), she found refuge in Port Everglades. The incident caused a strong protest by the US, which claimed that *Orion*'s act in US waters was a breach of international law. *Arauca* remained interned at the Florida port, proudly flying the Nazi flag but unable to leave, until she was seized by the US Navy on 20 April 1942. She served through the rest of the war as *Saturn* (AK49, later AF20).

After this flurry of activity, the Neutrality Patrol returned to the routine business of watching the US eastern seaboard. While the Phony War continued in Europe, the only belligerent activity in the Atlantic was the steady toll of shipping taken by the small number of U-boats then in service, all of which were operating well to the east of the Pan-American Security Zone.[†] Nevertheless, the United States continued to act increasingly in ways that aided the Allied side in the European war. On 22 December, the US Maritime Commission issued a directive to all US merchant shipping to avoid any mention in radio traffic of the presence of any other shipping in the vicinity, particularly information concerning the presence and course of convoys.[‡] The definition of neutrality as understood by the United States was evolving rapidly.

Following the capitulation of Denmark on 9 April 1941, that nation's several overseas possessions were without political leadership or military protection. The most strategically important of those was Greenland, the southern tip of which – Cape Farewell – lay within easy range of the northerly route followed by convoys between Canada and Great Britain. The other reason for interest in Greenland was a cryolite mine at the town of Ivigtut (Ivittuut), on the west coast near the southern cape. (Cryolite was used as a flux in the refining of bauxite to make aluminum.) On 3 May 1940, the Danish governors of the Greenland colonies turned to the United States for protection. The US declined to occupy Greenland at this time, fearing that a precedent would be set that the Japanese could use to occupy French and Dutch possessions in Asia, but

---

[*] Abbazia, *Mr. Roosevelt's Navy*, pp. 71–4; Cressman, *The Official Chronology*, pp. 13–14; Rohwer, *Chronology of the War at Sea 1939–1945*, p. 11.

[†] Tarrant, *The U-Boat Offensive*, p. 88. At the end of 1939, the Kriegsmarine had 54 U-boats. Of this number, only 33 were operational (the rest used for training or still working up) and, during December 1939, an average of only 8 were on patrol at any one time. The Phony War (often seen in the British spelling 'Phoney') was also called 'The Bore War' by the British, 'Der Sitzkrieg' by the Germans and '*La drôle de guerre*' by the French. This was the period between the fall of Poland in October 1939 and the start of the German attacks on Denmark and Norway in April 1940 when there was little actual combat between Germany and the Allies, at least on land.

[‡] Petrie, *American Neutrality*, p. 70, note 4.

that did not preclude showing the flag.* On 10 May, the Coast Guard cutter *Comanche* (WPG76) sailed, carrying newly appointed American diplomats to Ivigtut and the capital at Godthaab (Nuuk). The cutter/icebreaker *Northland* (WPG49) became the first US vessel primarily dedicated to patrolling the waters off Greenland.

In a related move, Royal Marines landed in Iceland on 10 May 1940, ending a month of sometimes tense negotiations between Great Britain and the stubbornly independent Icelanders, who rejected pressure to join the Allied side. The occupation of the capital, Reykjavik, and the strategically important anchorage at Hvalfjordur was uninvited, but also unopposed. The next day, 11 May, French and British troops occupied the Dutch islands of Curaçao and Aruba in the West Indies, following the German invasion of the Low Countries. These islands were of critical importance to the Allied war effort due to the presence of oil refineries supplied by crude oil from nearby Venezuela. President Roosevelt declared that these actions did not violate the Monroe Doctrine.

On 15 May, in his first correspondence with Roosevelt after becoming Prime Minister, Churchill raised several important issues. One was to request vital reinforcements for the Royal Navy's anti-submarine forces:

> Immediate needs are: first of all, the loan of forty or fifty of your older destroyers to bridge the gap between what we have now and the large new construction we put in hand at the beginning of the war. This time next year we shall have plenty. But if in the interval Italy comes in against us with another one hundred submarines, we may be strained to breaking point.[†]

Churchill's concern about the Italians entering the war was well founded. In particular, he was worried about the numerous and well-designed Italian submarines, more than double the number the Germans had in commission. He could not know in May 1940 that they would not be employed aggressively and would ultimately present far less a threat than their German counterparts. His concern about the submarine threat in general was, if anything, understated. After the war, he famously wrote: 'The only thing that ever really frightened me during the war was the U-boat peril.'[‡]

Churchill's request for the loan of warships from a neutral state was unusual, to say the least. The British and French had been placing large orders for war material of all types, including ships, once the arms embargo was lifted, but those had all been standard purchase arrangements. What Churchill was asking for could in no way be considered the act of a neutral state, but that fit well with his second unprecedented request of President:

---

[*]   Cressman, *The Official Chronology*, p. 22; Tilley, *The Coast Guard & the Greenland Patrol*; Abbazia, *Mr. Roosevelt's Navy*, pp. 86–8.

[†]   *Map Room File*, 15 May 40, WSC->FDR, #1216.

[‡]   Churchill, *The Second World War: The Gathering Storm*, p. 598.

But I trust you realize, Mr. President, that the voice and force of the United States may count for nothing if they are withheld too long. You may have a completely subjugated, Nazified Europe established with astonishing swiftness, and the weight may be more than we can bear. All I ask now is that you should proclaim nonbelligerency, which would mean that you would help us with everything short of actually engaging armed forces.*

As unusual as had been his request for the loan of warships, this request for a dramatic change in US foreign policy was more so. Churchill's request was not satisfied, at least not with an immediate and definitive public statement by the President, but had already effectively become the actual state of affairs.

No precise definition of non-belligerency exists in international law. The term is applied to those actions of a neutral state that assist one side in a war in preference to the other. For example, it was used to describe the actions of Italy before declaring war on France and England. By this definition, the US had been in a state of non-belligerency favoring the Allied side since October 1939. Still, Roosevelt was reticent because he was facing reelection in November. Until then, he had to avoid actions that would strengthen the Isolationist side of the American political debate.

He responded to Churchill the next day, 16 May 1940:

First, with regard to the possible loan of forty to fifty of our older destroyers. As you know a step of that kind could not be taken except with the specific authorization of the Congress and I am not certain that it would be wise for that suggestion to be made to the Congress at this moment . . . Furthermore, even if we were able to take the step you suggest, it would be at least six or seven weeks at a minimum, as I see it, before these vessels could undertake active service under the British flag.†

It probably was not coincidental, however, that the next day, Roosevelt ordered the recommissioning of 35 additional old destroyers, above and beyond those already being refurbished. Churchill was never one to accept the rejection of his ideas without a struggle, but there seemed to be a note of resignation in his reply on 20 May:

I understand your difficulties but I am very sorry about the destroyers. If they were here in six weeks they would play an invaluable part.‡

With that, the issue of the destroyers seemed to be overtaken by other events that dominated the minds of both men. The US Navy became indirectly involved in the Battle for France when, on 28 May 1940, just as the Dunkirk evacuation

---

* *Map Room File*, 15 May 40, WSC->FDR, #1216.

† *Map Room File*, 16 May 40, FDR->WSC, #872.

‡ *Map Room File*, 20 May 40, WSC->FDR, #1271.

SS Washington, *a passenger steamer idled by neutrality laws, was hired by the US Government to repatriate American nationals trapped in Europe by the outbreak of war. En route from Lisbon to Galway on 11 June 1940, she was stopped by U101 (Frauenheim) and her over 1,000 refugees ordered into lifeboats while the U-boat prepared to sink her. While the ship's fate was being negotiated between Frauenheim and* Washington's *master, the lifeboats were filled and swung out, as seen here, but not lowered. (USMM)*

was getting started, the French government requested a US warship be sent to Bordeaux with arms for the national police to put down a feared Communist uprising in the wake of French military defeats. This warship would then remove the 200 tons of French and Belgian bullion reserves which had been sent south to keep them out of German hands. That same day, the heavy cruiser *Vincennes* and two destroyers departed Hampton Roads, VA, for the Azores. The next day, the gold was sent from Bordeaux to Casablanca, French Morocco, to guarantee its safety. *Vincennes* reached Casablanca on 9 June and starting loading the gold that same day.

The liner *Washington* departed Lisbon the next day with 1,020 refugees for Galway, Ireland, where more US nationals had gathered. That same day, Italy declared war on Great Britain and France. FDR responded immediately. In a commencement address at the University of Virginia, he took the opportunity to confront American Isolationists with language that must have gratified Churchill:

> Some indeed still hold to the now somewhat obvious delusion that we of the United States can safely permit the United States to become a lone island, a lone island in a world dominated by the philosophy of force.[*]

He was equally open in his condemnation of the Italians:

> On this tenth day of June, 1940, the hand that held the dagger has struck it into the back of its neighbor.[†]

While the rhetoric certainly pleased the Prime Minister, the US remained ill-prepared to give the Allies much more than moral support. FDR knew full well what was required to address this problem. On 11 June, Congress passed the Naval Supply Act of 1940, which appropriated an additional $1.49 billion for

---

[*]   http://millercenter.org/scripps/archive/speeches/detail/3317
[†]   Ibid.

naval expansion.* The money, however, came with an interesting caveat. Aware that the British were seeking substantial naval aid from America, not just the destroyers, but also motor torpedo boats, submarine chasers and flying boats, and that Roosevelt was inclined to grant that aid, Congress tacked on to this bill the proviso that naval equipment could only be transferred to another nation after the CNO had certified that it was surplus to the needs of American defense.†

The Navy was ready for the money, awarding 22 contracts for new warship construction the next day. Forty-four more contracts were awarded on 1 July.

If Roosevelt wanted an 'incident' to convince reluctant Congressmen, the Germans co-operated by stopping *Washington* en route to Galway. At dawn on 11 June 1940, *U101* (Frauenheim), claiming to have mistaken the American liner for a Greek vessel, ordered the ship abandoned so that she could be sunk. Although Greece was still neutral in the war, Greek ships were singled out by the Germans for special treatment:

> Since the Greeks have sold and chartered numerous ships to England, Greek ships are to be regarded as hostile . . . U-boats must try to remain unobserved while attacking . . .‡

This order was to apply only within the blockade zone previously declared around the British Isles and the French Atlantic coast. However, the special note about remaining unobserved indicated this order was understood to be of questionable legality. Additionally, passenger liners were a special class of ship requiring special rules, especially since the controversial sinking of SS *Athenia* on the first day of the war:

> Immediate freedom of attack is permitted against liners showing no neutral markings, and against those darkened (except for navigation lights), provided they are within the area in which other darkened ships may already be attacked.§

Contemporary images show that *Washington* carried the required neutrality markings, with the ship's name and affiliation, along with two US flags, painted on both sides, nor was she within the German blockade zone, being 180 nm south-west of Vigo, Spain. Despite all this, Frauenheim, improbably mistaking her for a Greek ship, decided that she was liable to be stopped and sunk. It was only because he chose to ignore the 'remain unobserved' part of his orders, and surfaced to stop *Washington* and allow her passengers to disembark was a terrible tragedy prevented.

---

* Throughout this book, the word 'billion' is used in its American sense, to mean a thousand million (a milliard).

† Abbazia, *Mr. Roosevelt's Navy*, p. 92; Bailey and Ryan, *Hitler vs. Roosevelt*, p. 79.

‡ [Hessler] *The U-boat War in the Atlantic 1939–1945*, vol. 1, p. 44.

§ Ibid.

Like other cargo liners left underemployed by the outbreak of war, SS American Legion was taken over by the US Army to carry troops and supplies to distant outposts. She is seen here leaving San Juan, PR, early in 1940 on one of her regular supply runs between Charleston, SC, and Panama. In July, she was sent to Petsamo, Finland, to retrieve refugees and some secret cargo. (USA)

Nevertheless, it was a close-run thing.* At 0500, a signal light flashed the order to heave to and stop the ship. This was followed by 'Captain has ten minutes to leave ship' and 'Torpedo the ship'. While repeatedly flashing the message '*Washington* . . . American', the master ordered watertight doors closed and all passengers into lifeboats, which were swung out, but not lowered. Frauenheim repeated 'Ten minutes' once more and then, finally, seemed to realize that *Washington* was not Greek. After a few minutes of silence, Frauenheim responded with 'Thought you were another ship, please go on, go on.'

In Galway *Washington* took onboard an additional 767 refugees, exceeding her normal passenger load by 65 per cent, meaning that every bit of deck space, including the swimming pools, was used to accommodate the overflow. She arrived in New York on 21 June without further incident, with a full load of cramped, but happy, refugees.

Vincennes had arrived the day before, also without incident and docked at the New York Navy Yard with none of the fanfare that greeted *Washington*. The French and Belgian gold reserves were quietly unloaded and transferred to the Federal Reserve Bank in New York.

The rescue of US nationals from Europe was an on-going task. On 21 June,

---

*   *Ten Minutes to Abandon Ship!* (www.usmm.org).

destroyer *Herbert* (DD160) arrived at Casablanca to gather another load. That city had already become, along with Lisbon, a gathering point for refugees of all nationalities fleeing from Fascist Europe. When, in 1942, Hollywood writers were looking for a location in which to set a movie, featuring Humphrey Bogart as an American expatriate and Ingrid Bergman as the wife of a Czech resistance fighter, they naturally chose Casablanca.

While this was going on, a pair of heavy cruisers, *Wichita* (CA45) – the newest US heavy cruiser, built to a handsome flush-deck design – and *Quincy* (CA39), plus escorting destroyers, were dispatched to South America for some thinly disguised 'gunboat diplomacy'. It was no secret that several South American states, most notably Brazil and Argentina, had rightist governments that might be tempted to support the European Fascists. These two cruisers made a series of leisurely visits to the major Atlantic coast ports of South America. This 'goodwill' tour continued until September. The new light cruiser *Phoenix* (CL46) left Lahaina Roads, Hawaii, for an extended tour of South American Pacific ports for the same purpose.

One of the last, and definitely most spectacular, of rescue missions involved not a privately owned liner nor a Navy vessel, but the ATS ship *American Legion*. While the US Navy operated the nation's warships and during the war developed the capacity to transport the massive amphibious forces that assaulted enemy shores in the Atlantic and Mediterranean as well as across the Pacific, the Army was responsible both before and during the war for the transport and supply of Army troops in non-combat areas. For this purpose, the ATS operated a sizable fleet of owned and leased transports at a time when the Navy's auxiliary fleet had been allowed to shrink to negligible size. As war approached, many of ATS's larger transports were taken over by the Navy, but that was still in the future when *American Legion*, on 25 July sailed for Petsamo, Finland (Pechenga, Russia) on the Barents Sea.

The surrender of the last Norwegian units to the Germans in June had stranded a number of American nationals, who, not welcomed in Sweden, had fled further east into Finland. Crown Princess Märtha of Norway had fled to Sweden, the land of her birth, but the Swedish government feared her presence might antagonize the Germans. Having befriended the Roosevelts before the war, she received a personal invitation to come to the United States. *American Legion* was dispatched at FDR's specific instruction to pick up the Crown Princess and any US nationals in Finland desiring repatriation. The transport arrived at Petsamo on 6 August and departed again ten days later with the royal family, almost 900 additional refugees, including the well-known Danish musician/comedian Victor Borge. Also making that arduous journey from Stockholm to Petsamo – 800 miles in a straight line, probably 1,250 miles by road, skirting the Gulf of Bothnia – was a secret cargo. Purchased by British agents and transported with the tacit agreement of Swedish and Finnish authorities, a twin-mount 40 mm Bofors anti-aircraft gun complete with spare parts and 3,000 rounds made up part of *American Legion*'s manifest. She reached New York on 28 August, with the Bofors gun, but without the Norwegian royals. They had been taken off by a Coast Guard cutter the day before and carried directly to Washington, DC. The gun was transported to the naval weapons test center at Dahlgren, VA.*

On 17 June 1940, the same day German troops entered Paris, CNO Harold Stark appeared before Congress to request another $4 billion to prepare the US Navy to fight wars simultaneously in the Atlantic and Pacific. Specifically, he requested monies to build 257 new ships of 1.3 million tons. This would increase the size of the Navy by 70 per cent. Included were requests for authority to build seven battleships, 18 aircraft carriers, 33 cruisers, 115 destroyers, 43 submarines and 15,000 aircraft. Such a request would have been unthinkable even a few months earlier, but the rapid destruction of the French scared the American people and their representatives to the point that Stark's request was approved in its entirety. The Two-Ocean Navy Act passed Congress on 19 July and was signed into law by the President the same day.

The ships and aircraft authorized by this act formed the backbone of the US Navy in the second half of the war. With the exception of the smaller craft, such as the destroyers and submarines, few of these ships would join the fleet before 1943. Such is the lead time required to build capital ships, not one of the seven battleships authorized by this act – two additional *Iowa* class and five enlarged *Montana* class – would ever be completed.

At the time of the fall of France, three major French warships were caught in the Western Hemisphere: the obsolete aircraft carrier *Béarn* and the light cruisers *Jeanne d'Arc* and *Émile Bertin*. They put into Martinique, a French island in the Windward Chain of the West Indies, and awaited orders.[†] Only the last of the three was a warship of any consequence, but the Royal Navy could not, for political more than military reasons, allow them to escape to a Vichy port in Africa or France.

The Royal Navy blockade and the fear that the British would attempt a pre-emptive strike on the French ships, as they had at Mers-el-Kébir, Algeria, and Dakar, Senegal, seriously concerned the Americans. It would be a violation of the Monroe Doctrine to which the Americans would be forced to react. Fortunately, there was a way out. After a month of negotiations, towards the end of July, the US Navy took over the blockade of Martinique, assigning a heavy cruiser and six

---

* The US Navy found the Bofors to be superior in almost all respects to the indigenously designed 1.1-inch medium AA gun, but also found it to be ill-suited for mass production. The gun was completely redesigned for American manufacture. The first American-made quad mount was installed on a training ship in June 1942. By war's end, almost 40,000 guns had been produced.

† Abbazia, *Mr. Roosevelt's Navy*, pp. 113–17. Some sources place *Jeanne d'Arc* at nearby Guadaloupe.

destroyers to maintain the watch.* This would not be the last time the US Navy aided the British by the simple expedient of taking over tasks, freeing Royal Navy ships for other pressing duties.

On 31 July 1940, after a hiatus of two months, Churchill again raised the issue of the loan of American destroyers.

> It is some time since I ventured to cable personally to you, and many things both good and bad have happened in between . . .[†]

Any list of good things that Churchill could have enumerated would have been very short. The past two months had been little short of disastrous, so he wisely jumped directly into a series of pleas for assistance. Following a listing of 11 destroyers lost or damaged by German air attack in just the preceding ten days, he got to the heart of the matter:

> I am confident, now that you know exactly how we stand, that you will leave nothing undone to ensure that 50 or 60 of you oldest destroyers are sent to me at once. I can . . . use them against U-boats on the western approaches and so keep the more modern and better gunned craft for the narrow seas against invasion.
>
> Mr. President, with great respect I must tell you that in the long history of the world, this is a thing to do now. Large construction is coming to me in 1941, but the crisis will be reached long before 1941. I know you will do all in your power but I feel entitled and bound to put the gravity and urgency of the position before you.[‡]

Switching from cajoling to lecturing, Churchill's frustration at what he saw as foot-dragging in Washington is palpable. Standing now alone against the seemingly invincible German war machine, Churchill clearly could not conceive of a circumstance in which Britain would fail and democracy still survive in the world, and he did everything in his power to get this message across to the President.

Fortunately, Roosevelt needed no persuading. He had long since reached the same conclusion, and reacting as quickly as possible, he raised the issue at his next Cabinet meeting, on 2 August, asking the relevant Secretaries to get to work on making the transfer happen.

In the middle of all this, the Tizard Mission – officially the British Technical and Scientific Mission – arrived in the US on 8 September, meeting with Vannevar Bush, chairman of the US National Defense Research Committee. This led to a series of meetings between American and British scientists, the most famous of which was between the radar specialists of both sides. The meeting started with

---

* Abbazia, *Mr. Roosevelt's Navy*, p. 85.
† *Map Room File*, 31 July 40, WSC->FDR, #2490.
‡ Ibid.

The brand-new aircraft carrier Wasp *(CV7) is seen in October 1940 in peacetime livery. Intended for service in the Pacific, she was retained in the Atlantic when her working up was completed that month. She would be employed making Neutrality Patrol sweeps from Hampton Roads and later from Bermuda. (NHHC)*

some initial tension, as neither side wanted to reveal too much for fear of giving away critical secrets without equivalent return. The Americans described their microwave research which had led to excellent receivers, but underpowered transmitters. The British then revealed the existence of the cavity magnetron, which vastly exceeded the power of equivalent American amplifiers. This broke the ice, the Americans realizing they had as much to gain as did the British from scientific co-operation. The most immediate result was the contracting of the Bell Telephone Company to mass-produce the magnetron. By the end of October, they had made 30; by the end of the war, they made over a million.[*]

Roosevelt replied to Churchill's request on 6 August. He told the British Ambassador, Lord Lothian, that he was favorably inclined to meet Churchill's request for destroyers, but that in order to persuade Congress to go along, he had to show that fair value had been received. There were two specific items the President wanted in return. One was the long-term lease or sale of a list of naval facilities in the Atlantic and Caribbean. The idea of obtaining bases on British possessions off the American coast predated Vice-Admiral Andrews' comments after Fleet Problem XX. It had been mooted in the 1930s by some American legislators as a way to clear up Britain's lingering World War I debt. On 1 August, the idea was raised again by Navy Secretary Frank Knox in a meeting with Lothian, for the first time linked specifically to the request for destroyers.[†]

The other condition listed in Roosevelt's reply was for a formal guarantee that the Royal Navy would not be surrendered to Germany should Great Britain be defeated. This requires some explanation. Many in the US Cabinet, particularly Knox, were very worried that, should Great Britain fail – a prospect that seemed likely to many Americans in the late summer of 1940 – the Royal Navy might

---

[*]   Brown, *Technical and Military Imperatives*, pp. 159–66.
[†]   Abbazia, *Mr. Roosevelt's Navy*, p. 93.

Bermuda became available as a base for US warships as a result of the 'Destroyers-for-Bases' deal completed in September 1940. The 50 destroyers sent to the Royal Navy were all First World War-vintage flush-deckers, which suffered from poor seakeeping and a variety of mechanical ills, but nevertheless proved of great use to the British. One of them was Evans (DD78); *she was renamed HMS* Mansfield (G76) *by the British and immediately turned over to a Norwegian crew. In 1942, she was returned to the Royal Navy and then passed on to the Canadians, who actively employed her on convoy duty based at Halifax. She is seen here from her contemporary* Greer (DD145) *during the winter of 1942–3 in pancake ice. (NARA)*

have to be surrendered to the Germans as the price of a peace settlement. Were that to happen, the balance of power in the world would tip in favor of the Axis. The US Navy was confident it could succeed in a war against Japan, but adding the threat of a German-controlled Royal Navy in the Atlantic upset all plans for success in the Pacific. Many in the American leadership wanted a public statement from Churchill that the fleet would not be surrendered.

Churchill replied to Roosevelt's conditions on 15 August:

> We can meet both the points you consider necessary to help you with Congress and with others concerned, but I am sure that you will not misunderstand me if I say that our willingness to do so must be conditional on our being assured that there will be no delay in letting us have the ships . . . As regards an assurance about the British fleet, I am of course, ready to reiterate to you what I told Parliament on June 4th. We intend to fight this out here to the end and none of us would ever buy peace by surrendering or scuttling the fleet . . .
>
> As regards naval and air bases, I readily agree to your proposals for 99-year leases which is easier for us than the method of purchase.[*]

---

[*] *Map Room File*, 15 August 40, WSC->FDR, #2730.

This should have been sufficient for agreement to be reached, but some in the US wanted a legally binding agreement to be drawn up, showing exactly what was being exchanged for what, feeling this was necessary to persuade a reluctant Congress. Churchill not liking this idea at all, offered an alternative:

> Would not the following procedure be acceptable? I would offer at once certain fairly well-defined facilities which will show you the kind of gift we have in mind and your experts could then discuss these or any variants of them with ours . . . All this we will do free trusting entirely to the generosity and goodwill of the American people . . . But anyhow it is the settled policy of His Majesty's Government to offer you and make available to you when desired solid and effective means of protecting your Atlantic seaboard . . .
>
> If your law and your Admiral require that any help you may choose to give us must be presented as a quid pro quo, I do not see why the British Government have to come into that at all.*

The note clearly betrays Churchill's continued impatience with the negotiations. He was afraid for his country's survival and for the cost that may require, but mainly he was afraid that US help would come too late.

After this the process moved forward smoothly, though generally more slowly than Churchill wished. In a series of meetings on 27 August, the Cabinet approved the plan, with the Attorney General Robert Jackson rendering the opinion that the President could approve the transfer by Executive Order, obviating the need for Congressional approval, and then in a final, critical meeting attended by FDR, Stark, Knox, Secretary of State Hull and Lothian, the CNO certified that the agreed-upon 50 destroyers were indeed surplus to US needs.† Formal agreement between the two nations came on 2 September.

From that point, the transfer was rapid. The deal was announced by Roosevelt on the campaign trail to general approval. The first eight destroyers arrived at Halifax on 6 September, and were officially transferred to the Royal Navy three days later. (That same day, 9 September, using money provided by the Two-Ocean Navy Act, the US Navy awarded contracts for 210 ships, including 12 aircraft carriers, all of which would see action, and the seven battleships, which would not.) The transfers continued rapidly; the last batch of ten being handed over on 26 November.

As might have been expected, the destroyers were less of a help to the Royal Navy than had been hoped. No amount of paint could cover up the fact that they were old. Despite being delivered with a full complement of spare parts,

---

* *Map Room File*, 20 August 40, WSC->FDR, unnumbered.

† Abbazia, *Mr. Roosevelt's Navy*, p. 94; Cressman, *The Official Chronology*, p. 30. A small number of critics, mainly Republicans, publicly questioned Jackson's reasoning, but this was generally dismissed as 'politics as usual' given that the Presidential election was barely two months away.

their power plants were worn out. Mechanical breakdowns were frequent. The British found some equipment not up to their standards, particularly the sonar and anti-aircraft weapons. On the other hand, they found the provision of typewriters for yeomen and bunks for the enlisted crew to be unneeded luxuries. But the greatest problems involved ship handling. The flush-deckers had a notoriously large turning circle and generally poor maneuverability compared to their Royal Navy counterparts. Never good heavy-weather boats, their crews suffered in the turbulent North Atlantic, particularly in that first winter. Fortunately, they proved not essential to Britain's survival. The Battle of Britain reached its climax in September 1940, and while heavy raids continued to the end of the year, it gradually became obvious that Hitler had cancelled the planned invasion of Britain. This allowed the transfer to convoy duty of some of the modern destroyers held on Britain's Channel coast.

The question of whether the destroyers represented fair value to the British was debated then and since, but Churchill understood rightly that the issue never was old destroyers or island bases.[*] The message sent by this deal to the British people was that America stood by them. To the Germans, it spoke plainly that America may be neutral in name, but no longer in fact, and that, short of declaring war, there was little Hitler could do about it.[†] To neutrals, it said that America was no longer a passive observer of events across the sea and should not be taken lightly. To the Japanese, still technically neutral, the message should have been cautionary. Most importantly, it signaled clearly to the American people that their President was in no way neutral in his attitude towards the belligerents in Europe.

---

[*] Abbazia, *Mr. Roosevelt's Navy*, pp. 102–3, 106.
[†] *Fuehrer Conferences on Naval Affairs, 1939–1945*, p. 134.

2

Just Short of War
November 1940–December 1941

The American electorate had an opportunity to express their opinion on 5 November 1940, and gave Roosevelt a solid victory over the Isolationist Republicans. The date when the United States passed from neutrality to non-belligerence, might have been 2 September 1940, when the Destroyers-for-Bases agreement was signed, or it might have been that Election Day, when it was effectively ratified by the American people. Regardless, after the beginning of November 1940, the activity of the US Navy in the Atlantic increased steadily.

To acknowledge this increased importance, on 1 November, the name of the Atlantic Squadron was formally changed to Patrol Force, US Fleet. This put the force in the Atlantic on an equal footing organizationally with the two major formations in the Pacific. For all that, there was no significant reinforcement in the Atlantic at this time.

What did change significantly was the attitude of the leadership of the US Navy, with the acknowledgement, should war come, that the United States would commit to defeat Germany first, regardless of events in the Pacific. This came about because of insistence on the part of Admiral Stark that there be an agreed-upon position on the issue of fleet deployment going into combined staff talks with the British scheduled to begin in January.[*] The President probably would have preferred to begin the talks with no pre-determined position, but, of all the armed services, a navy needs to know where its ships are going to be months, if not years, in advance, so that ships can be maintained and the use of yard space optimized. Stark, therefore drafted a position paper in which he defined four possible plans for deploying fleet assets, labeled A to D. The first (Plan A) was a purely defensive posture with American forces staying out of the conflict; the other three assumed active US involvement in a war in both the Atlantic and Pacific. They differed in how US fleet assets were distributed. Plan B called for the deployment of most naval resources in the Pacific with an eye towards defeating Japan first. Plan C assigned equal forces to Atlantic and Pacific. Plan D called for

---

[*] Abbazia, *Mr. Roosevelt's Navy*, pp. 119–22; Stark, *Memorandum for the Secretary*, 12 November 1940, pp. 21–4.

a defensive posture in the Pacific with minimal forces while putting emphasis on the support of Great Britain and the defeat of Germany. He then analyzed the options, attempting to predict the consequences of each.

The conclusions were simple and grim:

> . . . if Britain wins decisively against Germany we could win everywhere; but that if she loses the problem confronting us would be very great; and, while we might not <u>lose everywhere</u>, we might, possibly, not <u>win anywhere</u>.[*]

He stated that following any of the first three options might well result in the defeat of Great Britain by the Axis, with the subsequent isolation of the US against Japan and Germany, an especially frightening prospect if, despite Churchill's assurances, some or all of the Royal Navy fell intact into German hands. Only by strengthening US forces in the Atlantic theater and giving Great Britain all possible aid could US maximize the chances of success in a war that was edging closer every day.[†]

On 9 January 1941, the President strongly endorsed Stark's conclusion and asked that the Navy determine how soon it could begin regular convoy escort operations in the Atlantic. Eight days later, the War Plans Division reported to Stark that such operations could start on 1 April.[‡]

— —

On 8 November 1940, a merchant ship struck a mine off the coast of Australia, in the Bass Strait between Tasmania and the mainland. This was not a part of the world where mines were expected; the crew of *City of Rayville* were taking no particular precautions as they entered the strait. The mine had been laid by the German auxiliary minelayer *Passat* at the end of October. The minefield claimed its first victim the day before, when the British steamer *Cambridge* sank. It is likely no one in *City of Rayville* knew of this sinking when she ran into the same minefield. All 38 crewmen were able to abandon the ship. One, however, reboarded the ship to recover some personal items and was lost when she sank. *City of Rayville* became the first American ship sunk in the Second World War, and the unfortunate, unwise James Bryan of Norfolk, VA, became the nation's first known casualty.[§]

Admiral Stark knew that, if the Patrol Force was going to become the predominant component of the US Fleet, it needed a more forceful leader than the incumbent commander, Hayne Ellis. He chose an old friend, a man who had been assigned duty on the General Board of the Navy in June 1939, a posting

---

[*]   Stark, *Memorandum for the Secretary*, 12 November 1940, p. 1. Emphasis in the original.

[†]   Because he recommended Plan D, this became known as the 'Plan Dog Memo'.

[‡]   Abbazia, *Mr. Roosevelt's Navy*, p. 134.

[§]   There must have been American casualties among the crews of merchant ships before this date, but Bryan was the first to have his fate widely documented in American newspapers.

generally regarded as a sinecure for superannuated flag officers. Many in the Navy would have been happy to see Vice-Admiral Ernest J. King go quietly into retirement. Tall, lean and of aristocratic bearing, he was generally admired for his intelligence and unrelenting drive, though some saw it as a streak of arrogance. He had a reputation for profanity and hard-drinking. He could be quite charming, but, reportedly, he reserved his charm mainly for the wives of fellow officers. Nevertheless, Stark saw in King the right man to prepare the Patrol Force for war, and, on 17 December 1940, King officially took over command of US forces in the Atlantic.

The state of the ships he took over was hardly encouraging. The most pressing issue was that they were seriously undermanned. There were multiple causes for this, including the nation's improving economy and the constant drain on trained personnel for new construction. During the depths of the Great Depression, the small US Navy could pick and choose among recruits and had no difficulty retaining men. The surge of orders for war production brought the nation's economy back to life, luring some skilled sailors away, while the increasing number of new ships needing to be manned with a cadre of experienced petty officers, meant that many ships in the Patrol Force found themselves with half the number of trained machinists and gunners they required.[*] A similar shortage of officers was addressed by the simple expedient of graduating the Naval Academy Class of 1941 six months early.

Aggravating the problem was the pace of operations for ships and men assigned Neutrality Patrol duty. In marked contrast to the relaxed peacetime routine enjoyed in the Pacific, ships spent as much as three-quarters of their time on active patrol, often steaming at high speed for days at a time. The strain on ships and men was beginning to wear both out. Maintenance was deferred for lack of time. Formerly 'spit-and-polish' ships now badly needed scraping and painting. Crews had little time for relaxation, much less overdue liberty. The strain affected morale, and lowered morale had an impact on re-enlistment rates.

An event critical to the future of Anglo-American relations passed almost unnoticed on 6 January 1941, the departure of Harry Hopkins from New York on his way to London. He was well known in the US, where he had headed the Works Progress Administration and had been Secretary of Commerce for two years, before resigning in 1940 due to ill health. (He had been diagnosed with stomach cancer in 1937 and fought health problems until his death in 1946. Feeling ill one evening in May 1940 while visiting the White House – he was close friend and confidant to both the President and the First Lady, one of the few friends they shared – he was put up in the Lincoln Bedroom, where he slept for the next three and a half years, even after he remarried in July 1942.)

Hopkins was sent to London as FDR's personal representative, with the unspoken task of assessing the likelihood of Great Britain's survival. This, and

---

[*] Abbazia, *Mr. Roosevelt's Navy*, p. 125.

Harry Hopkins, FDR's closest friend and confidant is seen boarding a Pan-Am Clipper in New York on 6 January 1941 on his way to England via Lisbon. His task was to assess the chances of Great Britain surviving the expected German invasion. (USLoC)

the President's January proposal of Lend-Lease, came about in reaction to a long year-end message sent by Churchill on 7 December in which he spelled out the precarious state of British resources. Roosevelt received the letter on 9 December on board *Tuscaloosa* in the Caribbean. He had set out a few days earlier for a two-week vacation cruise with three reporters, a handful of staff members and Hopkins.*

Churchill started by stating that it was not a question of will or manpower, but, with all that, the war could still be lost without the means to fight, and that Great Britain could fail not only catastrophically but by slow decline. He went on to detail recent shipping losses and the slow strangulation of Great Britain that would occur unless the losses were reduced. This was followed by a listing of the threats facing the British beyond shipping losses, ending this section with:

> . . . I feel entitled, nay bound, to lay before you the various ways in which the United States could give supreme and decisive help to what is, in certain aspects, the common cause.†

---

* When asked where he was going on this cruise, Roosevelt reportedly replied: 'We are going to Christmas Island to buy Christmas cards, and to Easter Island to buy Easter eggs.'

† *Map Room File*, 7 December 40, WSC>FDR, unnumbered, p. 8.

The list that followed was lengthy, including aid in escorting Atlantic convoys, the application of American pressure on the Irish government to allow Royal Navy use of Irish ports, the implementation of a plan to produce new merchant shipping for the British on the same scale as the Hog Islanders of 20 years earlier, the production of aircraft for the British at the rate of 2,000 per month and much more. Finally, on the thirteenth page of this magnum opus, he got to the crux of the matter:

> Last of all I come to the question of finance. The more rapid and abundant the flow of munitions and ships which you are able to send us, the sooner will our dollar credits be exhausted . . . The moment approaches when we shall no longer be able to pay cash for shipping and other supplies. While we will do our utmost and shrink from no proper sacrifice . . . I believe that you will agree that it would be wrong in principal and mutually disadvantageous in effect if, at the height of this struggle, Great Britain were to be devested of all saleable assets so that after victory was won with our blood, . . we should stand stripped to the bone.[*]

There is no question that Roosevelt was deeply impressed with the seriousness of the situation and wanted to help, but he had an ingrained suspicion, shared with many leading Americans, that the British were not to be trusted when it came to financial matters.[†] Indeed, each side saw the other as sharp traders out to position themselves to dominate the post-war world, and there was more than a grain of truth to the mutual suspicions. Nevertheless, Roosevelt agreed that Great Britain's survival was both essential to the US and not to be taken for granted. His problem was a political one, namely how to convince his allies in Congress, as well as enough Isolationists, that America's safety required the giving, as opposed to the selling, of massive aid to the British. The President had to walk a fine line, supporting Great Britain, but not the British Empire, which most Americans – Roosevelt included – thought was anachronistic.

It was obvious that the idea for Lend-Lease, a plan whereby the aid to Great Britain would be in the form of items being lent or leased with deferred payment, was conceived during this cruise on *Tuscaloosa*, with major input from Hopkins. The idea was first made public at a press conference on 17 December. The analogy FDR used was that of a man whose neighbor's house was on fire. If the man had a length of garden hose, he would not sell it to his neighbor, he would simply lend it to him with the expectation that it would be returned when the fire was out.[‡]

---

[*]   *Map Room File*, 7 December 40, WSC>FDR, unnumbered, pp. 13–14.

[†]   Olson, *Citizens of London*, pp. 7–8.

[‡]   As was pointed out then and since, war materials are far different garden hose, meant to be consumed.

When Roosevelt talked to the American people during one of his regular 'Fireside Chat' radio addresses on 30 December 1940, the danger of Britain's defeat was very much on his mind:

> If Great Britain goes down, . . It is no exaggeration to say that all of us in all the Americas would be living at the point of a gun – a gun loaded with explosive bullets, economic as well as military. We should enter upon a new and terrible era in which the whole world, our hemisphere included, would be run by threats of brute force . . .
>
> I want to make it clear that it is the purpose of the nation to build now with all possible speed every machine, every arsenal, every factory that we need to manufacture our defense material. We have the men, the skill, the wealth, and above all, the will . . .
>
> We must be the great arsenal of democracy.[*]

Staff talks between US and Great Britain began in Washington on 29 January. The US representatives had no problem endorsing the 'Germany first' principle approved by Roosevelt and went so far as to assure the British that US escort operations in the western Atlantic would start on 1 April.[†] Nevertheless, the British were disappointed by the unwillingness of the US to send a naval detachment to Singapore. There was disagreement too about the strategy to be employed once the Americans joined the war. The British were unwilling to commit to a direct assault on the French coast, something which the US Army already advocated. The British preferred working around the edges of Axis Europe, with attacks in North Africa and possibly the Balkans to secure control of the Mediterranean. For the moment, the discussion was purely theoretical, as the US was not in the war. The discussions continued into March, resulting in the ABC-1 Staff Agreement, signed on the 27th of that month. It stipulated that permanent combined staff committees would be set up in Washington and in London to foster ongoing co-operation.

— —

The news that Hopkins would be arriving on 10 January 1941 caught the British by surprise, as no one in London, Churchill included, seemed to have any idea who he was. In part this was because the British Ambassador to Washington, Lord Lothian, had died on 12 December.[‡] His replacement, Lord Halifax, was still in England when Hopkins arrived. When informed of Hopkins's imminent arrival, Churchill asked Brendan Bracken, his close confidant and advisor to

---

[*] www.americanrhetoric.com/speeches/fdrarsenalofdemocracy.html. Hopkins is generally credited with coming up with the phrase 'arsenal of democracy' for which this speech is remembered.

[†] Olson, *Citizens of London*, pp. 140–1.

[‡] Philip Kerr, 11th Marquess of Lothian, was a devout Christian Scientist and refused medical care that probably would have saved his life.

meet him on arrival at Poole Airport, and, no doubt, to size him up.* Bracken accurately judged that Hopkins was a man of great influence with Roosevelt, and Churchill went out of his way to assure that he saw all he wished of British military activities. Hopkins, who had arrived in London forewarned about Churchill's persuasive powers, nevertheless rapidly became convinced that Churchill would not allow the British to lose, and he passed this opinion on to the President. His visit, scheduled to last two weeks, stretched out to six, much of it spent at 10 Downing Street. During that time, he became very close to the Prime Minister, and at several critical points in the next year, Churchill communicated directly with Hopkins when he had messages for Roosevelt he did not wish to pass through normal channels.

The CNO had started his Plans Division, under Rear-Admiral Richmond Kelly 'Terrible' Turner, working on the problem of forming escort groups for service in the North Atlantic as early as mid-December 1940.† Turner's recommendation was for a force of 27 destroyers, supported by a wing of patrol aircraft and appropriate tenders. The President officially ordered Stark on 17 January to prepare ships and men to begin escorting convoys in the Western Atlantic starting 1 April. Rear-Admiral Arthur L. Bristol was selected to organize and run the Northeastern Escort Force, a post he assumed on 26 February. On 1 March, in order to disguise, for the moment, the intended use of Bristol's force, the name was changed to the more innocuous sounding Support Force.

A further reorganization of the US Fleet was ordered on 1 February. The Scouting Force and Battle Force would henceforth be called the Pacific Fleet, and the Patrol Force renamed the Atlantic Fleet. This may have been mainly a name change, but it did recognize the continuing increase in the importance of the Atlantic to the defense of the nation. This also meant an automatic promotion to full Admiral for Ernest King. On 1 April, the Atlantic Fleet comprised 159 ships, including two aircraft carriers (*Ranger* and the new *Wasp* (CV7)), three old battleships, four heavy cruisers, four light cruisers and 66 destroyers (mostly old flush-deckers). There were plans to bring more ships from the Pacific.

As the anticipated start of escort operations approached, King attempted to impress upon Stark and the President his opinion that the Support Force was not ready for this new assignment. His ships needed time to repair, replenish and train intensively in ASW. Roosevelt was more than willing to listen, as his political instincts were telling him that he was too far ahead of public opinion. He decided to postpone the start of escort operations until 1 May. Nevertheless, Stark ordered King to terminate the regular Neutrality Patrol in order to prepare

---

*   Churchill, *The Second World War: The Grand Alliance*, pp. 22–5.

†   Abbazia, *Mr. Roosevelt's Navy*, pp.142–3. Turner earned his greatest fame as the commander of amphibious forces in the Pacific.

his ships and crews. The delay would also allow crews a final peacetime liberty. In Stark's words: 'This step is, in effect, a war mobilization.'*

The delay also allowed an eastern terminus for the escorts to be identified where they could refuel and replenish. Four harbors were selected in Northern Ireland and Scotland, with Londonderry being the preferred site. At the same time, the idea was raised of using Iceland as the turn around point instead of any port in the British Isles. The idea was attractive because Iceland was already occupied by the British and because it was much closer to the point where US escorts could be expected to turn over convoy protection to the Royal Navy. It was decided, therefore, to send a team of naval experts to look over the island; the new destroyer *Niblack* (DD424) was selected to carry the team. After a brief stop at Halifax, the destroyer set out for Reykjavik on 7 April.†

On 10 April, at 1930, while still a day's steaming south-west of Iceland, a distress signal from a Dutch merchantman was intercepted. *Saleier* was sinking some 40 minutes after being hit by two torpedoes from *U52* (Salman). As the location of the sinking was not far off *Niblack*'s course, her commander, Lieutenant Commander E. R. Durgin, decided to search for survivors. Setting a course and speed that would bring *Niblack* to the location at first light, the destroyer's crew settled down to a nervous night. Sighting wreckage and three lifeboats at 0750, *Niblack* slowed and began a sonar sweep, as it was believed at the time that U-boats liked to lurk around the site of a sinking hoping for an easy shot at any ship that came to search for survivors. (In fact, the opposite was true. U-boats tended to leave the site of a sinking as rapidly as possible because any rescue ship was liable to be armed.) It was nearly 40 minutes later that *Niblack* slowed to a stop and began taking *Saleier*'s survivors on board. As the last were being hauled aboard at 0840, a sound contact was detected at close range which seemed to have the metallic character of a submarine. (Only hard-won experience would teach American sonar operators how to distinguish the echo of a submarine from that of a whale or thermal layer.) *Niblack* got underway, and Durgin ordered three depth charges dropped with no obvious result. Satisfied that any U-boat had been discouraged, *Niblack* headed for Iceland. Only after arriving at Newport, RI, on 28 April was the incident reported to Admiral Bristol, who dismissed the attack as the result of inexperience on the part of all involved. Post-war analysis proved him correct. The incident is memorable nonetheless as the first use of weapons by a US warship in the war.

Bristol made no report of the incident to King, but word nevertheless spread through the Atlantic Fleet and eventually reached King's ear. He ordered an investigation, word of which was reported to the public in June. This in turn led to feverish speculation in the press recounting imaginary engagements as far

---

*   Abbazia, *Mr. Roosevelt's Navy*, p. 145.
†   Ibid., pp. 191–4; Morison, *History*, vol. I, p. 57.

One of FDR's first acts under the new Lend-Lease law was to transfer ten Lake-class Coast Guard cutters to the Royal Navy. Unlike the 50 flush-deckers, these were handy, sea-worthy vessels that were immediately useful to the British. The first to be transferred was Saranac, *which became HMS* Banff *(Y43) on 30 April 1941. (USCG)*

afield as the Azores. The President was furious at the farcical handling of what was a very serious matter.

The Lend-Lease proposal was put before Congress on 10 January 1941. Two separate actions were required to put the plan into effect. One was the passage of the enabling law that modified the Cash-and-Carry provisions of the existing Neutrality Act, and the other was funding to pay for the materials to be lent or leased. The debate in Congress was spirited, but the passage of the bill came on 11 March and the first funding came on 27 March. Not only did the new law allow the US to transfer war materials to belligerents without payment, but, in a little-noticed provision, it also authorized the use of US Navy shipyards to repair or otherwise modify belligerent warships. Probably the first Royal Navy ship to take advantage was HMS *Malaya* (01).* Torpedoed on 20 March while escorting a convoy near the Cape Verde Islands, she entered the Brooklyn Navy Yard on 6 April, where she would be under repair until July.

The arrival of this ship, with a crew of upwards of a thousand men who would now be idle, proved timely. On 10 April, the President announced the transfer of all ten US Coast Guard Lake-class cutters under Lend-Lease. These were a generation newer than the 50 old destroyers, and would be immediately useful to the Royal Navy as convoy escorts. The first four – *Saranac, Mendota, Tahoe*

---

* *Naval-History.Net*; Blair, *Hitler's U-Boat War: The Hunters*, p. 261.

and *Pontchartrain** – were turned over in a ceremony at the Brooklyn Navy Yard on 30 April, being manned by sailors from *Malaya*. They were named, respectively, HMS *Banff* (Y43), *Culver* (Y87), *Fishguard* (Y59) and *Hartland* (Y00). Of these, *Hartland* was lost during the TORCH landings and *Culver* was torpedoed while escorting a convoy, but the other two survived the war and were returned to the US.

The passage of the Lend-Lease Act did not come without a price; as part of the political maneuvering that assured its passage, there occurred an incident that marred Anglo-American relations during and after the war.[†] As the act was being debated in Congress, the opposition, led by prominent Isolationists such as Charles Lindbergh, charged that the British were being disingenuous when they talked about their dwindling dollar reserves. They pointed to a number of large American companies that were British-owned or were subsidiaries of large British corporations.[‡] Among the largest of these were Lever Brothers, Shell Oil, Brown & Williamson Tobacco and Dunlop Tires, a collection of companies with an estimated value of nearly a billion dollars.[§] But, by far the largest British-owned company in the US was American Viscose, a subsidiary of Courtaulds, then a major textile and chemical producer. In order to quiet the critics, the US Secretary of the Treasury, Henry Morgenthau, proposed the forced sale of this company. FDR agreed and ordered Morgenthau to proceed rapidly, believing the fate of Lend-Lease hung in the balance. At the beginning of March, the British were informed that the sale of American Viscose was a political necessity and were given 72 hours to comply. The British Treasury hired Morgan Stanley and Dillon Read, a major investment banking house, to handle the sale. Morgan Stanley offered the British $54.4 million for the company, which was conservatively valued at more than twice as much. The British accepted the offer, being in no position to refuse. As rankling as the forced sale was to the British, they were positively furious when they learned that Morgan Stanley had turned around and sold American Viscose for $62 million, pocketing the difference.

On 30 March, acting on reports that some Italian ships interned at Newark, NJ, were being rigged with scuttling charges, the US Coast Guard boarded and seized 63 ships idle in US ports. These included two German, 26 Italian and 35 Danish ships. More than 900 German and Italian sailors were interned for the duration of the war. On the same day, *Vincennes* departed Simon's Town, South Africa, with a load of British gold for deposit in US banks. This was the second such transport; the first was by *Louisville* (CA28) in January. As with the controversial forced sale of American Viscose, this move was forced on the British by the Americans.

---

* Coast Guard cutters were not given hull numbers until they came under Navy control in late 1941.
† Churchill, *The Second World War: Their Finest Hour*, p. 573.
‡ Dixon, *The Great Marcus Hook Swindle*.
§ A 1941 dollar would be worth approximately $15.50 in 2011.

Churchill was none too pleased, but there was little he could do about it.*

In mid-April, Roosevelt again looked at the plans to start escorting convoys in the Atlantic and again postponed the starting date, this time indefinitely. At the same time, he rescinded the order to transfer ships from the Pacific. In the place of escorting convoys, he redrew the eastern limit of the Neutrality Zone at 26°W, just to the west of Iceland. This now overlapped the German's declared war zone by 12 degrees of longitude. Neither Stark nor King was able to dissuade the President, despite warning him that this would increase the strain on the already stretched resources of the Atlantic Fleet. The one concession he made to their protest was to promise, in somewhat vague terms, that an aircraft carrier and five destroyers would be transferred from the Pacific at the beginning of May.†

There is no question that this decision was driven by internal politics. Roosevelt wanted to bring the US into the war on Britain's side. However, he had promised repeatedly not to take the country to war, and he felt bound by that promise. Above all, he believed that the American people were not yet ready to support as big a step as escorting convoys. Instead, he returned to a policy of more incremental 'creep' towards war, hoping all the while that the Germans would provide him with the pretext he needed for bigger steps.

The decision to renew patrolling of the Neutrality Zone was announced to the Atlantic Fleet by King's OPPLAN 3-41 dated 18 April 1941. The warships of any belligerent not having possessions in FDR's expanded version of the Western Hemisphere would be considered unfriendly. This conveniently allowed British and French warships free access to the hemisphere, but excluded those of Germany and Italy.

> If any such naval vessels or aircraft are encountered within twenty-five miles of Western Hemisphere territory, except the Azores, warn them to move twenty-five miles from such territory and, in case of failure to heed such warning, attack them.‡

The official announcement of the new 26°W limit to the Neutrality Zone came on 24 April. On 26 April, the zone was extended south to 20°S latitude, covering the South American coast to just north of Rio de Janeiro. It was not entirely coincidental that the US Navy's Caribbean Patrol stood up on 18 April, comprising at this time just two destroyers, a squadron of patrol aircraft and their tender. At the same time, a South Atlantic Patrol, based at the Brazilian port of Recife (Pernambuco), started regular patrols as far east as the Cape Verde Islands.

To bolster the Atlantic Fleet, the President at this time authorized the transfer of significant forces from the Pacific, including: *Yorktown* (CV5); the three

---

*   Churchill, *The Second World War: Their Finest Hour*, p. 573.

†   Abbazia, *Mr. Roosevelt's Navy*, p. 154.

‡   OPPLAN 3-41, quoted in O'Connor, *FDR's Undeclared War*. Underlining in the original.

battleships of the *New Mexico* class (*New Mexico* (BB40), *Mississippi* (BB41) and *Idaho* (BB42)); four of the new light cruisers that had previously served in the Atlantic (*Brooklyn* (CL40), *Philadelphia* (CL41), *Savannah* (CL42) and *Nashville* (CL43)) and two DesRons (Destroyer Squadrons), a total of 12 new destroyers. Out of fear that the Japanese would take advantage of the weakening of the Pacific Fleet, every attempt was made to keep the moves secret as long as possible. Crews were not informed of the moves until ships were at sea. In some cases, ships' names were painted over and, to the extent possible, the Panama Canal was transited at night.

The appropriate diplomatic negotiations accomplished, the fast seaplane tender *Belknap* (AVD8, formerly DD251) arrived at Reykjavik and, on 26 May, began 12 days of flight operations with PatRon (Patrol Squadron) VP-52's PBY-5 Catalinas over the east coast of Greenland.*

That same day, another Catalina with an American pilot had a much greater impact on the war. With excellent range and reliability, the Catalina had by 1941 become the predominant maritime patrol aircraft in the US Navy's patrol squadrons and was among the most important pre-Lend-Lease purchases by the RAF. When the new German battleship *Bismarck* broke into the Atlantic in May 1941, Catalinas were flown by both US and British squadrons in wide sweeps from bases in Newfoundland and Northern Ireland. After encountering HMS *Hood* (51) and *Prince of Wales* (53) in the Denmark Strait early on 24 May, and famously destroying *Hood*, *Bismarck* had continued south-west and then south, shadowed by HMS *Norfolk* (C78). The main British fleet, well to the east, had detached the aircraft carrier HMS *Victorious* (38) to run ahead and launch an airstrike at the German battleship before dark. As a small flight of Fairey Swordfish of No. 825 Squadron approached *Bismarck* through low clouds and fading light, their ASV radars indicated a target ahead. Dropping out of the clouds, they were surprised to find not *Bismarck* but a US Coast Guard cutter. *Modoc* (WPG46) had *Bismarck* in sight, 6 nm further west, but her presence in these waters was not part of the combined search for that ship. She was looking for survivors from the convoy HX.126.† The 'Stringbags' at first lined up *Modoc* before realizing their mistake and heading for the correct target, leaving *Modoc* to her fruitless search.

After this attack, which scored one hit, *Bismarck* turned south-east towards Brest and seemed to disappear into the Atlantic. A massive search ensued, mainly by Catalinas of VP-52 flying from Argentia and two RAF Coastal Command

---

* It is more than a little anachronistic to label these PBY-5s Catalinas, as the assignment of official nicknames for aircraft types in US service was only approved in October 1941. Many aircraft, however, had been given nicknames by their manufacturer or by the men who flew them long before that date. Catalina was the name given to pre-war civilian versions of the PBY by Consolidated Aircraft Corp.

† Rohwer, *Axis Submarine Successes*, pp. 52–3; *Arnold Hague Convoy Database*; *Ships in Atlantic Convoys*; [Hessler] *The U-boat War in the Atlantic 1939–1945*, vol. 1, p. 73.

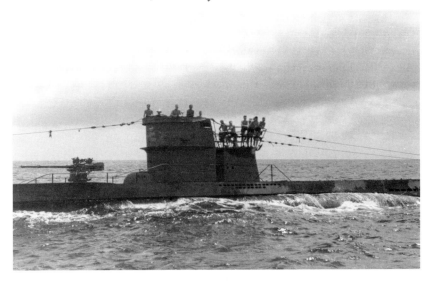

Robin Moor *was the first US merchantman sunk by a U-boat, on 21 May 1941. She was stopped by U69 (Metzler) in the Central Atlantic, midway between Dakar and Brazil. This U-boat is seen on 19 June, while awaiting the supply ship* Lothringen *at Punkt Rot, near Peter & Paul Rocks. The photo was taken from U107 (Hessler). The wait was in vain, the supply ship having been sunk four days earlier by HMS* Dunedin *(D93). (BAK)*

squadrons flying from Loch Erne, Northern Ireland. (In fact, *Bismarck* was never really lost. Her radio signals had been triangulated by HF/DF stations, clearly indicating her turn to the south-east.[*])

To help British pilots learn to handle their Catalinas, the US Navy had sent a number of experienced pilots to Loch Erne. One of those was Ensign Leonard B. Smith, who, though technically aboard only as an observer, was in the left seat on Catalina I (AH545) of No. 209 Squadron.[†] At 1010 on 26 May, Smith sighted a large warship through broken clouds, but then lost sight of it again. Emerging into clear air, the Catalina was taken under anti-aircraft fire by the ship, now positively identified as *Bismarck*. The fire was intense and accurate, and Smith turned the aircraft and flew an evasive course back into the clouds. When he turned back to begin shadowing the battleship, he was unable to relocate her. Fortunately, two other Catalinas, both also piloted by American 'observers', were able to find *Bismarck* based on Smith's contact report, leading Royal Navy units to the elusive

---

[*]   Winton, ULTRA *at Sea*, pp. 28–31. The HF/DF bearings sent to the Home Fleet flagship were correct, but were incorrectly plotted on HMS *King George V* (41). The error was not discovered for seven hours, during which time the British ships were converging on an incorrect position, well to the west of *Bismarck*'s actual location.

[†]   Smith *Report of Scouting and Search of PBY-5 No. AH545 'Catalina' for Bismarck 26 May, 1941.*

battleship. She sank the next day after being battered to a hulk by gunfire.

At 0225 on 21 May, about 700 nm off Freetown, Sierra Leone, the well-marked Hog Islander *Robin Moor*, carrying a general cargo to South Africa and Mozambique, was stopped by *U69* (Metzler).* Metzler had proposed a mining mission to West Africa to Vizeadmiral Karl Dönitz, the commander of German U-boat forces (Befelshaber der Unterseeboote, BdU). This mission was approved despite the fact that *U69* was a Type VIIC, smaller and with less range than the boats he normally sent into the South Atlantic. Dönitz apparently decided this would be an opportunity to test an idea that had been proposed before, using his more numerous Type VIIs on longer missions, extending their range by a combination of economical cruising and refueling from other U-boats or supply ships. Loaded with mines and torpedoes, *U69* departed Lorient, France, on 5 May, proceeding slowly on one engine.

U69 refueled from a tanker on 19 May, then continued south. Two nights later, a lighted ship was sighted. Following strict prize procedures, the steamer was instructed to stop, identify herself and make no radio transmissions, under threat of being immediately sunk. Metzler demanded that the master bring the ship's papers, including the cargo manifest, to be inspected. After examining the papers, he announced the steamer was carrying contraband, specifically radios and guns, and would therefore be sunk.[†] The 38 crewmen and eight passengers (four men, three women and a two-year-old child) were allowed to take to the four lifeboats, after which *Robin Moor* was hit by a single torpedo and then was shelled until she sank.

Metzler drew his U-boat alongside the lifeboat containing the master, gave him four tins of biscuit and two of butter for distribution among the four boats, and took the boats under tow. The slow-speed tow did not last long because later that same day, *U69* found and sank the British steamer *Tewkesbury* about 95 nm to the south-south-east, and the tow had been dropped some time before that. When he cut the boats loose, Metzler said he would radio the position of the lifeboats; if he did so, the transmission was never received. He told the survivors that they were close to shore and were in a favorable current that would bring them ashore in a few days. In fact they were still 670 nm from the nearest land and the current took them away from Africa. Three boats stayed together until 2 June, when they were rescued by a British steamer. The other lifeboat was found on 8 June, after drifting for 19 days and almost 875 nm to the south-west. Incredibly, only one person died during this ordeal, lost overboard after being rescued, an apparent suicide.

The reaction in America was outrage. From the President on down, most Americans expressed shock that an American ship on a peaceful voyage far

---

* Metzler's log reports the sighting occurring at 0525, but U-boats in the Atlantic kept Central European Time (CET), which was three hours ahead of local time in the mid-Atlantic.
† Wynn, *U-Boat Operations*, vol. 1, p 5.1.

from a war zone should be sunk and the passengers and crew abandoned on the open sea. (In fact, Metzler had scrupulously followed international law in his stopping and sinking of *Robin Moor*.) Almost the only official reaction by the US Government was to order the closure of all German consulates on 16 June 'for inappropriate activity'. This left the main embassy in Washington, DC, as Germany's only diplomatic outpost in the US. Five days later, all Italian consulates were similarly closed.

Units of the Atlantic Fleet, new and old, were kept busy during this period patrolling the extended Neutrality Zone. Typical patrols were uneventful, but they took a steady toll on material and men. For example, *Yorktown* arrived at Bermuda on 12 May, 30 days after leaving Pearl Harbor. She was held in harbor while *Bismarck* was loose in the Atlantic, but after the German battleship had been dispatched, she joined the rotation of US capital ships taking lengthy swings through the western Atlantic. She left Bermuda on 31 May on a patrol that lasted for 13 days and 4,550 nm, ending at Hampton Roads, VA. Two weeks later, she left on a 15-day patrol. This was a pace that was difficult to maintain by a navy trying to shake off the habits of a long peace.

One reason why these patrols were largely uneventful was that they were restricted to the western Atlantic, where U-boats were not yet regularly patrolling. Another was that they were often carried out at high speed, in part because the patrol areas were large and could not have been covered at cruising speed. The well-understood side effect of high speed was that a U-boat would have to be perfectly placed to get off a shot at a high-speed target. (A Type VIIC could make a maximum of 17 knots on the surface, but only under ideal conditions, and 7 knots submerged, but neither was a speed that could be maintained for long.)

On 20 June, on a sweep into the central North Atlantic, the old battleship *Texas*, accompanied by three new destroyers, steaming in the direction of Iceland, was sighted by *U203* (Mützelburg) south-east of Cape Farewell.[*] Mützelburg was well aware of nationality of his target, having correctly identified *Texas*, but chose to attack anyway. His reasoning was that the Americans were inside the German declared war zone and heading towards Great Britain. Additionally, they were zigzagging, which, according to prize law, was prohibited by neutral non-combatants. Because they were zigzagging he was able to keep them in sight for 16 hours, over 140 nm, at one point having a long-range trailing shot lined up when *Texas* zigged away. Eventually, he lost them when they reached the eastern limit of their patrol area and turned back into a gathering storm. The Americans remained unaware of *U203* throughout the entire encounter.

Still unwilling to commit the Atlantic Fleet to escorting convoys, the President decided on 4 June to send US ground forces to occupy Iceland, with

---

[*]   Blair, *Hitler's U-Boat War: The Hunters*, pp. 308–9; Abbazia, *Mr. Roosevelt's Navy*, p. 174; [Hessler] *The U-boat War in the Atlantic 1939–1945*, vol. 1, pp. 86–7; uboat.net.

Seen from Wasp, *the battleship* Arkansas *(BB33) departs Norfolk in late June 1941 to participate in Operation* INDIGO, *the convoy carrying the first detachment of US Marines to Iceland.* Arkansas *was the oldest American battleship to see combat in the Second World War. She would lose her cage foremast during a lengthy refit in mid-1942. (NARA)*

the intent of relieving the 25,000 Canadian troops.* The US Army had grown to almost a million-and-a-half men through the draft that was authorized in September 1940, but was still largely untrained and under-equipped, and further was hobbled by the requirement in the Selective Training and Service Act of 1940 that only troops who volunteered for military duty could be sent outside the Western Hemisphere.† No amount of redrawing of lines could legalize the sending of draftees to Iceland.

The only practical solution was to occupy Iceland with Marines, who, being volunteers, were not restricted in their movements. The Marines, just like the Army, were going through a rapid expansion and were just as untrained and, if anything, even more under-equipped. With the 1st Marine Division forming on the East Coast committed to a possible invasion of the French West Indies, the only possible source of Marines for Iceland was the 2nd Marine Division, forming in California. The 1st Marine Brigade (Provisional), cobbled together from pieces of all three regiments of that division and some support units from the East Coast, was formally organized at Charleston, SC on 16 June.

---

*   Abbazia, *Mr. Roosevelt's Navy*, pp. 197–204.

†   Clifford, *The United States Marines in Iceland*, p. 3.

On 22 June the last cargo was loaded and 4,095 Marines departed Charleston in six ships, initiating Operation INDIGO.* They were met by TF19 comprising the old battleships *Arkansas* (BB33) and *New York* (BB34), the new light cruisers *Brooklyn* and *Nashville*, 13 destroyers, an oiler and a tug. They arrived at Argentia on Newfoundland's south coast on the 27th, dropped anchor, and waited. The Prime Minister of Iceland proved to be a shrewd bargainer, holding out for favorable trading terms and an American promise to support Iceland's independence from Denmark after the war. Agreement was finally reached on 1 July and the task force departed Newfoundland the same day. The six transports were dropped off at Reykjavik at 1900 on 7 July, while the warships continued up the coast to the Royal Navy anchorage at Hvalfjordur.† A long inlet north of the capital, it soon became notorious among American sailors for the constant winds, frequent storms and poor anchorage, with a rocky seabed that allowed anchors to drag. Because Icelandic sounds very unusual to most American ears, Reykjavik became known as 'Rinky Dink' and Hvalfjordur as 'Valley Forge'.

The Germans were taken completely off guard by the American move; they had been aware of the troop movements, but believed the Americans intended to occupy the Azores. The American public overwhelmingly supported the move. Admiral King knew, as did FDR, that having Marines in Iceland made it necessary to run regular supply convoys to the island through waters in which U-boat packs operated. That this increased the odds of an 'incident' involving a US Navy warship was well-understood. It is safe to say neither the Admiral nor the President would have been unhappy should such an event occur.

One of the immediate needs in Iceland was for fighter aircraft to defend against possible German bombing raids. As none of the available aircraft had the range to fly to Iceland, they would have to be carried there by ship. As if preparing for this moment, the new aircraft carrier *Wasp* had, in October 1940, taken a deckload of USAAC P-40s and O-47A observation aircraft out from Norfolk and successfully launched them for flight back to land.‡ Thus, *Wasp* was chosen to transport the 30 P-40s and three trainers of the USAAC 33rd PS to Iceland in late July 1941 on INDIGO II.§ She sailed from Norfolk on 28 July, joining up with TF16 under Rear-Admiral Robert C. 'Ike' Giffen. Besides *Wasp*, the task force comprised *Mississippi*, *Quincy*, *Vincennes* and *Wichita*, eight destroyers, an oiler, a transport, a refrigerated store ship and USATS *American Legion* carrying

---

*   Abbazia, *Mr. Roosevelt's Navy*, pp. 201–4.

†   The official Icelandic spelling is Hvalfjörður, but for simplicity, the anglicized spelling is used here. It is pronounced roughly 'kvahl-fyoorthur'.

‡   The land-based military aviation of the US was known as the United States Army Air Corps (USAAC), until 9 March 1942, when it was subsumed under the United States Army Air Force (USAAF) .

§   Abbazia, *Mr. Roosevelt's Navy*, pp. 206–7.

An important task for the small number of aircraft carriers in the Atlantic was the delivery of land-based aircraft across the ocean. To demonstrate the feasibility of this operation, Wasp *took a detachment of early model P-40 Warhawks of the 8th PG out to sea from Norfolk on 14 October 1940 and successfully launched them for flight back to land. (NARA)*

the 1,100 men of the squadron's ground element.[*] At dawn on 4 August, the USAAC aircraft were flown off without mishap, and *Wasp*, *Vincennes* and *Wasp's* two plane-guard destroyers turned around for a high-speed run back to Norfolk. The remaining ships continued on to Reykjavik and Hvalfjordur, leaving again on 12 August. On the return trip, *U43* (Lüth) caught sight of *Mississippi* moving past at high speed, but was never able to line up a shot.

Finally, at the beginning of September, the US Army had a brigade-sized unit of volunteers ready to be transported to Iceland. The escort for the seven USATS transports, plus an oiler and a repair ship needed at Valley Forge, comprised *Idaho*, *Tuscaloosa*, *Vincennes* and 15 destroyers. INDIGO III assembled off New York on 6 September.[†] They arrived at Reykjavik on 15 September with no losses through generally calm, but often foggy, seas. The escorts made eight separate attacks on sonar contacts, but not one appears to have been a genuine target.

---

[*]   On her return from this voyage, USATS *American Legion* was acquired by the Navy, retaining her name, but now given the designation AP35.

[†]   Abbazia, *Mr. Roosevelt's Navy*, pp. 234–8; Rohwer, *Chronology of the War at Sea 1939–1945*, p. 96.

The second troop convoy to Iceland, INDIGO II, *is seen from* Wasp, *2 August 1941. Leading the column is the battleship* Mississippi *(BB41), followed by the Navy cargo ship* Almaack *(AK27) and* American Legion, *the latter in USATS service and colors. These were white hull, tan and black funnels with red-white-blue bands and the large flag on the side amidships. (NARA)*

BARBAROSSA, Germany's attack on Russia on 22 June 1941, surprised almost everyone, including the Americans. Admiral Stark argued that this was the ideal time for the US to announce its entry into the war, given that Germany's attention would be riveted elsewhere.[*] The President had no intention of declaring war without an act by the enemy that would assure him of overwhelming popular support. Nevertheless, he informed Stark at the end of June that it was his intention to begin escorting North Atlantic convoys in the near future. So convinced was Stark that FDR meant it this time, that he ordered King to ready Bristol's Support Force for immediate action.

Once again, the President blinked. Japanese moves against southern Indo-China, made evident by MAGIC decrypts, were planned for July.[†] Over Stark's objections, Roosevelt informed Japanese Ambassador Nomura Kichisaburo

---

[*] Abbazia, *Mr. Roosevelt's Navy*, p. 213.

[†] MAGIC was the codename given to intelligence derived from reading the Japanese 'Purple' diplomatic code.

As SS America, *she had been the flagship of the United States Line; as* West Point *(AP23) she started her naval service carrying refugees to and from Europe. Painted in overall Sea Blue (5-S), not yet an official camouflage scheme, she is seen arriving at New York from Lisbon with expelled American and Chinese diplomats on 1 August 1941. (navsource.org/ Paul Morrell)*

that the US would respond strongly to a Japanese occupation of southern Indo-China. (Stark wanted to give the Japanese no provocation to attack.) Nevertheless, on 24 July, the same day Roosevelt met with Nomura, the Vichy French colonial government in Saigon gave in to Japanese demands and agreed to Japanese occupation of the entire territory. In mid-July, FDR told Stark that the start of escort operations would again be delayed.

SS *America* had been the pride of the United States Lines' passenger service. Launched in 1939, she was America's attempt to compete for the lucrative trans-Atlantic passenger market. Not as fast as the Cunard–White Star's *Queen Mary* or the CGT's *Normandie*, she was every bit as luxurious. Unfortunately, the timing of her launch could not have been worse. Entering service in August 1940, she was unable to make the transatlantic runs for which she had been designed. She made a few cruises to the Caribbean and two to California, but it was no doubt with some relief to the management of the United States Lines that she was requisitioned by the Navy on 1 June 1941, being commissioned USS *West Point* (AP23) two weeks later.

On 16 July, having completed a rapid refit that converted staterooms and ballrooms into barracks, *West Point* anchored off the Staten Island quarantine station and took onboard the diplomats and their families from the closed Axis consulates.* In total, 137 Italian nationals and 327 Germans boarded. *West Point* left New York for Lisbon that same day, arriving on 23 July. She stayed there for three days, hosting receptions for Portuguese dignitaries, transferring supplies to the American station ship, the Coast Guard cutter *Ingham* (WPG35), and taking onboard 388 US and Chinese nationals, mostly diplomats and their families from consulates closed in retribution by Germany and Italy. She arrived back safely at New York on 1 August.

It was the intransigence of the Japanese after the occupation of French Indo-China that convinced FDR that there was nothing he could do to slow the approach of war in the Pacific and that, therefore, there was no reason to further

---

* *Dictionary of American Naval Fighting Ships.*

H.M.S.WARSPITE 14–42

One of the first and most important benefits the Royal Navy received from Lend-Lease was access to American shipyards. One of the first to take advantage of this was HMS Warspite *(03), seen at Puget Sound Navy Yard in early January 1942. She had been damaged by German aircraft off Crete in May 1941. After temporary repairs at Alexandria, she made the long trip to the US West Coast. A* Colorado-*class battleship is docked to the left. (NHHC)*

delay the decision on escorting convoys. Having reached this conclusion, it now became clear that this was the ideal time to go forward with an idea that had been pressed by Hopkins for some time: a face-to-face meeting between the President and Prime Minister.[*]

The obvious logistical problems were disposed of quickly. It would have been dangerous for Roosevelt to go to London. The last major raid of the Blitz had happened in mid-May, but the ensuing two-month lull was no guarantee that they could not resume at any time, particularly if the Germans got wind of FDR's presence. The ideal solution was a meeting afloat in some protected harbor as close as possible to mid-way between the two nations. The British proposed Loon Bay on the northern coast of Newfoundland for its remoteness. The Americans countered with Argentia for its better defenses. The British conceded this point, and plans were made for the two heads of state to meet at the end of the first week in August. With his love of chicanery, Roosevelt announced he was going on an overdue fishing trip off the Maine coast in the Presidential yacht *Potomac*

---

[*]   Churchill, *The Second World War: The Grand Alliance*, p. 427.

The second day of the Argentia Conference, 10 August 1941, was a Sunday, and a religious service was held on the spacious fantail of HMS Prince of Wales *(53). The destroyer leader* McDougal *(DD358) carried FDR to the British battleship. Waiting for the brow to be secured, Churchill leans over to pet the battleship's cat, to the amusement of onlookers; FDR waits patiently, seated behind mount 51, chatting with a naval aide. (NARA)*

(AG25).[*] *Potomac* overnighted in Menemsha Bight off Martha's Vineyard. There she met *Augusta* (CA31) and *Tuscaloosa*, and five destroyers. The President transferred during the night to *Augusta* and had departed before the sun rose, leaving *Potomac* still flying the Presidential pennant, with a middle-aged chief, dressed up to resemble FDR, enjoying a week of fishing around the bay.

Augusta and her escorts, in the meanwhile, made a high-speed run to Argentia, which she entered on 7 August. Churchill had left Scapa Flow on 4 August in HMS *Prince of Wales*, escorted by four destroyers. He arrived on 9 August, accompanied by Harry Hopkins, who had stopped in London after being dispatched by FDR to Moscow.

The first day together in Argentia was spent exchanging pleasantries and gifts.[†] The American sailors enjoyed visiting *Prince of Wales* because of the relatively free availability of alcohol; the President sent over a gift box containing cheese, apples, cigarettes and American magazines for every man on *Prince of*

---

[*]   Cressman, *The Official Chronology*, pp. 48–9; Morison, *History*, vol. I, pp. 69–70.

[†]   Abbazia, *Mr. Roosevelt's Navy*, pp. 219–22.

A few minutes later, FDR tries to make himself as comfortable as possible seated next to Churchill on Prince of Wales. *Standing immediately behind the President is Admiral Ernest J. King; next to him is the CNO, Admiral Harold R. Stark. To the left, further in the background, looking on with concern, is Harry Hopkins. Just visible between King and Stark is W. Averell Harriman. (NARA)*

Wales. The 'Limeys' enjoyed the food and the cigarettes immensely, but were bewildered by the magazines with their advertisements for cars, appliances and foods, particularly fresh meats, long rationed or totally unavailable in wartime Britain.

Churchill was perturbed that Roosevelt came to the meeting without a written agenda, but eventually accepted that all the President wanted from the meeting was a chance for the leaders of the two nations to meet face-to-face, so that, when the war came to America, close co-operation between the two nations would be possible from the beginning. Roosevelt most definitely did not want to make sweeping commitments to any new policy or strategy, in particular brushing aside Churchill's insistence that he set a firm date for American entry into the war.

The British wanted American agreement to the British strategy of fighting Hitler on the periphery of his dominions, securing Africa and the Middle East for starters, attacking Germany only with strategic bombing for the foreseeable future. The Americans disagreed, insisting that large-scale land warfare in

Heading back to England after the Atlantic Charter was signed, Churchill could not resist stopping off at Iceland and reviewing the US Marines recently arrived there, 16 August 1941. (USMC)

France would be necessary to defeat Hitler and should start as soon as sufficient forces could be assembled. This discussion was, at this point, purely theoretical, as the British understood that the US Army was struggling to train and equip its many new soldiers.

On naval matters, the major event was the formal announcement by the Americans of Roosevelt's decision to start escorting convoys in the western Atlantic as soon as possible. The basic mechanics of a chain of interlocking escort assignments was worked out, with the Canadians responsible for the westernmost leg between Halifax or Sydney, NS, and Cape Race – the south-eastern tip of Newfoundland – the Americans from there to a point south of the western tip of Iceland, and the British from there east. This worked out well for the Americans, in that it allowed them to use Argentia and Hvalfjordur as bases for their escort groups.

On other naval matters, though, the British were frustrated. They had hoped to get agreement that a sizable American naval detachment would be based at Singapore, but, lacking that, they requested that the new US battleships *North Carolina* (BB55) and *Washington* (BB56), both working up in the Caribbean, would remain with the Atlantic Fleet. This would allow the Royal Navy to transfer some units at Gibraltar to Singapore. The first three capital ships on the list to be transferred were HMS *Prince of Wales*, *Repulse* (34) and the new aircraft carrier *Indomitable* (92). Because she ran aground while working up in the Caribbean, *Indomitable* was delayed, but *Prince of Wales* – after returning Churchill to Scapa Flow – and *Repulse* were sent on in October without an aircraft carrier. They arrived at Singapore on 2 December in what proved to be very unfortunate timing.

Roosevelt now set 1 September as the target date for the US Navy to begin escorting convoys in the western Atlantic, but again that date came and went

FDR made a high-speed run back to the US aboard the heavy cruiser Augusta *(CA31), King's flagship, seen in the left foreground in this photograph, 14 August 1941. Notable by its presence was the first American escort carrier,* Long Island *(AVG1). The cruiser* Tuscaloosa *(CA37) is at the far right. (NARA)*

without the order to start. The only occurrence of note on that day was the issuance of OPPLAN 7-41, Admiral King's statement of the 'rules of engagement' for the upcoming escort missions. The language was plain and unambiguous, emphasized by being spelled out in all-capitals:

> MY INTERPRETATION OF THREAT TO UNITED STATES OR ICELAND FLAG SHIPPING WHETHER ESCORTED OR NOT, IS THAT THREAT EXISTS WHEN:
> 1) POTENTIALLY HOSTILE VESSELS ARE ACTUALLY WITHIN SIGHT OR SOUND CONTACT OF SUCH SHIPPING OR ITS ESCORT.
> 2) POTENTIALLY HOSTILE SURFACE RAIDERS APPROACH WITHIN 100 MILES OF SUCH SHIPPING, ALONG THE SEA LANES BETWEEN NORTH AMERICA AND ICELAND.
> 3) POTENTIALLY HOSTILE SURFACE RAIDERS OR SUBMARINES . . . ENTER THE PROCLAIMED NEUTRALITY ZONE.
> 4) ANY POTENTIALLY HOSTILE FORCES APPROACH TO WITHIN FIFTY MILES OF ICELAND.[*]

Equally unambiguous was the course to be followed should such a threat be detected:

> DESTROY HOSTILE FORCES THAT THREATEN SHIPPING NAMED ABOVE . . .[†]

---

[*]   O'Connor, *FDR's Undeclared War.*

[†]   Ibid.

Roosevelt still hesitated to give the final order to begin escorting convoys. He was apparently waiting for there to be a backlog of American and Icelandic shipping at both ends. Suspicion at the time was that he did this so he could claim that the American naval vessels were protecting American and Icelandic ships, and the fact that a British convoy also was being protected at the same time was a happy coincidence. Even at this late date, FDR was reluctant to make a move that appeared overly aggressive for reasons of both internal and international politics.*

Many of the President's closest advisors knew that he hoped that some incident would happen in the Atlantic that could serve as a pretext for escorting convoys. As if on cue, just such an incident occurred on 4 September, 125 nm south-west of Iceland. The flush-decker *Greer* (DD145) was carrying mail to the Marines on the island. Ten miles north-west of *Greer's* course, an RAF Hudson sighted *U652* (Fraatz) on the surface, forcing it to submerge. The Hudson then noticed *Greer* in the vicinity and passed on the contact information. As they were running short of fuel, the aircraft dropped four depth bombs which did no damage and then departed. *Greer* was able to establish sonar contact and trailed Fraatz for an hour-and-a-half. Frustrated, Fraatz fired a torpedo, which *Greer* was able to avoid and then responded with a pattern of eight depth charges, close enough to shake *U652*, but not do any damage.

Fraatz tried a second torpedo, which also missed, and *Greer* responded with a second pattern of depth charges, not as close as the first. Realizing that they needed to end the encounter if *Greer* was to reach Iceland before dark, the destroyer turned away and headed for Reykjavik at high speed. The first real encounter between an American destroyer and a U-boat had ended in a draw.

The diplomatic and military repercussions of the '*Greer* Incident' followed quickly and lasted longer than the encounter. On 10 September, Admiral King was finally able to issue orders to the Support Force to commence escort operations at the earliest possible date. In the meanwhile, the momentum towards active engagement in the war continued to build.

On 11 September, FDR took the occasion of another of his periodic 'Fireside Chats' to announce a further shift in his orders to the Atlantic Fleet. He started the address with a simplified version of the '*Greer* Incident', leaving out everything that occurred before *U652's* first torpedo attack. He then stated:

> This was piracy – legally and morally. It was not the first nor the last act of piracy which the Nazi government has committed against the American flag in this war. Attack has followed attack.
>
> . . .
>
> These Nazi submarines and raiders are the rattlesnakes of the Atlantic. They are a menace to the free pathways of the high seas. They are a challenge

---

*   Abbazia, *Mr. Roosevelt's Navy*, p. 247.

to our sovereignty. They hammer at our most precious rights when they attack ships of the American flag – symbols of our independence, our freedom, our very life.

. . .

It is no act of war on our part when we decide to protect the seas that are vital to American defense. The aggression is not ours. Ours is solely defense.

But let this warning be clear. From now on, if German or Italian vessels of war enter the waters, the protection of which is necessary for American defense they do so at their own peril.

The orders which I have given as Commander in Chief of the United States Army and Navy are to carry out that policy – at once.[*]

The next day, the Coast Guard cutter *Northland*, assisted by *North Star* (WPG59) – both part of the North-east Greenland Patrol – found and boarded the Norwegian sealer *Buskoe* near MacKenzie Bay, midway up the east coast of the island.[†] Warned of *Buskoe*'s mission by British agents in Norway, the two cutters had been able to find no trace of the sealer until a native sledge patrol told *North Star* they had seen a two-masted schooner dropping off men and provisions at a bay further north. *North Star* headed north to check out the landing party, while *Northland* searched further south for the sealer.

Both found what they were looking for on 12 September. *North Star* found the supplies, including provisions and a German portable radio, scattered on a beach, but no trace of the men. *Northland* stopped *Buskoe* because the otherwise innocent-looking schooner had an elaborate set of antennae, very unusual in an age when fishing boats rarely carried radio. *Buskoe* was ordered into MacKenzie Bay and boarded. At first the crew denied having put anyone ashore, but soon began to give details of two 'hunting' parties that had been landed further north. When it was discovered that not only was *Buskoe* equipped with a radio, but also had another portable set similar to the one found by *North Star*, the sealer was officially taken over by a Coast Guard prize crew, the first enemy warship captured by Americans in the Second World War. *Northland* located the second landing party and captured three men, one of them German, along with their radio and codes for reporting weather conditions. As the US was not at war with Germany, the three men were detained for violating Greenland's immigration law.

On 22 September, Admiral King issued a revision to OPPLAN 7-41, designated OPPLAN 7B-41.[‡] In this order, King further clarified the rules regarding the expected behavior of US Navy warships upon sighting a belligerent vessel:

The vessel may not be stopped and boarded. If there is conclusive evidence

[*]   *American Merchant Marine at War*, (www.usmm.org).

[†]   Abbazia, *Mr. Roosevelt's Navy*, pp. 233–4; Browning, *Coast Guard*, (www.uscg.mil).

[‡]   O'Connor, *FDR's Undeclared War*.

that she is a combatant naval vessel, either merchant type raider or a regular naval vessel, she shall be destroyed. Operate as under war conditions, including complete darkening of ships when at sea East of longitude 60 degrees West.[*]

It is difficult to distinguish this from a state of formal belligerence. Admiral Erich Raeder, head of the Kriegsmarine, certainly understood the implications of Roosevelt's speech and all that followed, and asked Hitler to rescind some of the restrictions on attacking warships within the declared blockade zone and to recognize the American Neutrality Zone only west of 60°W. This request was rejected.

With orders in hand, Admiral Bristol now had to organize and position his forces to begin escorting convoys. With only about 30 available escorts – all destroyers, about one-third new, the rest short-legged flush-deckers – it quickly became obvious that the Support Force would not be able to escort every convoy that passed between Newfoundland and Iceland.[†]

At this time, eastbound fast convoys, meaning convoys that could maintain better than 9 knots average speed, assembled at Halifax and were given an 'HX' designation; slow convoys assembled at Sydney and were given an 'SC' designation. Both types of eastbound convoys departed at six-day intervals, with SC convoys leaving a day or two after an HX convoy left Halifax, as this caused the least interference between convoys. Westbound convoys in ballast assembled at Liverpool. There was a similar six-day interval between each fast and each slow convoy. During this period, convoy size was generally between 45 and 60 ships. British escort groups were typically seven to ten ships, only a few being general-purpose destroyers, the rest smaller escort destroyers, sloops, frigates and corvettes designed specifically for convoy escort, a type of vessel the US Navy lacked.

Support Force staff calculated that, with escort groups based at Argentia and Hvalfjordur escorting convoys that averaged 10 knots speed of advance, it would take seven days between transfer points. (The transfer point south of Iceland was quickly dubbed 'MOMP', for Mid-Ocean Meeting Point. The transfer point south of Cape Race was sometimes called 'WOMP' or 'WESTOMP', for Western Ocean Meeting Point. These were not fixed locations; the exact meeting point varied a good deal due to convoys being re-routed to avoid U-boats or delayed by weather.) Allowing two days to reprovision and perform routine maintenance at the turn-around point, a round trip of 16 days was projected for an escort group. A simple application of queuing theory showed that with at most six groups of

---

[*] O'Connor, *FDR's Undeclared War*. The meridian at 60°W just touches the eastern tip of Nova Scotia.

[†] Morison, *History*, vol. I, App. V. This gives the strength of the Support Force at 27 destroyers in three squadrons on 18 March 1941.

destroyers available, the Americans would only be able to escort every other convoy back and forth, and only fast convoys, since the slow convoys would never be able to approach the necessary speed of advance. (The Americans soon learned that even fast convoys rarely were able to achieve 10 knots, the speed of advance being slowed by zigzagging, bad weather and frequent wide detours to avoid U-boat concentrations. By September 1941, between HF/DF and decryption of the radio traffic between Dönitz and his U-boats, convoys were routinely being routed around the wolfpacks.*) Escort for slow convoys between Iceland and Nova Scotia would be provided, to the extent possible, by the Canadians.

What the Americans lacked in experience and equipment, they made up in luck. For over a month, starting when TU4.1.1, comprising two new destroyers and three flush-deckers, picked up HX.180 at the WOMP on 7 September, no convoy protected by the Support Force was even sighted by a U-boat. In this they were aided not only by British Intelligence, but also by the typically atrocious weather found in the North Atlantic in the fall. Storm followed storm, making life miserable for merchant sailors and destroyermen alike, but reducing the U-boats in the North Atlantic to near impotence.

But, if the U-boats had no luck finding the convoys guarded by the Support Force, that did not mean American escort groups would not go looking for a fight. When, on 12 October, TU4.1.4 sailed from Iceland, their mission was to take over the escort of ON.24, a fast convoy of 56 merchantmen westbound in ballast. The convoy was met at the MOMP on schedule, and headed south-west to stay well clear of Cape Farewell. All was quiet except for a couple of attacks on false contacts until 2137 on 15 October when Captain Hewlett Thebaud in *Plunkett* (DD431) received orders to disperse the convoy and take his group to the aid of SC.48.[†]

This slow eastbound convoy of 52 merchantmen was supposed to have a strong escort – one Canadian flush-decker and seven Flower-class corvettes – but had the misfortune of being scattered by a storm, which meant that the main body of the convoy, now down to 42 steamers, was being escorted by only four of the corvettes when it was detected early on 15 October by the southernmost of a line of seven U-boats searching south-east of Cape Farewell.[‡]

The group converged on SC.48 and, on the first night, sank three merchantmen. Rain reduced visibility later that night, preventing further attacks by the gathering wolfpack. But the CIC Western Approaches, warned by ULTRA decrypts, expected that the attack would resume the following night and acted

---

* Winton, ULTRA *at Sea*, pp. 95–6; Sebag-Montefiore, *Enigma*, pp. 158–62. Starting in June 1941, the near-real-time reading of Enigma-encrypted messages caused the percentage of North Atlantic convoys sighted by U-boats to drop from 23 per cent for the period January to May 1941 to 4 per cent for June to August.

† Abbazia, *Mr. Roosevelt's Navy*, pp. 262–3.

‡ uboat.net.

On 17 October 1941, the war became very real for the US Navy. The new destroyer Kearny *(DD432) was torpedoed by U568 (Preuß) opening her forward fireroom to the cold Atlantic. She survived because of her stout construction and the design of her engineering plant that allowed her to keep way on and power to her pumps. This view shows the hole in her starboard side, as she lies tied up to* Monssen *(DD436) at Reykjavik. Both destroyers wear the newly authorized Ms12 Graded System camouflage. Neither as yet has radar. (NARA)*

to strengthen SC.48's escort, including ordering TU4.1.4 to steam at best speed to the aid of the convoy.* Only four of Thebaud's five destroyers arrived before dark; *Kearny* (DD432), one of the four, was ordered to sweep behind the convoy at twilight and drop four single depth charges at random intervals on the spurious notion that this would discourage U-boats trailing the convoy.

If anything, *Kearny*'s depth charges attracted more U-boats, because the attack that started after full dark on 16 October was even more intense. One of the escorts, the corvette HMS *Gladiolus* (K34), was hit soon after dark, exploded violently and sank with all hands. Two steamers and two tankers were also sunk before midnight. Nor did the attack end there; another steamer and another tanker were sunk after midnight. But, for the Americans, the last attack of the night was the most memorable. *U568* (Preuß) found a destroyer silhouetted against a burning tanker. Preuß fired four torpedoes, only one of which hit, but

---

*   ULTRA was the codename given to signals intelligence, including that obtained at GC&CS from the decryption of U-boat message traffic. The Germans considered this traffic secure, because it was encoded with Enigma machines, and, therefore, made no attempt to limit its use. However, Bletchley Park began breaking into U-boat message traffic in November 1940 and was able to read them concurrently (within 24 hours of intercept) in May 1941.

it staggered *Kearny*, hitting at the turn of the bilge in way of the forward fire room, killing 11 and wounding 22, and carving a huge gap in her starboard side. Fortunately, *Kearny* was a new *Gleaves*-class destroyer with split engineering spaces, which, in part, explains why she did not sink that night. The loss of her forward fire room did not mean the loss of all power. Within minutes of the torpedoing, *Kearny* was moving away from the convoy under her own steam. After dawn, she was met by *Greer* and then later by *Monssen* (DD436) with a medical officer from Reykjavik, which she reached after dawn on 19 October. She would be back, escorting convoys again, in April 1942.

To the surprise of many, Roosevelt did not use the '*Kearny* Incident' as an excuse for further commitment of American forces. He did however, use the occasion of Navy Day, 27 October, to make another grand pronouncement, stating bluntly: 'America has been attacked.'* If his goal had been to arouse public opinion, he had achieved his goal; a Gallup poll showed 65 per cent of Americans now favored intervention.† But, he knew better than most that the US was not ready to join the war as a full partner. The limited commitment of naval forces was as far as he was willing to go.

While the President may have seen the Navy's escorting of convoys as a limited commitment of American forces, to the sailors in the Atlantic, especially the sailors in *Kearny*, there was nothing limited about the risks they were running.

Salinas (AO19) had drained her tanks as station oiler at Hvalfjordur and was ordered back home with TU4.1.6, which left Iceland on 23 October to meet westbound ON.28. Because she was joining an already established convoy, *Salinas* was simply stuck at the end of an outside column, rather than in one of the inner columns where an oiler would normally be placed. There, on 30 October, she was hit by two torpedoes from *U106* (Rasch), one aft and the other amidships. She should have been fatally wounded, but she was in ballast and her crew reacted quickly, suppressing the fires and controlling flooding. *Salinas* reached safety under her own power on 3 November. Happily, there had been no deaths or even serious injuries among her crew.

TU4.1.3 met HX.156 on 24 October off Cape Race. They were directed far to the south to avoid a known wolfpack, only to encounter a new one in the process of forming. It was one of these boats, *U552* (Topp), that inflicted on the US Navy its first warship loss of this not-quite-a-war. Topp's victim was the flush-decker *Reuben James* (DD245). Just before dawn on 31 October, she was hit by one or two torpedoes port side below her bridge. The initial detonation was followed seconds later by a larger explosion, probably her forward magazines. When the smoke cleared, her bow was gone, as was most of her crew. The after end lasted less than five minutes, ready-use depth charges exploding as the stern sank. Only 45 men were rescued; 115 perished.

---

* *American Merchant Marine at War,* www.usmm.org/fdr/kearny.html.

† O'Connor, *FDR's Undeclared War.*

To the right in this photograph, taken some time early in 1941, the flush-decker Reuben James *(DD245) is tied up at New York Navy Yard. She would become famous as the first US Navy vessel sunk in the war, being torpedoed by U552 (Topp) on 31 October 1941. She is painted in a variant of the Ms2 Graded System authorized in January. To the left is the newly completed* Edison *(DD439) and behind both is the not-yet-completed* North Carolina *(BB55). (NHHC)*

The sinking of *Reuben James* impacted public opinion in the US far more than the earlier attacks on *Greer*, *Kearny* or *Salinas*. Within days, FDR invoked his executive authority to transfer control of the US Coast Guard to the Navy. Congress passed two amendments to the Neutrality Act that allowed the arming of US-flag merchant shipping and removed the prohibition against US shipping entering belligerent ports. Henceforth, US merchantmen could join the convoys to England. The sinking of American shipping would soon cease to be newsworthy.

——

On receipt of intelligence from ULTRA on 2 November that some of the Kriegsmarine's heavy units, most notably *Bismarck*'s sister *Tirpitz*, were ready to break out into the Atlantic, TG1.3 was organized at Hvalfjordur under 'Ike' Giffen to watch the Denmark Strait, the route used by *Bismarck* during her ill-fated sortie. Assigned to the patrol were *Idaho*, *Mississippi*, *Tuscaloosa*, *Wichita* and three destroyers, a force adequate to take on *Tirpitz* alone or in conjunction with the pocket battleship *Admiral Scheer*, also rumored to be ready to sail. In the event, *Scheer* suffered engine problems, which caused her participation in the planned sortie to be cancelled, and, once Hitler learned that *Tirpitz* was to sail alone, he cancelled the entire plan. The watch was stood down on 5 November.

On 4 November, TG3.6, comprising the old light cruiser *Omaha* (CL4) and

Three battleships of the New Mexico-*class were transferred to the Atlantic Fleet in June 1941. On a day like this, 25 September 1941, the sailors in* Mississippi *(BB41) no doubt wished they had stayed in the Pacific. She is painted in the Ms1 system that called for Dark Gray (5-D) up to the funnel top and Light Gray (5-L) above that. (NARA)*

the destroyer leader *Somers* (DD381), nearing the end of a routine South Atlantic Patrol, was ordered to join a Royal Navy search for a German raider reported just east of Peter & Paul Rocks.* The American ships were well to the north-west of the reported position, but nevertheless searched all through the next day, using *Omaha*'s two floatplanes to sweep large areas to the south-east. Neither this task group nor another based on *Memphis* (CL13) were able to find the reported raider. Late on 5 November, running low on fuel, *Omaha* and *Somers* turned back towards Recife, leaving *Memphis* to continue the search one more day.

At 0506 the next morning, just before standing down from dawn General Quarters, lookouts on *Omaha* sighted a small freighter heading just north of west, painted a worn light gray, showing no lights. Everything about this ship piqued the curiosity of Captain Theodore E. Chandler, *Omaha*'s CO. She was

---

*   CL4-1; CL4-2; DD381-1; Cressman, *The Official Chronology*, p. 55; Abbazia, *Mr. Roosevelt's Navy*, pp. 346–9; Roscoe, *United States Destroyer Operations*, pp. 40–1. Officially the St Peter and St Paul Archipelago, this group of 15 rocky islets is located in the Atlantic just north of the equator, almost midway between Brazil and the western tip of Africa.

In the meager protection of Hvalfjordur, Mississippi *is seen behind a pair of Royal Navy Tribal-class destroyers, HMS* Bedouin *(G67) to the left and* Punjabi *(G21), 4 October 1941. Within months,* Mississippi *and her sisters would be on their way back to the Pacific, and neither destroyer would survive the next year of battle. (NARA)*

far from normal shipping lanes, sailing alone, which would not be unusual for a neutral ship, but her name and all markings should have been well-illuminated. However, she bore none of the standard neutrality markings; where the national flag and ship's name should have been painted large on her sides, her crew had hung an actual flag – an American flag. She had the name *Willmoto* painted at her bow and the same name and her homeport – Philadelphia – across her stern. Additionally, she had the pennants for the letters 'KIFG' flying from her signal halyard, which was the correct international call sign for the American steamer *Willmoto.*

Altogether, these were enough to cause Chandler to increase speed and close the freighter. Closer examination did nothing to lessen his suspicions:

3. OMAHA continued cruising around the vessel and, noticing that some of her characteristics did not coincide with those of WILLMOTO in 'Merchant Ships of the World, 1940'; and, also, that some of her personnel were distinctly un-American in appearance, decided to send a boarding party to board her. At 0637, . . . a boarding party in charge of Lieutenant George E. Carmichael, U.S. Navy, left the ship to board the vessel. Immediately after the boat was lowered into the water the vessel hoisted 'FOX MIKE', meaning: 'I AM SINKING. SEND BOAT FOR PASSENGERS AND CREW'. At the same time they began abandoning ship . . .

4. At the time the boarding party reached the ship, about 0645, two explosions were heard which appeared to be in the after part of the ship. Two lifeboats had already been lowered into the water. The boarding officer ordered all other men back aboard the ship. At 0658 the boarding officer sent the following message to OMAHA:

'THIS IS A GERMAN SHIP X CREW IS TRYING TO LEAVE THE SHIP X THEY SAY IT IS SINKING AFT X I TRIED TO GET DOWN THERE BUT SMOKE PREVENTED X I AM BRINGING THE CREW BACK ABOARD.'*

The ship indeed was the German blockade-runner *Odenwald*, carrying a valuable cargo of raw rubber, truck tires, metals and foodstuffs from Yokohama, heading for Bordeaux. Having taken control of the ship, Carmichael's immediate problem was to determine if she really was sinking and, if so, whether she could be saved. At gunpoint, *Odenwald*'s first officer and chief engineer, the former speaking excellent British-accented English, led a salvage team into the motor room, which was beginning to flood.† The explosions had been in the after cargo holds, which were now open to the sea; watertight access plates in the motor room bulkhead had been left open, as had a sea suction valve, to facilitate the flooding of that compartment. Had the motor room flooded, *Odenwald* would likely have sunk rapidly, but fast action by *Omaha*'s salvage crew closed the suction valve, replaced the access plates and got drain pumps running to reduce flooding in the motor room. Some 400 sacks of oats and peanuts were jettisoned to lighten the ship.

Nevertheless, the ship continued to settle and by 1300 had taken on a serious list to starboard. The salvage crew managed to get the main diesels running by 1430, which powered enough pumps to gain on the flooding in the motor room. After jettisoning 20 bales of raw rubber and 75 tires, and draining the flooded starboard after fuel tank into the motor room bilge, the flooding was controlled to the point that *Odenwald* was able to get underway at approximately 1930. The three ships initially headed for Peter & Paul Rocks, in case *Odenwald* needed to be beached, but as she seemed to be stable, course was changed to northwest towards Trinidad. This was done despite the critical fuel situation on both *Somers* and *Omaha* – *Somers* crew rigged a sail which, they estimated, lowered fuel consumption by 5 gallons per hour.

Concerns about the still touchy political situation in Brazil caused Chandler to choose to head for Trinidad rather than Recife, despite the fact that this added more than 1,500 nm to their voyage. As the small convoy headed towards Trinidad at the most economical speed, *Omaha*'s engineers managed to pump out some of the fuel oil normally inaccessible at the bottom of fuel tanks. Even with the assistance of the jury-rigged sail, *Somers* had to resort to securing the

---

*   CL4-1, p. 2.

†   CL4-2, pp. 1–3.

In a move of dubious legality for a non-belligerent, Omaha (CL4) *lies near the stopped German blockade-runner* Odenwald, *the latter prevented from sinking by the quick work of a salvage party from the light cruiser, 6 November 1941. (NHHC)*

laundry, stopping fresh water bathing and burning diesel fuel and lubricating oil to reach the Royal Navy base.[*]

The capture of *Odenwald* created a tricky legal situation, as the United States was not at war with Germany and, therefore could not apply normal prize law to the capture. The admiral in charge of the US Navy's South Atlantic Force, Rear-Admiral Jonas Ingram, solved the problem by recalling the African Slave Trade Patrol established in 1820, which allowed US Navy ships to seize suspected 'blackbirders' carrying slaves to America. (Congress prohibited the importation of slaves in 1819, even though slavery was not prohibited until Lincoln's Emancipation Proclamation took force on 1 January 1863.) Claiming that *Odenwald*, sailing darkened and using a false name, was suspected of carrying slaves, the crew was interned and the ship and its cargo seized. After refueling at Trinidad, the three ships arrived at San Juan, PR, on 17 November, and the seizure was made official. When Hitler made his famous Reichstag speech on 11 December 1941 declaring war on the United States, he cited *Odenwald*'s seizure as one of the reasons for making that move. (After the war, the legality of *Odenwald*'s seizure was upheld, not because of the fiction that she was a slaver, but rather because, since she had signaled that she was sinking and her crew had been abandoning the ship, the actions of Carmichael's boarding party constituted an act of marine salvage. All crew members of both *Omaha*

---

[*] DD381-1, p. 3.

and *Somers* were awarded prize money; members of the boarding party each received $3,000. It was the first time prize money had been awarded to US Navy sailors since 1839.*)

——

Roosevelt's willingness to help the British was being tested in other ways. The British needed desperately to send reinforcements to strengthen the Eighth Army in Egypt. Ironically, they had the troops and equipment available in Great Britain, but lacked the transport capacity to move a sufficient number to the Middle East in a timely manner.

Churchill turned to Roosevelt for the needed transport. In a letter dated 1 September 1941 he asked for the loan of shipping sufficient to transport two divisions totaling 40,000 men – 12 liners and 20 cargo ships manned by American crews – from October through February 1942.[†] Restrained by US neutrality laws and available resources, Roosevelt nevertheless offered Churchill more than half of what he had requested.

> Replying to your 4014 of September 1, I am sure we can help with your project to reinforce the Middle East Army.
>
> At any rate I can now assure you that we can provide transports for 20,000 men. These ships will be United States Navy transports manned by Navy crews. Our Neutrality Act permits public ships of the Navy to go to any port.
>
> Maritime Commission is arranging to place ten or twelve additional ships in the North Atlantic run between American ports and Great Britain so that you could release ten or twelve of your cargo ships for carrying cargo to the Middle East.[‡]

Given the rudimentary state of American naval transport, this was in fact an extraordinary offer on Roosevelt's part. Six of the largest, most recently acquired US Navy transports – *Wakefield* (AP21), *Mount Vernon* (AP22), *West Point* (AP23), *Orizaba* (AP24), *Leonard Wood* (AP25) and *Joseph T. Dickman* (AP26) – were selected to participate. The first three were large, fast and relatively new liners of the United States Lines made idle by the war; the others were older ships of the ATS transferred to the Navy.

The final plan called for a complex movement of men and ships. On 25 October, the British 18th Division, embarked in the eight troopships of convoy CT.5, departed Liverpool under heavy escort. Three days later, six recently transferred Lend-Lease cargo ships left Halifax in a fast convoy codenamed TANGO escorted by TF14, comprising *New Mexico*, *Yorktown*, *Philadelphia*, *Savannah* and the nine destroyers of DesRon 2. As planned, the two convoys

---

*   *The Second World War – A Day by Day Account*, 6 November 1941.
†   *Map Room File*, 1 September 41, WSC>FDR, No. 4014.
‡   *Map Room File*, 5 September 41, FDR>WSC, unnumbered.

Under escort by US Navy warships and in US Navy transports, British troops for the Middle East sail south in convoy WS.12X. Two of the six transports – J.T. Dickman (AP26) to the left and Orizaba *(AP24) – are seen above the tailplane of an SB2U-1 Vindicator on* Ranger, *21 November 1941. Note the letter 'G' beneath the tail of the Vindicator, painted in yellow and partially obscured by Deck Blue (20-B) stain; the 'G' was the middle letter of 'RGR' painted at both ends of her flight deck for identification by pilots. (NARA)*

met at the MOMP on 2 November and exchanged escort groups. CT.5 arrived at Halifax on 7 November and the transfer of the troops and their equipment to the six US Navy APs began the next day.

The convoy, now named WS.12X, departed Halifax at 0830 on 10 November, heading down the US coastline for Trinidad. The initial escort was provided by a single Canadian destroyer. As U-boats had not yet made their way that far west, this meager escort was considered adequate for the first leg. Five hours later, responsibility for the escort of WS.12X was taken over by TG14.4, under the command of Rear-Admiral Arthur Cook. Coming out of Casco Bay, he led *Ranger, Quincy, Vincennes* and the eight destroyers of DesRon 8. Staying well to the west of U-boat waters, the convoy proceeded to Trinidad without encountering any enemy activity. The only real problem was a mechanical failure in *Leonard Wood* which lowered the planned speed of the convoy. WS.12X reached Trinidad in seven days and, now joined by the oiler *Cimmaron* (AO22), departed for Simon's Town, South Africa, on 19 November.

The convoy was now entering known U-boat hunting grounds, and, since speed was the single best defense against U-boat attack, Cook elected not to slow the convoy to accommodate *Leonard Wood*; she was detached with the destroyer *Moffett* (DD362) with instructions to make their way independently to South Africa. However, *Wood*'s engineers were able to make temporary repairs that allowed her to rejoin the convoy on 27 November.

Despite considerable U-boat activity in the South Atlantic, the convoy was able to remain undetected throughout the Atlantic passage. (ULTRA intercepts allowed one danger to be averted when HMS *Dorsetshire* (40) found and sank the raider *Python* in the act of refueling a pair of U-boats.) On 26 November, at latitude 15°S, confident there were no U-boats near the convoy's track, *Ranger* and two destroyers were detached to return to Trinidad. The convoy proceeded without incident through the next week, the most excitement being supplied by the weather, which built into a south-east gale on 6 December. Late the next afternoon, as the storm was abating, news of the Pearl Harbor attack reached the convoy. The warships of the US Navy that arrived in False Bay on 9 December were now fully at war, at least against the Japanese. (The US declared war on Japan on 8 December 1941; the declarations of war against Germany and Italy passed Congress on 11 December.)

While the entry of America into the war was a cause for joy in London, and certainly a relief for many in Washington, it complicated the plans for the six troopships in WS.12X. The original plan had called for the six ships to offload their troops at Basra, at the head of the Persian Gulf. This would keep them well clear of the more dangerous Red Sea and still allow the overland transport of the troops to Egypt. The outbreak of war in Asia and the unexpectedly rapid advance of Japanese troops on the main British outposts at Hong Kong and Singapore changed those plans. While the loss of Hong Kong would be embarrassing, it would not seriously alter the strategic picture. Singapore was another matter; if the British could hold Singapore, Japanese moves west into the Indian Ocean or south to the Dutch East Indies and Australia would be impeded. When the six troopships, now under British escort, departed on 13 December, the destination was now Bombay (Mumbai) rather than Basra.[*]

The convoy steamed peacefully, if nervously, up the east coast of Africa for eight days until HMS *Ceres* (D59) arrived with instructions to escort *Orizaba* to Mombasa, Kenya. From this point, the six troopships would never again be at the same place at the same time. The following are the highlights of the subsequent movements of the six ships of WS.12X:

23 December: *Mount Vernon* was directed to follow *Orizaba* at best speed for Mombasa.

25 December: *Mount Vernon* arrived at Mombasa. Neither *Mount Vernon*

---

[*]   AP22; AP23-1; AP23-2.

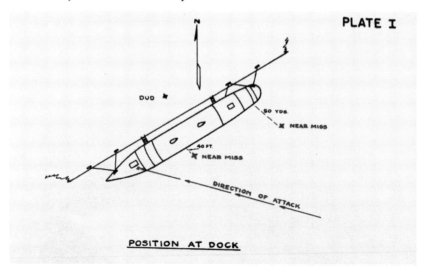

nor *Orizaba* unloaded troops.

27 December: *West Point* and *Wakefield* were instructed to make best speed for Bombay, arriving late in the afternoon. Unloading of *Wakefield* began immediately.

28 December: *Leonard Wood* and *Joseph T. Dickman* arrived at Bombay.

29 December: *Mount Vernon* departed Mombasa to join convoy DM.1 heading for Singapore. Some time later, *Orizaba* departed for Bombay.

2 January: Unloading of the four APs at Bombay was completed.

6 January: *Orizaba* arrived at Bombay. Unloading was completed the next day.

10 January: The three older APs (*Orizaba*, *Wood* and *Dickman*) were declared surplus to needs and left Bombay for Cape Town and eventual return to US East Coast. Convoy DM.1 transited Sunda Strait between Java and Sumatra.

13 January: *Mount Vernon* arrived at Singapore and began unloading troops.

14 January: *Mount Vernon* was near-missed by a Japanese bomb while unloading at Singapore. She departed that same day with orders to head for Aden via Sunda Strait, which she cleared three days later.

19 January: Having reloaded the same troops just offloaded, plus an additional unit of engineers, *West Point* and *Wakefield* departed Bombay for Singapore.

27 January: *West Point* and *Wakefield* cleared Sunda Strait.

28 January: The two transports were bombed by a single Japanese aircraft while transiting Bangka Strait; none of the bombs fell close.

29 January: *West Point* and *Wakefield* docked at Singapore and began unloading troops. All troops were unloaded that same day except the

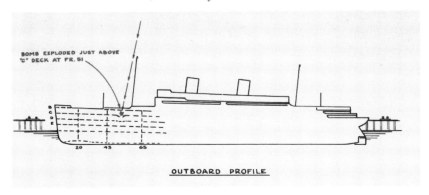

Above and opposite: two drawings from a War Damage Report filed for Wakefield *(AP21) showing the bomb hit made on 30 January 1942 while at Singapore during her epic voyage that took her from Halifax to New York via Bombay, Singapore, Batavia (Jakarta) and Colombo, a voyage of five months' duration. (NARA)*

engineers, who remained onboard.

30 January: Completed unloading the troops' equipment and supplies. *West Point* was near-missed and *Wakefield* hit by a single bomb during a Japanese air raid. The damage to *Wakefield* was not serious, killing five and wounding nine. Carrying more than 1,200 evacuees, the two ships left Singapore that same evening.

31 January: *West Point* and *Wakefield* arrived at Batavia (Jakarta), picking up more refugees.

6 February: *West Point* and *Wakefield* arrived at Colombo, Ceylon (Sri Lanka), where most of their passengers were discharged. Crowding in port led to the ships being redirected to Bombay for provisioning and repairs.

10 February: *West Point* and *Wakefield* arrived at Bombay and discharged their remaining passengers, including the engineering troops. Temporary repairs were begun on *Wakefield*.

16 February: *West Point* departed Bombay for Suez.

end February: *Wakefield* departed Bombay for Cape Town, carrying 336 American evacuees.

23 March: *Wakefield* arrived at New York.

31 March: *Mount Vernon* arrived at San Francisco, after carrying Australian troops from Aden to Fremantle, Australia.

1 April: *West Point* departed Adelaide, Australia, having disembarked the 5353 soldiers of the 7th Australian Division she had loaded at Suez.

24 April: *West Point* arrived at San Francisco, completing what may well have been the longest voyage of the war by a US warship.

As shocking and consequential as news of the Pearl Harbor attack was to the vast majority of Americans, to the sailors of the Atlantic Fleet, and particularly the Support Force, it was almost an anti-climax. They had been up to their necks in this war for months. Now, at last, the ambiguity of participating in something that was war in everything but name would be removed. If they hoped, however, that their past and future efforts in the cold and miserable North Atlantic would get a fair share of publicity and support, they were doomed to disappointment. For most Americans, Argentia and Hvalfjordur held none of the fascination of Samoa, Fiji and Guadalcanal.

3

The Learning Curve
December 1941–September 1942

The period between the formal entry of the US into the war and the first Allied invasions of Axis territory was a span of nine months, during which the US Navy learned how to fight a co-operative campaign against the common enemy. That it would be a difficult period for both of the major Allies quickly became obvious. Despite having been in what had been a shooting war in all but name for eight months, the US Navy was unprepared, both physically and mentally, for the start of full-scale conflict. To make matters worse for Admiral King, the heavy losses at Pearl Harbor necessitated the immediate transfer of some of the strongest units in the Atlantic Fleet to the Pacific. On 9 December, just two days after the Japanese attack, the three *New Mexico*-class battleships left for the Pacific. Except for the brand-new *North Carolina* and *Washington* still working up in the Caribbean, they had been the newest battleships in the Atlantic. The carrier *Yorktown* was in Norfolk, replenishing after a long sweep; she would depart for the Pacific on 16 December. For the moment, *Wasp*, along with the old *Ranger*, remained in the Atlantic. One encouraging sign was the presence of the first US escort carrier, *Long Island* (AVG1), the first in a long series of incredibly useful small aircraft carriers.* Unfortunately, every time a major unit transferred to the Pacific, it took with it an escort of destroyers which most often remained in the Pacific. The effect was a net loss in the category of ship the Atlantic Fleet would soon need most.

For most of the preceding decade, as American war planning increasingly focused on Japan as the likely opponent in any future war, the bulk of the nation's naval force was in the Pacific, and the post of CINCUS was generally held by the commander of the Battle Force or Scouting Force, both based in the Pacific. On 7 December 1941, that post was held by Admiral Husband E. Kimmel, who also

---

* The RN and the Americans first talked about merchant hull conversions to small aircraft carriers in 1940, and the American and British prototypes, *Long Island* and HMS *Audacity* (D10), both came into service in June 1941. The US type designator for escort carriers changed twice during the war. Originally AVG, which indicated a general-purpose aircraft tender, it was changed to ACV (auxiliary aircraft carrier) on 20 August 1942 and to CVE (escort aircraft carrier) on 15 July 1943.

commanded the Pacific Fleet, which had been formed by combining the Battle and Scouting Forces. Perhaps unfairly, Kimmel was blamed for the disaster at Pearl Harbor and was relieved of his appointments both as CINCUS and Commander of the Pacific Fleet on 17 December.

The next day, 18 December, FDR ordered that the position of CINCUS would include operational control of the three fleets – Atlantic, Pacific and Asiatic – and all coastal forces.* It was easy to foresee that this would cause confusion and potential conflict, as CINCUS now took over roles that had belonged to the CNO, who was now mainly responsible for fleet logistics support and long-term (but not current) planning. CINCUS and the CNO would have to co-operate closely to maintain control over a large and rapidly expanding fleet as it went to war. To encourage that co-operation, the Executive Order directed that CINCUS would be posted to the Navy Department in Washington, DC, not afloat as before. A great deal would depend on the personality of the man Roosevelt chose to replace Kimmel.

On 20 December, it was announced that Ernest King would be appointed CINCUS. (King was replaced in command of the Atlantic Fleet by Vice-Admiral Royal E. Ingersoll.) Almost his first act was to change the acronym CINCUS – which was pronounced 'sink us' and brought to many minds the image of battleships in the mud at Pearl Harbor – to COMINCH, an act that announced to all that there would be a complete break with the past. There is no question that King was the man for the job. King would have to manage a war on two-fronts with severely limited resources. There would undoubtedly be trials and setbacks, especially at the beginning. What was needed was a man with unshakeable self-confidence and unyielding determination, who demanded maximum effort from himself and would tolerate nothing less from those who served under him.† A congenial personality was not a requirement of the job.

In King FDR found the man to lead the Navy to victory. In making that choice, however, it is doubtful the President could have found a man less likely to work well with a co-equal CNO. Adding to the problem was FDR's loss of confidence in Stark, who inevitably bore some of the taint of being in command at the time of Pearl Harbor. This difficult situation continued until 26 March 1942, when King assumed the title and duties of CNO as well as COMINCH. Stark was given the posting of Commander, US Naval Forces in Europe based in London. This was rightly seen as a way of getting him as far as possible from King without actually forcing him to retire.

This effectively brings to an end Stark's role as a major player in this story. In London, he was the primary liaison between the US Navy and the Admiralty, a job that required exceptional tact and patience. He performed this difficult role

---

* Executive Order 8984, which can be found at wikisource.org/wiki/Executive_Order_8984.
† Anecdotal evidence suggests that King, a notorious hard drinker, swore off alcohol for the duration of the conflict.

very well, but that could have been done by a number of more junior officers. His place in history, however, is assured by the hard, often unrewarding, work he did seeing the US Navy through the last of the lean, pre-war years and then ably managing its rapid expansion once the nation awoke to the danger of war. He was denied the opportunity to wield the weapon he forged, but it is undeniable that the war was won with the Navy that Stark built.

In advance of the upcoming Arcadia Conference, which started in Washington on 22 December, King proposed a change in convoy routing that would take advantage of Great Circle routing. If he could devise a plan that moved merchant shipping across the Atlantic faster and with better utilization of available escorts, he could better prepare for what he felt with certainty was a coming storm, the 'imminent probability of a submarine attack' on the US East Coast.[*]

Dönitz had asked for sufficient warning from Hitler before Germany went to war with the US, so that he could mount a massive blow, a *Paukenschlag* (literally, a drumbeat), against the Americans. As with most in the U-boat service, he felt great resentment against the restrictions Hitler had imposed on attacking American ships and looked forward to a chance to openly assault American coastal shipping, which was rightly believed to be ripe for the picking. However, the Japanese gave Germany no warning of their planned attack on Pearl Harbor, and Hitler, as impulsive as ever, gave Dönitz only two day's notice of his intent to declare war on the US on 11 December. With that little warning, Dönitz could assemble only six long-range Type IXs to leave for the East Coast of the US and Canada at the end of December, with a further 12 shorter-ranged Type VIIs to operate off the Grand Banks to distract the Allies from the coming drumbeat. To make sure Operation PAUKENSCHLAG was a surprise, the six boats were ordered to ignore all but the largest targets during the crossing. Dönitz wanted them to have all of their torpedoes and as much fuel as possible when they arrived.

As much as King may have wanted to prepare for the anticipated blow, he simply did not have the necessary resources. Eleven Atlantic Fleet destroyers were transferred to the Pacific right after Pearl Harbor and more were off protecting WS.12X, which left 73 destroyers to allocate between Bristol's six escort groups and the on-going need to escort the Fleet's capital ships and troopship convoys. Also, it must be remembered that many of those destroyers had seen hard service over the preceding months and were in great need of repair and refit.

On 1 March 1941 Admiral Andrews was designated commander of the North Atlantic Naval Coastal Frontier, which, at the time, was an organization with little more than a name. As the war approached, the responsibilities of the

[*] Blair, *Hitler's U-Boat War: The Hunters*, p. 456, note. The quote is from a letter from King to Stark dated 17 November 1941.

command were defined and the extent of the command increased. By February 1942, the command extended from Canada to the northern border of Florida. On 6 February, its name was formally changed to Eastern Sea Frontier (ESF). Despite all the effort to organize the ESF and define its responsibilities, it remained little more than a shell. At the end of December 1941, ESF commanded 20 ships, the most useful of which were seven small, slow Coast Guard cutters.[*] None of the 73 Atlantic Fleet destroyers were permanently assigned to the ESF.

The sad fact was that the US Navy went to war with virtually no usable ASW craft smaller than destroyers. It was not a case of the need not being recognized. Stark, King and Roosevelt each understood the need for specialized ASW craft in large numbers, but, for a variety of reasons, they were not available at the beginning of February 1942. A program to build small submarine chasers (SCs) and patrol craft (PCs) had been started in mid-1941, but, as yet, none of these were close to being available. (These smaller patrol craft were ordered at FDR's insistence. Stark would have preferred that all available resources be put into accelerated production of full-sized destroyers, but the President believed correctly that these larger craft would not be available in the numbers needed soon enough. A possible compromise was an ocean-going escort vessel mid-way in size and capability between the small craft FDR preferred and full-size destroyers. An order for 50 of this compromise vessel was proposed in February 1941 by a board set up to study the problem of convoy escort and a formal request for these vessels was submitted to Knox, but Stark vetoed the order in May. The design, however, was resurrected in June when a Royal Navy request for just this type of vessel was submitted through Lend-Lease. The President approved the production of 50 British Destroyer Escorts (BDEs) in August 1941, though the first was not laid down until February 1942 and none were commissioned until January 1943.[†])

At the Arcadia Conference, the British would not consider King's convoy routing proposals unless the Americans agreed to a single, British commander for all convoy operations in the Atlantic. With the full backing of FDR, King refused to accept this arrangement, leading to later charges of Anglophobia. It was only on 12 January 1942, as the conference was winding down, that Commander Roger Winn, head of the Royal Navy's Submarine Tracking Room, was able to make a definitive declaration that an attack on the American East Coast was in the offing.[‡] Specifically, the Tracking Room weekly summary delivered that day stated that two groups of U-boats had been tracked as far west as Newfoundland. One group of six boats was said to be off Cape Race and St John's. (These were, in fact, the leading boats of Gruppe Ziethen, the 12 Type VIIs sent to operate in the Grand Banks area.) The second group, of five boats,

---

[*]   *War Diary, North Atlantic Naval Coastal Frontier, December 1941*, p. 10.

[†]   Friedman, *U.S. Destroyers*, pp. 139–50.

[‡]   Blair, *Hitler's U-Boat War: The Hunters*, p. 454.

Two of the best-known U-boats, and U-boat commanders, are seen leaving Lorient on patrol, 8 June 1941. To the left is U201 *(Schnee), commanded by a popular and successful officer, which took part in the fifth 'wave' of Operation* PAUKENSCHLAG, *having success off Cape Hatteras in April 1942. In the foreground is* U123, *with Kapitänleutnant Reinhard Hardegen in the white cap. Hardegen was bold and even more successful than Schnee, but not nearly as popular. (BAK)*

was reported to be approaching the East Coast between New York City and Portland, ME. (These were five of the six Type IXs assigned to PAUKENSCHLAG; the sixth had turned back due to a major oil leak. Three of the five – *U66* (Zapp), *U123* (Hardegen) and *U125* (Folkers) – were assigned patrol areas off the US coast – Cape Hatteras, New York City and New Jersey, respectively. The other two PAUKENSCHLAG boats – *U109* (Bleichrodt) and *U130* (Kals) – were ordered to operate independently in the Cabot Strait and the Gulf of St Lawrence.) Winn's report also mentioned two other groups further to the east, which appeared to be following towards the west.

When PAUKENSCHLAG began the next day, the five boats found a feast awaiting them. The first to achieve success was Kals in *U130*, who sank two steamers on 13 January in the Cabot Strait, close to the shore of Nova Scotia. The next day, Hardegen sank the Panamanian motor tanker *Norness* approximately 60 nm south-east of Montauk Point, the easternmost tip of Long Island. The war was brought home to American civilians for the first time when he struck again on 15 January, hitting the British tanker *Coimbra* at 0300 just off the south coast of Long Island. When the tanker's cargo of oil caught fire and began to

HMT Northern Duke *(FY11) was one of the 24 ASW trawlers of the 22nd A/S Strike Group lent by the Royal Navy to help the Americans deal with the devastation of the German assault on merchant traffic along the East Coast in 1942. She served out of Charleston, SC, and Norfolk, VA, between March and October 1942.*

burn brightly, it was plainly visible to residents of the Hamptons. Despite these successes and a brash reconnaissance into the outer harbor of New York City, Hardegen found the pickings slim off Long Island, and informed Dönitz he was moving south.[*] Kals had likewise found no targets after the first two, and, on 17 January, was also given permission to move south towards Cape Hatteras.

There they found that ship's masters had instinctively joined together in impromptu groups of up to five ships, which, according to Hardegen, only made his job easier.[†] The ease with which U-boats were able to attack these groups only reinforced King's belief that unescorted or weakly escorted convoys were not a good idea.

Between the five boats of this first 'wave', 23 ships were sunk and several more damaged, a massive toll considering the small number of boats involved.[‡] Not all of these were sunk off the American coast. Just counting those ships, 13 vessels, including six valuable tankers, were sunk in a period of two weeks. Almost all of those sinkings had taken place near Cape Hatteras.

As if this were not enough of a concern for King, there were problems with the safety of the bases in Iceland and Newfoundland. Both were subject to violent weather, particularly in the winter. A major storm hit Hvalfjordur starting 15 January. On the first day, as the winds reached 100 knots, the seaplane tender *Albemarle* (AV5) dragged her anchor – the seabed there was basically bare rock – as did the nearby freighter *West Nohno*. The heavy cruiser *Wichita*, downwind,

---

[*] *B.d.U. Op's WAR LOG*, 17.1.42.

[†] Gannon, *Operation* DRUMBEAT, p. 258.

[‡] Wynn, *U-Boat Operations*, vols. 1 and 2; Blair, *Hitler's U-Boat War: The Hunters*; Rohwer, *Axis Submarine Successes*; uboat.net.

The reality of war was brought home to many Americans for the first time when plumes of oily black smoke were seen off the eastern seaboard. One of the most spectacular resulted from the torpedoing of the tanker R. P. Resor *by U578 (Rehwinkel) on 27 February 1942 off the New Jersey shore.*

was able to avoid *Albemarle*, but fouled anchor cables with the freighter and the two ships collided, striking *Wichita's* bow a glancing blow. Now drifting free before the wind, *Wichita* hit a Royal Navy trawler, finally grounding bow-first on the lee shore. By morning the wind had abated enough that *Wichita* backed off the shore and anchored again in the roadstead. Examination revealed the damage to be minor; the ship's company performed repairs sufficient for her to sail to New York and the shipyard there, which she entered on 9 February.

Conditions at Newfoundland were not much better. On 18 February, *Pollux* (AKS2), a general stores issue ship, and her escort, the flush-decker *Truxton* (DD226), were caught up in a violent squall while entering Placentia Bay. Driven up against the shore near St Lawrence at the southern tip of the Burin Peninsula on the western side of the bay, both ships were run aground. *Truxton* broke up almost immediately, losing 110 crewmen to the high surf. *Pollux's* lookouts sighted the rocky shore just moments before she struck. When it became clear that the ship was hard aground, her captain ordered the engines full ahead to keep her from slipping off and sinking in deep water. Aided by townspeople from St Lawrence, lines were rigged to a rock ledge and most of her crew safely evacuated before she too began to break up. Nevertheless, 95 of her crew perished.

With no agreement in place on King's proposals, the Arcadia talks were followed a week later, on 22 January 1942, by a 'Convoy Conference', this time

One of the many destroyers temporarily assigned patrol duty in the ESF, only to be withdrawn again within days for higher priority duty, was Trippe (DD403), *seen at Norfolk in January 1942. (NARA)*

without Churchill or Pound present.* The British representatives again insisted on unified command of all Atlantic convoys, adding that in the eastern half of the ocean, the local escort commander would have to be British, even if there

---

* Blair, *Hitler's U-Boat War: The Hunters,* pp. 457–60; Hansen, *King, Canada, and the Convoys,* p. 68.

was a senior American officer present. Further, they pressed for the immediate formation of coastal convoys along the American East Coast. King's reaction was once again to reject the idea of a single commander for all Atlantic escorts, and to state emphatically his conclusion, based on rigorous analysis, that coastal convoys should not be started until adequate escorts could be found.* As he pointed out, a major objective of his plan was to free up sufficient American destroyers so that these convoys could be instituted.

Within two days the conference reached a compromise agreement.† The British agreed to split command of convoys, with Admiral Sir Percy Noble of the Western Approaches Command in charge east of Iceland and Bristol from there westward. They also agreed to the more southerly Great Circle routing. In turn, King agreed to provide 30 destroyers to fill out the convoy escort groups, actually five more than the number then assigned to this task. That left him approximately 40 destroyers to tend to the other needs in the Atlantic, including ten flush-deckers tentatively allocated for coastal escort.

The truth is that King was having to do what he had instructed his subordinates to do after taking over the Atlantic Fleet. 'We must all do all that we can with what we have.'‡ As COMINCH, King knew well the limits of the resources he had available to protect the shipping along the East Coast. Before the last of the ships lost to the first 'wave' of PAUKENSCHLAG had settled to the ocean floor, Andrews and King knew they had a problem. What they did not know, and had no way of knowing, was how serious it would become.

Experience told them that the Germans would not be able to sustain a major offensive off the American East Coast. The Germans simply did not possess enough of the long-range Type IXs to continue the assault begun in February. They might have known that the enemy would in fact be able to do so as a result of new tactics and techniques had the Germans not changed their codes, ending the flow of ULTRA decrypts for almost 11 months.§ By careful fuel management and the introduction of a sophisticated method of sharing fuel between boats, the Germans were able to extend their patrols and use the shorter-ranging Type VIIs off the American coast. By these means, Dönitz was able to maintain an uninterrupted presence off the East Coast.

The idea that U-boats could replenish at sea was not new. Boats operating in the South Atlantic had regularly replenished from surface ships since early in the war. That this kind of operation would be useful in the North Atlantic had also been foreseen. As early as 8 September 1939, Dönitz had proposed the

---

*   Hansen, Kenneth P., *King, Canada, and the Convoys*, pp. 63–9.

†   Blair, *Hitler's U-Boat War: The Hunters*, pp. 457–8.

‡   Atlantic Fleet Confidential Memorandum 2CM-41, quoted in Morison, *History*, vol. I, p. 53.

§   The ULTRA 'blackout' began in late January 1942, when the Germans changed their short weather report codebook on 20 January 1942. It was made worse by the introduction on 1 February of a new Enigma machine with a fourth rotor and a new reflector.

construction of 'submarine-tankers' to refuel boats at sea.* This suggestion was acted on with energy and the first Type XIV *Milchkuh* (Milk Cow), *U459*, was laid down in November 1940 and left on its first mission at the end of March 1942. The advantage to be gained from replenishing U-boats at sea was such that Dönitz ordered that *UA*, an oversized boat originally built for Turkey, also be employed as a replenishment boat. Her first supply mission began in mid-March 1942 and included the refueling of three Type VIIs in the fourth 'wave' of PAUKENSCHLAG in early April. New or not, Admirals King and Andrews were unaware of this critically important innovation in the deployment of U-boats because of the ULTRA 'blackout'.

Technically, Operation PAUKENSCHLAG was just the first 'wave' of five boats, all of which were on their way back to France at the beginning of February 1942. The four successive 'waves' of attacking U-boats that arrived without pause off the American coast between then and May were not officially part of PAUKENSCHLAG or any other named operation. Even then the assault did not end, it just moved further south into the Caribbean and the Gulf of Mexico. Dönitz would send his boats wherever there were targets to be found and the defenses were weakest. It was not until July that the Germans moved the last of their attacking U-boats away from the American coast and back into the North Atlantic, where the critical battle to sustain Great Britain would be won or lost.

It is not clear exactly when the Allies came to realize that a crisis was developing off the American coast. There is no question that it came to the attention of the British before the Americans, for which the American naval establishment, from FDR on down, has been roundly criticized. No-one has been targeted more frequently or harshly than Admiral King for this and for the failure of the Americans to respond more rapidly and effectively, but the critics often fail to take into account what King could have been expected to know and act on at the end of January 1942 or the resources available to him with which to act.

One fact the Americans knew for certain at the end of January was that, so far, more ships had been sunk in Canadian waters than their own. Also, King knew and had to be concerned that the Japanese had sunk two tankers and damaged five more off the West Coast that same month. At the time, it would not have been obvious that Japanese submarines would never return in strength to the American coast or that U-boat commanders would largely abandon Canadian waters in February, moving south along the American coast where there were more targets and the weather was more favorable. Not even in the earliest days of the war had they found so many ships sailing without any noticeable protection, lit up as in peacetime, silhouetted against undimmed coastal lights. So easy were the pickings in those first days that, among other names, the Germans began referring to area between Miami and New York as the 'American Shooting

---

* Rössler, *The U-boat*, pp. 146, 151–2.

Gallery'.* So many sinkings occurred around Cape Hatteras, the Americans took to calling the area 'Torpedo Junction'.

Expected or not, the Germans returned in strength in February and even began operating in the Caribbean, going so far as to shell an oil refinery on Aruba. The British were in no mood to be understanding of the problems faced by King, Ingersoll and Andrews. They knew that their survival depended on a steady flow of supplies from the New World, particularly the oil carried by tankers that seemed to be the favorite target of the U-boats operating in American waters. As early as 6 February, Churchill sent a note to Washington that read, in part: 'It would be well to make sure that the President's attention is drawn to the very heavy sinkings by U-boats in the Western North Atlantic.'† As the wording of the note indicates, it was not sent to Roosevelt or to King, but rather to Harry Hopkins, the one person in Washington Churchill felt certain was entirely sympathetic and had the President's ear. For all the intimacy of his correspondence with the President, Churchill obviously felt this subject was too sensitive to raise directly with FDR. There is, however, no indication that Hopkins ever delivered this message.

The carnage along America's East Coast only increased. Losses of shipping to U-boats in all areas had risen from 93,000 tons in December 1941 to 301,000 tons in January 1942 (with 202,000 of that being lost in American and Canadian waters and around Bermuda) and 429,000 tons in February (with 328,000 of that lost there and in the Caribbean). The losses in the ESF in February were 17 ships, with a further 19 lost in the western Caribbean and nine more near Bermuda. (Sinkings in Canadian waters had dropped not because Canadian defense was any better than the American, but because U-boat commanders found operating in the calmer and warmer waters further south to be easier.) Sinkings would rise again in March 1942 to 507,000 tons (with 384,000 lost in these same areas).‡ Churchill could not be blamed for believing that an existential crisis was developing in the Western Hemisphere.

When the Prime Minister next raised the subject with the Americans, in another message to Hopkins dated 12 March, he was even more concerned. After enumerating the known losses, emphasizing the loss or damaging of nearly 60 tankers in just over two months, he went on:

> 2. By rearrangement of Atlantic convoy duties a considerable number of American destroyers have been released from escort duties on the cross-Atlantic routes for other services. We have handed over 24 anti-submarine trawlers, of which 23 have now reached you.§

---

*   Hickam, *Torpedo Junction*, p. 34.

†   Churchill, *The Second World War: The Hinge of Fate*, pp. 117–18; Farago, *The Tenth Fleet*, pp. 58–9.

‡   Tarrant, *The U-Boat Offensive*, pp. 101, 105; Morison, *History*, vol. I, p. 413.

§   Churchill, *The Second World War: The Hinge of Fate*, p. 119.

Despite the correctness of both of Churchill's statements, it would be a mistake to take them at face value. The number of 'released' destroyers was far fewer than Churchill believed because of a misunderstanding about how many destroyers were available in the Atlantic. (The British persisted in believing the Americans had more destroyers in the Atlantic than they actually did.*) His statement that 23 trawlers had arrived was misleading. Of 24 trawlers lent to the Americans, one had been lost in transit and the rest required extensive refit after they arrived Only two of the 23 remaining boats were ready for service at the time the note was being written.

Churchill urged that immediate action be taken to protect the coastal shipping, even if that meant reducing the frequency of trans-Atlantic sailing or halting tanker sailings altogether. This message did get delivered and did get a reaction. Roosevelt sent a message to Churchill on 18 March that was surprisingly conciliatory in tone, especially considering the rather brusque manner in which the Prime Minister was telling the Americans how they should be disposing their forces.

FDR admitted that the US Navy had not been prepared for the U-boat campaign off its shores. He could have stated, but did not, that there were valid reasons for this state of affairs that explained, if they did not entirely justify, this lack of preparedness. He stated that his Navy had resisted building or acquiring vessels smaller than general-purpose destroyers, which was only partially true and more than a little self-serving. (The record of who should bear the blame for the American lack of ASW resources in early 1942 is far from clear, with a great deal of finger-pointing and buck-passing, including FDR's comments in his 18 March message. Even before he took over the Atlantic Fleet, King advocated the construction of large numbers of ocean-going escort craft, but Stark and Roosevelt were opposed for different reasons. He strongly supported the February 1941 request for 50 destroyer escorts that was rejected by Stark in May in favor of ordering more full-sized destroyers. The President remembered his First World War experience, when he had pushed through the Eagle boat program, and insisted on the construction of the SCs and PCs that, while they did become available much sooner than any other alternative, were of limited value.†)

Admiral King's reaction to Churchill's note was not as even-tempered as Roosevelt's. He drafted a response for the President that betrayed his irritation, which was forwarded by FDR without revision the next day. King repeated an

---

* Blair, *Hitler's U-Boat War: The Hunters*, p. 458. The British believed the Americans had committed 51 destroyers to the Support Force, when, in fact, that number never surpassed 40. So, when King's new proposal called for only 30 US destroyers for North Atlantic convoy duty, the British assumed 21 destroyers had been freed up for other duty, including coastal escort, when that number was in reality only ten, and, giving the many conflicting demands on these ships, their assignment to ESF duty was provisional at best.

† Morison, *History*, vol. X, pp. 32–3; Farago, *The Tenth Fleet*, pp. 73–4.

earlier demand that RAF assets be used to bomb U-boat bases, shutting down the movement of U-boats at the source. Some say this was simply an attempt to change the subject and find King's and Roosevelt's behavior unseemly.[*] However, Churchill's response, which was to state that such raids would have to wait for better weather and then would have to be considered along with other priority targets, calls into question his position on this contentious subject.[†]

None of which is to imply that mistakes were not made by King, Andrews and others in the first months of 1942. There were steps that could have and should have been taken sooner and would have likely had a beneficial effect. The most obvious would have been the more rapid darkening of shore lights. Time and again, U-boat commanders noted in their diaries the ease with which they found targets silhouetted against the brightly illuminated shoreline. Initial requests to local governments to reduce lighting near the shore met with surprising resistance. Merchants claimed it would interfere with business, and police said it would be an open invitation to criminals. It was not until 14 March that a 'dim out' of coastal lighting was ordered. This fell far short of an immediate and mandatory black out of coastal lights. That did not happen until July.

This is a clear and unmistakable instance of action that ESF and King could have and should have taken much sooner. That they moved too slowly setting up coastal convoys is far less obvious. Their contention that unescorted, or inadequately escorted, coastal convoys were worse than none must remain a matter for debate. However, there is one type of convoy that could have been instituted immediately and was not. The mistake was not distinguishing the value of tankers from the remaining merchant traffic running along the US East Coast. More than any other commodity, more even than steel, oil had become the indispensable commodity in warfare. Without a plentiful supply of bunker fuel, diesel, gasoline and avgas, no modern military force could operate, and for the US and UK, that meant moving large quantities in a steady flow between the oil fields in Venezuela and Texas, refineries in Trinidad, Aruba, Curaçao and the US, and the UK. Tankers were the vital link and, thus, the loss of a tanker meant far more than the loss of a ship, it meant the loss of a cargo and all future cargoes that tanker might carry, and a consequent reduction in the essential flow of fuels. The disproportionate loss of tankers in the first half of 1942 had impact far beyond the lost tonnage. The direct result of tanker losses in the first half of 1942 was rationing of petroleum products on both sides of the Atlantic and had a role in the postponement of operations planned for 1942 and 1943.

If so much dislocation of plans and discomfiture of people derived from this disturbance in the flow of oil, the obvious question is, could not some sort of special treatment have been devised to protect tanker traffic even if it was not possible to do so for all shipping? As will be seen, such special treatment

---

[*]   Gannon, *Operation* DRUMBEAT, p. 339.

[†]   *Map Room File*, 20 March 1942, WSC>FDR, No. 34.

was eventually forced on the Americans (and the other Allies) in mid-April. King and Andrews can properly be criticized for not having made such moves a month or more earlier.

———

The most important outcome of the Arcadia conference had been the decision to begin an immediate build-up of US troop strength in Iceland, Northern Ireland and England with the aim of launching a ground assault on French North Africa no later than May 1942 (Operation GYMNAST) and on Axis-held Europe in either 1942 (Operation SLEDGEHAMMER) or 1943 (Operation ROUNDUP). In the event, these projects all proved far too ambitious, and none were carried out on this projected timetable. Nevertheless, the US had committed to build up American troops in Iceland and Great Britain, and the process started with a pair of large troop convoys in January.

As much as King may have wanted to provide a sufficient number of destroyers dedicated to coastal escort, he simply did not have enough to go around. Even the ten short-legged flush-deckers he had intended to make available to Andrews were pulled away for other, higher-priority tasks. The troop convoy AT.10 departed New York City on 15 January with five troopships headed for Iceland and Londonderry, which required every available destroyer as escort. The destroyers that escorted AT.10 from New York returned in time to escort convoy BT.200 starting 23 January. This convoy comprised seven troopships carrying the first American contingent sent to the South Pacific. This escort took the convoy safely through to Key West, where they were detached and ordered to return to Casco Bay.

ESF had no chance to mount an effective anti-submarine campaign, much less begin organizing coastal convoys. Andrews was allocated seven new destroyers on 5 February, but before they could be deployed, they were withdrawn again for troop convoy escort. To make up for the loss of these assets, ESF was assigned three flush-deckers. One of them was *Jacob Jones* (DD130) tasked with making anti-submarine patrols off the entrance to New York City. Heading south along the New Jersey shore on 27 February, *Jones* found the burning hulk of tanker *R. P. Resor*, which had been torpedoed by *U578* (Rehwinkel) about 35 nm east of the Barnegat Light. After spending several hours looking for survivors, the destroyer headed south. Lacking radar, extra watch was set after dark as *Jones* continued past the mouth of Delaware Bay. Rehwinkel kept even better watch; at approximately 0500 the next morning, *Jones* was hit by two or three torpedoes and broke in two just aft of her bridge. Her bow sank quickly. No one from the forward part of the ship survived. Most of the rest of the crew died when another of the torpedoes demolished her crew quarters aft. It is estimated that 30 to 35 men made it into life rafts, mostly black gang, but many of them were killed when the aft end sank and armed depth charges detonated. The survivors

One of ten Flower-class corvettes lent to the US Navy by the British in 'Reverse Lend-Lease', Tenacity (PG71), formerly HMS Candytuft (K09), is seen outside the New York Navy Yard on 26 June 1942, soon after being commissioned into the US Navy. (NARA)

were sighted by a patrol aircraft soon after dawn and *Eagle No. 56* (PE56) had recovered 12 men when rising seas forced the rescue to be abandoned at 1100.

American destroyers had more than U-boats to fear.

On the night of March 18th the American freighter LIBERATOR bound for New York from Galveston was just a few miles off Cape Lookout. Her crew had spent a nervous day on constant alert for the submarines they knew were operating in Hatteras waters. In the early evening they had looked out over the stern and watched two vessels go to the bottom after enemy attack.*
. . . A little after midnight the watch saw a strange vessel that looked like a submarine about two miles off on the starboard beam. Word was passed to the gun crew who opened fire upon the target.[†]

The Naval Armed Guard that manned the guns mounted on American merchantmen had little opportunity to practice, but they were uncannily accurate that night. The first shell found its target. Unfortunately, that target was *Dickerson* (DD157), a flush-decker operating out of Norfolk. She reached the southern end of her patrol zone and had just turned back to the north when she was hit.

It is extraordinary what a single four-inch shell can do to a destroyer if it lands in a vulnerable place. This projectile passed through the spray shield on the starboard side and entered the chart house where it detonated. As it exploded it killed a seaman outright and inflicted mortal wounds upon the Commanding Officer, the sound operator and the Radar operator all of

---

*   Cape Lookout is approximately 65 nm south-west of Cape Hatteras. The two sinkings seen from *Liberator* were the American tankers *Papoose* and *W. E. Hutton*, sunk by *U124* (Mohr).

†   *War Diary, North Atlantic Naval Coastal Frontier, March 1942*, ch. III, p. 1.

Roper (DD147) was another destroyer on temporary duty out of Norfolk, but she distinguished herself when, on 14 April 1942, she caught and sank U85 *(Greger). She has an early model SC air search radar on her foremast. (NARA)*

whom were in the chart house. Two other officers were knocked unconscious . . .

Attempts to communicate with the land failed. The radio had been put out of order by the shell and the auxiliary spark transmitter did not work. In the morning the DICKERSON made Norfolk a few minutes after her Captain died.*

In the most exquisite of ironies, *Liberator* was sunk the next morning by *U332* (Liebe), just hours before Lieutenant Commander J. K. Reybold died in *Dickerson.*

The first U-boat sunk by American forces was *U656* (Kröning), sunk on 1 March 1942 by a Hudson flying from Argentia. The second was *U503* (Gericke), sunk on 15 March by a pilot who had mistakenly been credited with sinking another U-boat in late January. The third U-boat sunk by American forces, and the first by a surface ship, was *U85* (Greger) on 14 April. Just after midnight, the destroyer *Roper* (DD147) caught Greger on the surface near Cape Hatteras and made short work of the crew that tried to man the U-boat's deck gun. Within minutes, *U85* slid stern-first beneath the waves, leaving most of her crew in

---

* *War Diary, North Atlantic Naval Coastal Frontier, March 1942*, ch. III, p. 1.

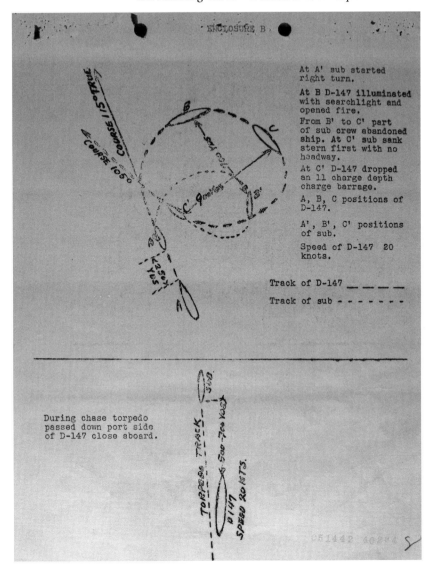

ENCLOSURE B

At A' sub started right turn.

At B D-147 illuminated with searchlight and opened fire.

From B' to C' part of sub crew abandoned ship. At C' sub sank stern first with no headway.

At C' D-147 dropped an 11 charge depth charge barrage.

A, B, C positions of D-147.

A', B', C' positions of sub.

Speed of D-147 20 knots.

Track of D-147 _ _ _ _

Track of sub - - - - - - -

During chase torpedo passed down port side of D-147 close aboard.

A pair of sketches from Roper's Action Report *show (below) the path of the torpedo that near-missed the destroyer, and the paths taken by the two vessels as U85 turned inside the flush-decker's large turning radius, all the while under fire. The U-boat sank at point C', the same point where* Roper *dropped a barrage of 11 depth charges. (NARA)*

the water. Unsure of what had just happened, *Roper* dropped 11 depth charges into the swirl where the U-boat had just disappeared, and then left the scene. Returning in the morning, *Roper* recovered 29 bodies, all of them killed by the

Part of the grim toll of that depth charge barrage, four of the 29 bodies recovered by Roper, *men who had been alive in the water, but were killed by the detonation of depth charges among them. (NARA)*

concussion of the depth charges dropped in their midst. No one of Greger's crew was found alive.

On 20 March 1942, King convened a conference to hammer out a coastal convoy plan. Its greatest challenge, as always, was to figure out how many escorts would be needed and where they would come from. When the conference submitted its report to King seven days later, it had concluded that 31 destroyers and half again as many smaller escorts would be needed. (At that time, ESF had on its rolls three destroyers on temporary assignment, no corvettes – although ten ex-Royal Navy Flower-class corvettes were in the process of being transferred to the US Navy and the first would reach ESF by the end of April – three 173-foot PCs, five 110-foot SCs and 14 of the 23 ASW trawlers lent by the Royal Navy, although there was uncertainty as to how to employ them, and approximately 70 antique Eagle boats, commandeered yachts plus Coast Guard rescue boats.*) It was estimated that necessary number of escort vessels would not be available until mid-May, not for another 45 days.

King had no choice but to accept this conclusion, though he urged Andrews

---

*   Hickam, *Torpedo Junction*, pp. 158–9.

to improvise as best he could. On 1 April, ESF introduced a voluntary 'Bucket Brigade' system around Cape Hatteras, under which merchantmen were urged to anchor at night in protected anchorages north and south of the cape and then travel together in informal convoys during daylight. By mid-month, it was possible to provide four escorts each way, but no attempt was made to make participation in a 'Bucket Brigade' mandatory and losses continued at a high rate at Cape Hatteras and further south.[*]

On 16 April, King took the drastic step of halting all tanker sailings in the ESF. A week later, facing a crisis in oil supply, the British ordered their tankers, piling up at Trinidad due to the sailing ban, to sail independently to Freetown where they would join an SL convoy to Great Britain. On 29 April, Andrews ordered sailings of US-flag tankers restarted. The Canadians came up with their own solution, running dedicated tanker convoys between the Caribbean and Halifax, passing near Bermuda and then north well clear of the American coast. These operated without loss from mid-May until September.[†]

The first mandatory American coastal convoy left New York City on 29 April, escorted as far as the entrance to Delaware Bay, after which the merchantmen could use inland waterways to reach Norfolk. The first regular convoy south from there sailed on 14 May. Sinkings in ESF dropped from 23 in April to five in May. It would be a mistake to credit this entirely to the introduction of convoys. It was also due to the movement of U-boats south, past the border between ESF and the Gulf Sea Frontier (GSF).

One of the last attempts by the Germans to regain the initiative along the American East Coast was the laying of mines at the entrances to several US ports. The first mines in American waters were 15 laid off the entrance to Delaware Bay on 11 June by *U373* (Loeser). The next day, ten more were laid by *U87* (Berger) off Boston. The only victim of these mines was the tug *John R. Williams*, which sank off Delaware, losing 14 men. The third, and by far most successful, of the minefields was laid by *U701* (Degen) off Cape Henry, east of Virginia Beach, VA, also on 12 June. This proved to be in the path of northbound convoy KN.109, approaching Hampton Roads on 15 June. Two tankers in that convoy – *Robert C. Tuttle* and *Esso Augusta* – struck mines. *Tuttle*'s bow sank quickly, but her stern remained above water and she was eventually salvaged and survived the war. *Esso Augusta* was damaged aft and lost power, but she was towed to Norfolk where she was repaired. Less fortunate was the trawler HMT *Kingston Ceylonite*. Escorting another merchantman from the convoy, she blundered into the now identified minefield. A Coast Guard cutter had been sent out to warn the trawler, but had missed the rendezvous. *Kingston Ceylonite* detonated a mine and sank quickly, taking her entire crew with her. The area was then swept for mines and declared safe, but two days later, while southbound convoy KS.511

---

[*] *War Diary, Eastern Sea Frontier, April 1942*, ch. III, p. 2.
[†] Fisher, *'We'll Get Our Own'*, p. 35.

One of two tankers to strike mines on 15 June 1942, in a minefield laid off Cape Henry by U701 (Degen) three days earlier, Robert C. Tuttle *settled on the shallow bottom forward, but was eventually salvaged. (NARA)*

was passing through these waters, the steamer *Santore* set off another of *U701*'s mines and sank within minutes, proving once again that minesweeping is an inexact process.

Mines can be a two-edged sword, sinking friend as well as foe. No better example exists than in the loss of the flush-decker *Sturtevant* (DD240). After a year making regular convoy runs across the North Atlantic, she was transferred to warmer climes in March 1942, when, after escorting Pacific-bound troopship convoy BT.201 from New York as far as Panama, she was assigned to the Caribbean Sea Frontier, based at Key West. On 26 April, *Sturtevant* departed Key West just past noon, heading west toward a rendezvous with a convoy forming off Southwest Pass, the westernmost channel in the mouth of the Mississippi River.* Two hours later, north of the Marquesas Keys, an explosion lifted *Sturtevant*'s stern out of the water and started a fire in her after deckhouse, but did not appear to cause serious damage to the ship. Assuming he was being attacked by a submarine, Lieutenant Commander C. L. Weigle, *Sturtevant*'s captain, ordered speed increased and depth charges dropped, but neither order could be carried out. Seconds later another larger explosion took place amidships which stopped her engines, and then, as the ship slowed, a third explosion broke her in two, the stern section sinking rapidly. Fortunately, the bow stayed afloat for two hours

---

* Roscoe, *United States Destroyer Operations*, p. 77; Parkin, *Blood on the Sea*, pp. 54–6.

before sinking slowly into the shallow water, leaving her crow's nest exposed. Rescue came quickly. Three of her crew were known dead and another 12 were missing, presumably killed by the explosion or trapped as the stern sank.

Sturtevant was sunk, however, not by a U-boat, but by poor communications. Two days before she sailed, the first mines in an extensive field had been placed west of Key West. The idea was to form a protected area close to Key West where convoys could assemble in safety. The existence and location of defensive minefields is rightly considered a valuable secret, but sufficient details must be made known to shipping using the mined waters. Sadly, when *Sturtevant* sailed, Weigle was not informed of the newly laid mines, and the result was the loss of a valuable warship and 15 men. Even more inexplicable was the loss of three merchantmen in the same waters over the next nine weeks to the same cause. Loose lips may sink ships, but overly tight lips can sometimes do the same.

The movement of the U-boats to the south relieved Andrews of responsibility for their actions, as his writ ran only as far south as Jacksonville, just south of the Georgia–Florida border. The sinkings off the Florida coast in early May took place in the GSF, which had been, until this move, a relatively quiet area under the command of a captain. But in May, this region suddenly became a center of U-boat activity (41 sinkings during May along the Florida coast and in the Gulf of Mexico, the most in any month in any of the coastal sectors during the war), along with the Caribbean (38 sinkings).* King reacted quickly, sending aircraft and escorts to these commands as soon as they became available. In July convoys started running between Trinidad, Aruba and Key West, and in September convoys had started between Galveston, TX, and Key West. A rationalized system of interlocking convoys was inaugurated at the end of September that ran from New York in the north, which was now the western terminus of trans-Atlantic convoys, and Galveston, Trinidad and the Panama Canal in the south, with mid-point stops at Key West and Guantanamo.

The U-boat attack of the American East Coast died out gradually, as U-boats were withdrawn from ESF waters in July, from the Gulf of Mexico in August and from the Caribbean in September. Attacks would continue sporadically and with occasional success for some time near Trinidad, but in general, by fall 1942, Dönitz had re-deployed his U-boats back to the North Atlantic convoy routes, where he knew the battle would be won or lost.

The losses in merchant shipping, particularly tankers, along the American coast had been terrible, and whenever a terrible event occurs, it is human nature to attempt to find the cause and to assign blame. For many British historians and a few American, the US Navy's reaction to this assault was tardy and inept, and the primary blame assigned to King. There is no question that King, Andrews and Ingersoll could have made other choices that, seen in the clear light of hindsight, might have reduced the toll, but to claim that they failed to make

---

*   *OEG Report No. 51*, ch. 4, p. 26.

those choices out of lack of concern or animus against the British is unfair and unfounded. They did the best they could given what they knew, what they could reasonably expect and what forces they had to deploy.

— —

Meanwhile, *Bismarck*'s sister ship, *Tirpitz*, had completed working up in the Baltic and transferred to Altenfjord in northern Norway in January 1942. From there she might break out into the Atlantic or sortie against the PQ-series convoys from Iceland to Russia that had started in September 1941. Her location was well-chosen, as Altenfjord has multiple exits and was so far from the nearest British naval or air bases that a close blockade would be impossible. The Royal Navy felt forced to keep adequate forces at the ready at Hvalfjordur and Scapa Flow to counter any move *Tirpitz* might make. Along the way, she became something of an obsession for Churchill and the Admiralty, tying up large forces that might have been better deployed elsewhere.

That elsewhere was the Indian Ocean. There was genuine concern in London that the Japanese might attempt to cut off sea communications with India by occupying the Vichy French island of Madagascar off the African coast. Remembering the ease with which the Japanese had taken over French Indo-China, this fear seemed well-grounded.

A plan was quickly developed and was approved by Churchill on 12 March involving assembling and transporting 10,000 troops to occupy Diego Suarez, a port at the northern tip of the island. To gather the necessary warships meant pulling Force H from Gibraltar. The only way to continue covering the western exit of the Mediterranean would be to pull units from the Home Fleet, which would, in turn, leave inadequate forces to contain *Tirpitz*. Churchill again turned to his friend across the Atlantic to solve this problem. He came directly to the point in a message dated 14 March:

> We have decided to do Bonus, and as it is quite impossible to weaken our Eastern Fleet we shall have to use the whole of Force H now at Gibraltar.* . . Would it be possible for you to send say two battleships, an aircraft carrier, some cruisers and destroyers to take the place of Force H temporarily? Force H would have to leave Gibraltar not later than March 30 and could hardly reach Gibraltar again before the end of June. We have not planned any operation for Force H inside the Mediterranean between April 1 and the end of June. It is most unlikely that French retaliation, if any, for Bonus would take the form of attacking United States ships by air . . . Cannot go forward unless you are able to do this. There are the greatest dangers in leaving Bonus to become a Japanese base.†

---

* Bonus was the original codename for Madagascar, later changed to Ironclad.
† *Map Room File*, 14 March 42, WSC>FDR, no. 44.

The newest US capital ship, Washington *(BB56), wearing Ms12 Mod, lies in Scapa in broad sunlight, April 1942. Behind her is HMS* Victorious *(38), while, to the far left, can be seen the bow of* Wasp. *(NARA)*

Churchill's request was demanding, quite specific and ended with what could certainly be interpreted as a threat, but Roosevelt took this in stride. Nor did he seem concerned that the British were asking for nearly every available major unit assigned to the Atlantic Fleet. On the other hand, FDR was very concerned that his 'leverage' with Vichy, based on a long history of Franco-American friendship, be maintained. He replied two days later that the US would supply the requested ships, but not at Gibraltar.

The Americans moved quickly to gather the forces requested by the British. In ten days, TF39, comprising *Washington, Wasp, Wichita, Tuscaloosa* and the eight destroyers of DesRon 8 set out from Casco Bay for Scapa Flow under the command of Rear-Admiral John W. Wilcox Jr. The only unit requested by Churchill not present in TF39 was the other new battleship in the Atlantic, *North Carolina*, which was attempting to overcome structural problems and was not yet ready for operational assignment.*

The task force immediately ran into heavy seas, such that the captain of

---

* *North Carolina* suffered from excessive vibration at certain speeds that sometimes made her after superstructure uninhabitable. She visited New York Navy Yard so often during her working up that she was nicknamed the 'Showboat'.

To free up Royal Navy units for the occupation of Madagascar, the US sent TF39, comprising almost all the major surface assets of the Atlantic Fleet to Scapa Flow, where they would be under the operational control of the Royal Navy. Seen from HMS Edinburgh (C16), which met TF39 on 3 April 1942, is Wichita *(CA45), one of the handsomest ships to ever serve in the US Navy. On a hull identical to the* Brooklyn-*class light cruisers, she mounted three triple 8-inch turrets. She is painted in Ms12 Mod, which broke up the three horizontal bands of the basic Ms12 in random swirls and splotches. (NARA)*

Washington ordered the forecastle and fantail kept clear of men not required to be there. Shortly after dawn on 27 March, informed that the aircraft on the catapults right aft were in danger of being damaged by the quartering seas, Captain Howard H. J. Benson ordered men to the fantail to reinforce their tie-downs. At approximately 1030, a cry of 'Man Overboard!' was heard and a man was seen flailing his arms in *Washington*'s wake. *Tuscaloosa*, directly astern of *Washington*, barely missed hitting the man. Two buoys were dropped and a destroyer ordered to rescue him. However, the search by *Ellyson* (DD454) found nothing.

Meanwhile, *Washington*'s crew was mustered and heads counted; no one was found to be missing. Sure that a mistake had been made, the OOD ordered a second muster, with the same result. Only then did the realization sink in that no one had seen Admiral Wilcox since 1030. At about 1000, he had been seen on the fantail, watching the work detail. Being unfamiliar with his new flagship, he had asked a bosun the location of the nearest ladder to the Upper Deck and had been directed forward on the port side. At 1015, he had been seen in his cabin and had talked briefly with his chief of staff. Soon after, a Marine guard on the starboard side saw him heading aft again, the last man to seen him alive. The

Under the 14-inch barrels of one of the main battery turrets of HMS Duke of York *(17), Vice-Admiral A.T. B. Curteis (right) talks with Rear-Admiral Robert C. 'Ike' Giffen, acting commander of TF39 after the loss of Rear-Admiral Wilcox on the passage across the Atlantic.* Wasp, *wearing Ms12 Mod, lies in the background. (NARA)*

next ranking officer in the task force, 'Ike' Giffen in *Wichita*, ordered the task force back and an extensive search was mounted, but Wilcox's body was never recovered.

After such an ill-omened start, the remainder of the crossing of TF39 was rough but uneventful. On 3 April, the Americans were met by HMS *Edinburgh* (C16), which escorted the task force into Scapa Flow the next day. If the Americans had thought they would sit peaceably in harbor while Royal Navy units went about their business, they soon found that Admiral Pound, who was granted operational control of the American ships, had other plans.

On 9 April *Wasp* was detached from TF39 for special duty. It was exactly the duty Churchill had said was not planned, a foray into the Mediterranean. A full-scale aerial assault of the island of Malta, situated astride the north-south convoy route between Italy and Tunisia, had been underway since December 1940. By April 1942, the situation was desperate.

> Air attack on Malta is very heavy . . . Malta can only muster now twenty or
> thirty serviceable fighters. We keep feeding Malta with Spitfires in packets of

Operation CALENDAR *saw* Wasp *used to carry RAF Spitfire MkVcs into the Mediterranean, where they were flown off to Malta, April 1942. Unfortunately, most of these aircraft, one of which is seen taking off, were destroyed soon after landing on that island. Note the FD (Mk4) fire control radar suspended off the front of* Wasp's *after Mk33 fire control director. (NARA)*

sixteen loosed from Eagle carrier from about six hundred miles west of Malta.

This has worked a good many times quite well but Eagle is now laid up for a month by defects in her steering gear . . . Argus is too small and too slow and moreover she has to provide the fighter cover for the Carrier launching the Spitfires and for the escorting force. We would use Victorious but unfortunately her lifts are too small for Spitfires. Therefore there will be a whole month without any Spitfire reinforcements.

Would you be willing to allow your Carrier Wasp to do one of these trips provided details are satisfactorily agreed between the Naval Staffs. With her broad lifts, capacity and length, we estimate that Wasp could take fifty or more Spitfires. Unless it was necessary for her to fuel Wasp could proceed through the straits at night without calling at Gibraltar until on the return journey as the Spitfires would be embarked in the Clyde.

. . . Operation might take place during third week of April.[*]

Roosevelt tried his best to find another option, but appears to have been persuaded about the need to reinforce Malta.

The Royal Navy wasted no time putting *Wasp* to work. Accompanied by destroyers *Lang* and *Madison* (DD425), *Wasp* departed Scapa Flow on 9 April, proceeding to Glasgow where her air group, except for the fighters, was landed and 47 RAF Spitfire Mk Vcs hoisted aboard her hangar deck. When she departed again on 14 April, *Wasp* was escorted by *Lang, Madison*, the battlecruiser HMS *Renown* (72) and four Royal Navy destroyers. This unit was christened Force W and their mission named Operation CALENDAR. The screen was supplemented by the anti-aircraft cruisers HMS *Cairo* (D87) and *Charybdis* (88) soon after passing the straits into the Mediterranean at dawn on 19 April. Force W steamed east at high speed, reaching a point east of the Balearics early on 20 April.

---

[*]   *Map Room File*, 31 March 42, WSC>FDR, no. 61.

Wasp *was sent into the Mediterranean a second time in May 1942, on Operation* BOWERY. *Accompanying her this time was HMS* Eagle *(94), seen from* Wasp, *with 17 additional Spitfires. These had better luck after reaching Malta. (NARA)*

Starting at 0400, *Wasp*'s fighters, 11 F4F-4 Wildcats of VF-71, were launched as CAP, while the Spitfires warmed up in the hangar. These were brought up one by one to the flight deck on the after elevator and launched, starting at 0530. Force W turned around and passed the strait again the next day. Swordfish aircraft of No. 812 Squadron of the Fleet Air Arm from Gibraltar flew on *Wasp* that same day, for delivery to Coastal Command. She arrived safely back at Scapa Flow on 26 April.[*]

All but one of Spitfires flown off on 20 April arrived safely at Malta, but they did not last long. Within four days only six remained operational. Again, Churchill appealed to the President:

> If the island fortress is to hold out till the June convoy, which is the earliest possible, it must have a continued flow of Spitfires. The last flying off from Wasp was most successful, although unhappily the enemy's attack broke up many after they had landed . . . I shall be most grateful if you would allow Wasp to do a 2nd trip . . . I do not think enemy have the slightest idea Wasp has been in and out of the Mediterranean.[†]

---

[*]   Hague, *The Supply of Malta.*

[†]   *Map Room File*, 24 April 42, WSC>FDR, no. 64.

Having demonstrated that land-based fighters could be launched from aircraft carriers, Ranger *was frequently used to carry USAAF aircraft across the Atlantic. Here, she is loading a P-40E of the 33rd PS at Quonset Point, RI, on 21 April 1942. All 68 of the squadron's Warhawks were successfully flown off to Accra, Gold Coast (Ghana) on 10 May. (NARA)*

FDR acquiesced, which garnered a witty reply from Churchill:

Most grateful . . . for allowing Wasp to have another good sting.[*]

Operation BOWERY, as the second run by *Wasp* was called, differed only in detail from the first. By dint of careful planning, *Wasp* was able to fit 50 Spitfires in her hangar. She departed Glasgow on 3 May, escorted by *Lang, Sterett* (DD407) and two Royal Navy destroyers. They were met on 8 May by HMS *Eagle* (94), back from refit, with 17 additional Spitfires, along with *Renown* and *Charybdis,* and passed the strait that night. The launch of the Spitfires the next day was more eventful than on the first mission. All of *Eagle's* got into the air without incident, but the first off *Wasp* lost power climbing out and crashed into the sea in the carrier's path. Another pilot was unable to draw fuel from his auxiliary fuel tank and, with no chance to reach Malta or any other friendly airbase, opted to attempt to fly back on *Wasp*. Incredibly, after the remaining 48 fighters were launched, Pilot Officer S. A. Smith managed to touch down on the moving flight deck and stop his aircraft barely 5 yards from its forward edge. As before, the force turned back and made a high-speed run for Gibraltar and the Atlantic. *Wasp* returned to Scapa Flow on 15 May.

---

[*]   *Map Room File,* 29 April 42, WSC>FDR, no. 73.

The delivery of aircraft for the war was also the main occupation of *Ranger*, the other US carrier in the Atlantic. Once again, this started with a request from Churchill for further aid. On 15 April, Churchill returned to his concerns over India and the Indian Ocean.[*] He complained that the Americans were not doing enough to distract the Japanese.

> We had hoped that by the end of April the American Pacific Fleet would be strong enough to reoccupy Pearl Harbor and offer some menace to the Japanese . . .[†]

It is not clear what Churchill meant, because the Americans never abandoned Pearl Harbor. The Japanese raid had left the oil storage area there intact and the three dry docks undamaged; Pearl Harbor remained a functioning navy base and headquarters of the US Pacific Fleet throughout the war. Furthermore, what remained of the striking power of that fleet, primarily based on the aircraft carriers *Lexington* (CV2), *Yorktown* and *Enterprise* (CV6), joined in March by *Hornet* (CV8), had been busy raiding Japanese positions across the Pacific from Wake to Papua New Guinea and even the Home Islands, though the British had not yet been informed of some of these activities. Nevertheless, Churchill, panicking over the perceived threat to India, wanted more.

> If you do not feel able to take speedy action which will force Japan to concentrate in the Pacific, the only way out of the immense perils which confront us would seem to be to build up as quickly as possible an ample force of modern capital ships and carriers in the Indian Ocean . . . If you would consider sending North Carolina and Ranger from Task Force 22 to join Somerville temporarily, he would . . . be better off . . .[‡]
>
> Alternatively if you preferred to place North Carolina alongside Washington at Scapa we could send Duke of York to join Somerville in the Indian Ocean and Ranger could go direct to Capetown to meet her.[§]

FDR's reaction was mild, but he was wary about sending more ships to serve under Royal Navy command. He was willing to send aircraft flown by American pilots, as long as it was understood the aircraft would come from those awaiting shipment to the RAF. He would even expedite their shipment across the Atlantic. He sent this proposal to General Marshall and Harry Hopkins, both then in London, for personal delivery to Churchill. Above all, he hoped to temper Churchill's sense of desperation. He obviously hoped Hopkins's special ability to transmit Churchill's words would work in the other direction as well.

---

[*]   *Map Room File*, 15 April 42, WSC>FDR, no. 52.

[†]   Ibid.

[‡]   Admiral Sir James Somerville commanded the Royal Navy's Eastern Fleet based at Kilindini, Kenya, from March 1942 until August 1944.

[§]   Ibid.

FDR was willing to commit to using *Ranger* to ferry aircraft across the Atlantic, which could then protect India as effectively as additional ships would.

> These plans, however, involve use of *Ranger* as a ferry boat and prevent her use as carrier with her own planes. The *Ranger* is of course best suited for ferrying as we are not proud of her compartmentation and her structural strength.[*]

Churchill had little choice but to go along with Roosevelt, but that did not mean he was happy about it.

> There is no question of our seeking battle against superior forces, but we do not want to be sought out and found at a disadvantage . . .
>
> I should be only too willing to release Kittyhawk aircraft for *Ranger* for despatch in *Ranger* were it not that this would mean taking grave risks in Middle East and possibly compromising the coming offensive.[†] Egypt is now more than ever dependent on this type because of large despatches of Hurricane fighters to India . . . perhaps it would be possible to use any vacant space to hasten shipment of Kittyhawk destined for Middle East but at present waiting for ships.[‡]

Ranger arrived at Quonset Point, RI on 17 April and landed her air group.[§] The 68 P-40Es, previously allocated to the RAF but hastily rechristened with USAAF tactical numbers, were loaded into her hangar deck on 21 April. Only four of *Ranger*'s own air group, SB2U-2 Vindicators, were retained to fly anti-submarine patrols.

Ranger departed Narragansett Bay the next morning on what had now been named Project 157, escorted by *Augusta* and five destroyers, and made a high speed run to Trinidad where bunkers were topped off. Departing there on 29 April, TF22 headed out into the Atlantic. The target was a fly-off point less than 100 nm south-west of Accra, Gold Coast (Ghana). This was reached on the morning of 10 May. All 68 fighters flew off safely. The return trip to Trinidad was uneventful for *Ranger*, though two of the escorting destroyers, *Hambleton* (DD455) and *Ellyson*, collided in a rain squall, the former getting much the worse of the encounter. The aircraft flown off *Ranger* proceeded across Africa and eventually ended up reinforcing the 51st FG in India and the 23rd FG, successors to the famous American Volunteer Group Flying Tigers that had been fighting the Japanese in the air over China and Burma since November 1941.

Even before *Ranger* departed Rhode Island, the President was offering her

---

[*]   *Map Room File*, 16 April 42, FDR>WSC, no. 134.

[†]   Kittyhawk was the RAF designation for the Curtiss P-40D Warhawk and later models.

[‡]   *Map Room File*, 18 April 42, WSC>FDR, nos 57 and 58.

[§]   Cressman, *USS* Ranger, pp. 183–6.

services to Churchill for further ferrying missions.* After a brief interlude at Argentia training pilots, *Ranger* was back at Quonset Point on 1 July, loading 72 P-40Fs of the 57th FG.† This mission went much as the previous. After a stop at Trinidad, *Ranger* sailed east until within range of Accra where, on 19 July, all 72 Warhawks were successfully launched. These fighters went on to Egypt, flying combat missions in support of the Eighth Army starting 9 August.

— —

On 28 April most of TF39, reconstituted as TF99, left Scapa Flow along with Royal Navy units to provide cover for convoys PQ.15/QP.11 between Reykjavik and Murmansk. Force Distaff comprised *Washington, Tuscaloosa, Wichita* and four US destroyers, along with HMS *King George V, Victorious*, the cruiser *Kenya* (C14) and ten Royal Navy destroyers. All went smoothly for three days, as *Tirpitz* showed no sign of budging, but bad weather and worse luck did what the Germans could not. *Washington's* captain reported:

> 1. At about 1545, May 1, 1942, while this ship was following H.M.S. KING GEORGE V in column, speed eighteen knots, distance 800 yards, in a dense fog, the KING GEORGE V had a collision with H.M.S. PUNJABI, cutting the latter in two. Circumstances compelled this vessel to pass between the two sections of the PUNJABI. Her depth charges were exploding as we passed and several exploded under and very near this ship, resulting in heavy shocks to the ship, some serious damage, much minor damage, and numerous derangements.‡

Washington suffered no structural damage, but her gunnery control systems, including the main battery rangefinders, control computers and radars were temporarily knocked out. *Tuscaloosa* was detached to search for survivors from *Punjabi* (G21). In all, 209 of *Punjabi's* crew were recovered. *Washington* put into Hvalfjordur on 5 May.

TF99, this time with *Wasp*, was joined at Valley Forge on 17 May by a Royal Navy detachment that included HMS *Duke of York* (I17), *Renown* and *Victorious* to provide escort for PQ.16/QP.12. The northbound convoy departed three days later, but, since no German moves appeared in the offing, TF99 detached east of Iceland, conducted anti-aircraft training and retired again to Hvalfjordur. *Wasp* continued westward, heading for Norfolk and a quick refit. *Lexington* had been lost at the Battle of the Coral Sea on 8 May, and all signs pointed to another major Japanese move in the direction of Midway Island. *Wasp* was needed desperately in the Pacific. On 22 May, *Washington* and *Wichita* departed for Scapa Flow with Royal Navy units, arriving on 3 June after a rough passage.

---

*   *Map Room File*, 21 April 42, FDR>WSC, no. 137.

†   Cressman, *USS Ranger*, pp. 190–1.

‡   BB56, p 1.

American sailors mustered on the fantail of Washington *are inspected by HRH George VI at Scapa, 7 June 1942, under the wing of an OS2U Kingfisher observation aircraft. (NARA)*

Washington was inspected by King George VI, the reigning British monarch (and father of Queen Elizabeth II), on 7 June.

Ill-fated convoy PQ.17 left Iceland on 27 June 1942.* Most of TF99 was involved in providing cover. Near support for the convoy came from four cruisers and three destroyers, which included *Wichita*, *Tuscaloosa*, *Wainwright* (DD419) and *Rowan* (DD405). This group had orders to remain to the north of, but close to the convoy until east of Spitsbergen (Svalbard). More distant cover was provided by *Washington*, *Mayrant* (DD402), *Rhind* (DD404) and the heavy units of the Home Fleet. This time the Germans reacted with Operation RÖSSELSPRUNG, a planned attack on the convoys by *Tirpitz*, three heavy cruisers and supporting destroyers which were moving north from Trondheim and Narvik. During the day on 4 July, PQ.17 sustained multiple attacks by Luftwaffe torpedo bombers that succeeded in sinking three merchantmen and damaging another, although the attacks had been largely deflected by effective anti-aircraft fire by the escort, particularly *Wainwright*.

The further east the convoy proceeded, the more nervous Admiral Pound got. Available evidence indicates that he had decided even before the air attacks on 4 July, that should the German attacks increase and, in particular, if they should include surface ships, he would order the convoy dispersed. The dispersal of a convoy is a drastic, irreversible move. Under certain circumstance, it is the best

---

* Morison, *History,* vol. I, pp. 179–92; Winton, John, ULTRA *at Sea*, pp. 61–72.

Convoy PQ.17 was first sighted by Luftwaffe *reconnaissance aircraft on 1 July 1942, beginning a sequence of air and U-boat attacks that led to the convoy being dispersed three days later. Twenty-four ships were lost to German attacks. (NHHC)*

response to a threat to a convoy. However, a convoy threatened by surface attack and also by air or submarine attack, will probably suffer less staying intact.

Under normal circumstances, a decision of this sort would be left to commanders on the spot, especially since Admiral John Tovey, in command of the Home Fleet aboard *Duke of York*, and Rear-Admiral L. H. K. Hamilton in command of the cruiser force, were competent and respected. However, Pound's access to ULTRA, which for legitimate security reasons could not be passed on to Tovey or Hamilton, caused him to intervene at the tactical level. The problem was that ULTRA was giving Pound an incomplete picture of what the Germans were about. In the late afternoon on 4 July, Pound received an ULTRA intercept that indicated that *Tirpitz* had arrived at Alta that morning and was to be assigned an anchorage, and also that her accompanying destroyers were to complete with fuel at once. Nothing in this message indicated that a sortie against the convoy would follow. In fact, the lack of any further signals regarding *Tirpitz* that day led the analysts at GC&CS to presume that the German heavy units remained in port, but this did not persuade Pound. Believing that *Tirpitz* could reach the convoy soon after midnight, at 2111 Pound ordered the cruiser force to withdraw to the west at high speed, and at 2123 ordered the convoy dispersed with ships to scatter and make for Russian ports as best they could. The larger units of the

On 5 July 1942, U88 (Bohmann) tracked and torpedoed the American steamer Carlton, *from the dispersed convoy PQ.17, due north of North Cape. For the Germans, it was like old times, with the sea full of independently sailing merchantmen. Forty-three of the steamer's 45-man crew managed to get into one lifeboat and four rafts, seen from the U-boat beyond the flotsam in the foreground. All but one of those men survived, to be taken prisoner by the Germans when they made shore in Norway. (NHHC)*

convoy's immediate escort was ordered to join the cruiser force heading west, leaving the remaining merchantmen and auxiliaries with nine smaller escorts.

What Pound could not know was that Hitler withheld permission to execute RÖSSELSPRUNG until reconnaissance showed that Allied covering forces were well clear of the convoy, which meant that *Tirpitz*, along with *Admiral Scheer*, *Admiral Hipper* and nine escorts, did not exit Altenfjord until mid-afternoon the next day. Nor could he have predicted that, seeing the carnage wrought by U-boats and the Luftwaffe, the German ships would be recalled before midnight before they sighted a single ship. In the event, only 14 of the 41 merchantmen and auxiliaries that left Hvalfjordur would reach Russia. Three turned back to Iceland. The rest, 22 merchantmen and two auxiliaries, were lost to enemy attack, all but three after the convoy was dispersed.

— —

On 25 May, *Blakeley* (DD150) was patrolling off the west coast of Martinique to make sure the French warships there stayed put. What should have been easy duty was anything but, because there was every reason to believe there was a

Four of the U-boats that so devastated PQ.17 are seen on their return to Narvik after the attack, July 1942. These are all the medium-sized Type VIIC boats, the most numerous type, (NHHC)

U-boat about, two small freighters having been sunk in the vicinity the day before. At 0945, after two sonar contacts that proved to be false alarms, *Blakeley*'s sonar was taken off-line for maintenance. There is no way of knowing whether that act in any way affected *Blakeley*'s fate, but at 1000 without warning, her bow was demolished in a massive explosion. Despite losing her bow, *Blakeley* remained stable, and, with her power plant intact, she was able to power the pumps necessary to control flooding. Within 15 minutes, she was underway again, heading towards Fort-de-France, tying up alongside *Béarn* at 1324.

The French were hospitable, offering to accommodate *Blakeley*'s crew on the carrier while emergency repairs were made. These consisted of shoring up the forward bulkhead and removing all unnecessary topside weight. *Blakeley* cast off from *Béarn* about two days later and limped one island south to Port Castries, St Lucia, a British possession, where a wooden bulkhead was fitted across her bow and the torn shell plating that made navigation difficult was bent in to secure the bulkhead. She then proceeded by stages to San Juan, where a false bow was fitted, and on to Philadelphia, where, in short order, the bow was removed from *Taylor* (DD94), a sister ship that was being used as a damage control training hulk, and grafted onto *Blakeley*. She was back in the Caribbean again, escorting convoys, in September.

The flush-decker Blakeley *(DD150) was assigned the simple task of keeping tabs on the Vichy warships holed up in Fort-de-France, Martinique. Unfortunately, two U-boats were there looking for American ships and U156 (Hartenstein) managed to put a torpedo into the destroyer forward that demolished her bow, 25 May 1942. With luck and excellent seamanship,* Blakeley *survived, having the bow of a sister-ship grafted on to replace her missing stem.* Blakeley *is seen here soon after that successful surgery at the Philadelphia Navy Yard. (NARA)*

Admiral King was furious when he heard about the PQ.17 debacle, and he took steps to end the stay of TF99 under Home Fleet command. The US Navy detachment returned to Hvalfjordur on 8 July, and was disbanded piecemeal. On 14 July, *Washington* sailed for New York and a month-long refit before heading for the South Pacific. *Wichita* briefly became Admiral Giffen's flagship again, but she had been suffering from a damaged propeller that caused excess vibration at speeds over 20 knots. She departed on 19 July for Scapa Flow and then Rosyth, where she entered dry dock on 24 July. Despite the best efforts of that dockyard, the vibration persisted, and, on 14 August, *Wichita* left Rosyth and after a stop at Valley Forge headed for the Brooklyn Navy Yard, where the problem was resolved.

Alone among the major American units in TF99, *Tuscaloosa* was given further tasking. The destruction of PQ.17 was blamed in part on the long days in early July in the far north, and the Royal Navy suspended further convoys to Murmansk until September. Not surprisingly, this brought a loud protest from the Russians, who claimed the long hiatus would threaten their ability to continue the war. To placate Stalin and show good faith, the decision was made

The destroyer Mayo *(DD422) stands by while the veteran transport* Wakefield *(AP21) burns. She was returning to the US with 850 construction workers after dropping off a full load of troops in Great Britain, 3 September 1942. The fire was soon out of control and the passengers and crew were taken off. The still burning hulk was towed to Halifax where she was beached and written off as a total loss. (USN via navsource.org)*

to mount a high-speed supply run, dubbed Operation EASY-UNIT.[*] *Tuscaloosa*, accompanied by destroyers *Rodman* (DD456) and *Emmons* (DD457), arrived at Greenock on 12 August and immediately began loading 300 t of cargo that included explosives, radar equipment and medical supplies, plus 11 officers and 167 other ranks of the RAF and Royal Navy. Each of the destroyers took on an additional 39 t of supplies, mostly the kit needed to support two RAF ground units. They sailed the next day, arriving at Seidisfjordur on 19 August, where

---

[*]   Morison, *History,* vol. I, pp. 358–60; Roscoe, *United States Destroyer Operations*, p. 133.

The German commerce raider Stier *(Schiff 23) had the misfortune to run into an American merchantman,* Stephen Hopkins, *in the South Atlantic, 27 September 1942.* Hopkins *was hopelessly outgunned by the raider, but managed to damage the German before she was sunk. The damage was such that* Stier *could not be saved; she is seen here burning, from the German transport* Tannenfels. Stier's *crew was rescued by* Tannenfels. *That of* Hopkins *was not as lucky; they were left with one small lifeboat by the Germans, only 14 of her crew surviving to reach the coast of Brazil. (NHHC)*

they refueled and immediately departed with three Royal Navy destroyers as added escort. They were sighted by a Luftwaffe reconnaissance aircraft the next evening, but darkness, a course change and providential fog allowed them to reach the Kola Inlet, and the docks at Vaenga (Severomorsk) on 23 August. By 0700 the next morning, the cargo and men had been landed and more than 500 stranded merchant sailors and four Russian diplomats were distributed between *Tuscaloosa* and the five destroyers. Despite being sighted by German aircraft several times on the return trip, no attacks developed and the six ships reached Iceland on 28 August, refueled and pressed on to the Clyde, where the seamen were dropped off on 30 August. *Tuscaloosa* and the two destroyers headed for Iceland and then the US East Coast for yard availability. *Tuscaloosa* was the last major unit of TF99 to depart British waters.[*]

— —

---

[*] Some sources state this was the last time King allowed American capital ships to operate under Royal Navy command, but this is not true, as will be seen in chapter 5.

A fitting way to end this painful period, almost a year long, during which the US Navy learned much that was needed to fight the war in Europe, is to relate an extraordinary event that occurred on 24 July 1942. The US may have been slow to address the need for ASW ships, but, once set on the right course, had the industrial 'muscle' to make good the deficit. The first two BDEs, HMS *Bayntun* (K310) and *Bazely* (K311) were launched at the Boston Navy Yard on 27 June 1942. (The fact that two were launched on the same day was not co-incidental; destroyer escorts were often built in slips large enough to accommodate two or more hulls.) The next DEs took the water at the Philadelphia Navy Yard on 24 July, when no less than six were launched.* This was something of a stunt. The next was not launched until 24 August, and a total of 21 more were launched by the end of the year, but the pace rapidly accelerated as smaller yards came on line. No less than 378 were launched in 1943.

By the end of September 1942, US Navy forces had sunk (or collaborated in the sinking of) 11 U-boats with another two sunk by USAAF aircraft.

---

* One of these became HMS *Drury* (K316), the other five were taken over by the US Navy.

4

Friends & Enemies:
The Landings in North Africa
October 1942–November 1942

The war in the Pacific was primarily naval. The premise was simple – control the sea and Japan would lose. In contrast, the war in Europe could be lost at sea but not won there. To win the war in Europe, the lands won by the German Army would have to be taken back by carrying Allied armies across open water and landing them on hostile shores, all on a scale never attempted before.

The war in Europe differed from that in the Pacific in another critical dimension. While there was frequent disagreement between and even within the services of the US military over strategy in the Pacific theater, the President did his job and a unified strategy was hammered out with little regard to America's allies. By 1942, the war in Europe was being fought by a pair of theoretically equal Allies, and every decision had to accord with their often divergent strategic goals. The British were mainly concerned with the Mediterranean, with the occasional nervous glance in the direction of India, and consistently urged the 'liberation' of Vichy North Africa and the subsequent defeat of the Afrika Korps as the necessary first step on the road to victory in Europe. The Americans necessarily had to pay equal attention to two fronts separated by half a world, and to them, the shortest path, across the English Channel to France and thence to Berlin, was the only sensible course. The Russians' only interest in this discussion was that another front be opened as soon as possible to divert as much of Hitler's attention and resources as possible.

Thus, the question of when and where the western Allies would invade Axis territory would not be easily resolved. The Arcadia Conference in January 1942 called for an assault on French North Africa no later than May 1942 (Operation GYMNAST) followed by an invasion of France proper late in the year or early in 1943. It is doubtful that anyone at the conference really believed those goals could be met, but, since no one knew yet what it would take to mount a large-scale amphibious assault, they were as good as any.

Although FDR was in favor of landings in North Africa, resistance from military leaders on both sides of the Atlantic caused the plan to be dropped in March.* Even Churchill reluctantly went along with the decision. However, pressure built in the early summer to reinstate GYMNAST. One factor was the visit of Soviet Foreign Minister V. M. Molotov to Washington in June, which caused Roosevelt to promise a 'second front' in 1942. Another was the fall of Tobruk to Rommel, also in June. Churchill, backed by Pound and Field Marshal Sir John Dill, expressed the firm conviction that a cross-Channel landing was not feasible before 1944. The Americans could disagree with, but not refute, the British arguments. When the staff discussions moved to London in July, with King, Marshall and Hopkins, but without FDR, the Americans faced unified opposition to a landing in France in 1942. On 25 July, realizing they could not go forward without British support, the Americans agreed to landings in Vichy North Africa within four months.

Despite the short time allowed for preparations, planning for what was now called Operation TORCH got off to a slow start. Overall naval and ground forces commanders – Admiral Sir Andrew B. Cunningham and Lieutenant General Dwight D. Eisenhower – were not appointed until mid-August. From that point, progress sped up with the basic outlines set by 9 September. The plan called for three widely separated simultaneous landings in French Morocco and Algeria. The naval components broke down as follows:

> *Western Naval Task Force* (Rear-Admiral H. Kent Hewitt, USN) transporting most of three US Army divisions commanded by Major General George S. Patton, Jr., from ports on the US East Coast to landings at Safi, Fédala-Casablanca and Mehedia-Port Lyautey, French Morocco.[†]
>
> *Center Naval Task Force* (Commodore Thomas Troubridge, RN) transporting parts of two US Army divisions from ports in Great Britain to beaches either side of Oran, Algeria, while an American airborne regiment would be dropped on two airfields outside the city.
>
> *Eastern Naval Task Force* (Rear-Admiral Sir H. M. Burrough, RN) transporting brigades from two American and one British infantry division, plus two British Commando units from ports in Great Britain to beaches either side of Algiers (al-Jazaïr), Algeria.

The naval components of the Center and Eastern Task Forces was supplied by the Royal Navy, although a number of the troopships were American. These ships had to pass through the Straits of Gibraltar, which they did during the night of 5/6 November. Not surprisingly, this passage was noted, causing Vichy forces in both Algeria and Morocco to be placed on alert. Nevertheless, an attack on French North Africa was considered unlikely; German intelligence believed

---

[*]   Morison, *History,* vol. II, pp. 12–15.

[†]   Fédala is now Mohammedia; Mehedia is now more often spelled Mehdia; Port Lyautey is Kenitra.

A few of the troops assigned to the Torch *landings had the opportunity to train in landing craft – LCPs and LCVPs – in the calm waters of the Chesapeake Bay, 12 October 1942. It hardly prepared them for the much rougher conditions they met off the coast of French Morocco. Most of the troops and their Navy boatmen did not have even this limited training. (NARA)*

this shipping was part of a Malta convoy.

To a number of the French in North Africa, the TORCH landings came as no surprise at all. While the relations between Vichy and Great Britain had soured, those with Americans remained cordial. Hoping to take advantage of traditional friendship between France and the US, the entire operation was to have an American 'flavor', with British elements staying discreetly in the background. In a further attempt to influence the French military in North Africa to support (or at least not resist) the landings, the Allies staged Operation FLAGPOLE, in which American Major General Mark W. Clark was carried by HMS/M *Seraph* (P219) to a meeting on 23 October with General Charles E. Mast, chief of staff of the French XIX Corps in Algeria.* Mast was known to be in sympathy with de Gaulle's Free French movement, but, despite promising to issue orders to his command to welcome the Americans, he was not trusted enough to be told the exact date of the planned landings.

At Mast's insistence, the Americans also reached out to General Henri

---

*   Eisenhower, *Crusade in Europe*, p. 87.

The destroyer Ellyson *(DD454) refuels alongside the escort carrier* Santee *(ACV29) in November 1942 as they approach North Africa.* Santee *shows the effects of a depth charge exploding under her bow, her shell plating deformed and paint chipped away. While* Ellyson *is painted in a complex, late variant of the Ms12 Mod scheme,* Santee *appears to be one of a small number of ships painted in Ms17, an experimental disruptive scheme. (NARA)*

Giraud. He had fought in May 1940, been captured, escaped from Germany and was living quietly near Lyon, where he was contacted by Allied agents. A plan was developed whereby Giraud would be picked up by submarine from the south of France, transported to Gibraltar, where he would meet Eisenhower and be placed in charge of all French forces in North Africa. To placate Giraud's anti-British sentiments, a ruse was devised whereby *Seraph*, sent to pick him up on 5 November, flew an American flag and was nominally commanded by Captain Jerauld Wright, USN. The British crew got into the spirit of the moment, affecting American accents learned from Hollywood movies. Giraud was not fooled.

The landings in North Africa would not be the first large-scale landing carried out by the US Navy, but they would be by far the largest to date. Elements of the 1st Marine Div had been put ashore on Guadalcanal, Tulagi and Florida (Nggela Sule) Islands in August. Those landings, however, had involved 14,000 Marines, theoretically well-trained and equipped for amphibious assaults. The

Chenango (ACV28) carried 76 P-40Fs of the 33rd FG to North Africa for the TORCH
*landings. Sixty-two of them can be seen parked on her flight deck. Delays in capturing the
airfield at Port Lyautey meant these aircraft were not launched until two days after the
initial landings. (NARA)*

TORCH landings would involve over 70,000 American troops landing on beaches
separated by 700 miles with Army units having only rudimentary amphibious
training. Even the naval personnel involved were largely untrained: of 30
transports and cargo vessels used for TORCH, only 14 were in commission and
available for training at the beginning of August.[*] Finally, the number and size of
the landing craft available for this operation were understood to be inadequate,
as would be amply borne out by events. Small wonder that Eisenhower grew
increasingly nervous as the invasion drew closer.[†]

Another area of major concern was control of the air over the convoys and
the landing beaches. The landings in the southern Solomons had been several
hours flight away from the nearest Japanese airbase at Rabaul. In contrast, there
were airbases near all the proposed landing beaches, and the French Armée de
l'Air was estimated to have 168 aircraft available to defend the Moroccan Atlantic
coast. To counter this, the US Navy had very limited resources. The attrition of
aircraft carriers was such that by the end of October 1942, there were only two
left afloat in the Pacific and both of those were under repair. To support TORCH,
therefore, there was only *Ranger* and the four newly converted large escort
carriers of the *Sangamon* class. These had been built as commercial tankers

---

[*]   Morison, *History,* vol. II, p. 26.
[†]   Eisenhower, *Crusade in Europe,* pp. 96–7.

*One of the P-40Fs of
the 33rd FG catapults
off* Chenango, *10
November 1942. All 76
arrived at Port Lyautey
airfield safely.*

to a Navy-approved design.* The decision to convert four of them to aircraft
carriers was made early in 1942; they were recommissioned as ACVs in August
and September. To be available for TORCH, their working-up periods were
abbreviated. One of the four, *Chenango* (ACV28), ferried 76 land-based P-40F
Warhawks of the 33rd FG. The other three carried escort carrier air groups of
between 26 and 31 aircraft (except that *Suwannee* (ACV27) also carried 12 F4F-4
Wildcats of *Chenango*'s VF-28). *Ranger*'s air group comprised 72 aircraft. In all,
the carriers assigned to TF34, the Western Naval Task Force, carried 171 aircraft
(not counting the Warhawks), of which 109 were Wildcats and the rest were
SBD-3 Dauntlesses and TBF-1 Avengers.

The various components of TF34 departed their ports and assembled on a
tight schedule. Aircraft and ground units began moving towards the departure
ports in early October. The first naval unit to depart was SubRon 50, which
left New London, CT, starting on 19 October. These were five new *Gato*-class
submarines assigned reconnaissance and beacon duty related to the landings.
Four of the submarines would reconnoiter the beaches before the landing forces
arrived and then act as guides for scout boats that would mark the beaches. The
fifth, *Blackfish* (SS221), was to keep an eye on Dakar to make sure *Richelieu*, the
more complete of two unfinished French battleships that fled to African ports,
did not sortie against the landings. The Northern and Southern Fire Support
Groups, along with *Chenango*, left Norfolk on 23 October. The transports and
cargo ships departed Hampton Roads on 24 October, the same day that the
Center Fire Support Group left Norfolk and the Covering Group left Casco Bay.
The Air Group, comprising the remaining four aircraft carriers, left Bermuda on
25 October. These groups all joined into a single massive convoy heading east
on 28 October.

---

* Friedman, *U.S. Aircraft Carriers*, p. 173. The first of the class of 12 became *Cimarron* (AO22)
in 1939. The need for oilers was such that only four were made available for conversion to
escort carriers.

Bernadou (DD153) was one of two flush-deckers modified to carry assault troops into Safi harbor on 8 November 1942. The loss of her fourth funnel was a standard modification for flush-deckers in which they exchanged a boiler for added bunkerage and accommodation space. Non-standard modifications for TORCH included the removal of masts and torpedo tubes, the addition of a ramp-layer aft and extra splinter protection around her bridge and amidships. (NARA)

The passage was mostly uneventful and not sighted by any U-boats or German aircraft. The most excitement took place on 30 October, when a Dauntless being launched on ASW patrol from *Santee* (ACV29) lost a 325-lb depth bomb, which fell to the flight deck and rolled off the front. It exploded under *Santee's* bow, denting her shell plating forward, carrying away her rangefinder and a searchlight, and damaging her radar antennae. She was not otherwise damaged and continued with the convoy.

The convoy followed an evasive course well south of the Azores and then north of Madeira, until 7 November when the Southern Attack Group (TG34.10), heading for Safi, and the Northern Attack Group (TG34.8), heading for Mehedia and Port Lyautey, split from the main convoy, The remainder, the Center Attack Group (TG34.9), including the Covering Group (TG34.1), continued straight on towards Fédala and Casablanca. To minimize the chance for resistance on the beaches, debarkation to the landing craft was scheduled to begin right after midnight on 8 November, with the first landings at 0400.

—–—

The Southern Attack Group comprised five transports and a cargo ship, covered by three destroyers and three minecraft. Air support came from *Santee*, gunfire support from the old battleship *New York*, light cruiser *Philadelphia* and three more destroyers. *Barb* (SS220) was the beacon submarine. The landing beaches were widely separated and deemed poorly suited for landing armor, so a plan was devised to capture the small port of Safi intact and to unload vehicles directly to

A close-up of the bridge area of Cole *(DD155) before* TORCH *shows the splinter mats added around her bridge and the absence of a foremast. She has a pair of navigation lights on a pole at the front of her bridge and a TBS antenna aft. (NARA)*

the quay from *Lakehurst* (APV3), a ship originally built to carry railroad cars. To assure the rapid capture of the port facilities, two flush-deckers, *Cole* (DD155) and *Bernadou* (DD153), had been specially modified to carry assault troops into the harbor. As with many flush-deckers, both destroyers had already lost their after boiler and the associated funnel, which gave room for added fuel tanks and for space to hold troops and equipment. The modifications made specifically for this mission included the removal of masts, torpedo tubes and other top hamper, the addition of an extending ramp-layer on the after superstructure and splinter mats around the flying bridge and along the railings amidships.

In the pre-dawn gloom, a truck was being lowered over the side of *Dorothea L. Dix* (AP67) off the southern 'Yellow Beach' when the ship rolled with a wave, causing gasoline to spill from a tank in the truck's bed. The gasoline fell onto the engine of the waiting landing craft and caught fire with a bright flash. Word rapidly spread through the nearby shipping that *Dix* had been torpedoed. At that moment, two nearby YP 'crash boats' were mistaken for French torpedo boats and taken under fire by several nearby APs. Fortunately for all concerned, the inexperienced gun crews missed.

Undeterred, *Bernadou* took on 197 Army raiders from *Harris* (AP8) and departed for Safi harbor at 0345; *Cole* followed with a similar load at 0403. It was still dark when *Bernadou* approached the shore north of the harbor. In the

The oiler Merrimack (AO37) *carried a pair of YP 'crash boats' for use off the beaches after the* TORCH *landings. On more than one occasion, these were mistaken for enemy torpedo boats by twitchy gun crews on the invasion transports. (NARA)*

darkness, she was initially mistaken for a returning fishing boat and was fired on only after she replied incorrectly to a flashed challenge. She was then taken under fire by at least three shore batteries. She fired off a specially prepared 'flag' shell – a starshell with an American flag streaming from its parachute shrouds – but this seemed to have little effect. She then opened fire with her 3-inch and 20 mm guns, effectively silencing the French fire, but in the confusion of the melée, she missed the quay and beached at 0430 deeper in the harbor than intended. Her troops went over the bow using cargo nets and soon controlled the immediate vicinity.

Cole followed in the dark, sighted a ship she mistook for *Bernadou* towards the south, and only by the best of luck managed to avoid ramming the outer jetty, entering the harbor at 0517. She came alongside the quay at 0545 and put her troops ashore without problem. The two destroyers suffered no deaths and only one man wounded. High tide mid-morning allowed *Bernadou* to float off and moor alongside *Cole*. Safi was effectively secured by the afternoon of D-Day.

— —

The Northern Attack Group comprised six transports and two cargo ships, with a screen of five destroyers and three minecraft. *Texas* and *Savannah* provided fire support. *Sangamon* (ACV 26) and *Chenango* with her deckload of Army fighters intended for Port Lyautey were screened by two destroyers. *Shad* (SS 235) was the guide submarine. This site for the northern landings was chosen because Port Lyautey had the only paved airstrip in French Morocco. The village of Mehedia was on the south bank of a river that split the two northern landing beaches from three in the south. Port Lyautey was a much larger settlement approximately 5 miles inland, also on the south bank, with the airstrip between in a sharp bend of the river.

No surprise was achieved by this group.[*] When it was pulling into position offshore soon after midnight on 8 November, a coastal convoy of five well-lit steamers passed through the transport area and then continued down the coast, but not before broadcasting a warning. Adding to the problem, the boarding of landing craft from the troopships took longer than planned; although the landings were scheduled to start at 0400, the first troops did not come ashore until 0515. Resistance to the landings increased as dawn approached, most of the French fire coming from a battery of six 138.6 mm guns sited near Mehedia. These were taken under fire by *Savannah* and the destroyer *Roe* (DD 418) and temporarily silenced, a process that would have to be repeated several times during the day. French shelling did not seem to seriously hamper the landing craft or the men already ashore, but fell close enough to some of the transports that the loading of landing craft was halted while they moved out of range. Adding to the difficulties, French aircraft showed up at 0630 and began bombing and strafing the landing craft. Wildcats from *Sangamon* (and later also from *Ranger*) were launched and soon cleared the sky over the beaches, and later attacked French aircraft on the ground at Port Lyautey and Rabat.

The fight on the ground was a hard slog, resisted in part by French armor that was effectively counterattacked by naval gunfire and *Sangamon*'s air group. By nightfall on 9 November, neither Mehedia nor Port Lyautey had been captured. The flush-decker *Dallas* (DD 199), modified in a similar manner as *Cole* and *Bernadou*, was intended to move up the river and put Army raiders ashore at the airstrip. She had not gone in as planned on 8 November because a net barrier across the river had not been cut. Finally, in the early morning dark on 10 November the barrier was rammed and *Dallas*, guided by a Free French river pilot, forced her way against heavy fire and around shoals and blockships more than 7 nm up the river, putting her raiders ashore. Neither *Dallas* nor the raiders suffered a casualty. During the day on 10 November, with the airfield captured, *Chenango*'s Army fighters were flown ashore. The town of Mehedia was taken and resistance there came to an end the same day. The river pilot, René Malavergne, became the first non-US civilian to be awarded the Navy Cross.

---

[*]   Morison, *History*, vol. II, pp. 117–33.

As expected, most of the naval action took place off Casablanca, the major French naval base on the Atlantic coast of Africa. Besides the battleship *Jean Bart*, in port on 8 November 1942 were one light cruiser, three destroyer leaders, seven destroyers, 19 smaller craft and 11 submarines. *Jean Bart*, which had fled metropolitan France in June 1940 in an incomplete state at the same time as *Richelieu*, had remained at Casablanca ever since, effectively immobilized and with only one main battery turret completed.* The four 380 mm guns in her single working turret were operational.

The Center Attack Group, carrying the largest of the three landing forces, comprised 12 transports and three cargo ships with a screen of six destroyers and six minecraft. Direct fire support was provided by *Augusta*, *Brooklyn* and four destroyers. The air component was supplied by *Ranger* and *Suwannee*, screened by the brand-new light cruiser *Cleveland* (CL55) and five destroyers.† Two submarines, *Gunnel* (SS253) and *Herring* (SS233), acted as guides. More distant support was provided by the Covering Group, comprising the new battleship *Massachusetts* (BB59), heavy cruisers *Wichita* and *Tuscaloosa*, and four destroyers, led by Rear-Admiral Giffen.‡ The landings were to be at four beaches north-east of the town of Fédala, itself slightly more than 5 miles north-east of Casablanca. The main defenses at Fédala were: Batterie de Pont-Blondin – north-east of the landing beaches, four 138.6 mm guns; Batterie du Port – south-west of the landing beaches, three 100 mm guns; two fixed 75 mm guns on Cape Fédala across a narrow bay from the landing beaches; and a battery of mobile 75 mm guns.§ At Casablanca, there were: Batterie d'El Hank – due west of the city, four 190 mm and four 130 mm guns and Batterie d'Oukacha – north-east of the port, four antique 100 mm guns; however, the most dangerous weaponry available to the French were the main battery guns of *Jean Bart*.¶ She was moored alongside a pier with her bow – and her operational turret – facing seaward. She had a new air/surface search radar, which had begun operation just a month earlier, but it was not usable for fire

---

* Breyer, *Battleships and Battle Cruisers*, pp. 435–6. *Jean Bart* escaped St-Nazaire on 19 June 1940 under German air attack.

† *Cleveland* was the lead ship of a large class of flush-deck light cruisers, essentially 6 inch-gunned versions of *Wichita*. In all, 52 *Clevelands* were ordered, of which nine hulls were completed as light aircraft carriers and 14 cancelled towards the end of the war.

‡ *Massachusetts* was the third of the new *South Dakota*-class battleships to commission. In an attempt to improve protection on the same displacement as the *North Carolinas*, the *South Dakotas* were 48 ft shorter, allowing thicker armor over a smaller citadel. They were considered cramped, with too much interference between the various medium- and small-caliber guns on their foreshortened superstructure.

§ Batterie du Port was the name used by Americans; the French refer to this position as Batterie de la Falaise.

¶ American sources generally refer to Batterie d'Oukacha as 'Table d'Oukasha' or 'Table d'Aoukasha'.

control against either surface or air targets.*

The landings at Fédala got off to a slow and confused start. The first line of transports arrived in position on time, a few minutes past midnight on 8 November. Behind the troopships came the three cargo ships which carried additional landing craft. As at the other landing sites, four hours were allowed to put all the men into boats and for the first wave to reach the line of departure. Ten minutes before H-hour, planned for 0400, beach marking boats were to be in position off their designated beaches and begin firing off appropriately colored flares. The inexperience of all involved began to show immediately, as in this account from *Leonard Wood*:

> 5. . . . 0009 began lowering boats. 0010 first boat waterborne. 0021 Beach marking boat departed to locate and mark the landing beach Red 2 . . . Some delay was encountered in lowering the tank lighters . . . The first three waves of assault boats departed at 0350 for the landing on designated beach. H hour was delayed from 0400 to 0445 by Commander Task Group Thirty Four Point Nine. The fourth wave departed at 0400 and the fifth wave at 0540. Some time was lost in loading the first wave because of failure of six boats (LCP(L)'s) to arrive from the U.S.S. PROCYON. Boats of succeeding waves were loaded and dispatched to the beach singly or in groups of two or three in order to expedite the disembarkation.

> 6. As boats of the first wave approached the shore they were illuminated by a searchlight from the direction of Chergui.† Support boats immediately opened fire on the light. Shortly thereafter firing was observed between land batteries at Chergui and Fedala and control vessels (destroyers) near the lines of departure.

> 7. Twenty one boats from this vessel were lost in making the initial landing due to striking rocks at the shore line and to surf conditions. Eight additional boats were lost during the day in landing thru the surf. Casualties to personnel as a result of this as well as the firing were very light. Continued to transfer troops and equipment between ship and shore as boats became available. Due to the loss of so many boats this method of unloading was extremely slow . . .‡

As seen from *Augusta*, firing was first observed at 0530 when the same coastal convoy seen off Mehedia now approached the transports off Fédala.§ This quickly died out, as did the firing at the searchlight at Pont-Blondin. Informed at 0617

---

* This was a DEM (Détecteur Electro-Magnétique) set with separate rotating antennae for transmission and reception operating in the 16 cm band.

† 'Chergui' is a misspelling of Cherqui, the location of Batterie de Pont-Blondin. Morison, *History,* vol. II, spells it 'Sherki'.

‡ AP25, pp. 2–3.

§ CA31, Enc A, pp. 1–3.

that resistance was being encountered, *Augusta* proceeded to launch all four floatplanes, but was unable to establish radio communications with any of them.

> 0700 Took position in area west of meridian of Fedala, about 14,000 yards off-shore, for counter-battery bombardment of Batterie du Port . . . Visibility very poor, with coastline obscured by haze and by heavy black smoke from one or more burning oil storage tanks on Cap Fedala. The cause of this oil fire was not definitely known, but it may have been caused by gunfire from Support Boats or Fire Support Groups 61, 62 and 63 (destroyers in close support of landing), which had been in progress.[*]

Augusta fired off 72 rounds of 8-inch gunfire at Batterie du Port to little effect. When the battery was captured, it was found that shelling had shot away the rangefinder, but had not damaged any of the guns.

The story was different further north, where *Brooklyn* fired off 757 rounds of 6-inch in 85 minutes at Batterie de Pont-Blondin before concluding with a two-minute burst of continuous fire that ended at 0742. Shortly thereafter, the French gunners, mostly unenthusiastic colonial troops, surrendered readily to forces advancing off the beaches. By 1100, the last resistance on the ground ceased at Fédala. The only US naval casualties in this phase occurred when *Murphy* (DD603), which had also been engaging Batterie de Pont-Blondin, was hit by a single 138.6 mm round, which penetrated her after engine room, killing three and wounding seven.

— —

The most consequential naval action of TORCH took place off Casablanca, where the Covering Group kept one eye on the French warships in the harbor and the other on the southern horizon in case the Dakar squadron sortied. The French were at an obvious disadvantage. Even if the two cruisers off Fédala are discounted, the Americans outnumbered and outgunned the French in every category, especially in the air, where the French were outclassed by more capable American aircraft. In the most significant encounter, 18 Wildcats of VF-41 off *Ranger* attacked Les Cazes airfield near Casablanca on the morning of the invasion.[†] They found ten Dewoitine D.520s and six Curtiss Hawk 75As over the airfield. The former was a modern low-wing monoplane with a 20 mm cannon and four rifle-caliber machine guns, the latter was an American-built version of the USAAF P-36 Hawk, slower and less well-armed than the Dewoitine. The Wildcat was less maneuverable than either French fighter, but better-armed with

---

[*]   CA31, Enc A, pp. 1–3. According to Morison, *History,* vol. II, p. 77, the oil fire was indeed caused by gunfire from *Wilkes* (DD441) or *Swanson* (DD443).

[†]   Morison, *History,* vol. II, pp. 88–9.; Cressman, *USS* Ranger, pp. 211–18.

The battle off Casablanca started with AA fire over the landing beaches as a 20 mm gun crew on Massachusetts *(BB59) waits nervously for the surface battle to begin, 8 November 1942. The coast was completely obscured by low clouds and mist. (NARA)*

six .50 caliber machine guns and capable of absorbing tremendous punishment. The Americans had learned from bitter experience fighting Zeros in the Pacific how to minimize the Wildcat's weaknesses (poor maneuverability and climb rate) and maximize its advantages (firepower, ruggedness and dive rate). The result of this engagement over Les Cazes was eight French fighters shot down and 14 more destroyed on the ground. Four Wildcats were lost, two to ground fire. All four pilots were captured by the French and later released. This effectively ended all but sporadic French resistance in the air. The Americans lost 44 aircraft during the entire campaign; most of the aircrew survived.

The naval battle began even earlier, at dawn on 8 November. It was a complex affair, best understood if divided into its several more or less discrete phases. (The times given to delineate these phases are approximate.)

0650–0800   Bombarding the Harbor

As *Ranger's* aircraft began receiving anti-aircraft fire and the shore batteries at Fédala were firing at the landing boats, the Covering Group assumed battle formation with the four destroyers in front followed by *Massachusetts*, *Wichita* and *Tuscaloosa*, in that order.* As seen from *Mayrant*, one of the screening destroyers, the visibility was far from ideal.

---

* The general description of this long engagement comes from Mordal, *La Bataille Navale de Casablanca*, Morison, *History*, vol. II, pp. 91–112 and O'Hara, *The Battle of Casablanca*.

Two huge national ensigns fly from fore and mainmasts of Massachusetts *in the vain hope that the French would not fire on American ships. The upper ensign is partially obscured by the two-star flag of Rear-Admiral Giffen. The upper ensign was reported holed by a shell from* Jean Bart. *(NHHC)*

Visibility was very good except in the direction of the land where a light haze over the coast obscured targets and navigational aids considerably. The Sun, rising over the land, added to the difficulty of target observation.

... At 0652 bursts of AA fire were observed over coast near CASABLANCA, and the order 'PLAY BALL' was received.[*] This was the signal to take vigorous offensive action against the enemy ...

At 0705 message was received from Flagship directing MAYRANT to stay astern and not to cross the line of fire, as by this time the JEAN BART and shore batteries had commenced firing on the MASSACHUSETTS. The MASSACHUSETTS then opened fire, apparently using divided fire in accordance with plan, engaging JEAN BART and shore batteries.[†]

The shore batteries commenced ranging the heavy ships so all ships started steering evasive courses to confuse shore spotters. A number of splashes landed near at hand and one was reported landing 50 yards on port quarter.[‡]

The Americans drew first blood at 0718, when VS-41 Dauntlesses off *Ranger* put a 500-lb bomb on *Jean Bart*'s port catapult base, starting a small fire, and

---

[*]   Baseball terminology was used for important orders: 'BATTER UP' signaled that French resistance had been encountered and 'PLAY BALL' that the French should be engaged.

[†]   According to BB59, Enc A, p 2, *Massachusetts* opened fire on *Jean Bart* at 0704.

[‡]   DD402-1, pp. 1–3.

Two gun flashes shine out of the low mist that obscured the shore during the morning action off Fédala as seen from Augusta, *8 November 1942. It is easy to see why the shore batteries and later the 2ème Escadre Légère proved difficult to hit until the mist dissipated.* (NARA)

another quayside which perforated her hull near the bow.[*] French return fire was steady and accurate, achieving straddles in the first few salvos, but the American reply, aided by spotting aircraft, was even better. In 22 salvos over 36 minutes, *Massachusetts* hit or near-missed *Jean Bart* five times with 16-inch shells:

0725   Hit aft that exploded in an empty 15.2 cm magazine;[†]
0735   Shell that splashed alongside and continued into the bow;
0736   Shell exploded on quay alongside, sending debris into the hull; and
0737   Hit passed through the funnel and part of the hull before exiting above the waterline; and a second shell, from this salvo or the next, that glanced off quay and *Jean Bart*'s belt armor.

By 0740, *Massachusetts*, which had been leading the Covering Group towards the north-east for the last half-hour, was approaching the transport area off Fédala. She checked fire and led the force around, settling on a course due west and started firing again at 0748, obtaining three more hits in 24 salvos before fire ceased again 40 minutes later:

---

[*]   O'Hara, *The Battle of Casablanca*, p. 52; Cressman, *USS Ranger*, p. 220.
[†]   Special thanks to Richard Worth for this chronology.

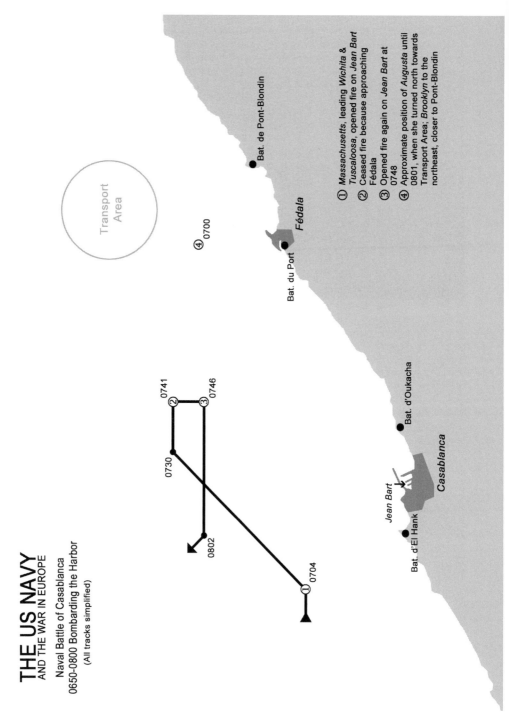

THE US NAVY
AND THE WAR IN EUROPE

Naval Battle of Casablanca
0650-0800 Bombarding the Harbor
(All tracks simplified)

Transport Area

Bat. de Pont-Blondin

Fédala

Bat. du Port

④ 0700

0741
②

③
0746

0730

0802

0704
①

Bat. d'Oukacha

Jean Bart

Casablanca

Bat. d'El Hank

① *Massachusetts*, leading *Wichita* & *Tuscaloosa*, opened fire on *Jean Bart*

② Ceased fire because approaching Fédala

③ Opened fire again on *Jean Bart* at 0748

④ Approximate position of *Augusta* until 0801, when she turned north towards Transport Area; *Brooklyn* to the northeast, closer to Pont-Blondin

A Benham-class destroyer, probably Mayrant *(DD402), is dwarfed by a pair of shell splashes from Batterie d'El Hank, 8 November 1942. (NARA)*

0806 Hit that deformed the forward main battery barbette, jamming the forward turret in train, and ricocheted into central Casablanca without exploding, whence it was recovered and put on display at the city hall; a second shell from the same salvo hit the barbette of the incomplete superfiring main battery turret, also without exploding; and

0810 A final hit penetrated her quarterdeck and the 100 mm armored deck protecting the auxiliary steering compartment, exploding there and holing her outer shell below the waterline.

While *Massachusetts* was dueling with *Jean Bart*, the two heavy cruisers in the Covering Group were attempting to silence the shore batteries and bombers from *Ranger's* VS-41 and *Suwannee's* VGS-27 went after ships in the harbor, damaging three submarines (*Amphitrite*, *Oréade* and *La Psyché*), as well as numerous merchant ships. Of the remaining French warships in Casablanca harbor, the following were to some degree unavailable:

Two destroyers [*Tempête* (T 62) and *Simoun* (T 61)] were repairing damage from a collision two months earlier and were not immediately able to get underway;

The power plant of the light cruiser *Primauguet* had been under repair and was being hastily restarted, but it would be more than an hour before she had steam sufficient to maneuver;

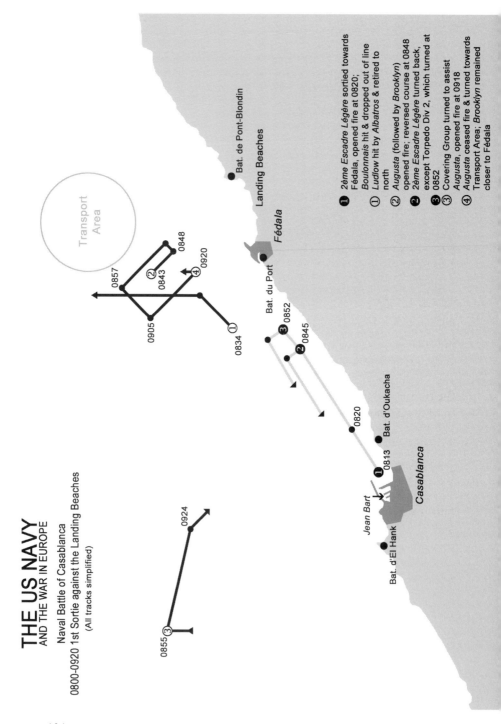

THE US NAVY
AND THE WAR IN EUROPE

Naval Battle of Casablanca
0800–0920 1st Sortie against the Landing Beaches
(All tracks simplified)

Transport Area

Bat. de Pont-Blondin

Landing Beaches

Fédala

Bat. du Port

Bat. d'Oukacha

Jean Bart

Casablanca

Bat. d'El Hank

① *2ème Escadre Légère* sortied towards Fédala, opened fire at 0820; *Boulonnais* hit & dropped out of line

① *Ludlow* hit by *Albatros* & retired to north

② *Augusta* (followed by *Brooklyn*) opened fire; reversed course at 0848

② *2ème Escadre Légère* turned back, except Torpedo Div 2, which turned at 0852

③ Covering Group turned to assist

③ *Augusta*, opened fire at 0918

④ *Augusta* ceased fire & turned towards Transport Area; *Brooklyn* remained closer to Fédala

Destroyer leader *Le Malin* was undergoing refit and would not be available at all;

The submarine *Le Conquérant* was in a floating dry dock, but was floated out minutes before the drydock was hit by gunfire from *Massachusetts*. The submarine put to sea without any torpedoes or working periscope in an attempt to reach the safety of Dakar.[*]

Of the ships available at dawn on 8 November, the first to sortie were five submarines which took up assigned defensive patrol positions. A semi-circle traced from Pointe d'El Hank was split into four pie-shaped zones, each roughly a 40° slice, occupied, from west to east, by *Orphée*, *Méduse*, *Antiope* and *Amazone*. These left the harbor starting just before 0600. The easternmost zone was supposed to have been occupied by *La Sybille*, but her captain had not arrived from town in time to sortie with the others, so his boat was assigned a patrol zone off Fédala. *La Sybille* departed just before 0700.[†] Also at around 0700, *Le Tonnant* sortied with *Sidi-Ferruch*, with orders to head for Safi. Both had sustained strafing attacks by Wildcats, both their captains had been wounded in these attacks and both departed under the command of their executive officers.

0800–0920   First Sortie against the Landing Beaches

The remaining French warships began to move, assembling in the outer harbor starting at 0715. After *Albatros* joined at 0813, the ships of Rear-Admiral Raymond Gervais de Lafond's 2nd Light Squadron (2ème Escadre Légère) steamed out of the harbor and, setting their speed at 18 knots, headed east-north-east up the coast towards the landing beaches.[‡] They were ordered by divisions: Destroyer Division 11 (*Milan* (X 111) and *Albatros* (X 72)), followed by Torpedo Division 5 (*Brestois* (T 51) and *Boulonnais* (T 52)) and Torpedo Division 2 (*Fougueux* (T 21), *Frondeur* (T 22) and *L'Alcyon* (T 23)).

Milan, leading the French line, opened fire at 0820, soon scoring a direct hit on a landing craft off Yellow Beach west of Cape Fédala. Initially, the only opposition to the French destroyers came from the Wildcats of *Ranger's* VF-9 and VF-41 which spotted the line heading towards Fédala at 0815.[§] The fighters made several strafing passes at the destroyers, causing considerable damage to the upperworks of several of the ships, killing and wounding a number of officers and men. The most heavily damaged of the French ships was *Boulonnais*, whose captain was mortally wounded and the forward control and hydraulic steering put out of action. The ship stopped briefly while command was switched to after

---

[*]   Mordal, *La Bataille Navale de Casablanca*, p. 250.

[†]   Ibid., p. 244.

[‡]   Gervais de Lafond had gained fame for his brave and skillful handing of a small destroyer squadron against much stronger Royal Navy formations off Lebanon in June 1941.

[§]   Cressman, *USS* Ranger, pp. 222–4; Mordal, *La Bataille Navale de Casablanca*, pp. 435–6.

control and manual steering established, rejoining the squadron at 0915 along with *Primauguet*.

The Wildcats soon had to withdraw, low on ammunition and fuel, but the action was taken up by the destroyers *Wilkes* (DD441), *Swanson* (DD443) and *Ludlow* (DD428), which had been providing direct gunfire support to the landings since dawn and were starting to run low on main battery rounds. Hoping to lead the French away from the beaches and transport area, *Wilkes* and *Swanson* turned to the north and retired at high speed. *Ludlow*, however, delayed her turn and exchanged fire with the French squadron long enough to obtain a hit and be hit in turn. A hit on *Milan* started fires that were soon extinguished, but the hit on *Ludlow* at 0834 by *Albatros* penetrated her forecastle, exploding in the wardroom, starting a serious fire. *Ludlow* retired from the fight and spent the next three hours making repairs.

Meanwhile, *Augusta* and *Brooklyn* had been summoned and came charging through the transport area to the cheers of the sailors on the transports. *Augusta's* report gives the sequence of events:

0817 Information received from planes that a number of French men-of-war had sortied from Casablanca harbor and were heading toward Fedala and the transport area. Number and disposition of enemy ships uncertain because of haze and smoke screen being laid by their destroyers.

0825 Enemy ships tentatively identified as 2 CL and 6 DD. This ship changed to southerly course to intercept and engage.

0837 Enemy ships sighted. Two largest (later established as DL) nearest coast, proceeding northeastward, roughly parallel to coastline. A number of smaller ships (DD), variously estimated at 5 to 6 in number, outboard of the two DL, on northeasterly courses. Haze and smokescreen made visibility very poor.

0838 This ship and BROOKLYN under fire from enemy ships, medium caliber (5 to 6 inch), red and green splashes.[*]

Having sighted the oncoming cruisers, Gervais de Lafond ordered his ships about to a southwesterly course back towards the harbor, but in the smoke and confusion, Torpedo Division 2 missed the signal and continued towards Fédala.

0843 Commenced firing on enemy ship target . . . Ship on southeasterly course, firing to starboard.

0848 Enemy fire (red splashes) very close. Ship commenced turn left to

---

[*] CA31, Enc A, pp 4-5. It was common practice on both sides for shells to contain dye packets that would color shell splashes, different colors for different ships, allowing them to track their gunfire. *Milan* fired red-dyed projectiles.

Brooklyn *(CL40) fires to port as she trails* Augusta *(CA31) during the Battle of Casablanca, 8 November 1942. A smaller ship, almost certainly the damaged* Ludlow *(DD428), is crossing in front of* Augusta. *If that identification is correct, then this photograph was taken at about 0857, when the two cruisers turned towards the south-west to close the ships of the 2ème Escadre Légère as they sortied towards Fédala. (NARA)*

reverse course for another run. During above run, 20 mm. gun mounts No. 11 and 12, on fantail, damaged by blast from turret 3. Higgins boat rigged in at starboard rail also damaged by blast, and was therefore dropped overboard.[*]

The LCP(L) had been swung out to take Patton ashore, a move that was put on hold when *Augusta* turned to engage the French squadron. At 0852, the CO of Torpedo Division 2, Commander Louis S. Sticca, realized his division was alone and exposed and ordered a turn away to the south-west.

0853 Ship on northwesterly course . . . Resumed fire on ship target.
0857 Changed course toward targets, to southwesterly course, to close range

 . . .

0905 Changed course to left, to southeasterly course.[†]

---

[*] Ibid.
[†] CA31, Enc A, pp. 4–5.

The heavy cruiser Wichita *exchanges fire with a shore battery, 8 November 1942. (NARA)*

For the last few minutes *Augusta* and *Brooklyn* had been primarily exchanging fire with *Primauguet*, which was now underway and joined by *Boulonnais*. Neither side appears to have scored a hit. Not wanting to get too far from the transports they were assigned to protect, the two cruisers did not pursue the French further to the south-west.

> 0920 Enemy ships retiring to Casablanca. Ceased firing. Changed course to north, returning to transport area. Covering Force (MASSACHUSETTS, TUSCALOOSA, and WICHITA) observed to westward, firing toward shore near Casablanca.

Despite this, Gervais de Lafond found himself in an unenviable position. He had not gone far towards the south-west before he came under fire from the Covering Group. Sighting the oncoming *Massachusetts*, he reversed course again, circling outside the entrance to the harbor.

0920–1016   The Covering Group in Action

So far, the French had proved to be very hard to hit. They were maneuvering skillfully behind a dense smokescreen laid by the destroyers, which, added to the coastal haze and the fires at Fédala, made tracking fall of shot nearly impossible. *Primauguet* and Batterie d'El Hank engaged *Massachusetts* well enough that at 0935, she turned away towards the west to open the range. As seen from *Mayrant*, the action was furious. Sticca's destroyers were the most visible of the French:

> . . . At 0915 sighted three French destroyers of the 'L'Alcyon' class bearing 160 true, range about 16,000, target angle about 240.* Reported sighting to flagship over TBS.† At 0920 flagship signalled 'commence firing' and MAYRANT opened fire at 0922. The enemy destroyers were in column, firing quite rapidly and apparently had found the range, as a very radical zig-zag was necessary during this phase to avoid straddles.
>
> The leading destroyer was chosen as our target . . . The destroyers were also under fire from our cruisers to the N.E. and were frequently obscured by their splashes. The gunnery officer observed three straddles and a direct hit during the third straddle made by guns of the MAYRANT, after which target emitted a cloud of steam, lost headway rapidly and headed for the beach apparently well down by the stern.‡

Fougueux, the lead destroyer, may or may not have been hit by *Mayrant*, but also drew fire from the heavy units of the Covering Group and was hit by one shell from *Massachusetts* and a salvo from *Tuscaloosa* forward at approximately 0940. She did indeed turn away, losing way, with her bow a mass of flame as far aft as the bridge. The crew, forced aft by the fire, began lowering boats for the wounded. *Frondeur* slowed to allow Sticca to transfer over, but was herself hit twice by *Tuscaloosa*, killing the gunnery officer on her bridge and damaging her steering, and was ordered to proceed. At 0955 *Fougueux*'s crew began to abandon ship, and at approximately 1,000, out of sight of the Americans, she exploded and sank. At about the same time, *Milan* was hit by a shell from *Massachusetts* that entered under her starboard bridge wing and burst in the petty officers' country. The explosion damaged the forward fire room and started a fire in the signal rocket store that spread into the chart house one deck up. Two more 16-inch hits followed, one in the forecastle, adding to the fire already burning under the bridge. Fighting this fire proved very difficult, because the fire mains had previously been damaged by Wildcats. It soon became necessary to abandon the bridge and stop all internal ventilation to prevent the spread of smoke to after compartments. Losing power, *Milan* turned towards the shore north-east of the harbor.§

At almost the same time, *Massachusetts* was hit by a single 190 mm shell

---

* The times given in this excerpt all seem to be about a ten minutes early. The action described started at approximately 0925. This kind of time discrepancy is common in action reports.

† TBS was a high-frequency, tactical, voice radio system introduced in 1939.

‡ DD402-1, pp 3-4. The gunnery officer referred to in this excerpt was Lieutenant Franklin D. Roosevelt, Jr.

§ Mordal, *La Bataille Navale de Casablanca*, pp. 436–7; O'Hara, *The Battle of Casablanca*, p. 57.

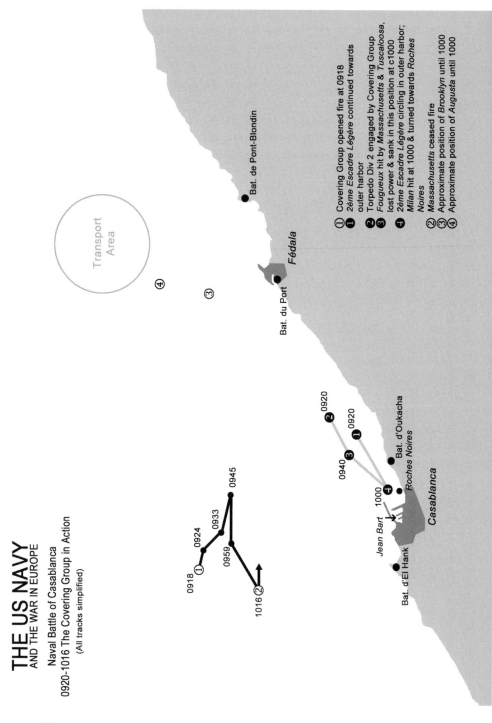

THE US NAVY
AND THE WAR IN EUROPE

Naval Battle of Casablanca
0920-1016 The Covering Group in Action
(All tracks simplified)

Transport Area

Bat. de Pont-Blondin

Fédala

Bat. du Port

Bat. d'Oukacha

Roches Noires

Casablanca

Bat. d'El Hank

Jean Bart

① Covering Group opened fire at 0918
❶ 2ème Escadre Légère continued towards outer harbor
② Torpedo Div 2 engaged by Covering Group
❸ Fougueux hit by Massachusetts & Tuscaloosa, lost power & sank in this position at c1000
❹ 2ème Escadre Légère circling in outer harbor; Milan hit at 1000 & turned towards Roches Noires
② Massachusetts ceased fire
③ Approximate position of Brooklyn until 1000
④ Approximate position of Augusta until 1000

130

from Batterie d'El Hank, which penetrated her main deck abreast No. 2 main battery turret and exploded in a second deck compartment for minor damage and no injuries. A few minutes later at 1003, she was near-missed by a spread of four torpedoes from one of the French submarines, probably *Méduse*. Not long after, *Tuscaloosa* was missed by torpedoes from *Antiope*. The Covering Group continued on to the west, losing sight of the squadron outside the harbor at about 0950.[*] *Massachusetts* then turned her attention back to the harbor; at 0955 she hit *Le Malin* with a 16-inch shell that ricocheted off the stone jetty, failed to explode, but nonetheless punched large holes in her shell plating in way of her engine room. Seven of her crew were killed and seven more wounded. *Massachusetts* ceased firing at 1016.

1000–1025   The 'Death Ride' of Torpedo Division 5

By 1000, the French squadron was in disarray. Gervais de Lafond was no longer able to communicate with his division commanders, who now began to operate independently. Making matters worse, two of his division commanders, Commander Sticca in *Fougueux* and Commander Mariani in *Brestois*, were incapacitated. Additionally, the captain of *Boulonnais*, Lieutenant Commander de Préneuf, who should have taken over command of Torpedo Division 5, had been seriously wounded by strafing Wildcats early in the battle, so command of the division fell to *Boulonnais*'s XO, Lieutenant Chazereau. On his own initiative, Chazereau decided that the only way out of the crossfire between the two cruisers to the north and the Covering Group to the west was make a potentially suicidal torpedo attack on *Brooklyn* and *Augusta*.[†]

Brooklyn was to the south of the transport area off Fédala. *Augusta* was further east, but stopped with a landing craft alongside ready to take General Patton ashore. When gunfire was heard to the south, the landing craft was cut loose and she bent on all speed. For the second time, Patton would be delayed. (He would finally be put ashore around 1100.[‡]) Fortunately, neither ship had far to go before they had the two French destroyers in sight. At about 1010, *Boulonnais* and *Brestois* charged at *Brooklyn*, but were met with a hail of gunfire that rapidly overwhelmed *Boulonnais*. Chazereau ordered the torpedoes fired when the range reached 13,000 yards, but before the order could be obeyed, the ship was hit by six shells out of a full salvo fired by *Brooklyn*. The time was 1012. One shell penetrated the magazine for main battery gun No. 2, which was saved from exploding by rapid flooding. Other shells damaged her engine room. The ship was obviously beyond saving and the order was given to get the wounded into boats. Meanwhile, the two working guns continued firing and *Brooklyn* shot back, hitting with two more shells, at which point *Boulonnais*

---

[*]   DD402-1, p. 4.

[†]   Mordal, *La Bataille Navale de Casablanca*, pp. 439–41.

[‡]   Cherpak, *The Memoirs of Admiral H. Kent Hewitt*, p. 136.

The heavy cruiser Augusta *looses a salvo at a target somewhere in the thick haze obscuring the shore near Fédala, 8 November 1942. (NARA)*

was ordered abandoned. *Brestois* stopped briefly to pick up survivors, but *Brooklyn*, now joined by *Augusta*, continued firing until *Brestois* turned and headed back towards *Primauguet* and the cover of the smokescreen outside the harbor. Miraculously, she survived this sortie relatively unharmed. It is not known whether she fired any torpedoes. What is known is that captain of the submarine *Amazone* claimed to have fired a spread of five torpedoes at *Brooklyn* at 1010 at a range of less than 1,100 yards. *Brooklyn* turned sharply to port to thread the wakes; all the torpedoes missed.[*] *Boulonnais* remained afloat until 1107, when she rolled over and sank. Survivors were rescued around 1330 by the armed trawler *Servanaise*.[†]

1015–1100   The End of the 2ème Escadre Légère

Brooklyn and *Augusta* were now on an east-south-east course firing towards the French squadron milling around the harbor entrance. The haze and smoke were becoming patchy, so that the French were intermittently visible to the American cruisers. At 1015, one such moment occurred and *Brooklyn* opened fire on *Primauguet*, which took one hit with a 6-inch shell that caused little material damage, but inflicted numerous casualties. She was hit again five minutes later

---

[*]   Morison, *History*, vol. II, p. 106.

[†]   Mordal, *La Bataille Navale de Casablanca*, p. 442.

by three shells that passed through her without detonating.

At this time, the Fédala battery chimed in, near-missing *Augusta* several times. Patton was on the foredeck near main battery turret No. 2 when a shell landed near enough to drench him in the splash; he found the experience amusing.*

There were now five ships remaining in the French squadron, *Albatros*, *L'Alcyon*, *Frondeur* and *Brestois* milling around off the outer breakwater (Jetée Delure), under the questionable protection of a thinning smokescreen and the guns of *Primauguet* and Batterie d'El Hank. Under constant fire from *Massachusetts* and four cruisers, it was just a matter of time before the remaining French ships were incapacitated. The next was *Brestois*, hit at 1020 by an 8-inch shell from *Augusta*, which exploded in the crew's quarters and caused flooding amidships. *Frondeur* took a hit aft at 1025, almost certainly also from *Augusta*. The explosion lifted her stern out of the water and, when she settled again, water was pouring into her engine room, which had to be abandoned. Incredibly, though, her turbines continued to operate and she turned away from the battle, setting a course for the inner harbor.

Albatros was hit hard at about 1030.† An 8-inch shell damaged No. 2 main battery mount and started a fire in the ammunition hoist that proved difficult to contain. A near-miss at 1040, possibly by a 16-inch shell, opened a 23-foot long tear in her hull. Despite this, she maneuvered along the coast for another hour-and-a-quarter.

Primauguet had remained the primary target of the American warships, and had been hit at least five times at or below the waterline by 6-inch or 8-inch shells during this period, but she continued maneuvering outside the harbor and firing back until 1045, when she was hit by a bomb on her after fire control station dropped by a Dauntless of VS-41. A few minutes later a second bomb destroyed her engineering office. With this, she finally turned away and headed towards the outer harbor, though her guns continued to fire.

The only revenge the French could exact for all this destruction came when *Brooklyn* was hit once at 1046 by a shell of unknown caliber, probably from *Albatros*, which glanced off a 5-inch mount and continued overboard without exploding, nevertheless wounding six men. Then at 1057, *Primauguet* managed a hit on *Massachusetts* on an unmanned 20 mm mount for minor damage.

1030–   Odds & Ends, Mostly Ends

By 1030, *Milan* had been reduced to a crawl; she was heading slowly towards the outer harbor, her entire forward superstructure engulfed in flame with munitions starting to cook off in the forward magazines. The only communication between crew trapped in the forecastle and the rest aft of the fire was by messages carried by two strong swimmers of the ship's water polo team. At 1045, the tug *Lavandou*

---

*   O'Hara, *The Battle of Casablanca*, p. 59.

†   Mordal, *La Bataille Navale de Casablanca*, pp. 443–4.

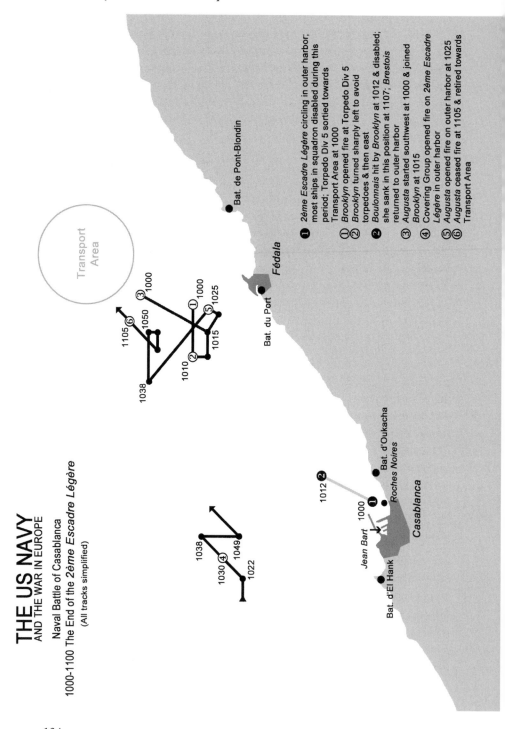

THE US NAVY
AND THE WAR IN EUROPE
Naval Battle of Casablanca
1000-1100 The End of the *2ème Escadre Légère*
(All tracks simplified)

Transport Area

Bat. de Pont-Blondin

Fédala

Bat. du Port

Bat. d'Oukacha

Roches Noires

Casablanca

Jean Bart

Bat. d'El Hank

1 *2ème Escadre Légère* circling in outer harbor; most ships in squadron disabled during this period; Torpedo Div 5 sortied towards Transport Area at 1000

① *Brooklyn* opened fire at Torpedo Div 5

② *Brooklyn* turned sharply left to avoid torpedoes & then east

2 *Boulonnais* hit by *Brooklyn* at 1012 & disabled; she sank in this position at 1107; *Brestois* returned to outer harbor

③ *Augusta* started southwest at 1000 & joined

④ *Brooklyn* at 1015

⑤ Covering Group opened fire on *2ème Escadre Légère* in outer harbor

⑤ *Augusta* opened fire on outer harbor at 1025

⑥ *Augusta* ceased fire at 1105 & retired towards Transport Area

134

Primauguet *(left) and* Albatros *are seen from the beach. The Jetée Transversale is in the background in this view. (NARA)*

came alongside and began taking off the wounded. The aviso-dragueur (small minesweeper) *Commandant Delage* (A 63) took off Gervais de Lafond and transported him back to his flagship, *Primauguet*. *Milan* was steered towards the beach to the north-east of the Jetée Transversale (or Jetée des Phosphates) that separated the inner from the outer harbor, finally running aground near a pair of large rocks known as the Roches Noires at 1346, with 31 dead and over 70 wounded.

Gervais de Lafond and *Primauguet* were already there, having anchored in shallow water just off the Jetée Transversale soon after 1100. The Americans were not done with her. During the afternoon, she was a frequent target for Wildcats, but it appears to have been the 325-lb bombs of Avengers from *Suwannee* which completed her destruction later that afternoon. One hit her bridge, killing her captain and eight others, wounding Gervais de Lafond and starting a fire that burned all night, gutting her forecastle.[*] *Wichita* fired on *Primauguet* between 1444 and 1505, but caused no further damage.

Frondeur, which dropped out of the fray soon after *Milan*, anchored in the inner harbor at 1125, where she became the regular target of Wildcats with nothing better to shoot at. She capsized that night.

Having expended 60 per cent of her main battery ammunition and concerned that she might not have enough should *Richelieu* appear, *Massachusetts* ceased

---

[*] Mordal, *La Bataille Navale de Casablanca*, pp. 438–9; Cressman, *USS* Ranger, pp. 232–8; CA31, Enc D, pp. 3–4.

Milan is seen beached near the Roches Noires. She has two red bands on her second funnel, the pennant number (X III) is brick red with black shadowing and the shields of the fore and aft superfiring gun mounts have blue-white-red national markings which were originally adopted during the Spanish Civil War Non-Intervention Patrol. (NARA)

fire and turned away to recover aircraft soon after 1100. At the same time, *Augusta* turned back toward the transport area. *Brooklyn* continued to patrol back and forth on a line perpendicular to the coast off Fédala. After *Massachusetts* turned away, *Tuscaloosa* and *Wichita* again approached the harbor from the north, hoping to engage the remaining French ships. The only French warships still moving outside the outer breakwater were now *Albatros*, *Brestois* and *L'Alcyon*, all three with varying degrees of damage.

During her evolutions along the coast after 1100, *Albatros*, chased by 8-inch shells from *Wichita* and *Tuscaloosa*, was hit at least five more times. However, she still was moving at 1145, when, passing Batterie d'Oukacha, a pair of Dauntlesses of VS-41 each placed a bomb amidships, which destroyed her after machinery spaces, knocking over her third funnel, and opened the forward engine room to the sea, bringing her to a halt. At least 25 of her complement were killed and another 80 wounded. *Albatros* was towed later in the day to the same area where *Milan* and *Primauguet* had already found refuge.

Brestois did not last much longer. At 1146, a bomb burst just off her port side, causing progressive flooding. She anchored just inside the outer breakwater (Jetée Delure) at about 1230. Losing the battle against incoming water, her crew was taken off at 2100, only a few minutes before she capsized.

This left only one warship moving outside the harbor, *L'Alcyon*, which remained largely undamaged.

The only retribution the French could exact at this time was a hit on *Wichita*

The destroyer Frondeur *(T 22) lies on her side in the inner harbor, Casablanca. The American transport* John Penn *(AP51) is being unloaded in the background on the inner side of the Jetée Transversale. (NARA)*

at 1128 by a shell from Batterie d'El Hank, which exploded on her second deck, wounding 14 men and starting fires that were quickly controlled. At 1150, *Tuscaloosa* and *Wichita* were ordered to disengage and head west again on receipt of a false report that a French cruiser had been sighted down the coast. *Massachusetts*, *Augusta* and *Brooklyn* maintained positions beyond the range of shore batteries.

There was one more burst of action later in the day. At around 1245, *Tempête* was towed out of the way, allowing *Simoun* to move slowly out of the inner harbor and moor to a buoy in the outer harbor, hoping to act as a floating battery with the hope of drawing the Americans back within the range of Batterie d'El Hank. While this was going on, the aviso-colonial (large colonial sloop) *La Grandière* (A 61) and the two avisos-dragueurs *Commandant Delage* and *La Gracieuse* (A 65) slipped out of the harbor and joined up with *L'Alcyon* with the intent of rescuing survivors of *Boulonnais*.[*] They were sighted by American aircraft and reported as a light cruiser and two destroyers at 1258.[†] *Augusta* was the closest American ship, but she slowed to launch two aircraft, the second while under fire from *La Grandière*. *Brooklyn* opened fire at 1315, *Augusta* at 1326. The two cruisers exchanged fire with the French ships and with *Albatros*, which was

---

[*]   O'Hara, *The Battle of Casablanca*, pp. 59–60.

[†]   CA31, Enc A, pp. 7–8; Morison, *History*, vol. II, pp. 108–10.

The three French ships beached in the outer harbor at Casablanca are seen from the Jetée Transversale. Note the discoloration of the burned-out forecastle of Primauguet *to the left. To the right are* Albatros *and* Milan. *(NARA)*

being towed towards Roches Noires, but no hits were achieved by either side. However, American aircraft continued to score as the French pulled back into the inner harbor. A single bomb hit *La Grandière* for damage and another near-missed *Commandant Delage*, causing minor flooding. *L'Alcyon* now headed towards her berth alongside the Jetée Delure. She was strafed and bombed by Dauntlesses of VS-41 off *Ranger* at 1315, one bomb exploding close enough that it opened up the fuel tanks on that side. This caused her to take on a list that led most onboard to believe she would capsize, but her engineers managed to bring her back to an even keel and control the flooding.

This ended the major action on D-Day, 8 November 1942, but not the Naval Battle of Casablanca. There was more to come. The Americans could look at the day's activities with some satisfaction, but certainly not with smugness. The troops had been put ashore, enough at least to secure the beachheads and initial objectives, but there was still much to be learned before an opposed landing against a well-equipped and determined enemy could be attempted. The French fleet had been defeated – two ships sunk outright, three more beached and another two sinking – but with overwhelming superiority on the surface and complete control of the air, any other result would have been embarrassing, if not disastrous. And, it had been achieved only with an exorbitant expenditure of munitions; many of the US warships were down to less than 20 per cent of magazine capacity. It is safe to say that had the ships at Dakar sortied, the Americans would not have had enough shells to defeat them.[*]

— —

The next day proved quiet, a lull that the French used to advantage. The jammed turret on *Jean Bart* was freed and again available for use; sailors off sunken French warships were organized into infantry units and dug defensive positions east of the city.

Action started early on 10 November, with *Ranger's* aircraft supporting troops of the 7th Infantry as they approached the French lines near Roches Noires. She was in the process of recovering a flight of six Dauntlesses, when, at approximately 0910, two torpedoes were seen passing close astern. These were from a spread of four fired by *Le Tonnant*.

To support the defenders at Batterie d'Oukacha, Vice-Admiral François Michelier, commanding the naval forces at Casablanca, ordered gunfire support. The two small avisos-dragueurs, *Commandant Delage* and *La Gracieuse*, again slipped out of the harbor unnoticed and had begun at about 1120 to lob shells at the American troops. *Augusta* was the closest large warship, but was about 15 nm north-east of the two minesweepers. Two American destroyers, *Edison* (DD439) and *Tillman* (DD641), were closer than *Augusta* and opened fire first at 1125. *Augusta* joined in at 1137.

However, *Augusta* was in for a nasty surprise when, at 1145, two large yellow shell splashes, a good 100 feet tall, appeared just 600 yards short of the ship.[†] When the third or fourth two-gun salvo were straddles, *Augusta* turned away, being chased by these splashes until she was 30,000 yards from their only possible source, *Jean Bart*. One fell close enough that Admiral Hewitt was drenched by seawater. While *Augusta* was heading the other way, the destroyers kept firing at the two avisos and obtained two hits on *Commandant Delage*, one in the radio shack and another, at 1203, that hit the after gun shield. *La Gracieuse* made smoke to cover the two ships, which slipped back into the harbor, having suffered nine dead and 26 wounded.[‡]

It was not until 1430 that the Americans turned their attention to *Jean Bart*. A flight of nine Dauntlesses armed with 1,000lb bombs took off from *Ranger*. Only two of the bombs hit – one forward of the operating turret, blowing out her bow, the other on the starboard side alongside her aircraft hanger, peeling

---

* Morison, *History,* vol. II, p. 111. BB59, Enc A, p. 13, states that *Massachusetts* fired 786 rounds and ended the day with 387 remaining, including a 110-round reserve. She had fired off just over 67 per cent of her capacity.

† O'Hara, *The Battle of Casablanca,* p. 52, note 11. This states *Jean Bart* was firing orange-dyed shells, but most American observers reported them as yellow.

‡ CA31, Enc A, pp 10-1; Morison, *History,* vol. II, pp. 162–3; Mordal, *La Bataille Navale de Casablanca,* p. 449.

Augusta, *her angular Ms17 camouflage evident, cautiously approaches Casablanca for surrender negotiations, 11 November 1942.* Primauguet *can be seen beached to her right, with* Albatros *visible at the left of this image. (NARA)*

back the deck like the lid of a sardine can – and another just missed to port, raising a column of muddy water that inundated her bridge. While her turret was still operational after this attack, her stern settled in the mud; she fired no more that day.[*]

Army units were ready to assault Casablanca the next day when word came that the French were willing to surrender the city.

— —

The Battle of Casablanca was over on the ground, but at sea it continued, involving submarines. Of the 11 French submarines at Casablanca at the beginning of 8 November, three were damaged beyond repair in the initial attack on the harbor and a fourth escaped without any means to attack the Americans. The other seven all attempted to attack the invasion fleet; on at least four occasions, torpedoes were fired at American ships at close range, not one hitting. The cause of this general lack of success was probably inexperience on the part of the French and great good luck on the part of the Americans.

Of these seven, three survived to fight on: *Orphée* returning to Casablanca, where she surrendered; *Amazone* and *Antiope* reaching Dakar, where they remained under Vichy orders for the moment. *Le Tonnant* reached Cadiz on 15 November and was scuttled by her crew rather than be interned. US Navy aircraft on ASW patrol accounted for three:

Méduse was attacked and damaged by patrol aircraft from *Santee* on 9

---

[*] Cressman, *USS* Ranger, pp. 272–4; Mordal, *La Bataille Navale de Casablanca*, p. 449.

Seen from her port side, Jean Bart *looked relatively intact and undamaged, except for the bulging in the shell plating of her bow caused by a 1,000-lb bomb. (NARA)*

From quayside aft, the seriousness of the damage to Jean Bart *becomes more obvious. (NARA)*

141

Beached at Mazagan (El Jadida), south of Casablanca, the French submarine Méduse *was attacked by US Navy floatplanes on 9 November 1942 and again the next day, causing her to be abandoned. (NARA)*

November. With no means of caring for the men wounded in this attack, the decision was made to beach the boat down the coast at Mazagan (El Jadida), long enough to get the casualties ashore. She was found there the next morning by a floatplane off *Philadelphia* and damaged to the extent that she was abandoned;

Sidi-Ferruch was sunk on 11 November near Batterie d'El Hank by aircraft from *Suwannee*.

Le Conquérant was sunk on 13 November by two Catalinas of VP-92 off Villa Cisneros (ad-Dakhla), Western Sahara, having made it about halfway to Dakar.

That left only one boat, *La Sibylle*, unaccounted for. The exact cause of her disappearance is unknown, but it is most likely that she stumbled into a defensive minefield laid by the Americans around the transport area off Fédala.

The submarines that achieved the greatest success during Operation TORCH were neither French nor American. They were German U-boats. The normally reliable B-Dienst (the Kriegsmarine's signals intelligence unit) failed utterly to pick up on the preparations for TORCH. It was only on 7 November, the day before the landings, that Dönitz was ordered to investigate the 'giant massing of forces for landing operations in the Western Mediterranean'.* The approach of the Americans to French Morocco was not detected by the Germans, thus, it was only on 8 November that the nine closest boats were ordered to make best speed towards the landing sites.† The first of these boats – *U572* (Hirsacker) – arrived on 9 November, but failed in several half-hearted attempts to penetrate the ASW screen around the transports. This was not the first time that Hirsacker

---

* *B.d.U. Op's WAR LOG*, 7.11.42.

† Ibid, 8.11.42.

was suspected of excessive caution, and, upon his return to France, he was tried and found guilty of cowardice, the only U-boat commander to be so accused.

Most of the other boats of Gruppe Schlagetot (Death Blow) likewise failed to penetrate the American defenses, several being damaged in the attempt.* Only two had success. *U173* (Schweichel) was on only her second war patrol, the first under the very young Schweichel. The boat was eight days outbound from Lorient, approaching the Canary Islands, when she was diverted towards Casablanca. Soon after full dark on 11 November, Schweichel took *U173* through the destroyer screen around the transport area off Fédala. He made this move on the surface, undetected by any of radars of the screening destroyers. At about 1945, he fired at least one torpedo at *Joseph Hewes* (AP50) and, quickly calculating a new solution, at least two more at the oiler *Winooski* (AO38). *Hewes* was hit, opening No. 2 hold to the sea. Still loaded with 93 per cent of the cargo she carried across the Atlantic, she sank quickly by the bow. *Winooski*, on the other hand, had delivered most of her cargo. She was hit by one torpedo at 1955, which tore a hole in an emptied fuel tank just abaft the bridge, causing an 8° list that was quickly corrected by shifting her remaining cargo. The crew fit a temporary patch on the damaged tank and resumed fueling operations the next morning.

Another torpedo in that same spread was probably aimed at the transport *Hugh L. Scott* (AP43), but missed and continued on towards a target that was only there coincidentally. The destroyer *Hambleton* had been part of *Sangamon's* screen off Port Lyautey, but, running low on fuel, she was relieved by *Corry* (DD463) and sent south at 1650 to refuel from *Winooski*. She hoped to arrive before dark so that the process could be started immediately. The approach took longer than anticipated because of the need to navigate the newly laid defensive minefield around the transport area. As related by *Hambleton's* captain:

> At about 1845, voice radio communication was established with WINOOSKI and we were advised that she would not receive us alongside until daylight . . . Commander Destroyer Squadron 13 . . . ordered us to proceed to the Eastward of the convoy and anchor . . . At about 1940, I went below to have dinner in the Wardroom. At 1951, the officer of the deck telephoned to me in the Wardroom that a ship had exploded to port, and while I was still holding the telephone he reported further that a torpedo wake was coming straight for us. Before I could put down the telephone we were struck, the torpedo apparently coming from the north-west, narrowly missing HUGH L. SCOTT across her bow and striking us at frame 97, port.†

The explosion opened her forward engine room and after fire room to the

* Blair, *Hitler's U-Boat War: The Hunted*, pp. 107–11; *Dictionary of American Naval Fighting Ships*.
† DD455, p. 2.

A victim of bad timing, Hambleton *(DD455) was only anchored off Fédala the night of 11 November 1942 because she arrived at the anchorage too late to refuel before dark. There, she was hit port side amidships by a torpedo from U173 (Schweichel). The hole caused by the explosion and the deformation of her hull can be seen as she lies tied up alongside* George Clymer *(AP57) in Casablanca harbor. (NARA)*

sea and caused an immediate starboard list of 10°, increasing periodically to 15° as she rolled with the swell. As bad as this was, the ship remained stable in this attitude. and, confident she would not sink, the crew was put to shifting fuel oil and jettisoning such topside weights as depth charges and the starboard smoke generator. In this manner, the list was reduced by half. Her forward and after parts worked in the swell, but never to the point that the ship appeared liable to break up.

Schweichel, still on the surface, attempted to slip out between two destroyers of the screen. She showed up on the radar of the brand-new destroyer *Bristol* (DD453), but her captain was afraid the contact might be a stray landing craft and ordered the target be illuminated by searchlight before opening fire. That delay gave *U173* enough time to submerge and make good her escape.

The next day *Hambleton* was towed to Casablanca, where she tied up alongside *George Clymer* (AP57). Despite having an intact fire room and engine room, her structural integrity was considered insufficient to permit a safe passage across the Atlantic. Therefore, a novel expedient was devised; a 40-foot section of her hull was removed by SeaBees, the two remaining halves reattached, allowing the

Seen from New York *(BB34), two transports in the Fédala anchorage explode, hit by torpedoes fired by* U130 *(Kals), 12 November 1942. The explosion on the left is* Hugh L. Scott *(AP43); the one on the right is* Tasker H. Bliss *(AP42). Both sank, along with a third transport. (NHHC via Ed Rumpf)*

ship to reach Boston under her own power on 28 June where permanent repairs were made.[*]

Hugh L. Scott may have literally dodged a bullet that night, but she was not to live much longer. The next day, *U130*, a veteran of Operation PAUKENSCHLAG on her last patrol under the popular Kals, slipped down the coast submerged, approaching the transport area off Fédala from the landward side. The water was so shallow in places that the U-boat scraped bottom but, in the late afternoon, managed to reach a position to fire a spread of five torpedoes at the assembled transports. All of the torpedoes found targets. The first hit was *Edward Rutledge* (AP52) at 1728. She was obviously sinking, and the crew attempted to run her aground, but power failed before she could reach the beach, and she sank stern-first, losing 15 of her crew. The second was *Tasker H. Bliss* (AP42). She sank more slowly, burning on into the night before sinking at 0230 the next morning. The last was the twice-targeted *Hugh L. Scott*. She burst into flames and settled quickly, taking 59 of her crew with her. Kals slipped away undetected up the coast. Alarmed by these losses, the unloading of transports was moved as rapidly as possible to Casablanca harbor, where the process was faster and safer.

On 15 November, Schweichel attacked again, putting a torpedo into *Electra* (AK21), carrying wounded soldiers from Safi towards Fédala. She was badly

---

[*] 'SeaBees' was the common name used to designate the US Navy's Construction Battalions (CBs), originally recruited from experienced construction workers.

After the surrender of Casablanca on 11 November, the US Navy moved some of their major units into the harbor, anchored stern-first to the Jetée Delure towards the left in this image. These included Augusta, Chenango *and* Brooklyn. Jean Bart *lies to the right of the broad Môle du Commerce, her stern resting in the mud.* Primauguet, Albatros *and* Milan *are beached towards the upper left outside the Jetée Transversale. (NARA)*

damaged, but did not sink; after removing all the wounded soldiers and unnecessary crew, she was safely beached near Casablanca and the rest of her cargo off-loaded. Over the next four months, her crew repaired her to the point that she could cross the Atlantic to Charleston.

—‑—

In reaction to TORCH, Operation ANTON began after dark on 10 November, with German troops entering unoccupied France from the west and north, and Italians from the east. The outskirts of Toulon, the main French naval base on the Mediterranean coast, were reached late on the next day, but the Germans halted there while negotiations began for the surrender of the Marine Nationale. These dragged on for days until, losing patience, the Germans ordered an assault on the port before dawn on 27 November. Sentiment among French seamen ran the gamut from loyalty to Vichy to sympathy for the Free French, but they all agreed that the fleet should not fall into German hands. As Panzers crashed through the gates of the naval base in the pre-dawn gloom, the order went out

Major General George S. Patton, Jr and Rear-Admiral H. Kent Hewitt share a laugh onboard Augusta, *10 November 1942. They commanded the land and sea forces, respectively, for Operation* TORCH. *(NHHC)*

to scuttle the fleet. This was done with remarkable efficiency. The battleship *Lorraine*, battlecruisers *Strasbourg* and *Dunkerque*, heavy cruisers *Dupleix*, *Foch*, *Algérie* and *Colbert*, three light cruisers and dozens of destroyers, torpedo boats, submarine and smaller vessels were sunk, totaling more than 70 vessels. A few, mostly submarines, escaped to North Africa or Spain. A number were raised by Italian engineers in 1943, most too damaged to be repaired; these were scrapped or re-sunk by Allied air raids. Seven of the scuttled destroyers were given Italian designations and were in various states of repair when Italy surrendered in September. At least one destroyer survived to fight on under German command.

The convoluted story of the leadership of French North Africa needs to be brought to its bizarre conclusion. Once at Gibraltar, Giraud demanded command of all Allied forces in North Africa, but was convinced by Eisenhower to accept a lesser role. At the same time, it was discovered that Admiral François Darlan, head of the Marine Nationale and some-time deputy to Pétain, had arrived in Algiers the day before the landings. The trip was ostensibly to visit an ailing son, but there was a lingering suspicion that the timing was not coincidental. Despite the fierce opposition of the Free French, the Allies backed Darlan as leader of the liberated French colonies in North Africa, with Giraud as his military deputy. Darlan, with Pétain's apparent approval, ordered the surrender of French forces on 10 November, but rescinded the order that evening when he learned that

Pétain, under intense pressure from the Germans, had changed his mind. The surrender order was reinstated the next day when Darlan learned of Axis moves to occupy Vichy France.

Darlan proved to be something of an embarrassment for the Allies. For example, he retained and enforced Vichy's anti-Semitic decrees with FDR's tacit approval.* The embarrassment did not last long, as Darlan was assassinated in Algiers by a French Monarchist on 24 December. Giraud succeeded to the mostly symbolic position of High Commissioner for North Africa and briefly shared leadership of the Free French with de Gaulle. Starting in February 1943, major French naval units, such as *Richelieu*, headed for American naval yards for long-overdue refits. The last French hold-outs, such as Admiral Godfroy at Alexandria and the small squadron at Martinique, agreed to join the Allies. On 1 June 1943, de Gaulle took formal control of the Marine Nationale, and proceeded to remove the last remaining Vichy officers, most notably Vice-Admiral Michelier.

---

*   Medoff, '*Megillat Hitler*'.

5

Climax in the Atlantic
November 1942–October 1943

With the surrender of the Vichy forces in Morocco, the battle for North Africa became, from the point of view of the US Navy, a land war. Much of the naval force assembled for the TORCH landings was redeployed, either to the Pacific or to the renewed struggle against the U-boat menace in the Atlantic. A significant number of the major ships involved were slated for transfer. *Massachusetts* and three of the four *Sangamon*s were headed for the Pacific as soon as they completed hasty refits. Of the escort carriers, only *Santee* was retained; along with destroyers *Livermore* (DD429) and *Eberle* (DD430), she was assigned to TU23.1.6, based at Trinidad, tasked with patrolling the South Atlantic for German surface raiders and blockade-runners. The light cruiser *Savannah* soon joined the South Atlantic patrol. *Ranger* was also retained in the Atlantic and employed transporting fighters to North Africa in January and again in February. (*Ranger* was retained in the Atlantic mainly because she was not wanted in the Pacific. Her long, fine hull made her a poor sea boat; anything more than a moderate swell limited her ability to launch and recover aircraft.)

The Allied success in North Africa – by 17 November, forces that had landed at Algiers had pushed east as far as Bizerte, Tunisia – accelerated the need for a decision about what would come next. Churchill and Roosevelt met in Casablanca starting on 14 January. Bowing to British resistance to a direct assault on France in 1943, the US agreed to postpone Operation ROUNDUP until 1944 and to proceed with an invasion of Sicily in mid-1943. Part of the reason the Americans agreed to the postponement of ROUNDUP was the mounting concern over the resurgence of the U-boat threat to the North Atlantic convoy routes.

The Allies, particularly the Americans, no doubt sighed in relief when the U-boat assault on the American East Coast, the Gulf of Mexico and the Caribbean was finally mastered in mid-1942, but the battle was far from over in the Atlantic. If anything, the German Ubootwaffe (Submarine Fleet) was more powerful in November 1942 than it had been the preceding January. Compared to a monthly average of 42 U-boats at sea each day in January, by July, that number had risen to 70 and in November reached 95. These boats were

Ranger *was often employed delivering Army fighters to Africa, whence they flew on to the Middle East or India. Here some of the 75 P-40F Warhawks of the 325th FG launch on 19 January 1943. (NARA)*

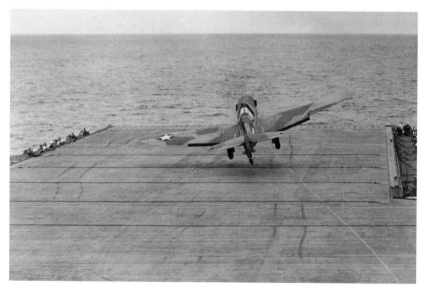

The take-offs were sometimes wobbly, but all 75 of these Warhawks flew safely to Casablanca, 19 January 1943. The take-off required application of full power, which caused the aircraft to roll in a counter-clockwise manner and turn left as soon as it unstuck. The pilot is correcting with his ailerons and rudder. (NARA)

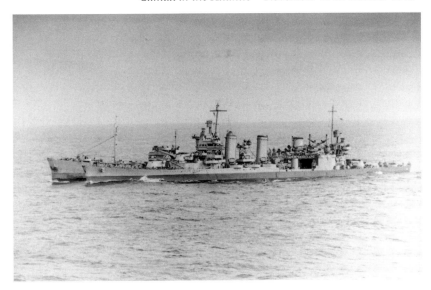

After TORCH, many of the major naval units departed for the Pacific. One that stayed was Tuscaloosa *(CA37), seen here refueling from* Chickopee *(AO34), 14 January 1943. Both wear the Atlantic standard Ms22 Graded System camouflage, which differed from the earlier Ms12 in that it used only two colors – Navy Blue (5-N) and Haze Gray (5-H) – the dividing line between the two being carried horizontally from the lowest point of the main deck. (NARA)*

increasingly spread over many theaters, so that, at any one time, only about one-third were in the North Atlantic.

There were a number of factors working in Dönitz's favor as fall turned into winter in 1942, besides having more boats to deploy. He had better and more useful intelligence of convoy sailings than the Allies did of U-boat dispositions. This was because, as of 1 November, GC&CS was still unable to read the four-rotor Shark cypher.[*] On the other hand, B-Dienst had broken into the British Naval Cypher No. 3, the convoy code, in February 1942 and knew the course and location of convoys with remarkable accuracy. Also that fall, U-boats received the first radar warning device, the FuMB 1 Metox receiver, which could detect the radio waves used by the first-generation British airborne radar, the ASV MkI, which operated in the 1.4 m band.[†] In the hands of an experienced radio operator, Metox could detect the approach of a radar-equipped aircraft in sufficient time for a U-boat to dive to safety. Finally, this period also saw the introduction of new torpedoes that made each shot by a U-boat potentially more effective. These included the fitting of an improved dual magnetic/

---

[*] 'Shark' was the name given by the British to the cypher net for U-boats in the Atlantic, called Triton by the Germans.

[†] FuMB stood for *Funkmessbeobachter*, literally radar detector.

contact pistol, Pi 2, to the workhorse G7e electric torpedo, which was renamed T3. This detonator, though still not perfect, had a reliable magnetic detonator. More important was the introduction of a clever anti-convoy torpedo, the Federapparat (Spring-operated) Torpedo (FaT), which could be set to loop back and forth across the path of a convoy. Thus, as the improved defenses decreased the likelihood that a U-boat could set up a well-aimed shot at specific targets, this new torpedo offered an alternative. It could be fired in the general direction of a convoy with a reasonable chance of finding a target as it crossed the rows of ships multiple times.

Against these advantages, the Allies continued to develop counter-measures in an attempt to reclaim the initiative in the tonnage war. The most straightforward response was the allocation of more escorts with better sensors and weapons to the defense of the convoys. In part this was because, with the success of the TORCH landings, many destroyers which had been dedicated to escorting troop convoys were released for use in the North Atlantic, and, in part, this was because American wartime production was beginning to gain momentum.

At the same time, the Allies began to gain a decisive advantage in the technology war. Just as Metox detectors were being installed in all U-boats, the British introduced the microwave ASV MkIII, which not only performed better than the MkI, but operated on a shorter wavelength outside the range of the Metox set. Thus, when early in 1943, U-boats with functioning Metox sets found themselves again being surprised by RAF aircraft, there began a period of almost comical confusion on the part of Dönitz and the U-boat arm as almost every possible explanation was explored. For example, it was believed for a time that Metox sets radiated a signal that British aircraft were homing on. This belief was so strong that by mid-1943, U-boats were ordered to avoid using their Metox sets. In fact, the idea that the RAF were using a centimetric-wavelength radar was suggested, but was rejected because German radar developers claimed such a set could never be made small enough to fit in an airplane. It was only after an RAF bomber with a prototype H2S microwave ground mapping radar was shot down over Rotterdam in February 1943, that the Luftwaffe realized that airborne microwave radar was feasible, and it was not until months later that they bothered informing the Kriegsmarine. It was only in November 1943 that the first radar warning devices capable of detecting the ASV MkIII were distributed to U-boats.[*]

The introduction of the improved ASV radar would have been useful, but not decisive, if it had not been accompanied by the introduction of aircraft to cover the 'air gap', the area in the middle of the North Atlantic that was beyond the range of aircraft then based in Newfoundland, Iceland and Northern Ireland. The were the VLR (Very Long Range) Liberator GR I patrol bombers. They

---

[*]   These were FuMB 7 Naxos or FuMB 10 Borkum sets

had started out life as Consolidated B-24As ordered in 1940 for the USAAC. So desperate was the RAF's need for heavy bombers that 20 of the original order of 38 were sold directly to Great Britain. It took very little time for the RAF to determine that these aircraft were not suited to fly bombing missions over Germany, as they lacked self-sealing fuel tanks and had very limited defensive armament. But they possessed excellent endurance and they were immediately passed along to RAF Coastal Command for use as long-range anti-submarine aircraft. By June 1941, No. 120 Squadron was stood up with nine operational aircraft, modified with auxiliary fuel tanks, ASV radar and additional forward firing armament. However, their most important feature was the ability to carry 2,500 lb of ordnance over a range of 3,000 nm. The first confirmed sinking by a VLR Liberator came on 12 October 1942 about 750 nm south-west of Iceland, when Liberator 'H' of No. 120 Squadron sank *U597* (Bobst) with the loss of all hands. What was most significant was that the sinking occurred in direct defense of a convoy in the most dangerous part of the ocean. (By war's end, flying successive marks of the VLR Liberator, No. 120 Squadron had sunk 15 U-boats, making it the most successful squadron in Coastal Command.)

— —

As these trends developed, the war between U-boats and convoys seemed to be reaching a climax at the beginning of spring 1943.[*] After sinking more than 600,000 GRT in the Atlantic in November 1942, the numbers had slipped sharply over the next three months, reaching a low of 182,000 GRT in January 1943. There were two proximate reasons for this trend. The renewed recovery of the German Shark cypher starting on 13 December was one of those reasons. The other was terrible weather. A succession of storms, climaxing in January 1943, shortened patrols and reduced visibility, reducing the value of B-Dienst intelligence.[†] Patrol lines were established, but, as often as not, failed to sight the expected target.

The Allies had every reason to expect the pressure on the North Atlantic trade routes to increase again. Looking at the current rates of U-boat construction and U-boat sinkings, the Allies anticipated a steady increase in the number of U-boats operating in the Atlantic. On top of this on 8 March, Bletchley Park warned that the Germans were about to again replace their short weather report codebook, and that there would be another months-long blackout in reading Shark messages until the new codes could be captured or deduced.[‡]

---

[*]   The numbers in this section come from [Hessler] *The U-boat War in the Atlantic 1939–1945*, vol. 2, plans 59 and 60.

[†]   Morison, *History*, vol. I, pp. 410–11. In January 1943, 181,767GRT of shipping was lost to U-boats in the Atlantic and Arctic areas; during the same month, 110,512GRT were lost to 'marine casualties', mainly foundering in the violent storms.

[‡]   Sebag-Montefiore, *Enigma*, p. 318. Possession of the short weather report codebook allowed the development of cribs which could be used to break each day's Enigma settings.

A second Convoy Conference was convened in New York starting 1 March 1943 to address these issues. Agreement was reached on a stepped-up pace of convoy sailings (HX-ON convoys would start sailing every five days) and that responsibility for the escorting of North Atlantic convoys would be split between the Royal and Royal Canadian Navies. The US Navy would remain responsible for the Central Atlantic convoys, the coastal and tanker convoys, as before, and would lend the first of its 'hunter-killer' groups, based on the escort aircraft carrier *Bogue* (ACV9) and four flush-deckers, to the British for the North Atlantic runs, starting on 20 March. The Royal Navy's first escort carrier groups, based on HMS *Biter* (D97) and *Archer* (D78), also began operating with Western Approaches Command in March 1943.

Typical of the action at this time was the attack on ON.166. Starting on 20 February, parts of three U-boat packs converged on the convoy and over four days and nights sank 14 ships for the loss of two U-boats. One of these was sunk by depth bombs dropped by a VLR Liberator, the other after being depth charged and then rammed by the Coast Guard cutter *Campbell*.

An early success attributable to the deployment of escort carriers in the Atlantic was the interception of the German blockade-runner *Karin* (the former Dutch *Kota Nopan*).* On 11 October 1942, she had sailed from Bordeaux heading for Japan; she succeeded in eluding Royal Navy patrols that stopped three other blockade-runners leaving at about the same time. By March 1943, she was on her way back with a cargo of vitally needed tin and rubber, passing through the South Atlantic 'Narrows' between Recife and Freetown.

Karin's passage through this area was anticipated by ULTRA intercepts, but the exact timing and route were not known, and it was exactly this circumstance which demonstrated yet again the value of escort carriers such as *Santee* and of her embarked air group. She was part of TG23.1 which included *Savannah* and two destroyers. One of *Santee's* scouts sighted a solitary ship north-east of Peter and Paul Rocks at 1500 on 10 March. *Savannah* and the destroyer *Eberle* immediately detached and headed at high speed towards the the steamer, which was believed to be German. As seen from *Savannah*, the encounter was brief.

1630 Cut in boilers #1 and #2 on main steam line. Speed was now 31 knots.
      EBERLE hoisted international signal WBA meaning:–
          'DO NOT LOWER BOATS'
          'DO NOT SCUTTLE'
          'DO NOT USE RADIO'
          'IF YOU DISOBEY I SHALL OPEN FIRE'.
1632 Having reached a point about 6,500 yards from unidentified ship, commenced maneuvering ... to circle and inspect her at a safe distance.

---

* Launched as SS *Kota Nopan* in 1931, she was captured by the German raider *Komet* (Schiff 45) on 14 August 1941 near the Galapagos Islands.

Some sailors got nice weather. Here, Eberle *(DD340) and* Savannah *(CL42) maneuver in the vicinity of* Santee *in the warm waters off Brazil, 19 January 1943. Considering the number of men on* Eberle's *rail and the deployed fenders, this probably was the beginning of a refueling maneuver. (NARA)*

She is flying the Netherlands flag. (Upside down)* . . .

1636 'KOTA TJANDI' hoisted international signal FM meaning 'I am sinking. Send boats to pick up crew and passengers.'†

1637 O.T.C., ordered EBERLE to board her.‡

This order was to have tragic result. At the same time that *Eberle's* boat, with a boarding party of 14 officers and men was approaching the steamer, *Karin's* crew was abandoning ship in four lifeboats. *Savannah's* scout plane flew along the length of the steamer, firing bursts of machine gun fire into the water under the lifeboats, but the boats continued to be lowered and it was soon obvious why, as smoke and then flames were seen rising from *Karin's* midships superstructure

---

*   The Dutch national ensign is three horizontal bands of (from the top) red, white and blue. *Karin's* crew had in their haste hoisted it with the blue band at the top.

†   *Kota Tjandi* was a sistership to *Kota Nopan*, but was still in Dutch service and carrying cargo in the African coastal trade until sunk by *U515* (Henke) near Freetown on 30 April 1943.

‡   CL42-1, p 3. 'O.T.C.' stands for Officer in Tactical Command.

Eberle and Santee *again steam in parallel, but on a much sadder occasion. A memorial service is being held to honor the seven officers and men from* Eberle *who died in the sinking of the German blockade-runner* Karin, *11 March 1943. (NARA)*

and her boat deck aft. Despite spreading flames, the salvage crew from *Eberle* drew alongside the steamer and boarded, hoping to find a way to save the ship or, at the very least, to recover some materials with intelligence value.

> 1656 Two heavy explosions were observed amidships and one aft on the 'KOTA TJANDI'. These appeared to result from very powerful time bombs located deep in the ship . . . Immediately after the explosions, she commenced settling rapidly by the stern. EBERLE boarding party boat was wrecked by explosions . . . SAVANNAH boat rescued three (3) EBERLE personnel (1 officer and 2 men) from water where they had been blown by explosions . . .
>
> 1657 'KOTA TJANDI' sank stern first.*

Seventy-two officers and crew of *Karin* were taken prisoner. Seven officers and crew off *Eberle* were killed in the sinking of *Karin*.†

---

* CL42-1, p. 4.

† CL42-1 states that *Eberle* reported nine men missing. Morison, *History,* vol. I, p. 384, states that eight men lost their lives. *Dictionary of American Naval Fighting Ships* puts the number at

Even late spring in the Central Atlantic can bring lousy weather. The Coast Guard cutter
Spencer *(WPG36) guards the port side of a convoy, almost certainly UGS.9, in mid-June*
1943. With their high freeboard and broad beam, the Secretary-class cutters were excellent
sea boats. She appears to wear the rare Ms16 Thayer System of camouflage, with Thayer
Blue (5-B) and White (5-U) designed to hide ships in foggy conditions. (NARA)

On 10 March, as expected, the Germans switched to the new codebook, and,
as expected, Bletchley Park lost the ability to break into the Shark cypher. This
led directly and almost immediately to the biggest and most costly convoy battle
of the war. In what proved to be very poor timing, a slow convoy – SC.122 – left
New York City on 5 March, followed three days later by the fast HX.229 along
an identical track, so that each day that passed brought them closer together.
U-boat contact with SC.122 was made on 16 March, but when U-boats began
to converge on the reported position, they instead found the trailing HX.229,
40 merchantmen escorted by three old destroyers and two corvettes. It was not
a fair fight; by nightfall nine U-boats had made contact with HX.229 and 23
more had been summoned. By the time the escort was reinforced on 18 March,
17 ships had been sunk. By the time the two convoys had reached Great Britain,
22 out of 105 merchant ships in the two convoys had been sunk for the loss of
one U-boat.

No one could be blamed if they believed the Germans were on the verge of

---

seven, and, being the most recent of the sources, I have used that figure.

Two months earlier, on 17 April 1943, while escorting HX.233, Spencer *depth charged* U175 *(Bruns), forcing her to the surface where she was then brought under fire from several nearby ships. Nineteen officers and men were rescued from the U-boat.* Spencer *suffered 25 casualties from 'friendly fire' including one dead. (USCG)*

cutting the vital lifeline across the North Atlantic.

Dönitz had every reason to be pleased with this action and the normally restrained BdU stated in his war diary: 'This is so far the best result obtained in a convoy battle'.* With more boats than ever in service and the Baltic full of new boats working up, the future must have looked bright, but for one small cloud on the horizon.

> After the first surprise coup the enemy increased his anti-submarine forces constantly, but probably no boat was lost . . . 2 boats were heavily damaged by aircraft bombs, so that they had to break off. Nearly all the boats were bombed or depth-charged but without serious consequences except for the above 2.†

The next operation, against HX.230, gave a foretaste of the future. Terrible weather limited the ability of U-boats to concentrate and to keep up with the convoy, but the presence of the *Bogue* escort carrier group on its first patrol proved to be even more problematical. On 26 March, the presence of an aircraft carrier with the convoy was reported by two U-boats, one of which described

---

*   *B.d.U. Op's WAR LOG, 20.3.43.*

†   Ibid.

Bogue as a carrier of the Illustrious class.[*] When the operation was called off four days later, the convoy had lost only one ship and that one was a straggler.

Better weather in early April led to a series of attacks on convoys, but they in no way approached the success of March. There was a clear trend of declining results, in particular a worsening 'exchange rate', the ratio of U-boats lost to victims sunk. However, nothing in these numbers could have prepared the Germans for the disaster that would overtake them in May. This reversal of fortune was as sudden as it was dramatic. In the first three weeks in May, major attacks by dozens of U-boats against successive convoys produced meager results and, more alarmingly, increased losses of U-boats. Attacks on SC.130, HX.239 and ON.184 netted not a single sinking for the loss of six U-boats. The presence of escort carrier air groups was important, but by no means the only reason for this reversal of fortune. More escorts of all types were becoming available, both new construction and those released from escorting troopship convoys to the Mediterranean. Also, those escorts were more likely to be equipped with microwave radar and shipborne HF/DF. All of these factors combined to create a 'tipping point' that tilted the balance of power away from the U-boats.

On 24 May, Dönitz ordered the redeployment of U-boats away from the North Atlantic towards the Central Atlantic, where he hoped they would have more success.

What Dönitz could not know was that at the same time as he was deciding to shift his U-boats south against the American-escorted Gibraltar convoys, decisions were being being made across the Atlantic that would doom this move to failure. On 30 April, as previously agreed, the US Navy turned over sole responsibility for convoy escort on the North Atlantic routes to the Royal and Royal Canadian Navies, ending a 20-month experiment in shared responsibility that often was anything but smooth. The Americans took full charge of escorting convoys between the Western Hemisphere and Gibraltar and the Mediterranean. Thus in June 1943, the *Bogue* 'hunter-killer' group was released from the North Atlantic and joined three other groups, two of them new, based on *Santee*, *Card* (ACV11) and *Core* (ACV13), protecting the convoy lanes in the central Atlantic.

What these groups found was not always what they expected. On 23 June, the second day of her first patrol, *Card*'s fliers found not a submarine but an American floatplane drifting nearly 1,000 nm south-south-east of Bermuda. Even more surprising was the fact that it was occupied; two men in the OS2U greeted the VC-11 Avenger with green flares. *Card* changed course to approach the aircraft and found the pilot and his radioman/gunner in good condition, despite having been adrift for ten days. They had launched from the light cruiser *Boise* (CL47), newly assigned to the Atlantic Fleet.[†] Presumably, they lost radio

---

[*]   *B.d.U. Op's WAR LOG*, 26.3.43.

[†]   *Boise* was already a veteran, having been seriously damaged in the Battle of Cape Esperance (11–12 October 1942) off Guadalcanal.

On 23 June 1943 fliers off Card *(ACV11) spotted this OS2U Kingfisher afloat hundreds of miles from the nearest shore. It had been flown off* Boise *(CL47) and had been forced down by mechanical problems. Despite drifting for ten days, the crew of two was in good shape. They have inflated their life raft and placed it on the starboard wing in case they were forced to abandon the aircraft. A parachute has been opened and draped over the cockpit area both to make them more visible from the air and to protect them from sun and rain. (NARA)*

communications with their ship while on anti-submarine patrol and were forced down by mechanical problems, and, presuming them lost, *Boise* continued on to her appointment as fire-support ship in the Mediterranean. Thanks to very good luck, Ensign Farley and RM3c Gibson lived to tell their tale.*

In a four-day period, starting on 13 July 1943, Lieutenant R. P. Williams, flying an Avenger off *Core*, made three separate attacks on U-boats resulting in two sinkings. On the first day, Williams found *U487* (Metz), a Type XIV *Milchkuh*, on the surface, damaged it on the first pass and continued to harass the boat until more aircraft arrived to finish it off. The next day Williams sighted and attacked *U527* (Uhlig), one of the boats that had savaged HX.229. He dropped four depth bombs for damage, but the U-boat escaped for the moment. Two days later, acting on a Tenth Fleet tip, Williams found *U67* (Müller-Stockheim)

---

*   ACV11, pp. 20–1.

and in a remarkable attack, sank the boat in a single drop of four depth bombs.* No other pilot would ever come close to repeating this feat.

During that same four-day period, three other U-boats were sunk by US Navy aircraft and another was sunk by Royal Navy ships assisted by a Catalina of VP-92, making for an extraordinary total of sinkings. In July 1943, US Navy assets sank 22 U-boats with another shared sinking, making this the first month that the US Navy sank more U-boats than the Royal Navy.

Invoking a mutual protection treaty dating from 1373, on 8 October 1943, a convoy of transports and cargo ships, accompanied by the escort carrier HMS *Fencer* (D64), approached Faial and Terceira islands in the Azores and flew ashore an ASW squadron and landed ground support personnel to manage Lajes airfield. At first, Portugal refused to permit American aircraft to land there, but by late-November this problem was resolved.

On 27 October, a PBY-5A Catalina of VP-73 flying out of Agadir, Morocco, encountered a Spanish aircraft – a license-built Italian Fiat CR.32 – near Gran Canaria island. The Spanish fighter fired on the Catalina and forced it to turn back towards base. The Americans reacted quickly. Overnight they flew in a pair of Lockheed PV-1 Venturas, a twin-engine patrol-bomber armed with three forward-firing .50 caliber machine guns, which were sent out the next day. They were intercepted as the Catalina had been the day before, but they surprised and damaged the lone fighter, which made a forced landing on a beach. Thereafter, Catalinas flew patrols around the Canary Islands without interference.

In no sense did this mark the defeat of the U-boats, but they would not again pose the same level of threat to the Allied war effort as they did at the beginning of 1943.

---

* Tenth Fleet was set up in May 1943 at King's instigation to co-ordinate the use of intelligence and fleet assets to improve ASW performance. No ships or aircraft were directly assigned to Tenth Fleet, but it had the warrant to direct the use of any assets in the Atlantic theater. To make sure that Tenth Fleet 'orders' were treated with the necessary respect, the fleet was nominally commanded by King, but the actual commander was the fleet's chief-of-staff, Rear-Admiral F. S. Low. At no point did the fleet's staffing ever exceed 50 people.

6

Into the Middle Sea
November 1942–May 1944

Quite literally, the US Navy was born to fight in the Mediterranean. Interference with American merchant shipping by the so-called 'Barbary Pirates' led to the establishment of the Navy in 1794. Since then, there had often been an American presence in the Mediterranean, but the US Navy's commitment to the Middle Sea never was central to its mission and, after France fell to the Axis in June 1940, no US warships operated regularly in that sea until after the TORCH landings.

The TORCH plan had called for American and British ground forces to push east from Algiers immediately after the landings and capture Tunisia, cutting Rommel's supply line. The plan, however, over-estimated the speed at which the newly landed Allied forces would be able to advance, and under-estimated the speed of the German reaction. British airborne troops were supposed to secure Bône (now Annaba, Algeria), Bizerte and Tunis, with the hope that the French in Tunisia would resist German moves to occupy those ports. Bône was duly occupied on 12 November, but the drops on the Tunisian ports were called off when it was learned that confusion among the French had led to the Germans gaining control of Bizerte and Tunis; French forces retreated to a line in the mountains west of those ports. When the British reached the Atlas Mountains on 17 November, the Germans were already present in enough strength to halt the Allied advance. What was supposed to be a rapid occupation of Tunisia and the strangulation of Rommel's forces instead turned into a stalemate made worse by the beginning of winter rains. Reinforcements from Italy and Rommel's orderly withdrawal to the southern border of Tunisia allowed the Germans to establish a strong defensive position.

It was in this situation that Roosevelt and Churchill met at Casablanca in mid-January 1943. (Stalin had been invited but declined due to the ongoing battle for Stalingrad.) Both Giraud and de Gaulle were invited and put on a stage-managed display of cordiality, but it was pure sham, as the two men intensely distrusted and disliked each other. The real work of the conference was done by the Prime Minister and President and their senior staffs. There was much work to be done; despite the failure to secure Tunisia rapidly, there was no doubt in either nation that victory there was only a matter of time, and that agreement needed to be reached concerning the next moves to be made against the Axis.

The Americans still wanted to shift emphasis immediately to a rapid build-up of forces in Great Britain with the aim of a cross-Channel landing in France in 1943. This view was supported by Admiral King because he believed it would require a relatively small commitment of American naval forces, freeing up resources for the Pacific. The British fundamentally disagreed with this position point-for-point. To them, the conquest of the entire North African coast brought little in the way of strategic advantage beyond relieving Egypt of the threat of imminent invasion. The major strategic goal of re-opening the Mediterranean to the free passage of convoys heading to and from India was only partially achieved by victory in North Africa; that required the control of the Sicilian Narrows.[*] Additionally, Churchill, with his characteristic long view of history, was very concerned that a Soviet victory might have consequences as serious as a Soviet defeat, including Russian domination of the Balkans as far south as Greece. Knocking Italy out of the war, which was a hoped-for consequence of a victory in Sicily, would put the Western Allies on the flank of any Russian move into the Balkans or Austria.

Despite the objections of his military advisors, FDR was convinced by Churchill's arguments in favor of an attack on Italy, even if that meant postponing the cross-Channel invasion into 1944. That left only the decision whether the target should be Sardinia or Sicily. The argument in favor of Sardinia, whether or not it was followed by an invasion of Corsica, was that it could be invaded with smaller forces, and therefore as much as three months sooner than an attack on Sicily. The Joint Planning Staff, arguing for Sardinia, stated that an invasion of Sicily could not be mounted until the end of August.[†] Churchill was insistent that Sicily was the better target and, again, convinced Roosevelt. The invasion of Sicily, Operation HUSKY, was ordered for the full moon period of July.

One further decision of consequence came out of the Casablanca Conference, though it is not at all clear this was a considered decision agreed to in advance by both principals. At a news conference held at the end of the meetings, Roosevelt announced that the Allies demanded the 'unconditional surrender' of the Axis nations. While there is no doubt that the concept was discussed by the two leaders and informally agreed upon, it was not mentioned in the official communiqué released at the end of the conference.[‡] Churchill recalled being surprised, but not upset, by Roosevelt's use of the term. Much time and effort was later spent explaining what was meant by 'unconditional surrender'; as stated, it was taken to mean that the Allies refused to accept anything short of the complete submission of the existing Axis governments and that there

---

[*] Eisenhower, *Crusade in Europe*, p. 159.

[†] Churchill, *The Second World War: The Hinge of Fate*, p. 678.

[‡] Ibid, pp. 684–91.

In April 1943, the new battleship Alabama *(BB60), seen here from* Ranger *a month earlier, sailed with TF22 to Scapa Flow to reinforce the Royal Navy Home Fleet while British units were busy supporting the landings on Sicily. (NARA)*

would be no separate peace with individual Allied states. In practice, the Allies proved to be quite flexible in their treatment of Axis states, offering the Italians lenient terms to encourage their early surrender and allowing the Japanese to retain their emperor while those who served him were held responsible for their actions.

While there may have been no doubt in the Allies' minds that victory would come in Tunisia, it proved to be a hard slog against a tough opponent. The inexperienced Americans were roughly treated by German Panzers before stopping Rommel at Kasserine Pass in February 1943. After that, the Allies slowly pushed the Axis forces into a smaller and smaller pocket around Tunis and Bizerte. A final assault starting 4 May broke the last lines of resistance and led to the capture of both cities on 7 May, and the final surrender of over 275,000 Italians and Germans on 13 May completed the campaign to clear Africa of Axis forces.

Having decided upon the invasion of Sicily, a significant build-up in naval forces began in the Mediterranean even as the fighting in Tunisia wound down. Part of this build-up included the transfer of major units of the Royal Navy's Home Fleet to the Mediterranean in May, including battleships HMS *King George V* and *Howe* (32), the latter having completed working up only in mid-February. The threat posed to convoys in the North Atlantic and Barents Sea by

German surface forces based in Norway, particularly *Tirpitz*, had not gone away, so the British requested and received the temporary reinforcement of the Home Fleet by equivalent units of the US Navy.

TF22, commanded by Rear-Admiral O. M. Hustvedt in *Tuscaloosa*, included two battleships – *South Dakota* (BB57) and *Alabama* (BB60), the former returning to service after being damaged at the Naval Battle of Guadalcanal, the latter having just completed working up – and five destroyers. They departed Casco Bay for Argentia on 2 April, remaining there for most of a month before proceeding to Scapa Flow, where they arrived on 19 May, being re-designated TF61 and put under Royal Navy tactical command.

TF61 spent most of the next three months safely ensconced in Scapa Flow, waiting for what was hoped would be a sortie by some or all of the German surface units. However, at the end of May, the decision was made to make a re-supply run to the Allied garrison on Spitsbergen Island in the Svalbard Archipelago. These operations had been run regularly since 1941 under the rubric 'Operation GEARBOX'. This one was labeled 'GEARBOX III/FH', and involved two Royal Navy cruisers carrying supplies with distant cover provided by TF61 along with HMS *Duke of York*, *Anson* (79), the aircraft carrier *Furious* (47), two cruisers and six Royal Navy destroyers.* This was a force ready to take on any threat the Kriegsmarine might devise, but the Germans stayed home at Altenfjord, and TF61 detached on 12 June, heading for Hvalfjordur. On 21 June, they were back at Scapa Flow and again part of the Home Fleet.

Allied intelligence services had conjured an elaborate deception to distract the Germans from HUSKY, playing on Hitler's obsessive belief that the British intended to invade and re-capture at least part of Norway while he was deeply committed to the Kursk Offensive in Russia. As part of this, the Home Fleet mounted Operation CAMERA starting on 6 July. This was a complex series of fleet movements starting with cruisers sailing from Hvalfjordur. The next day, a simulated convoy left Scapa, sailing northward, west of the Shetlands then turning east as if approaching the Norwegian coast north of Bergen. Ten hours later, *Duke of York*, *South Dakota*, *Furious*, a light cruiser and all five American destroyers turned north-east at high speed, arriving at a point about 400 nm west of Trondheim at noon on 8 July. The force then turned south-east, heading for the same part of the Norwegian coast as the fake convoy. At that point, the fleet was sighted by a Luftwaffe reconnaissance aircraft, which was, after all, the whole point of the exercise. (Once it was certain the Bv 138 had transmitted its sighting report, it was shot down by a Martlet II off *Furious*.†) They continued

---

*   The various iterations of Operation GEARBOX during 1942 were given the Roman numeral 'II' and those in 1943 the numeral 'III'. The designator 'FH' identified this operation as one in a series of operations in the Barents Sea, designated 'Fx'.

†   The Martlet II was a Grumman-built F4F-3 Wildcat with folding wings, armor and self-sealing fuel tanks.

towards the south-east until 2100, reaching a point about 250 nm from the coast, and then turned back towards Scapa, arriving there unhindered at 1000.

Operation CAMERA had succeeded in distracting the Germans, but it failed to draw out the heavy units of the Kriegsmarine, so a repeat operation, this one named GOVERNOR was planned for later in the month. If anything, this was a bigger operation with forces approaching the Norwegian coast at several points. This time, the simulated invasion convoy sailed from Scapa Flow on 25 July, heading for the Shetlands. The first of two main forces, based on *Anson*, *Alabama* and the aircraft carrier *Illustrious* (87), just back from a major refit, sailed the next day from Hvalfjordur for a point north-east of the Shetlands, from which it then began a slow drag towards the east. On 27 July, the other main force, comprising *Duke of York*, *South Dakota*, the new light aircraft carrier *Unicorn* (F72), a light cruiser and nine destroyers, left Scapa on a similar course south of the first main group.[*] Again this failed to cause a German sortie, and, after the two main forces met the next day at a point 100 nm off the Norwegian coast and were sighted by Luftwaffe aircraft, they headed back to Scapa.

On 1 August, TF61 was released from Home Fleet duty and returned to Norfolk for a brief yard availability before heading out for the South Pacific. Other US Navy warships, particularly *Augusta*, *Tuscaloosa* and *Ranger* continued to operate in the Central and North Atlantic, occasionally in conjunction with the Royal Navy. For example, *Augusta* was seconded to the Home Fleet from 19 August to late November, providing cover for convoy RA.54A, one of the renewed Murmansk convoys, which left Kola Inlet on 1 November and arrived at Loch Ewe, Scotland, on 14 November.

— —

Key to the success of HUSKY was controlling the air and water between North Africa and the Axis harbors and airbases in Sardinia, Sicily and southern Italy. Neither would be easy. Land-based airpower was built-up in North Africa within range of all these areas, so that, unlike TORCH, there would be no need of aircraft carriers to protect the invasion fleets or support the troops once ashore.[†] The enemy mounted periodic air raids on shipping in ports along the North African coast, but never with enough intensity to delay the invasion preparations.

More serious was the threat posed by the Italian surface fleet and submarines of both the Regia Marina and Kriegsmarine. The Italians still had the modern battleships RM *Roma*, *Littorio* and *Vittorio Veneto*, three light cruisers and 11 destroyers at La Spezia, well up the west coast of the Italian peninsula, and two

---

[*] HMS *Unicorn* was originally classified as an aircraft maintenance ship, but with two hanger decks and a full-length flight deck, she resembled a diminutive *Ark Royal* and was used as a conventional aircraft carrier for much of the war.

[†] This refers only to the American landings. The Eastern Naval Task Force, supporting the British landings east and north of the American beaches, was supported by HMS *Formidable* (67) and *Indomitable*.

modernized First World War-vintage battleships RM *Andrea Doria* and *Caio Duilio* at Taranto, on the Ionian Sea.* However, the threat presented by these ships was much reduced by their lack of modern electronics, particularly radars, and the increasing scarcity of fuel oil, particularly at Taranto, which forced long periods of inactivity and left their crews essentially untrained.

The most effective weapon available to the Axis was the small number of U-boats operating from La Spezia (17 U-boats in July 1943). More numerous, but less effective, were Italian submarines based at Cagliari, Sardinia, and Pola, on the upper Adriatic, as well as other Italian naval bases. Axis submarines began to take a toll of American shipping as soon as it entered the Mediterranean. Probably the first such loss was the steamer *Arthur Middleton* sunk by *U73* (Deckert) on 1 January 1943 while waiting to enter the port of Oran. At the same time, the US Navy suffered its first loss in the Mediterranean. *LCT21*, a tank landing craft, was being carried as deck cargo on *Middleton* and was lost when the Liberty ship sank. Her 11-man crew, along with 67 merchant sailors and Armed Guards, died in the sinking.

The plan for the HUSKY landings called for landing 160,000 men and 14,000 vehicles, including 600 tanks, in the first days of the invasion, fully 50 per cent more men and vehicles than participated in the TORCH landings. To carry this amount of men and materiel, the naval forces, under the overall command of Admiral Cunningham, would deploy a number of specialized landing craft for the first time in European theater. The American Western Naval Task Force, under now Vice-Admiral Hewitt, would include hundreds of landing craft of new types. As an example, the 'Joss' Force that landed the US 3rd Infantry Division, 3rd Ranger Battalion and Combat Command A of the 2nd Armored Division, were carried ashore on 150 landing craft comprising 37 LSTs, 48 LCI(L)s and 65 LCTs[†]; two of the LSTs had been modified with a flying-off platform for L-4 Grasshoppers – liaison/observation aircraft – and 12 of the LCTs held in reserve were Royal Navy boats. The Royal Navy also contributed some specialized support landing craft: eight LCG(L)s and seven LCF(L)s to provide close-in support for troops ashore. Nine American destroyers further off-shore provided fire support for 'Joss' Force, along with the light cruisers *Brooklyn* and *Birmingham* (CL62).

'Joss' Force was the westernmost of three American landing forces. It was to put troops ashore either side of Licata, the most useful seaport on Sicily's south shore. 'Dime' Force landed at and just east of Gela, about 20 miles east of Licata, supported by *Boise*, *Savannah* and 13 destroyers; 'Cent' Force landed either side

---

* O'Hara, *Struggle for the Middle Sea*, pp. 215–16.

† Cf. Appendix B for a description of the landing craft types referenced in this book. 'Joss' Force had the bulk of the available large landing craft, which were still relatively scarce; the other two landing forces were, for the most part, carried in attack transports (APAs) and landed from smaller LCMs and LCVPs.

The new light cruiser Birmingham *(CL62) fires towards Licata, Sicily, in support of the* HUSKY *landings, 10 July 1943. Her primary task was the suppression of enemy artillery batteries on Monte Desusino, seen in the background. (NARA)*

of Scoglitti, another 20 miles further east, supported by *Philadelphia*, the new monitor HMS *Abercrombie* (F109) and 15 destroyers. All three landing sites were on the Gulf of Gela, a shallow indentation in the southern coast of Sicily. The afloat reserve, designated 'Kool' Force, was escorted by ten destroyers. There were two British landing zones, 'Bark' and 'Acid', to the east of the American zones, stretching from Cape Passero, the south-eastern tip of the island, up the east coast to just south of Syracuse (Siracusa), a span of about 40 miles. Because most of the troops coming ashore were British (or Commonwealth), they were to make the primary push to the north, skirting Mount Etna, heading as rapidly as possible to Messina in the north-eastern corner of the island, Patton's Seventh Army protecting their left flank.

The landings took place in compliance with the accelerated schedule endorsed at Casablanca Conference. The various task forces departed their North African assembly ports towards the end of the first week in July 1943. For example, *Philadelphia* departed Mers-el-Kébir on 5 July, sailing east along the coast, joining with other American support forces as they emerged from Algiers and other ports, providing cover for TF80, the Western Naval Task Force, as it passed through the Tunisian War Channel.[*] Once out of the channel, TF80 continued south along the Tunisian coast to pass south of Pantelleria, which

---

[*] CL41-1, p. 1, Morison, *History*, vol. IX, p. 65. The Tunisian War Channel was a mine-protected channel ten miles wide and 50 miles long across the mouth of the Gulf of Tunis from just east of Bizerte to Cape Bon.

Unlike the TORCH *landings, the* HUSKY *landings made extensive use of large landing craft, particularly the LSTs seen here off Licata from* Brooklyn, *10 July 1943. (NARA)*

had been captured a month earlier after a ten-day air and sea bombardment, joining with the landing craft west of Malta on 9 July, then turning north to approach the Sicilian coast. Despite the Home Fleet demonstration off Norway and an elaborate deception codenamed Operation MINCEMEAT, the enemy was well aware of the build-up in shipping at North African ports, the progress of the invasion fleet was monitored by aerial reconnaissance and the correct target deduced.[*] Yet no air attacks developed.[†]

The biggest problem faced by the invasion fleet was the weather. On 9 July, the day before the landings, the infamous mistral – a cool, dry wind that gains momentum as it sweeps down the Rhône valley – sprang up, at one point reaching a strength of 40 knots. As many of the troops were making the crossing from North Africa in the landing craft that would put them ashore, life became miserable for the soldiers, particularly for those in LCIs, in which the troops were carried below decks, and LCTs, on which troops and heavy vehicles were exposed to a drenching spray.[‡] As the sun set, Admiral Hewitt considered recommending to Admiral Cunningham that the invasion be postponed, but

---

[*] Operation MINCEMEAT involved the planting of documents describing an invasion of Greece and Sardinia on a dead body that was dressed up in a Royal Marines uniform and allowed to float ashore in southern Spain at the end of April 1943.

[†] CL41-1, p. 1.

[‡] Morison, *History*, vol. IX, pp. 66–9.

the wind had in fact been abating since 1800 and the meteorologists agreed that it would continue to decrease through the night, so the landings went ahead the next morning as scheduled, though high surf and wind caused them to be more difficult than expected.

Hoping to achieve tactical surprise, the landings were scheduled to begin at 0245, a full three hours before sunrise, but the wind and the complexity of the operation caused 'H-HOUR' to be delayed an hour. The pre-invasion bombardment began at Scoglitti at 0334 and lasted 28 minutes.[*] Enemy air attacks began at 0430 and continued regularly throughout the day. Four SOC-3 Seagulls were catapulted off *Philadelphia* shortly after dawn and two more at 1000 to spot gunfire. One of these, piloted by Lieutenant (Junior Grade) Paul Coughlin, performed an even greater service. While scouting behind Green 2 Beach on the eastern end of the Scoglitti landing zone, he sighted some men working on a defensive position and made a diving attack.

> 4.   After pulling out of the dive, I circled past some of our soldiers, a forward patrol, on the beach at the foot of a cliff . . . They waved and pointed at the hill, which they were evidently having trouble gaining. I circled low over the hill and spotted some movement on the ground. Upon my next sweep I saw a group of soldiers run into a hedge. I immediately released a bomb on this position. The bomb, however, did not detonate, because the low altitude from which it was dropped did not give it sufficient time to arm itself . . . I then began to strafe this position, and after four (4) runs of fixed and free gun fire, white flags and Italians began appearing from the hedge. I flew low and motioned for them to go in the general direction of our troops; their movement was hurried and guided by the very accurate fire of the Radioman.[†]
>
> Looking at the top of the hill for a way to direct them, where they would be in the open, I saw white flags waving over four entrenchments. As the prisoners from the hedge would get close to one of these positions, I would fly over and wave for them to come out and go in the direction of the others. They were a little slow coming out; until a few shots were fired close to them. In this way we got all out into the open, and headed for the beach.
>
> We rode herd on them, very much the same as in handling cattle; when one would start to stray or would start spreading, shots were placed close to the guilty ones. This worked very well and they gathered force as they went forward, resulting in what appeared to be better than a hundred by the time they reached the soldiers on the beach.[‡]

At the end of this episode, Coughlin's floatplane was jumped by a pair of German fighters, which had just shot down another of the cruiser's aircraft. The

---

[*]   CL41-1, p. 3.

[†]   Coghlin's radio operator/gunner was Richard Shafer, ARM2c.

[‡]   Coughlin's report of this action is quoted in CL41-1, pp. 4–5.

The beach shelf on the south coast of Sicily is so shallow that LSTs could not get close enough to unload directly to the beach. The expedient of building a causeway of barges, as here at Licata, solved the problem neatly. (NARA)

Bf 109s were driven off by anti-aircraft fire from *Philadelphia*.

The landings at Licata and Scoglitti were confused, but achieved their initial goals against generally light opposition. The confusion was in part a result of the decision to make the initial landings in the dark, exacerbated by a shallow shelf off the beaches that stranded many landing craft and by the high surf. They were further hampered by soft sand on the beaches that bogged down vehicles and the supplies they carried, and by the general lack of experience of most of the participants. Many of the landing craft that were able to extract themselves from the beach did so still loaded because poor planning and the inexperience of the beach control parties left them no place to unload. There was so little call for fire support off Scoglitti that *Abercrombie* was detached to support the Gela sector, where the need was greater.

It was at Gela that the landings met the most resistance both on the ground and in the air. A column of Italian tanks started towards the beaches before dawn. They had approached within 3 miles of the coast when they were spotted at 0900 by one of *Boise*'s scout planes. The light cruiser's gunfire stopped that column, aided by shore-directed gunfire from *Jeffers* (DD621). A second column of 25 light tanks was engaged by *Shubrick* (DD639), which knocked out most of them. Nine or ten reached Gela, where they were taken on by US Army Rangers. After two were destroyed and one surrendered, the rest withdrew.[*]

Without aircraft carriers to provide close-in air support, air units supporting the American landings had to make the lengthy transit from Tunisian bases. This combined with poor communication and inexperience led to a failure to maintain air superiority over the invasion fleet and the landing beaches until airfields ashore were captured two days after the landings. The result was that Luftwaffe attacks occurred with distressing regularity, opposed primarily by anti-aircraft guns of the invasion fleet. Few of the attacks resulted in damage, but those that did took a terrible toll. The first ship to be hit was *Maddox* (DD622), dived on by a Stuka in the pre-dawn twilight.[†] *Maddox* was on patrol off Gela when the dive bomber attacked from astern, undetected by her radar.[‡] One of two bombs missed aft, but the second struck her starboard propeller guard and detonated. This explosion apparently demolished the shell plating on that side and set off one or both of the after main battery magazines. The explosion was so bright that, according to observers, the still-dark sky was briefly lit like day.[§] It demolished *Maddox*'s after end and opened the bulkhead of the after engine room, which began flooding. The destroyer rolled onto her beam ends and slid beneath the water stern-first in less than two minutes, taking most of her crew with her. Only 74 survivors were rescued.

Sentinel (AM113), a minesweeper, was also attacked before dawn. The attacks started at 0430 while she was patrolling to seaward of a sister ship sweeping the inshore approaches to Licata harbor. She was illuminated by flares at about 0500 and then holed by a series of near-misses that opened her after engine room to the sea. Attacked four more times over the next hour, one bomb hit her forward gun mount, wounding most of the occupants of her bridge. Soon after dawn, now drifting without power, taking on water and starting to draw the attention of shore batteries, she was ordered abandoned at 0615. Most of the crew and all of the wounded were taken off over the next hour. A skeleton crew remained onboard until the list reached 28°. She capsized at 1030, soon after the last man was taken off, and sank at 1045. She suffered ten dead and 51 wounded out of a complement of 101 officers and men.

The unloading of landing craft was moving so slowly that it was dusk before

---

[*]   Morison, *History*, vol. IX, pp. 103–4.

[†]   Stuka is a German contraction for *Sturzkampfflugzeug*, meaning 'dive bomber', the nickname given to the Ju 87.

[‡]   Sources differ on exactly what *Maddox* was doing at the time and exactly when the attack occurred. *Dictionary of American Naval Fighting Ships* and Morison, *History*, vol. IX, p. 100 state she was on anti-submarine patrol well offshore and that the attack occurred at 0458; Parkin, *Blood on the Sea*, pp. 145–6 states she was providing fire support, which would require her to be much closer to shore, and that it occurred five minutes earlier. The accounts agree on what happened next.

[§]   Morison, *History*, vol. IX, p. 100.

LST313 approached Beach Green 2 east of Gela with a tank deck full of motor vehicles, anti-tank guns and land mines. A single bomb dropped by a German bomber exploded there, igniting an inferno of burning vehicles punctuated by crates of munitions cooking off. Only through heroic rescue efforts were losses limited to 20 soldiers and a single seaman.[*]

The next day brought more air attacks and more timely fire support. At 0640, American troops of the 26th RCT, 1st Infantry Div., advancing north from the beachhead encountered German armor as they approached the Ponte Olivo airfield, some 6 miles inland. The troops had no anti-tank artillery, because it had been lost in the destruction of *LST313*, and no armor because congestion on the beaches had delayed the unloading of American tanks until mid-morning. It was not until 0830 that the call came in for naval gunfire support, but the Navy's response was rapid. Within minutes *Savannah* was lobbing 6-inch shells at a concentration of Panzers less than 2 miles from Gela and then shifted fire to another group a mile further inland.[†] Another German attack at 1040 was broken up by shellfire from *Boise* and *Glennon* (DD620). By 1100, multiple groups of Panzers had come so close to the beaches that no further fire support was requested for fear that the defenders might be hit. This lasted until shortly after noon, when enough tanks had come ashore. Enemy aircraft sank *LST158* and damaged transports *Barnett* (APA5) and *Orizaba*. By far the most spectacular success for the Luftwaffe was the sinking of the new Liberty ship *Robert Rowan*. Fully loaded with munitions and 334 men of the 18th Infantry, she arrived off Gela during the morning of 11 July and was idling in shallow water, waiting her turn to unload. That process had just begun when a flight of about 30 Ju 88s attacked the roadstead at 1540. Three bombs hit the cargo ship; one failed to explode, but two detonated in her holds and the resulting fires were soon out of control. Well aware of the nature of her cargo, the ship was rapidly abandoned, so that when her bow disintegrated in a massive explosion, not a single life was lost. *Rowan* continued to burn for two days; on the first night, the flames were so bright that *McLanahan* (DD615) was tasked with sinking the hulk, but this proved impossible, as the water was too shallow.

Fire support for the landings continued for one more day, but during the day on 12 July, the beachhead expanded to the point where the 6-inch guns of the light cruisers could no longer reach enemy positions. The last shells fired over the beaches came from *Boise* at 2048 aimed at retreating enemy forces 8 miles inland. By the next day, Allied fighters were flying from captured airfields.

The job of fire support did not end with the expansion of the beachheads, it just moved as elements of the 7th Army pushed towards the larger Porto Empedocle, 30 miles west of Licata, which fell on 16 July, and Agrigento, which was captured the day after, both attacks supported by naval gunfire. After that, the fast-moving

---

[*]   Ibid, pp. 107–8.

[†]   Ibid, pp. 111–18

The cargo ship Robert Rowan *was anchored off Gela on 11 July 1943, waiting her turn to be unloaded. An attack by 30 Luftwaffe bombers put two bombs in her and caused her to be abandoned. This took place not a moment too soon, because her forward hold, filled with munitions, detonated in this spectacular cloud of smoke and streaking artillery shells which, because of the speed of her abandonment, caused no loss of life. (USA)*

Army forces turned inland and headed north-west across the western part of the island, taking Palermo on 23 July. As the troops entered the city, they were greeted by the sight of DesRon 8 – the veteran destroyers *Wainwright, Rowan, Rhind* and *Mayrant* – escorting four minesweepers of MinDiv 17 already at work clearing channels to the harbor. Those four destroyers were patrolling east of the city three days later when they came under air attack. Along the northern coast of Sicily, Allied air superiority had yet to be established.

At 0931, *Mayrant's* radar detected enemy aircraft at a range of five miles and the ship went to General Quarters. They were visually identified as a flight of three Ju 88s and were taken under fire by the main battery. Speed was increased and a hard starboard turn ordered.

> Before the ship had even begun to swing a stick of 3 or 4 bombs was dropped on the starboard side, distance about 150 yards, by a plane approaching from astern, which had not been previously sighted . . . This was followed by a stick of one or two bombs dropped approximately 500 yards ahead of the ship by one of the three planes in the initial contact group. At this time it is believed that all guns which were manned were firing on the initial contact on the port bow. However, one of these planes dropped his stick of 4 bombs

With friendly ports available along the north coast of Africa, ships of the Allied invasion fleet rotated back on a regular basis to replenish and refuel. The problem with this was that these ports were within range of Luftwaffe bombers, which raided regularly. Here, Savannah *leaves Algiers on 16 July 1943, after one such raid. (NARA)*

which straddled the MAYRANT. One bomb landed approximately 5 feet off the port beam . . . A second bomb landed off the starboard beam at a distance of about 40 yards . . . The ship listed heavily to port and nearly all personnel were thrown to the deck or against bulkheads.[*]

Despite being only near-missed, *Mayrant* was seriously wounded, her port side opened to the sea. Within seven minutes, all main power had been lost, the after fire room and forward engine room had completely flooded and the other two large engineering spaces were filling rapidly with water. Moments later, the emergency diesel generator failed, meaning the ship also had no electric power.

At 0945 the after engineroom was reported completely flooded and the forward fireroom flooded to within 4 feet of the water line. The ship had approximately 14" of freeboard and a list of 4 degrees to starboard. All 5 gasoline handy billy pumps had been ordered rigged to the forward fireroom[†] . . . The 3 electric submersible pumps had been similarly rigged but stopped when the diesel generator failed.

It was apparent that the ship was in serious danger of sinking and at 0953

---

[*]   DD402-2, p. 2.
[†]   A 'handy-billy' is a small gasoline-powered pump.

the whaleboat was put in the water and all topside weights were ordered to be jettisoned.[*]

Incredibly, *Mayrant* did not sink. The destroyers *Wainwright* and *Rhind* and the minesweepers *Skill* (AM115) and *Strive* (AM117) came to *Mayrant*'s assistance, passing over additional handy-billies and, in the case of *Strive*, coming alongside and supplying electricity so that the submersible pumps could be powered. *Skill* towed the two ships to Palermo, where they tied up alongside the Santa Lucia pier at 1615. *Mayrant* had suffered five dead and 18 wounded; topping the list of wounded was Lieutenant Franklin D. Roosevelt, Jr. After a stop at Malta, she was able to make Charleston Navy Yard, where she was repaired, returning to service on 15 May 1944.

The capture of Palermo coincided with the culmination of a plan by Italian King Vittorio Emanuele III to oust Benito Mussolini as head of state. On 25 July, after a vote of no-confidence by the Fascist Grand Council, the King summoned Mussolini, dismissed him and had him arrested. Marshal Pietro Badoglio was named Prime Minister and immediately began to make secret overtures to the Allies regarding an armistice.

On 27 July, the American naval forces remaining in Sicilian waters were designated TF88, under the command of Rear-Admiral Lyal A. Davidson, with orders to provide support for the 7th Army.[†] The force that arrived at Palermo on 30 July comprised *Philadelphia*, *Savannah* and six destroyers. Over the next several weeks, TF88 was busy providing fire support for Patton's troops and, on two occasions, providing sealift for a battalion of the 30th Infantry which was landed behind German defensive positions.[‡] Another, larger landing at Spadafora on 16 August also failed to trap the enemy, who were rapidly evacuating the island. Empty Messina was entered the next day by Patton's troops, bringing the Sicilian campaign to an end. Between 3 August and the morning of 17 August, over 100,000 Axis troops, 10,000 vehicles, 135 guns, over 17,000 t of munitions and stores, and 12 mules were evacuated to the Italian mainland with no significant interference from Allied naval or air forces.[§]

The armistice negotiations proceeded rapidly. Badoglio wanted an Allied landing on the Italian mainland to precede the armistice, but the Allies made no such promise and, on 1 September, the Italians decide to accept the terms as offered. In the event, on the same day that General Giuseppe Castellano signed the armistice agreement onboard HMS *Nelson* (28), 3 September, two divisions of the British Eighth Army (General Sir Bernard L. Montgomery) crossed the

---

[*]   DD402-2, p. 3.

[†]   Morison, *History*, vol. IX, pp. 191–208.

[‡]   These landings took place on 8 August at Sant' Agata and on 12 August at Brolo. They were mounted in a pair of LSTs, plus LCTs andd LCIs.

[§]   Ibid, pp. 215–16.

The 'Fritz X', officially named FX 1400, was a 1,400-kg (3086.5-lb) armor-piercing bomb with radio-controlled tail section incorporating spoilers and air brakes that allowed limited guidance after it was dropped. Its great disadvantage was that it required the bomber that dropped it, usually a Do 217, to remain in visual range of the bomb as it fell. Nevertheless, it was a significant threat to Allied invasion shipping until countermeasures could be deployed.

Strait of Messina on landing craft to Reggio di Calabria (Operation BAYTOWN). The armistice was originally set to come into effect (and be made public) on 12 September, but was pushed forward to 8 September because, on the next day, Allied troops were to land at two more locations along the Italian coast.

Marshal Badoglio had no choice but to go along, broadcasting news of the surrender at 1945 on 8 September. However, he did not issue instructions to Italian military units, which were left on their own to deal with the immediate German reaction. This included the remnants of the Italian Navy, most of whose operational units were at La Spezia. At 1700, unaware of the impending armistice, the Italian fleet had been ordered to attack the Allied forces sighted approaching Salerno; they were in the process of getting underway when the announcement was made. Bound by terms of the armistice to sail for specified Allied ports, the fleet was ordered instead to sail for La Maddalena, Sardinia. A force of three battleships – *Roma*, *Vittorio Veneto* and *Italia* (formerly *Littorio*) – along with three cruisers and eight destroyers departed La Spezia at 0300 on 9 September.[*] However, at 1340, heading east in the Strait of Bonifacio between Corsica and Sardinia, they learned that the Germans had occupied La Maddalena and the fleet commander, Admiral Carlo Bergamini, ordered a turn to the west, through

---

[*]   O'Hara, *Struggle for the Middle Sea*, pp. 219–23.

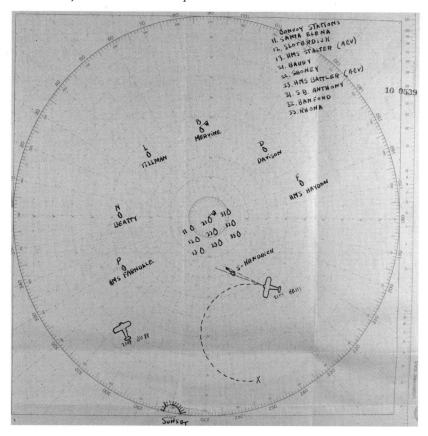

While escorting part of convoy UGF.10 on its last leg towards Bizerte on 2 September 1943, Kendrick (DD612), in the trailing position, was attacked by a He 111 which dropped a pair of torpedoes. As this excellent chart shows, the attack occurred at sunset, the aircraft approaching from the starboard quarter, turning away to the left and splashing well aft of the convoy. The torpedo hit Kendrick right aft, demolishing her rudder, but leaving her able to steam. (NARA)

the Gulf of Asinara and then south towards Malta. The first German attack came 20 minutes after turning west.

Six Do 217 K-2 bombers of III/KG100, each armed with one of the new Ruhrstahl FX 1400 radio-guided bomb were approaching from the north. The 'Fritz X' was a 1,400-kg armor-piercing bomb fitted with an aerodynamic nose-cap, four stub wings for stability and a tail unit with radio receiver and a ring-shaped air brake with controllable spoilers. Once dropped, the bombardier would visually follow the bomb's path by means of a bright flare in the bomb's tail. He would be able to make minor corrections to the bomb's ballistic trajectory in both range and deflection. The first known use of a 'Fritz

X' was against Augusta harbor on the east coast of Sicily on 21 July 1943, but that and a few subsequent attacks were not particularly successful and it is not clear that the Allies were aware that they were being attacked with a radically new weapon.

The first of the 'Fritz X' bombs dropped this day, starting at 1535, near-missed *Italia*, briefly jamming her rudder. Ten minutes later, *Roma* was hit on the starboard side; the bomb passed completely through her hull and exploded beneath the keel, flooding an engine room and two fire rooms, reducing her speed to 10 knots. At 1602, she was hit again, this time further forward. This bomb exploded in her forward engine room and triggering a secondary explosion in her No. 2 main battery magazine, tearing the ship in two and causing her to sink rapidly, taking Admiral Bergamini and nearly 1,400 men with her. This brought the full potential of the 'Fritz X' to the notice of the Allies and set off a scramble to develop countermeasures.

The rest of the Italian fleet, joined by three cruisers from Genoa and the two old battleships, two cruisers and a destroyer from Taranto, were interned at Malta the next day. Most units were eventually sent to sit out the war in the Great Bitter Lake in the middle of the Suez Canal.

——

Even before the end of the Sicilian campaign, the pressure on Eisenhower to move quickly onto the Italian mainland forced his hand. When asked in June what moves he would recommend after the capture of Sicily, he stated that, given that seven Allied divisions would be withdrawn from the Mediterranean theater by November to prepare for the cross-Channel invasion the next spring, that only small moves, either capturing Sardinia or crossing the Strait of Messina with a token force, would be possible. He estimated that it would be October before a Sardinia operation could be mounted, or November if the choice was to push into Calabria.[*] At a meeting at Eisenhower's headquarters in mid-July, the Americans remained adamant that no new forces be introduced into the Mediterranean, but accepted Churchill's argument that it would be a mistake to have no active front against the Germans for almost a year. As a compromise, Eisenhower was instructed to exploit any victory in Sicily with the forces at his disposal, with a move to capture Naples, if not Rome, especially if it looked like this would hasten the collapse of Italian resistance.

The plan for landings on the Salerno Plain south of Naples, was codenamed Operation AVALANCHE. Moving with the assurance of forces now approaching their third landing operation, planning for AVALANCHE proceeded with remarkable speed. Because the landings would take place in a relatively small area – less than 20 miles separated the northernmost and southernmost

---

[*] Churchill, *The Second World War: Closing the Ring*, pp. 35–9; Eisenhower, *Crusade in Europe*, pp. 168–9.

By the time the Allies landed at Salerno on 9 September 1943, they had obviously mastered the art of rapidly landing troops and the massive amounts of equipment and supplies they required, but not yet how to move either off the beach fast enough. (NARA)

beaches – both land and sea forces were unitary commands, both commanders being American, Admiral Hewitt and now-Lieutenant General Clark.[*] The initial landings, by one American and two British infantry divisions, plus American Rangers and British Commandos, was scheduled for before dawn on 9 September. In order to achieve tactical surprise, the landings were to take place without preliminary air or naval bombardment. Fire support for the southern beaches, where the US 36th Infantry Div was to land, was provided by *Philadelphia*, *Savannah* and *Brooklyn*, supported again by HMS *Abercrombie*, and four destroyers.[†] Overall cover was provided by the Royal Navy's Force H, based on battleships HMS *Nelson*, *Rodney* (29), *Warspite* (03) and *Valiant* (01) with air support coming from fleet carriers *Illustrious* and *Formidable*, light carrier *Unicorn* and escort carriers *Battler* (D18), *Attacker* (D02), *Hunter* (D80) and *Stalker* (D91), the last four US-built.

British troops were landed at Taranto (Operation SLAPSTICK). The only major American naval unit involved in SLAPSTICK was *Boise*, which, along with four Royal Navy cruisers, deposited the British 1st Parachute Div ashore on 9 September, the same day as the AVALANCHE landings. The approaching

---

[*] Clark remains a controversial figure. He was brought in from Eisenhower's staff to replace Lieutenant General Omar Bradley, who was sent to England to command the US Army forces massing there for the upcoming cross-Channel invasion. Clark has been criticized for the rigid planning that slowed the build-up of ground forces at Salerno and for failure to exploit a number of tactical opportunities.

[†] The US beaches were approximately a mile from the three Greek temples at Paestum, one of the world's great historical treasures, which, fortunately, were unharmed in the battle.

SLAPSTICK force encountered the Italian fleet units departing Taranto to surrender at Malta. There were a few tense moments as the two forces passed. The Germans had evacuated the city and the Italians proved co-operative, so many of the troops were landed dockside. *Boise* unloaded her 788 passengers and more than 60 light vehicles carried in her hanger and was on her way towards Salerno the next morning.[*]

The weather co-operated on 9 September and the initial AVALANCHE landings went much more smoothly than either TORCH or HUSKY, but the German 16th Panzer Div was in defensive positions behind the beaches and soon made life difficult for both main landing forces. Naval forces provided essential fire support, breaking up tank concentrations. By the end of the first day, the Allies held four separate beachheads. The next two days were spent joining the Allied beachheads, but by 13 September the position was still shallow and the German forces, which had been gathering around the beachhead, launched a major counterattack along the Sele River, where the Allied sectors met. At one point, Clark asked Hewitt to prepare to carry troops from the American sector south of the Sele to reinforce the northern sector, but this proved unnecessary.[†] That night and the next, parts of the 82nd Airborne Div dropped into the beachhead and provided vital reinforcement to the lines. Renewed German attacks on 14 September were defeated and, the next day, the Germans went over to the defensive. Montgomery's Eighth Army coming up from Calabria reached the beachhead on 16 September.

The naval forces supporting the landings offshore became the target of German naval and air forces. The first important attack was by three S-boats – *S151, S152* and *S158* – fast motor torpedo boats (known to the Allies as E-boats) that had sortied from Civitavecchia, north of Rome, after dark on 10 September.[‡] At 2215 that same night, the convoy SNF.1 started forming up, 16 cargo ships and assault transports returning empty to Oran, escorted by ten destroyers.[§] The convoy had not completed assembling when destroyer *Rowan* took station on the convoy's starboard bow at 2240. She was still at that station just after midnight when the quiet night suddenly became very busy.

> 3.   About 0015, 11 September the Officer of the Watch reported a torpedo wake crossing starboard bow, distant about 100 feet. This was confirmed by the sound operators. Speed was increased to 15 knots, full right rudder was ordered and a turn made to run down torpedo track . . .[¶]

---

[*]   Morison, *History*, vol. IX, pp. 235–6; Eisenhower, *Crusade in Europe*, p. 189.

[†]   Morison, *History*, vol. IX, p. 290.

[‡]   German *Schnellboote* (*S-boote,* S-boats), literally 'fast boats', were often called 'E-boats' by Americans after the British practice.

[§]   Whitley, *German Coastal Forces*, p. 94; Rohwer, *Chronology of the War at Sea 1939–1945*, p. 273; Morison, *History*, vol. IX, pp. 298–9; Parkin, *Blood on the Sea*, pp. 155–6.

[¶]   DD405, p. 1.

Jumping to the logical conclusion that the torpedo had come from a U-boat, the captain, Lieutenant Commander R. S. Ford, ordered depth charges armed and set for shallow detonation. However, it became clear almost immediately that the torpedo must have come from a surface craft.

> At the same time SG radar contact was made on bearing 335° True, distant about 5,000 yards. Initial ranges appeared to be closing and then began to increase rapidly. Speed was increased successively to 20 knots, 25 knots and 27 knots within a period of a minute. A report over the TBS had been made . . . that we were investigating possibility of "E" Boats . . . Ranges commenced to decrease slowly and at about 4,800 yards fire was opened with the forward 5" guns, full radar control. Ranges now appeared to increase and a report was received from the SG radar operator that the "E" Boats were separating and proceeding on diverging courses.[*]

The two S-boats rapidly pulled away, and *Rowan* ceased firing, increased speed to 32 knots and turned back towards the convoy.

> After proceeding on this course for approximately 4 minutes, SG radar operator reported another contact on the port quarter, range 2,800 yards . . . FD radar was coached on this target by SG and control was ordered to open fire.[†] It was reported by control that guns 1 and 2 could not bear, and control was ordered to open fire with 3 and 4. In the meantime a turn to 140° true was made to bring all guns to bear. This course of 140° had just been reached when the range to the target was reported at 2000 yards. Believing that this would be the range at which a torpedo would be fired, full right rudder was ordered to bring the target astern . . . The ship was swinging rapidly to starboard with full right rudder and had swung about 30° when torpedo struck. It is believed the torpedo struck the port quarter and exploded the after magazine. The ship sank . . . in a total of about 40 seconds.[‡]

So sudden and cataclysmic was *Rowan's* sinking that only men whose duty station was above deck had any chance of survival, and the fact that any men were pulled alive from the oil-covered sea was due to the initiative of a torpedo-man who, without waiting for orders, had disarmed the depth charges after learning the target was not a U-boat.[§] Seventy-five out of her complement of 273 were pulled from the water, many of them badly wounded; four of those later died of their injuries.

Later that same morning, the Americans got their first taste of the 'Fritz X'

---

[*]   DD405, pp. 1–2.

[†]   SG was the centimetric surface-search radar that made the original contact; FD was the Mk 4 fire-control radar fitted to *Rowan's* Mk 33 main battery director.

[‡]   DD405, p. 2.

[§]   Ibid., pp 2–3. The enterprising sailor was Walter F. Garrigus, TM2c.

Rowan *(DD405), seen here in November 1942, engaged three S-boats on the night of 11 September 1943 and was hit by a single torpedo which detonated her after magazine. The destroyer sank in less than a minute. (NARA)*

So cataclysmic and sudden was Rowan's *sinking, that the 75 survivors, one of whom is seen here wiping away the oil from which he had been pulled, were too stunned to yet register the tragedy they'd survived. (NARA)*

Later that day, 11 September 1943, the Americans made the acquaintance of one of Germany's newest weapons, the 'Fritz X' guided bomb, one of which hit Savannah *on main battery turret No. 3, setting off this massive explosion. (NHHC)*

Damage control teams pour water into turret No. 3 on Savannah, *11 September 1943, while others look to the wounded in the other turrets. One man to the right of turret No. 2 is beyond all help. Note the damaged life rafts on the turret tops, stocked with containers of water and rations. (NARA)*

The hole made in the 2-inch STS armor plate atop turret No. 3 on Savannah *by the 'Fritz X', clearly visible once the fire was knocked down, demonstrates the threat this large and powerful weapon was to even well-defended warships. (NARA)*

guided bomb. Again, it was a flight of Do 217s from Southern France, attacking *Savannah* at 0944.

13   The bomb made only a 'whooshing' noise as it hit. Considerable debris from balso [sic] life rafts stowed on top of turret #3 was thrown high into the air. A heavy jolt was felt at the same time. Dense clouds of smoke poured from turret #3 and many small fires were started on deck, probably from flaming bits of the life rafts . . . A tremendous turbulence of water abreast turret #3 to port and the venting of much smoke from the explosion within the ship through this turbulence led many topside personnel aft to think that the bomb had been a near miss.[*]

That simple description does not do justice to the devastation done by the missile or to the incredible luck and skill that allowed the ship to survive what could well have been a fatal blow. When the bomb hit the turret roof, made of 2-inch STS – a homogeneous nickel-steel armor plate used for decks and other structural uses not requiring face-hardening – it punched a 21½-inch hole, demolished a rammer, deflected off the turret roller path straight down

---

[*]   CL42-2, p. 5.

A casualty is passed down through the rear escape hatch under turret No. 2 on Savannah, *11 Sepember 1942. Men died not only in the turret that was hit by the 'Fritz X' and the handling rooms below it, but the blast injured and killed men in the two other forward turrets and their magazines. (NARA)*

through two armored decks before exploding in the handling room of Turret No. 3. The explosion blew smoke and flame upward into the turret, killing the entire gun crew, also blowing out the bulkheads fore and aft, causing heavy casualties among the magazine and gun crews of the two other forward main battery turrets. Most seriously, it started powder fires in several of the forward magazines. Fortunately, the explosion was of such magnitude that it also blew a hole, 28 feet in length, in *Savannah's* bottom and pushed out her shell plating on her port side for a length of 45 feet, opening the riveted seam below the armor belt.[*] The inrushing water from these hull breaches extinguished the powder fires, undoubtedly preventing a magazine explosion.

The damage to *Savannah* was serious, but never life-threatening. She immediately took an 8° list to port and was down 11 feet at the bow, but no additional flooding occurred after the first five minutes, and counterflooding corrected the list to 3½° by 1121. By 1758 that same day, *Savannah* was underway for Malta at 12 knots, later increased to 18 knots. She was docked at Malta on 19 September, where she was repaired sufficiently to allow her to depart for

---

[*]   CL42-2, p. 5; CL42-3, pp. 1–2, 12–13.

Steaming to Malta later in the day on 11 September 1943, Savannah *is obviously down by the bow. (NARA)*

Philadelphia on 7 December, where she began an eight-month overhaul that lasted into September 1944. Her damage and her survival were best summed up in the *War Damage Report*:

> The bomb that struck SAVANNAH was the largest, both in total weight and size of charge, to have scored a hit on a U.S. naval vessel. Further, the bomb also detonated in the midst of main and secondary battery magazines – a location usually regarded as certain to cause the immediate and violent destruction of the vessel. Finally, the hit was the first made on a U.S. naval vessel by a German radio-controlled bomb.[*]

Her survival was rightly attributed to her rugged construction – the *Brooklyn* class was the first to use a new longitudinal framing system that added strength without adding weight – and to the resourcefulness of her crew. Nevertheless, she paid a heavy price; 206 officers and men were killed outright or later died of their wounds.

The Allies moved quickly to develop counter-measures to defeat the 'Fritz X' and the equally dangerous Hs 293 rocket-boosted glide bomb.[†] Both used the same transmitter/receiver combination for the radio link from aircraft

---

[*] CL42-3, p. 1.

[†] The Hs 293 was 500-kg fragmentation bomb fitted with wings and stabilizers at the tail and a rocket motor to provide initial velocity. Unlike the 'Fritz X', it was designed to attack unarmored targets.

A DUKW, commonly called a 'Duck', was one of the most ubiquitous and useful amphibious craft, seen here from the command ship Ancon (AGC4) *off Salerno, 12 September 1943. A DUKW was basically a 6x6 GMC 2-1/2t utility truck with a watertight body and a propeller. They could carry men and supplies over open water, across the beach and inland as far as needed, which made them very popular. (NARA)*

The 82nd Airborne was supposed to be dropped on Rome on 8 September 1943 to capture airfields and railyards, but the drop was cancelled when it was realized how strong the German defenders were around the Italian capital. Part of the division was landed at the north end of the British zone to reinforce troops tasked with seizing the road across the Sorrento Peninsula. Three Lend-Lease LCIs loaded with American paratroopers are seen from Ancon, *13 September 1943. (NARA)*

A Lend-Lease LST – HMS LST404 – *is seen from* Ancon *off Salerno, 12 September 1943. In the foreground are two American PT boats, the nearer wearing a novel 'dazzle' paint scheme. In the background are an 'alphabet soup' of landing craft, including five LCIs, another LST, an LCT and an attack transport. (NARA)*

After the surrender of Italy was confirmed on 8 September 1943, the Italian fleet had been instructed to proceed to Malta for internment. One Italian submarine, RSmg Nichelio, *chose to surface in the midst of the Salerno invasion fleet, causing some initial consternation before its intent to surrender was determined, 12 September 1943. (NARA)*

A warning, chalked on a ventilation duct in Philadelphia *(CL41) off Salerno, September 1943, reminded sailors to keep their eyes out for nightly visitors – German aircraft – some of which had acquired nicknames, including 'Freddie the Flare Dropper' and 'Zoom Gidgit'. Carelessness could lead to an unwanted result – 'The Flaming Liberty'. (NARA)*

Opposite, top: The light show to which that warning humorously referred is captured in this image taken from Ancon *off Salerno, 12 September 1943. Dropping flares can be seen left and right while AA fire sprays upward from the invasion fleet offshore. (NARA)*

Opposite, below: That same night, 12 September 1943, Lyminge, *a British cargo ship loaded with gasoline, land mines and gas cylinders, was near-missed by a guided bomb and began to burn, as seen from* Ancon. Lyminge's *crew, understandably concerned for their safety, quickly abandoned ship. A salvage crew from* Biscayne *(AVP11), flagship of RAdm Richard L. Conolly, USN, commanding the support for the American Ranger forces, was put aboard and contained the fires, saving the ship and valuable cargo. (NARA)*

to guided-bomb.* The US Naval Research Laboratory (NRL) had a jamming transmitter ready and installed in two destroyer escorts by late September, but the XCJ jammed the wrong frequencies and proved ineffective. The modified XCJ-1, which jammed the correct frequencies, was ready by the end of the year. The British introduced the Type 650 jammer at the same time, which had the advantage of not requiring the operator to search manually through the 18 possible command frequencies available to the transmitter.

— —

On 10 September, the Germans began to evacuate Sardinia, using the same barges and ferries that had enabled the evacuation of Messina. They carried 25,000 troops, 2,300 vehicles and 5,000 t of supplies across to Corsica, and then by air and sea to the Italian mainland. French naval forces began transporting troops to occupy Corsica starting on 11 September; the German evacuation and French re-occupation were complete by the end of the month.

— —

In Norwegian waters, on the day before the Salerno landing, major units of the *Kriegsmarine* carried out Operation SIZILIEN (also known as ZITRONELLA), a raid on the Norwegian outpost on Spitsbergen, involving *Tirpitz*, the battlecruiser *Scharnhorst* and nine destroyers carrying a battalion of troops. Setting out undetected on 6 September, they arrived off Spitsbergen two days later, landed the troops, shelled some facilities and burned others – killing 11 Norwegians and capturing 74 more, though most of the garrison simply fled into the surrounding hills – and then reboarded their troops and returned to Alta, having sustained minor damage to three of the destroyers. The Royal Navy's Home Fleet, reinforced by *Ranger*, *Tuscaloosa*, *Augusta* and five American destroyers, sortied from Scapa Flow on 8 September, but turned back the next day when it was learned that the German ships were already back at Alta. The survivors of the Norwegian garrison returned after the Germans departed and re-established the outposts as best they could, until a small task force comprising *Tuscaloosa*, *Fitch* (DD462) and three Royal Navy destroyers brought supplies and additional troops on 19 October. *Tuscaloosa* claims that this was the farthest north any US warship reached in the Second World War.†

Operation SIZILIEN was to be the only time *Tirpitz* fired her main guns in anger. On 22 September, she was attacked in Altenfjord by Royal Navy midget submarines, two of which planted mines that immobilized her for six months. Soon afterwards, the 'pocket battleship' *Lützow* was transferred from northern Norway to the Baltic. The Royal Navy had hoped to intercept *Lützow* as she

---

* The transmitter was codenamed Kehl and the receiver Straßburg, which operated in the low VHF range. Kehl and Straßburg (Strasbourg) are cities on opposite banks of the middle Rhine.

† Morison, *History*, vol. IX, p. 231n.

sailed south near the Norwegian coast, planning strikes by *Ranger*'s air group, but those attacks never materialized.*

Still, wanting to take advantage of *Ranger*'s presence, another operation was planned, an attack on shipping and port facilities at Bodø, just above the Arctic Circle. The Home Fleet sortied on 2 October for Operation LEADER, arriving at the planned launching position 100 nm west of Bodø at 0600 on 4 October. The launch of the first attack was delayed almost 20 minutes while *Ranger* was searching for wind over the deck. Because she lacked catapults, *Ranger* needed 31 knots of relative wind over her deck to launch combat-loaded aircraft. Even at her best speed, 29 knots, she needed help from at least a 2-knot breeze to launch her attack, but, at 0600, she found dead air. Like a sailing ship caught in the Doldrums, her lookouts searched for any change in the flat calm of the sea surface that might betray a patch of wind. At 0618, she had found enough of a breeze that she could launch her CAP and anti-submarine patrol, followed by the 20 Dauntlesses – armed with single 500-lb or 1,000-lb bombs – and eight Wildcats of the Northern Attack Group which quickly assembled and headed straight for Bodø at 0640. At 0730, ten Avengers – armed with four 500-lb bombs each – and another six Wildcats, comprising the Southern Attack Group, were on their way to Sandnessjøen, almost exactly 100 miles down the coast from Bodø. For most of the pilots, this would be their first combat missions.†

The plan called for a low-level approach to avoid detection. A division of four Dauntlesses and a section of two Wildcats were detached from the northern group soon after passing the outer lighthouse at Myken, with orders to search a side lead north of Åmnøya. Almost immediately, at 0724, they found a good target, the large steamer *La Plata* in the outer fjord near Bolga Island.

Flying at 135(IAS) knots, at 50–100 feet . . . made landfall at Myken light, 18 miles from beginning of area to be searched.‡ Commenced slow climb, about 10 miles in from Myken light, to 1,500 feet . . . The detached division sighted target, LA PLATA at 0824 1/2 mile South of Aamno . . . and first section attacked following strafing runs by 4 VF . . . Mast head bombing attack delivered by two VB, bombing run at 200 knots, one release from sixty feet. Lt. (jg) Gordon reporting, 'I went in very close, so close in fact, I had to pull up severely to miss foremast.'§

Believing *La Plata* to be seriously damaged, the other two Dauntlesses retained their ordnance and all six aircraft flew north to rejoin the main strike.

---

* Cressman, *USS* Ranger, pp. 326–44.

† CV4, cover letter, pp. 1–2.

‡ IAS stands for Indicated Air Speed, the speed of an aircraft relative to the air it is passing through, as opposed to ground speed. For example, an aircraft flying at 200 knots IAS into a 20-knot headwind would have a ground speed of approximately 180 knots.

§ CV4, 1st Aircraft Action Report, p 4. The account in CV4 differs in many details from that in Cressman, *USS* Ranger; I have opted to follow CV4.

Operation LEADER was an air attack on shipping in the vicinity of Bodø, Norway, by Ranger's air group, CVG-4, 4 October 1943. The Northern Attack Group (NAG), Dauntlesses and Wildcats, found the steamer La Plata and attacked, but, as noted in this post-attack photograph, she was undamaged, although the fliers at the time thought otherwise. Note the painted-out national insignia on this Dauntless's upper right wing. This complied with instructions, issued in February 1943, to remove the roundels from the upper right and lower left wings. (NARA)

The main strike passed up several small fishing boats and finally coming upon a small convoy, identified by the fliers as comprising a large motor vessel, the coastal tanker *Rigmor* and a small escort variously described as a 'flakship' or a former Norwegian destroyer.* They were, in fact, the steamer *Kerkplein*, the tanker *Schleswig* and the small minesweeper *M365*. Two SBDs attacked *Kerkplein* and obtained one hit, and eight went after *Schleswig*, claiming two hits. Both ships were believed to be afire and sinking; one Wildcat was damaged by defensive fire, but managed to return to *Ranger*.†

The eight SBDs that still had bombs then proceeded to Bodø harbor. Four ships were attacked in the harbor, each by one section of two Dauntlesses: *Malaga* was near-missed for minor damage; the small steamer *Rabat* was sunk and *Cap Guir* badly damaged in the inner harbor; the fourth ship attacked was

---

* Flak is a German contraction of *Flugzeugabwehrkanone*, which literally means 'anti-aircraft gun'. The term was picked up and used by the British and Americans, and is still in common use today, though often to connote sharp criticism.
† Ibid, pp. 4–6.

The second attack by LEADER's *NAG, 4 October 1943, was on this small convoy of (left-to-right)* Schleswig, M365 *(a small minesweeper) and* Kerkplein. *The two larger ships were believed to have been hit and left in sinking condition, but neither was seriously damaged. (NARA)*

A bomb splashes just aft of the tanker Schleswig, *which was believed to be burning from a fire just forward of the after superstructure. While hit by at least one large bomb, she was not seriously damaged, 4 October 1943. (NARA)*

The main attack by Operation LEADER*'s NAG on 4 October 1943 was at Bodø harbor, where Dauntlesses hit and sank two small steamers and another was damaged by strafing by Wildcats. In this view, the sky seem to be full of SBDs and Wildcats, one of which is strafing the steamer at the bottom right, visible against the mountainous background only by the puffs of smoke left by its .50-cal mgs. (NARA)*

The steamer Topeka *was hit for damage by the Southern Attack Group (SAG) of Operation* LEADER, *4 October 1943. She was last seen like this, aground and giving off a heavy plume of white smoke, but she was in fact not seriously damaged. (NARA)*

Opposite, top: The larger steamer Malaga, *misidentified here as* Saar, *was near-missed for minor damage in Bodø harbor, 4 October 1943. (NARA)*

Opposite, below: One ship that was sunk in Operation LEADER *was* Vaagan, *caught by the SAG, and, though not hit, was near-missed with enough force to break her back, as seen here, 4 October 1943. (NARA)*

196

CV-4 SORTIE #7. 10-4-43. ALT.? 6·⅜" FL.
"SAAR", UNDER ATTACK IN BODO HARBOR, NORWAY.
NEW TYPE GERMAN M/V. APPROX. 3000 G.T.
SETTLING BY STERN WHEN LAST SEEN.

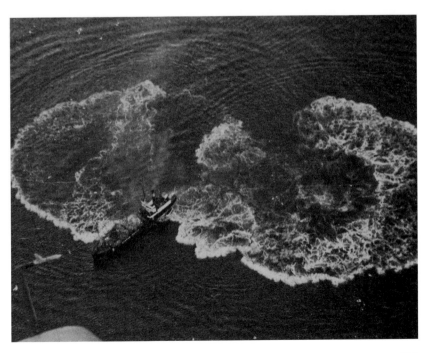

probably *Ibis*, a small steamer which was hit by machine gun fire. A Dauntless was damaged by defensive fire and hit the water at a steep angle; both airmen were killed. Another Dauntless was hit in the engine, but managed to make a safe water landing; the two crewmen were taken prisoner by the Germans.

Meanwhile, the Southern Attack Group made landfall. They found the steamer *Topeka* near Sandnessjøen, which was strafed and bombed by two Avengers despite her prominent Norwegian neutrality markings, leaving her beached and on fire. One of the attackers was shot down by anti-aircraft from the shore; the pilot was seen to bail out. Working their way north, they attacked the small Norwegian tanker *Vaagan* obtaining near misses sufficient to break her back. They attacked and ran aground the ferry-barge *F231* and then found and attacked *La Plata*, which had survived the initial attack with only minor damage. This time, she was hit with two bombs and left in sinking condition. So was the transport *Skramstad*, which was carrying over 800 soldiers, of which more than 200 were killed.[*] After this, all aircraft had expended their ordnance and were returning to *Ranger*.

Three German aircraft came snooping around *Ranger* around 1400, a pair of Ju 88 bombers and an He 115 reconnaissance floatplane. One of the bombers and the floatplane were splashed by *Ranger*'s CAP; the other bomber was not sighted and apparently turned back towards Bodø after seeing the reception the other two received.

It is difficult to assess how many of the dozen ships attacked by *Ranger*'s air groups were actually sunk, as a number of them had beached, which made their repair and return to service at least a possibility. It appears that *Vaagan*, *Cap Guir*, *Rabat*, *La Plata* and *Skramstad* were indeed sunk or damaged beyond repair, accounting for approximately 17,000 GRT of German shipping. The disruption caused to the enemy's coastal convoy system was probably more valuable than the actual loss of shipping.

— —

On 1 October 1943, the Allies captured Naples and the Foggia airfield complex on the eastern side of the Italian peninsula, which satisfied the objectives of AVALANCHE. Again there was uncertainty as to what should come next. The British, particularly Churchill, were terribly disappointed that this success was not immediately followed by more attacks. In particular, Churchill was incensed that the Italian-held Dodecanese islands had been allowed to fall to the Germans when the Italians surrendered.[†] He wanted to remain on the offensive in Italy, possibly even expanding the front to include Greece and the Balkans, even if that meant postponing the cross-Channel invasion until this and the pressure

---

[*]   CV4, 2nd Aircraft Action Report, pp. 1–4.

[†]   Churchill, *The Second World War: Closing the Ring*, pp. 329–32; Eisenhower, *Crusade in Europe*, p. 191.

One of the Luftwaffe aircraft that came looking for Ranger *was this unfortunate He 115 floatplane, which was splashed by a Wildcat of the carrier's CAP, 4 October 1943. (NARA)*

from the Russians caused the Germans to strip France of combat troops.[*] While Churchill was careful never to call for the outright cancellation of the cross-Channel invasion, now called Operation OVERLORD, he was not shy about expressing his desire that it be postponed until its success could be guaranteed. Nevertheless, when he and FDR met at Cairo in late November before proceeding together to meet with Stalin at Tehran, he reluctantly agreed that OVERLORD should proceed as planned in spring 1944. Nevertheless, he managed to win the postponement of the transfer of some landing craft and troops from the Mediterranean theater and the approval for another landing between Naples

---

[*]   Eisenhower, *Crusade in Europe*, pp. 194–5, 198–200.

and Rome to sidestep the strong German defenses north of Naples.

Even without this new landing, the needs of the forces already engaged in Italy meant that a steady stream of convoys were running to and from Naples. For the most part, the capture of the Foggia airfields and the construction of new fields in North Africa, Sardinia and Corsica meant the Allies could run these convoys with a relatively low risk of German interference. But low risk is not the same as no risk, and on occasion the Germans were able to make an effective attack on this traffic. One such occasion was on 6 November, when a force of Luftwaffe bombers took advantage of a lapse in Allied air cover to attack convoy KMF.25A off Cape Bougaroun, Algeria, approximately midway between Algiers and Tunis. The convoy comprised 26 merchantmen, escorted by an anti-aircraft cruiser (HMS *Colombo* (D89)), seven American destroyers (all *Benson-Gleaves* class), five Hunt-class escort destroyers (three Royal Navy and two Greek) and two American destroyer escorts (*Frederick C. Davis* (DE136) and *Herbert C. Jones* (DE137)). These last two were of some interest; they had departed Norfolk together on 7 October on their first combat assignments after spending some time in the hands of NRL where they were fitted with the prototype XCJ jammers that proved ineffective.

The Germans attacked in strength, an estimated 25 aircraft of two different types with three different weapons systems – Do 217Ks armed with 'Fritz X's and Hs 293s and Ju 88s armed with torpedoes. They attacked in small groups in a well-coordinate attempt to reach the convoy, which included nine troopships.[*]

The attack appears to have started a half-hour after sunset on the convoy's port quarter, where *Tillman* was stationed.

> . . . attack consisted of a glider bomb attack, aimed at this vessel, by 3 or 4 Dornier 217's, followed by torpedo attack in vicinity of JONES and PARKER by about 5 Junkers 88's, action ending with torpedo attack on this vessel by 5 Junkers 88's . . .
>
> About 1803A SC-1 radar picked up aircraft bearing 320° true, closing, director was matching up when almost simultaneously plane was sighted 325° true, 8,000 yards, identity not yet determined, but actions definitely not friendly . . . Ordered main and machine guns batteries to open fire . . . Machine guns were firing within a few seconds of sighting, before orders could be relayed. Range was hopelessly long but this battery provide quickest means of warning other units.[†]

In fact, it was this gunfire that gave *Beatty* (DD640), on the opposite quarter of the convoy, first warning of the attack.

> At 1803 machine gun fire was observed on the port hand of the convoy . . . A

---

[*]   DD640, 1st Endorsement, p. 1.

[†]   DD641, pp. 2–3.

number of small pips on the SG radar were observed in the vicinity of U.S.S. TILLMAN . . . She was seen to be firing and at 1804 1/2 a large caliber bomb was seen to explode close aboard her.[*]

Tillman indeed got a very close look at an Hs 293:

> About time main battery opened fire plane was identified as Dornier 217 and a glider bomb (type HS 293) was observed towing under and slightly aft of plane by what appeared to be a 10-15 foot connection. At this time ordered full left rudder to bring plane on bow. After a few seconds observed sparks of combustion coming from tail of glider after which it was apparently cut free . . . it appeared that this vessel was target; ordered engines emergency full, continuing swing to left with full rudder. Glider crept forward until under nose of aircraft, after which it turned sharply and headed direct for this vessel in a shallow glide at terrific speed . . . As glider straightened out, parent aircraft, under heavy 5" fire, turned sharply away. Bursts were coming very close when plane disappeared . . . the glider was taken under a terrific volume of fire by port machine guns. Beginning at a range of about 1,000 yards observed what were believed to be 20 mm hits on glider. At about 600 yards, when a hit on the ship seemed inevitable, the glider went into a steeper dive, crashed and exploded violently about 150–200 yards on the port bow.[†]

Even at this early date, it was known that the guide aircraft had to fly a straight and level course after launching a 'Fritz X' or Hs 293 to have any chance of hitting a target. By forcing the Do 217 to turn away, *Tillman* probably guaranteed that the bomb would miss, though her CO believed that the anti-aircraft fire also contributed to the splashing of the Hs 293.

Tillman had no chance to admire this achievement, because almost immediately, a second Do 217 was approaching off the port beam. This glide bomb passed ahead of the ship and was seen to turn back towards *Tillman*, crashing 150 yards off her starboard quarter. The guide aircraft was shot down, but only after the bomb hit the water. A third attack followed immediately; once again, the guide aircraft was forced to turn away by defensive fire and, once again, the Hs 293 fell short, apparently out of control.[‡] *Tillman*'s survival so far, was due to the effectiveness of her evasive maneuvering and to the density and accuracy of her defensive fire, which caused two of her three attackers to lose control of their bombs.

So far the attacks on the convoy had been by glider-bombs, which, while extremely powerful, proved difficult to use successfully against a small, well-defended target. Torpedoes were a different matter. *Beatty*, along with the rest of

---

[*]   DD640, p. 1.

[†]   DD641, pp. 3–4.

[‡]   DD641, p. 4.

the escort, had been ordered to make smoke, which factored into the subsequent action:

> At about 1805 at least two planes, showing American IFF, were observed by SC radar to be passing astern of the convoy* . . . One was tentatively identified as a JU 88 by control and in view the circumstances it was decided to disregard the IFF on low flying planes in a position to attack. By this time our smoke was drifting off to starboard and was low lying and dense. From the bridge the sector from 135° relative to dead astern was partially obscured . . . and the main battery director had very little visual sight in this direction. At about 1810 control picked up two planes dead astern about 10,000 yards by visual but before fire was opened these planes disappeared into the smoke.†

At the same time, radar showed five or six aircraft at 8,000 yards off the starboard beam. At 1811, two Ju 88s, possibly the same two seen before, briefly emerged from the smoke and then were lost to sight again. Radar tracked these aircraft as two passed ahead of *Beatty* and two more worked their way aft again. The picture only got more confusing:

> Almost at the same time fire was opened by all 20 mm guns on the starboard side at two JU 88s which appeared close aboard out of the smoke on the starboard quarter. These planes were not observed by the bridge until several seconds later when one was passing close aboard on the starboard side headed forward. The other turned away and flew into the smoke further from the ship than the first . . .
>
> About twenty or thirty seconds after fire was opened on the latter planes (probably about 1813) this ship was hit at frame 124 by a torpedo . . . The SC was tracking two planes on the starboard bow and a plane had just dropped a torpedo about 3,000 yards astern and this torpedo appeared to run in the direction of the convoy. This plane was lost track of in the subsequent excitement.‡

The 'excitement' in question was the result of the 250-kg warhead of an air-dropped F5B torpedo detonating against the starboard shell plating just aft of the bulkhead separating the after fire room and engine room. Both of those compartments flooded within a minute, but, even worse, the starboard shaft from the forward engine room was bent and the bulkhead between that compartment and the after fire room ruptured at the gland, leading to slow flooding of that engine room and the loss of all power. Despite the best efforts of

---

* IFF (Identification Friend or Foe) is an interrogation/response system that allows an aircraft with the appropriately encoded transponder to identify itself when illuminated by a friendly radar.

† DD460, pp. 1–2.

‡ Ibid, pp. 2–3.

the crew, the battle to keep *Beatty* afloat was lost; by 1825, it was determined that the keel was broken and the ship was sagging and listing to starboard. All crew were brought on deck preparatory to abandoning ship. Incredibly, 20 minutes later, the list had decreased and the ship appeared more stable, and, with the jettisoning of topside weights continuing, an attempt was made to restart one of the forward boilers. This proved impossible as there was water in the forward oil tanks and a fire could not be kept lit. After that, the ship's condition deteriorated slowly, but steadily. The fantail was abandoned at 2200 and the rest of the ship by 2230; *Beatty* broke in two and sank at 2305.[*]

Tillman was attacked by torpedo-carrying Ju 88s as well.

> At about 1814 . . . picked up a group of low flying planes at 325° true, 7,000 yards, closing slowly . . . began turning left with full rudder, all engines ahead emergency full. Main battery opened fire on these planes when visible, believe about 5,000 yards. At 3,000 yards backed port engine emergency full to swing ship as much on her heel as possible . . . Planes apparently launched torpedoes and turned to their right at 2,200 yards. At about 1818, with ship swinging hard left, two torpedo wakes passed down starboard side . . . About 20-30 seconds after wakes had passed a heavy explosion shook ship violently. This is believed to have been due to torpedo exploding in the wake, or possibly to a torpedo fired at longer range and exploding at end of it's run.[†]

Tillman was shaken again, but not damaged. There is no doubt that part of the reason why she survived, when *Beatty* did not, was due to the adroit shiphandling by her CO, Lieutenant Commander C. S. Hutchings, who handled his 1,630 t destroyer as if it were a speedboat. Eleven men died in *Beatty's* sinking. Two transports in the convoy were also torpedoed; one sank soon after, the other limped into the outer harbor of Philippeville (Skikda), Algeria, where she settled to the bottom.

— —

The least well-executed of the landing operations conducted in the Second World War was undoubtedly Operation SHINGLE, which put 36,000 Allied troops ashore at Anzio and Nettuno on the west coast of Italy south of Rome on 22 January 1944. Tactical surprise was achieved and might have cut off the German forces on the Winter Line in front of Cassino, but the general in charge, Major General John P. Lucas, took a week to organize the advance out of the beachhead and by then the Germans had the surrounding mountains well-defended and the breakout failed. Blame for this failure was placed on the general commanding the beachhead, as it should have been, but the entire operation was hastily prepared and poorly conceived from the beginning. When briefed on the final plans,

---

[*]   Ibid, pp. 3–7.

[†]   DD641, pp. 5–6.

General Eisenhower, who was preparing to take over planning for OVERLORD, stated his belief that the initial landing force would be insufficient and the post-landing build up too slow.[*] Sadly, his concerns proved well founded.

Whatever failures there were in the planning and execution of the land campaign, the US Navy's role of carrying the landing force to the beaches and supporting them as long as they remained within range of their naval rifles, was carried out with skill and bravery, even though fire support for the beachheads was required not for a few days, as had been the case in previous landings, but for more than four months.

The initial plan assumed that the two divisions being landed would be able to link up with General Clark's Fifth Army within a week, so supplies for seven days were to be landed, and naval support withdrawn after a week, as they were needed elsewhere to prepare for OVERLORD and for Operation DRAGOON, the planned landings in Southern France. When Lucas was told of this plan, he complained loudly enough that he was allocated enough LSTs to maintain supplies for 12 days, after which they would incrementally be withdrawn.[†]

Coming at the same time as another push by the Allies in the Cassino area, the actual landings on 22 January went smoothly, against only token resistance. Casualties on D-Day were remarkably small; the minesweeper *Portent* (AM106) sank after setting off a mine and *LCI20* was hit by a bomb dropped by a German fighter-bomber which passed through the landing craft and exploded beneath, blowing out her bottom. By the end of the day, 90 per cent of the men and materiel of the assault force were ashore, the towns of Anzio and Nettuno were captured and landings were deemed a success.[‡] The need for naval gunfire support on D-Day had been minimal.

Yet this successful start was not followed up, and the result was disastrous for all Allied forces involved, including naval forces. The next day saw more activity. *Brooklyn* used her 6-inch guns to break up an early morning counterattack. Numerous ships were near-missed by the inevitable Luftwaffe attacks, including *Brooklyn* and the minesweeper *Prevail* (AM107). Hits were obtained on *Plunkett* and on the Royal Navy hospital ship *St David* on 24 January. The former became the focus of persistent attacks starting at 1738. She was missed by a pair of glider-bombs and at least two torpedoes, but at 1757 was hit by a 250 kg bomb dropped by an Fw 190 fighter-bomber. This bomb exploded amidships and destroyed her after engine room, but she was able to limp to Palermo on her starboard engine. Twenty-three men were killed and 28 were never found. Three Royal Navy hospital ships were attacked, despite being marked and illuminated in accordance with the Hague Convention. *St David* was hit by a bomb and sank rapidly; fortunately, most of the casualties she was carrying were 'walking

---

[*] Eisenhower, *Crusade in Europe*, pp. 212–13; Morison, *History,* vol. IX, pp. 317–19.

[†] Morison, *History,* vol. IX, pp. 325–8.

[‡] Ibid, pp. 336–43.

One of the lessons learned by the time the Allies were ready to put troops ashore at Anzio, 22 January 1944, was not to attempt a pre-dawn landing. Having light sufficient to find the correct beaches was more important than any tactical surprise landing at night could gain. Here, a line of five YMS coastal minesweepers heads inshore as the setting sun sinks into low clouds and a hazy horizon. (NARA)

wounded' and were able to abandon ship and stay afloat until rescued. Later that evening, the destroyer *Mayo* (DD422) struck a mine while maneuvering off-shore; she survived, but suffered seven dead and 25 wounded.

Losses of that magnitude were expected and accepted as the price of landing troops closer to enemy airfields and further from one's own. What was clearly not expected was that losses at a low, but sustained level would continue not for a week, but for four months, as the troops remained pinned down within a shallow beachhead. But while some ships were damaged or sunk, others spent extended time off Anzio, witnessed the mayhem at close quarters, but seemed to lead a charmed life. One such was the destroyer *Ludlow*, which supported SHINGLE from D-Day through 8 February, when cumulative damage finally caused her to be sent Stateside for repair and refit:

January 24 – D plus 2 Day
    . . . At 1859 a heavy explosion was seen to the south of Fire Support Area Two and it was soon learned that the PLUNKETT was hit. On her call for assistance *LUDLOW* stood toward her in Fire Support Area Three while

An unidentified Benson-Gleaves-class *destroyer makes smoke during a Red Alert, meaning enemy aircraft had been detected, as seen from* Philadelphia, *22 January 1944. The black smoke was created by spraying oil into hot funnel gasses; the white smoke closer to the water was created by smoke generators at the destroyer's fantail. (NARA)*

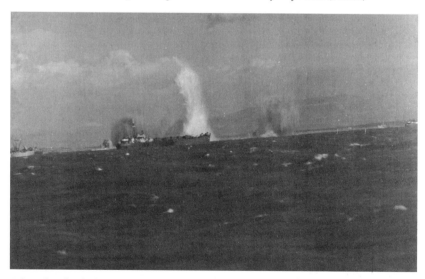

A huge bomb splash rises near the bow of a fully loaded LST as it approached the coast at Anzio, as seen from Frederick C. Davis (DE136), *22 January 1944. (NARA)*

Minesweeping was undoubtedly one of the most dangerous tasks facing an invasion fleet; small ships went in harm's way to clear a path for larger ships. Sometimes those small ships paid a price, as happened to the minesweeper Portent *(AM106), when she set off one of the mines she was sweeping off Anzio, 22 January 1944. NARA)*

The destroyer Mayo *(DD422) comes under fire from shore batteries a few minutes later, 22 January 1944, while* Portent's *bow (to the right) is all that can be seen of the minesweeper.* Mayo *would be hit by an aerial torpedo and seriously damaged two days later. (NARA)*

Biscayne *was a small seaplane tender that had been fitted out as an amphibious force command ship by forward forces at Mers-el-Kébir in April 1943, though she would not be redesignated as a command ship until October 1944. At Anzio, where she is seen in this view, 22 January 1944, she was flagship of Rear-Admiral Frank J. Lowry. The mottled appearance of the sky in this image is an artifact of the film development. (NARA)*

still laying smoke for the BROOKLYN. At 1815 a rocket bomb was seen approaching from east but it reversed course about a thousand yards away and was seen to hit on or near a lighted hospital ship standing out the swept channel . . .

January 26 – D plus 4 Day

. . . At 1151 received following coordinates from NLO 50, 090200. While getting into position to fire on this target the ship was attacked by three FW 190s. Three near misses resulted. Due to confined waters and no fighter cover it was decided to retire to Transport Area until cover could be obtained.

Target was not fired on during remainder of day due to constant Red Alerts and lack of spotting plane . . . At 1745 several rocket bombs were seen in the area. At 1757 one approached the ship and was taken under fire by 40mms. One rocket bomb while under fire from this ship and several others appeared to crash without exploding . . .

January 27 D plus 5 Day

. . . While retiring from Fire Support Area Five, 4 ME 109 fighters passed over area to attack beach. Planes were taken under fire at 0849 by 5"/38 guns and 11 rounds of AA common and 6 Mk. 32 shells were expended. One plane was seen to go into a shallow dive and crash on the beach . . .

January 29 – D plus 7 Day

... At 1739 while close to H.M.S. SPARTAN and DIDO during Red Alert, sighted six DO 217 to east of Anzio over assault beaches. Planes were fired on immediately. Several rocket bombs were seen to be released. At 1754 H.M.S. SPARTAN was hit and commenced burning. At 1756 another rocket bomb hit close astern with a tremendous explosion.* This bomb was under fire of LUDLOW's 40mms at the time ...†

On 30 January, *Ludlow* developed a serious steam leak caused by a failed cruising throttle valve gasket. She requested and was granted an availability at Naples to effect repairs. When it turned out that the facilities at Naples were insufficient to repair the casualty, she proceeded to Palermo, where she was under repair until 5 February, when she departed for return to Anzio. When she arrived the next morning, she found the situation on the ground, if anything, more dire than when she left and she was immediately assigned fire support targets well within reach of her 5-inch guns. For the next two days, *Ludlow* was far busier supporting the beachhead than she had been the seven days of her previous rotation. Even more alarming, she found herself coming under fire from shore batteries, which had not been true before.‡

February 7 – D plus 16 Day

... NLO 10 sent "Troops on the move at 088158". This target was taken under fire at 1043 and given one minute of rapid fire twice, expending eighty-eight rounds ... Throughout this firing a shore battery fired intermittently at this vessel but was always about 1,500–2,000 yards short ...

February 8 – D plus 17 Day

At 0815 NLO 50 requested a U.S. Destroyer to fire on an urgent target of troops and artillery near Ardea, Italy, as no British destroyer was available in that area.§ At 0840 LUDLOW entered Peter-Xray Channel for north-west Fire Support Area.¶ While enroute LUDLOW passed H.M.S. LAFOREY and Capt. D., 19th D.F. asked our mission and when informed, requested we return and close him in Xray anchorage.** He also said a British destroyer was

---

* HMS *Spartan* (C95) sank an hour and a half after being hit by a single Hs 293 which exploded in an engine room and touched off secondary explosions.

† DD438, pp. 2–6.

‡ Ibid, pp. 6–7. *Ludlow's* 5-inch/38 main battery guns had a maximum range of 17,500 yds/8.64 nm/9.94 miles firing common rounds from a gun with average barrel wear.

§ Ardea is a town 12 miles north-west of Anzio, just in from the coast, on the road to Rome. At this time it was still in German hands.

¶ 'Peter-Xray Channel' was a swept channel paralleling the coast that connected the American (Xray) beaches and the British (Peter) beaches.

** The CO of the Royal Navy's 19th Destroyer Flotilla – Capt (D) in RN parlance – was also SOPA (Senior Officer Present Afloat) for the fire support units.

One of the more interesting adaptations of the basic LST platform was its use as a flying-off ship for Army L-4 Grasshopper light liaison aircraft. LST16 is seen about to launch an aircraft off Anzio, 22 January 1944. (NARA)

available and would handle fire missions in Peter area. LUDLOW reversed course at 0917 to 148° T for Xray area. Speed at this time was five knots . . . At 0932 . . . LUDLOW was hit on director deck by what is estimated to have been a six-inch shell. Two others hit at the same time close aboard to port and exploded. The angle of fall was about 60° and the shell next hit the forward port bridge structure about 34" above the deck . . . One or two fragments remained inside the pilot house, one of which seriously wounded the commanding officer. The shell next hit the starboard twenty-millimeter ready box, bursting it wide open and carrying many of the loaded twenty-millimeter magazines with it into the Captain's cabin. Minor damage and fires resulted from these magazines, many of which exploded. The shell passed through the deck in the Captain's head . . . hitting the confidential locker in the wardroom passageway . . . the shell continued through the main deck . . . severing the firemain and drain to Captain's head . . . The collision bulkhead at frame #45 was penetrated four feet above the 1st platform deck into the scullery. The 1st platform deck was not penetrated and the shell was found spent and unexploded three feet from skin of the ship at frame #43, port side. Chief Gunner's Mate J. D. JOHNSON, USN, picked the shell up and carried it to the main deck, . . . where he threw it overboard. The shell . . . was almost wholly intact with the exception of the nose, which was later found in several large fragments in the after mess hall.*

---

* DD438, pp. 8–10. Morison, *History*, vol. IX, pp. 361–2 adds the detail that the shell passed between the CO's legs, burning him badly.

Plunkett (DD431) was hit amidships by a single 250 kg bomb dropped by a Ju 88 off Anzio, 24 January 1944. Despite losing an engine room and sustaining 51 casualties, she survived to navigate back to Palermo under her own steam. (NARA)

The fires were minor, but were difficult to fight due to the severed fire main. The shell punched holes in four decks and two bulkheads. It is easy to imagine how much worse it would have been had it exploded. The damage was sufficient to send *Ludlow* to Naples and then New York, after the facilities at Oran were found to be insufficient to effect repairs.

Throughout the month of February, the beachhead was under intense attack, at times appearing to be on the verge of being overrun, but by the end of the month the situation had stabilized and remained relatively static until late May, when the breaking of the German lines to the south allowed the troops in the Anzio beachhead to advance towards the north. The intervening period of almost four months saw a steady rotation of Allied warships in fire support and convoy protection roles off the beaches and south to Naples. For the most part, these duties were routine, but dusk air attacks were an almost daily event and attacks by U-boats and S-boats, while rarely successful, added further excitement.

One day stands out during that period as being particularly busy and dangerous. On 15 February, a Luftwaffe attack developed as usual after the fighter protection provided by Allied air forces departed at dusk. The first victim that

The stalemate around the beachheads at Anzio led to extended tours of fire support for naval units. Here, Brooklyn *fires at enemy positions at Cisterna on 30 January 1944, eight days after the landings. (NARA)*

evening, ironically, was *Herbert C. Jones*, which had been fitted with the improved XCJ-1 jammer, though it still required manual tuning and could be ineffective if multiple bombs were in the air at the same time. That appears to be what happened this evening. *Jones* was damaged when an Hs 293 near-missed; fortunately, the damage was not serious. That was not the case with a second glide-bomb, which hit the merchant steamer *Elihu Yale*, which was off-loading artillery shells into *LCT35* alongside. The bomb exploded in an empty hold, but the fire soon spread to the LCT, which blew up in a violent explosion, causing more damage to the freighter. The fires on *Yale* were eventually controlled and she remained afloat, but the damage was such that she was written off as a total loss.

When the troops massed at Anzio – eventually they comprised seven divisions, more than 150,000 men – finally advanced out of the beachhead on 23 May 1944, the need for naval support again increased. The light cruiser *Philadelphia*, along with the destroyers *Kendrick* (DD612) and *Laub* (DD613), approached the swept channel off Anzio well before dawn.

> Comdg officer had just settled with the navigator that course was to be changed to 037 into the channel at 0434 x Laub had been ordered to take station astern by TBS at 0425 in anticipation of entering in normal formation with one DD

The stalemate on the ground also meant that support fleets of transports and cargo ships spent more time in vulnerable anchorages off the coast, where they were subjected to nightly raids by the Luftwaffe. One victim of one such raid was the steamer Samuel Huntington *off Nettuno, hit by an Hs 293 rocket-boosted glide bomb on the night of 29 January 1944. She burned well past midnight and then exploded in this violent blast seen from* Herbert C. Jones (DE137), *ironically one of the ships equipped with jamming equipment meant to protect against such attacks. (NARA)*

ahead and one astern x At 0434 when TBS signal quote speed one five course zero three seven unquote was executed a DD was noted coming out of the dark to port at high speed x She was about 30 degs on port bow target angle approximately 40 degs x Distance was short x Comdg officer at first assented to execution of change of course to right but immediately thereafter changed the order to full left cma and followed with stop all engines x Back full x Back emergency full x Collision followed in less than a minute x Philadelphia bow struck the Laub on starboard side abaft number two stack at an angle of 30 degs x Philadelphia backed clear[*]

Laub's captain was not on the bridge at the time of the accident; a lieutenant had the conn. Rather than slowing to allow *Philadelphia* to pass ahead or circling to port, he attempted to circle to starboard which took his ship directly into the path of the cruiser. The only good thing was that neither ship was moving very fast and both were slowing at the time of impact. *Laub* was sliced open on her starboard side in way of her after engineering spaces, which immediately flooded. *Philadelphia*'s bow bent the starboard propeller shaft as well, which left the destroyer without power. Nevertheless, damage control on *Laub* was effective; flooding was limited to the after fire room and engine room and electric power was soon restored, keeping her pumps in operation. She took a 9° list to starboard, but counterflooding and jettisoning of topside weights reduced that to 5°. She had suffered two dead and four injured. *Laub* was towed to Naples and repaired there sufficiently to allow her to steam to Boston under her own power. She was back at Oran again on 2 December. *Philadelphia*'s bow was bent and her shell plating crumpled as far back as Frame 12, but she was not seriously damaged. She was repaired at Malta and was back in time to support DRAGOON in August.

The last fire support for the troops at Anzio was provided by the veteran destroyer *Kearny* on 3 June.

— —

One further incident from this period must be described, though it does not reflect well on the Allied services involved. Because the Allies feared the Germans might turn to the use of chemical warfare, as their situation grew more desperate, they decided it was necessary to bring some chemical weapons of their own into the theater. This decision was approved by FDR in August 1943, but remained a highly classified secret lest it provoke the very act it was supposed to counter. It was Allied policy that, as the front advanced, a quantity of chemical weapons follow close behind so that it might be available for prompt retaliation.[†]

Thus, in great secrecy, 1,350 t of bombs containing mustard gas were loaded on the Liberty ship *John Harvey* at Oran on 18 November 1943. The ship sailed two days later for Augusta, where the cargo was inspected and cleared for Bari,

---

[*] CL41-2, Enc D, pp. 1–2. In this excerpt, 'x' indicates a period to end a sentence and 'cma' means a comma.

[†] Atkinson, *The Day of Battle*, pp. 271–8. Most of this account comes from this source, but it should be noted that no two sources agree on the details of this incident. Much of the information on this incident was classified for many years after the war, and much misinformation circulated. The author has attempted to be very careful that this account at least approximates what actually happened.

the closest port on the Adriatic coast to the British Eighth Army then fighting along the Sangro River. On 2 December, the port was overcrowded and a large number of recently arrived cargo ships were parked stern-first at the outer mole awaiting their turn at a quay. These included *John Harvey*, which had arrived four days earlier. The harbor was well-lit that evening as the unloading of merchant ships continued into the night. There was no particular alert as the Luftwaffe had been largely inactive on the east side of the peninsula for some time. The port authority had been informed of the nature of *Harvey*'s cargo, but that information was restricted to only a few officers and no effort was made to expedite her unloading.

Therefore, it was against no significant opposition that a force of Ju 88 bombers came in from the north-east starting at 2030. The only opposition was anti-aircraft fire from individual ships in the harbor. A primary target was the line of ships berthed side-by-side along the outer mole. At least 14 ships were parked there, of which ten would be sunk by bombs or by secondary explosions caused by fire that spread across the harbor, fed by fuel oil from a broken pipeline. The raid was over in less than half-an-hour.

It is likely that *John Harvey* was not hit during the raid, but, with burning, sinking ships on either side and fire all around her, she exploded soon after the Germans left, an explosion strong enough to break windows miles inland. Much of the mustard gas, actually dichlorethyl sulphide, a liquid that vaporizes slowly, was burnt off in the explosion, but the rest dissolved in the oil coating the harbor, which splashed over ships and quays not damaged directly by the air raid. As many as a thousand men died that night from the explosions, burns or drowning; at least 16 ships were sunk and another seven badly damaged. Symptoms of mustard gas poisoning began to appear within hours – skin blisters, swollen eyelids, vomiting and respiratory distress – getting worse and more prevalent during the next day. Sadly, because knowledge of the gas was restricted, triage nurses and doctors treating the many wounded turned first to men with serious injuries, leaving for later many less injured men covered with the mustard-saturated oil. It was only the next day that doctors at military hospitals began to suspect gas poisoning. By then, men were dying of the effects. The official reports list 617 cases of gas poisoning and 83 confirmed deaths, but it is generally agreed that this was a very low estimate. Additionally, an unknown number of Italian civilians were affected by the fumes that spread from the harbor until dispersed during the night.

The cover-up began immediately, when a meeting of British and American officers at the port met the day after the attack and agreed that the presence of poison gas at the port should continue to be kept secret. Yet the secret was impossible to contain completely. For example, two Royal Navy escort destroyers – HMS *Zetland* (F59) and *Bicester* (F134) – escaped from Bari soon after the raid and showed up at Taranto the next day unable to navigate the entrance channel because both bridge crews had been blinded by effects of the gas. Rumors spread that the Germans had dropped chemical bombs on the harbor. German radio accurately reported the incident. Within a month, the US officially admitted that there had been an accidental release of a small amount of mustard gas, but claimed that there had been no injuries due to the gas. This remained the official line in the US for the next 16 years. For example, Eisenhower, in his postwar memoirs, stated:

> One of the ships was loaded with a quantity of mustard gas, which we were always forced to carry with us because of the uncertainty of German intentions in the use of this weapon. Fortunately the wind was offshore and the escaping gas caused no casualties.[*]

Churchill ordered all references to mustard gas be deleted from all public records. The US finally declassified records of the event in 1959. The British agreed to pay retroactive pensions to sailors injured by the gas only in 1986.

---

[*] Eisenhower, *Crusade in Europe*, p. 204. Morison, *History,* vol. IX, p. 319, has an almost identical two-sentence statement.

7

Assaulting Fortress Europe
August 1942–April 1945

The movement of American forces to Great Britain had started before the US officially entered the war, but it was only in the second half of 1943, with the U-boat threat in the North Atlantic contained and the industrial capacity of the US approaching its full potential, that the training, equipping and transporting of the massive numbers of men needed to invade continental Europe began in earnest. The arrival of Eisenhower in London in mid-January 1944 to take command of OVERLORD was a major milestone.

Under the codename Operation BOLERO, the build-up of American land and air forces in Great Britain specifically for the invasion of France had been underway since April 1942. The initial planning for a major cross-Channel invasion in spring 1943 (Operation ROUNDUP), called for the transport across the Atlantic of a million US troops and their equipment. These included the men and aircraft for 38 bomber groups and 17 fighter groups. When it became obvious to the Americans in late summer-early fall 1942 that ROUNDUP would not occur in 1943, the pace of BOLERO was slowed, both to allow forces to be accumulated for TORCH and for the landings at Tarawa towards the end of November, which marked the beginning of Nimitz's drive across the Central Pacific.

Active planning for ROUNDUP, which became OVERLORD, began in earnest with the establishment of COSSAC (Chief of Staff to the Supreme Allied Commander) in March 1943. Lieutenant General F. E. Morgan, RA, who served in this post for almost ten months before the Supreme Allied Commander was named, oversaw the creation of the initial three division plan for landing on the north coast of the Calvados region of Normandy. This plan would be chewed over countless times, both before and after Eisenhower took over as Supreme Allied Commander. It eventually became a plan involving the simultaneous landing of five infantry divisions, along with three airborne divisions, on and behind five beaches stretching almost 50 miles.* Eight more divisions were ready

---

* The total forces landed or dropped on 6 June equalled eight divisions, though some were composite division-sized forces.

to follow immediately across the approximately 85 nm separating the southern coast of England from the Normandy beaches. All that remained was the final training of the landing forces and the setting of a date for D-Day.

D-Day for OVERLORD had been tentatively set for 1 May 1944 at the Quadrant Conference in August 1943, but this was postponed a month in early 1944 when Eisenhower and Montgomery, who had been selected to command the landing forces, both demanded that the initial three-division landing force be increased. The exact date and timing of the landings became the subject of sometimes rancorous disagreement between land and naval commanders. The ground force commanders wanted the landings to take place at high tide, because the beaches were wide and gently sloping, so that the difference between high and low tide meant an extra hundred yards or more of open beach to be covered before finding the shelter of the coastal bluffs. The naval commanders, however, insisted that the landings take place at low tide, so that the numerous beach obstacles would be exposed and could be avoided by landing craft drivers. This argument carried the day because any significant loss of landing craft in the initial phases would doom the follow-up to failure. A moon more than half-full was needed to provide light for the paratroopers, who would be dropped during the early morning hours well before dawn. The days in June on which low tide would come approximately 90 minutes before dawn along with a bright moon were the 5th to the 7th, with the 18th to the 20th as a second option should bad weather make the landings impossible at the beginning of the month.

Compared to the landing beaches used for the three Italian landings, these beaches were far more suitable, with a gentle slope – often as little as one foot rise per hundred feet – and firm sand in most places. Behind the beaches were, in order, a shingle slope a few feet high composed of smooth stones, a flat shelf and then sandy bluffs as much as 90 feet high. A small number of gaps in the bluffs, called 'draws', offered exit off the beaches, but these were where German defenses were concentrated. On some beaches, there were short sections of wood and concrete seawall as much as 12 feet high, built before the war to reduce beach erosion. The westernmost of the beaches, Utah Beach, had tidal ponds between the shingle and the bluffs with only a few narrow passages between the ponds. The two American airborne divisions were dropped behind Utah Beach specifically to capture and hold these crossings until the infantry could relieve them.

Eisenhower and his staff were well aware of the difficulties experienced at Salerno and particularly at Anzio and hoped that the much more favorable topography, without high mountains only miles from the beaches, would benefit the Allies. They were also well aware of the fiasco at Dieppe in August 1942. There, some 6,000 men, mostly Canadian but including a small contingent of American Rangers, had been put ashore on the French coast south of the Pas de Calais. The plan was to hold the small port at Dieppe for about 18 hours and withdraw with

Slapton Sands is a stretch of beach on the south coast of Devon that bore an uncanny resemblance to UTAH *Beach, the westernmost of the five beaches chosen for the Normandy landings. It had a shingle bench backed by tidal pools with narrow crossings between bench and coastal bluffs. It is not surprising that this location was chosen as the site of landing exercises, such as that seen here, with troops and vehicles landing from LCI(L)s and LCTs. All that was lacking was the urgency caused by enemy fire. Part of that was supplied by German S-boats, which sank two LSTs and damaged another during one such exercise early on 28 April 1944. (NHHC)*

all forces and equipment intact. From the beginning, the exercise was a tragic series of blunders: the pre-assault intelligence was inadequate and sometimes completely wrong; the British did a poor job of disguising the preparations, as a result of which the Germans knew when and where the attack was coming; offshore gunfire support was sporadic and inadequate; inexperienced landing craft operators often put troops ashore on the wrong beaches; air support was at the extreme limit of the short-ranged RAF fighters; armor support was late in arriving and often bogged down on the beaches. With all these problems, it is not surprising that the raid was a disaster, with over 3,500 ground troops killed or captured. Warship losses included a destroyer and 33 landing craft. The RAF lost over 100 aircraft, the Luftwaffe less than 50.

To assure maximum realism in the preparation of the assault troops, several training beaches were identified in southern England where troops could come ashore in landing craft and face topography similar to the Normandy beaches. Beach obstacles, minefields and pillboxes were emplaced, at least in simulated form. The primary American training beach was at Slapton Sands on Start Bay on the western side of Lyme Bay on the Devon coast. This location had been selected because of its similarity to the topography of Utah Beach, with a shingle bench backed by tidal pools. Several exercises were held there in the spring of 1944. One, Exercise TIGER, scheduled to run from 22 April to 30 April, went terribly wrong. The initial 'landings' had been carried out successfully on 27

The forces gathering for the OVERLORD landings assembled off the English Channel coast, 2 June 1944. Among the capital ships visible are Arkansas *(left) and* Texas *(BB35). (NARA)*

April, as the whole 'alphabet soup' of landing craft sailed from Devon ports and after a simulated shore bombardment, landed their troops.* The trouble started that night, when a follow-up convoy of eight LSTs carrying troops and vehicles of the American 1st Engineer Brigade left Plymouth and Brixham and began maneuvering outside Start Bay so they would be in position to land at dawn. Cover for these ships was provided by the local Royal Navy district commander. There were supposed to have been two escorts, a Flower-class corvette – HMS *Azalea* (K25) – sweeping ahead of the convoy, and a destroyer close aboard, but the destroyer originally assigned this duty had been damaged the day before and was unavailable. A replacement – HMS *Saladin* (H54) – received orders late and was well to the south at 0130 when sporadic gunfire broke out astern of the convoy. *LST507*, the last of the eight LSTs, in line-ahead and steaming at a leisurely 3½ knots, had sighted a German S-boat and had taken it under fire.

That there were S-boats about that night should have come as no surprise. The Allies knew there were two flotillas of the fast torpedo boats based at Cherbourg, at the tip of the Cotentin Peninsula, barely 85 nm south-east of Lyme Bay, and that they regularly sortied on nights when the weather was

---

* Morison, *History*, vol. XI, pp. 65–6; Whitley, *German Coastal Forces*, p. 71; *The Exercise Tiger National Foundation*; Crapanzano, *World War II Oral History*.

The beach obstacles awaiting the landing craft along the Normandy coast included posts topped with contact mines as are seen to the right in this image, driven into the sand at an angle to a height that would be just covered at high tide, the presumed timing for an invasion attempt. The ramps further up the beach, which would also be submerged at high tide, were intended to capsize landing craft that ran up on the sloped rail.

calm and visibility was good, as was the case this night. More specifically, the Royal Navy had received a warning from their standing patrol off Cherbourg that S-boats had been seen leaving the harbor. In fact, nine S-boats departed at 2200 and set a course straight for Lyme Bay at full speed (36 knots). Even after the brief exchange of gunfire at 0130, which died out quickly and caused no damage, the convoy remained in the same formation at same speed, and *Azalea* maintained her position ahead of the convoy, even though the firefight had broken out astern.

The S-boats took a half-hour to organize a co-ordinated attack. It started when, at 0204, a single torpedo hit *LST507* in way of her auxiliary engine room, breaking the ship's back; power was knocked out, and, with no pressure on the firemains, the ship was soon engulfed with flames and had to be abandoned. A number of the soldiers jumped overboard with their combat packs, which dragged them under before they could release them. A few minutes later *LST531* was hit by two torpedoes; she rolled over and sank within six minutes. At 0228, while exchanging fire with several of the S-boats, *LST289* was hit by a single torpedo, but maintained power and was able to make port the next day. Another LST was hit by 'friendly fire' causing minor casualties. More than 600 soldiers and sailors died that night due to the torpedo attacks; the S-boats fled at high speed when they began receiving intense gunfire from the remaining LSTs.[*]

---

[*]   Morison, *History*, vol. XI, says 638 died in the 'Battle of Lyme Bay'; Crapanzano, *World War II Oral History* says 639; a letter from the US Secretary of the Navy dated 30 March 2011 at *The Exercise Tiger National Foundation* gives the figure 749.

Three additional Royal Navy destroyers arrived on the scene in time to help rescue survivors.

The mass of ships allocated to OVERLORD was unprecedented, as should be expected given the size of the 'over-the-beach' sealift planned, not only on D-Day, but over the weeks or even months it would take to procure adequate harbor facilities. The landings at Utah Beach had been added to the plan specifically to facilitate the rapid capture of Cherbourg, although it was understood that the port facilities there, even if they could be captured relatively intact, would not be adequate to handle the volume of supplies needed by Allied armies in France. The strategic plan for the breakout from the Normandy beachhead called for an immediate pivot on Caen and a drive to the north-east with the goal of capturing Antwerp, the only port along the lower North Sea coast of Europe with the capacity to handle the necessary volume. It was hoped that Antwerp would be captured before winter, but clearing the approaches and repairing what was expected to be significant destruction might take several additional months.

But even before Cherbourg could be captured, much less brought to full operating capacity, the armies would need harbor facilities where cargo ships, as opposed to landing ships, could be unloaded in all but the worst weather. To solve this problem, a proposal was generated in mid-1943 by COSSAC to create artificial harbors that could be constructed in England, towed across the Channel and positioned as needed.* The eventual project, presented and approved at the Quadrant Conference, was a complex scheme involving blockships, gigantic floating caissons, pontoon causeways and four-legged pierheads that could be raised and lowered to follow the tides, which can rise and fall 20 feet twice a day along the Normandy coast. This massive project was given the codename MULBERRY, and proved one of the great successes of OVERLORD.

As the first set of potential D-Days in June approached, weather became the main concern. Storms are possible in the English Channel in any month and, in those narrow waters, are notoriously dangerous with high winds and heavy surf. When Eisenhower met with his meteorologists before dawn on 4 June, some of the landing craft with the longest distances to travel, those coming from ports in southern Wales, Essex and Suffolk, were already at sea.† One minesweeping unit was only 35 nm from the French coast when recalled. When the forecast called for a day of high wind and rain, the landings were reluctantly postponed a day and the landing craft at sea ordered back to their ports with orders to refuel and sail again anticipating landings on the following day. The total cost of the one postponement was one American LCT that foundered. The local weather the next morning, 5 June, was no better but the weathermen predicted a 36-hour

---

* Churchill, *The Second World War: Closing the Ring*, pp. 72–5; Morison, *History,* vol. XI, pp. 24–7. The idea for the adjustable pierheads seems to have originated as early as spring 1942.
† Eisenhower, *Crusade in Europe*, pp. 249–50; Morison, *History,* vol. XI, pp. 80–2.

Most of the troops riding this LCVP towards Omaha Beach, the most hotly contested of the five landing beaches on D-Day, 6 June 1944, were very 'green', and seem lightly equipped with M1 carbines and M1903 Springfield bolt-action rifles. (USA)

window of calmer weather would start the next morning, and the decision was made to proceed with the invasion of France on 6 June 1944.

This was a courageous decision with significant risks should the forecast be wrong, or even if it was right and storms returned the afternoon of 7 June and prevented resupply and reinforcement of the invasion forces. Against this Eisenhower weighed the 'costs' of waiting, which included the erosion of morale and the ever-present risk that Germans would get wind of what was going on. Adding to this was the warning by Admiral Sir Bertram Ramsay, overall naval commander, that another postponement would require at least 48 hours for the fleet to 'reset', which in effect meant a delay until 18 June at the earliest. The decision to go was reached quickly and was unanimously supported.* That it succeeded was clearly a case of Fortune smiling on the bold.

Operation NEPTUNE was that part of OVERLORD involved with cross-Channel transport and naval beachhead support. The force that sailed on 4 and 5 June was the largest armada ever assembled. Almost 7,000 vessels, anything seaworthy enough to carry weapons, troops or supplies across the Channel or from ship

---

* Morison, *History,* vol. XI, pp. 80–2.

On D-Day, Texas *shelled the bluff at Pointe-du-Hoc, just west of Omaha Beach. This was the site of a suspected German shore battery that was assaulted by US Army Rangers in a daring climb up a near-vertical cliff face, 6 June 1944. (NARA)*

to shore, were put to use. Of those vessels, more than half were landing craft, almost evenly split between American and British, though about half of the British landing craft were American-made. Of the remaining ships, over 800 were chartered cargo ships and more than 1000 were miscellaneous small craft, meaning there were somewhat more than 1200 warships in sizes ranging from trawlers to the six battleships (three American and three British) assigned to provide fire support.

Rear-Admiral Alan G. Kirk was CTF122, the Western Naval Task Force responsible for transporting and supporting the 1st US Army (Lieutenant General Bradley). TF125, the Utah Beach assault force, besides the landing craft and transports, comprised a large minesweeper group, an escort group of seven destroyers and assorted anti-submarine craft and Rear-Admiral Morton L. Deyo's Bombardment Group. This latter comprised the battleship *Nevada* (BB36), the monitor HMS *Erebus* (F02), heavy cruisers *Tuscaloosa, Quincy* (CA71), HMS *Hawkins* (I86), light cruisers HMS *Enterprise* (D52) and *Black Prince* (C81), along with the Dutch gunboat *Soemba*, eight American destroyers and two destroyer escorts. A truly eclectic group, these included a Pearl Harbor survivor (*Nevada*), a new-construction heavy cruiser carrying on the name of

Pearl Harbor veteran Nevada *(BB36) shells enemy concentrations behind Utah Beach, as seen from* Quincy *(CA71), 6 June 1944. (NARA)*

an Atlantic veteran lost at Savo Island (*Quincy*) and a new anti-aircraft cruiser (*Black Prince*) along with assorted older ships well suited to relatively static duty.

TF124, the Omaha Beach support force, was similarly constructed and included a Bombardment Group under Rear-Admiral C. F. Boyer that comprised battleships *Texas* and *Arkansas*, light cruisers HMS *Glasgow* (C21), *Bellona* (C63), *Montcalm* and *Georges Leygues* – the latter two French – nine American destroyers and three British Hunt-class escort destroyers.

Following a carefully orchestrated plan, all the support ships arrived in position off their assigned beaches at approximately 0230 and then waited patiently for 'call fire' assignments or to return fire from shore batteries. Unlike previous invasions, the preliminary bombardment was primarily delivered by waves of medium and heavy bombers and, for a while, all the bombardment groups could do was watch the 'terrific air bombardment in progress'.* *Nevada* did not note any shore battery fire off Utah Beach until 0515 and no fire close to any ship until *Forrest* (DD461) was near-missed at 0534 and returned fire.

The plan was to start the naval bombardment at 0550, 22 minutes before sunrise and 40 minutes before the troops were to hit the shore, but *Nevada* started up three minutes early because shore batteries were already pouring

---

*   BB36-1, Enc A, p. 6. This was in the entry for 0230 on 6 June 1944.

Passing Arkansas's *bow is a 'Rhino' tug pulling a 'Rhino' ferry (RHF5) loaded with 'SeaBee' (CB – Construction Battalion) equipment, 6 June 1944. (NARA)*

One of the ubiquitous DUKWs passes Arkansas's *bow fully loaded, heading towards Omaha Beach, 6 June 1944, while an empty LCVP heads in the other direction. (NARA)*

Four LCMs and an LCI (LCI323) towing a barrage balloon head towards the beach while an LCT heads out for another load, 6 June 1944. (NARA)

'Rhino' ferries, such as RH7 seen here on D-Day, 6 June 1944, were six pontoon units wide and were self-propelled, compared to the two unit barges seen earlier. They were used to carry vehicles from LSTs that grounded well away from shore. (NARA)

227

A pair of 'Rhino' ferries – RHF2 in the foreground and RHF18 in the middle – struggle in the surf off one of the Normandy beaches, June 1944. A petrol barge is behind the two ferries, and an LCM behind it. Dozens of other landing craft and transports form the background. (USA)

sustained and accurate fire on the invasion fleet. At 0545, *Nevada*'s log reported a landing craft hit 1,000 yards astern and a Coast Guard cutter capsized on her port bow.[*] A more spectacular incident occurred 25 minutes after H-Hour:

> 0655 U.S.S. CORRY observed hit by shells from shore batteries and enveloped in cloud of smoke.
>
> . . .
>
> 0714 CORRY reported she was under fire from target No, 86. Other support ships ordered to take target No. 86 under fire.
>
> 0718 CORRY sinking.[†]

As seen from *Corry*, the destruction was sudden and devastating. Her action started when she arrived at her assigned fire support position, Station 3 opposite the town of St-Marcouf, at approximately 0600. This position was 4,000 yards

---

[*] BB36-1, Enc A, p. 7. There was no Coast Guard cutter sunk that day; the ship seen capsized off *Nevada*'s bow was probably PC1261, hit by German gunfire at 0532 off Utah Beach. She rolled on her side, but remained visible for several hours.

[†] Ibid., p. 8.

Corry (DD463) was a victim of a mine or German shore battery fire, 6 June 1944, or possibly both. Regardless, her back was broken, and she settled on the shallow bottom with her bow and stern initially visible above the water. (George K.S. Hardy via uss-corry-dd463.com)

off the coast, in a narrow swept channel between the rocky Îles St-Marcouf and the beach.[*] *Corry* and the destroyer *Fitch*, at the next position to the north, were taken under accurate fire by a battery of three 210 mm guns at Crisbecq.

> . . . After approximately 15 minutes of firing counter battery fire, firing was commenced on assigned numbered targets adjacent to the beachhead. While firing on these numbered targets, batteries previously assumed to be silenced resumed firing on this vessel. Rapid continuous fire was then reopened on the principal battery firing on this vessel and evasive movements were used within the confines of the assigned fire support station. At approximately H-hour, CORRY was hit by a salvo of two or three 8″ projectiles that detonated in the engineering spaces and broke the keel, causing the immediate flooding of one engineroom, one fire room, the subsequent flooding of the other fire room, and the breaking in half of the vessel. An attempt was made to clear the area to estimate damage but all electric power was lost, and the rudder was jammed, causing the ship to go in a circle until stopped. When the main deck was awash word was given to prepare to abandon ship, and then followed a few minutes there-after by the word to abandon ship.[†]

This is a clear account of the sinking of a ship caught in a position where effective maneuvering was impossible, hit by large caliber shells from a well-protected shore battery and lost within minutes with six dead, 16 missing and another 33 injured. Not all of those men died in the initial explosion; while the ship was being abandoned, a shell appears to have hit the smoke generator on *Corry*'s fantail, unleashing a noxious cloud of white smoke that sickened some

---

[*]   These islets were in fact the first French territory seized on D-Day, being occupied by two squadrons of US cavalrymen, totaling 132 men, at 0430 on 6 June 1944.

[†]   DD436-1.

of the survivors in the water and obscured the sinking ship from both enemy and friendly eyes, delaying rescue efforts by *Fitch* and *Hobson* (DD464).[*]

However, by the time the official loss report of *Corry* was filed 13 days after the event, the cause of the loss had been changed.

    (6)   At about H minus 20 minutes, smoke screens were laid so completely by planes that all vessels in force UNIT appeared to be screened very effectively except the CORRY . . .

    (7)   Immediately after the laying of the smoke screen, at about H minus 15 minutes, fire was concentrated on this vessel. The anchor was lifted from short stay and abrupt maneuvers were commenced to throw off salvos, by giving ahead flank speed, stop, backing, right full rudder, and left full rudder, giving due regard to the reefs which extended nearly the entire seaward side.

    . . .

    (9)   At 0633 (H plus 3 minutes) this vessel hit a mine under the engineering spaces that caused the immediate flooding of the forward engineroom, the forward fire room and the flooding of the after fire room very shortly thereafter.[†]

The reason for changing the cause of the sinking was addressed at the end of the report:

3.   Because of the fact that just prior to H hour, the ship was being heavily fired upon by shore batteries, emitting large flashes, it was believed for a long time that the cause of the fatal damage of the ship was a salvo of heavy caliber projectiles. However, as a result of the review of the concussion effect throughout the ship and the revelation of the fact that practically every man on the ship was thrown from his feet regardless of the location of his battle station, it is now fully believed that the major damage was due to a mine and that the shelling received simultaneously and shortly thereafter resulted in merely incidental damage.[‡]

Before D-Day was over, all five landings were safely established; Omaha Beach had proved the toughest, but even there, the assault troops had cleared the

---

[*] The white chemical smoke made by the smoke generators located right aft on American destroyers was produced from titanium tetrachloride ($TiCl_4$), which hydrolyzes in damp air to form a fog of droplets of titanium oxychloride and hydrochloric acid. While not immediately toxic, the smoke is highly irritating to eyes and skin and can cause breathing difficulties. It is not known how many of *Corry*'s casualties were the result of breathing the chemical smoke.
[†] DD463, p. 3.
[‡] Ibid., p. 10. In itself, it is not unusual for a final loss report to differ from preliminary reports, but many of *Corry*'s surviving veterans are unconvinced that her loss was caused by a mine; cf. http://www.uss-corry-dd463.com.

During a lull in the action on D+1, 7 June 1944, sailors on Arkansas *relax, going so far as to toss around a medicine ball (left). The sentiment scrawled on the top of turret No.2 and on the barrels of that turret's two 12-inch guns, no doubt sums up the attitude of the entire crew: 'YOU NAME IT BOSS, WE'LL HIT IT' (on the turret top) and 'HITLER'S', 'DOWNFALL' (on the gun barrels). (NARA)*

landing beach and began to move inland by nightfall. The Canadian and British forces that had landed at Gold, Sword and Juno Beaches had linked; The two American landings at Utah and Omaha Beaches were still isolated footholds at the end of the first day. Besides *Corry* and *PC1261*, American losses on D-Day included 18 landing craft lost to mines (one LC(FF), 12 LCTs and five LCI(L)s), three lost to shore battery fire (one LCT and two LCI(L)s), two LCTs which ran aground and one which was swamped and sank. The many losses to mines were due to the density of the German minefields and the fact that they had laid a variety of mine types, including magnetic, contact, delayed-action magnetic and the new air-droppable pressure mines – the so-called 'oyster' mines set off by the change in water pressure caused by a ship steaming as slowly as five knots – so that a single sweep of an area would not necessarily clear all mines. Additionally, starting on the night after D-Day, the Germans planted new mines from aircraft and S-boats.

The Germans attempted to attack the invasion fleet with the relatively meager naval forces they had available. That night three torpedo boats from Le Havre approached the Royal Navy's eastern patrols and managed to sink the Norwegian-manned destroyer *Svenner*. Two S-boat flotillas sortied from Cherbourg and claimed the sinking of an LST and an LCT against the loss of two S-boats in a minefield laid by Royal Navy MTBs off Cap Barfleur.[*] In fact, there were no losses to German action that night west of the landing beaches.

There were still many targets within range of naval gunfire when the sun rose on D+1, and still many German shore batteries able to hit back at the fire support groups. *Jeffers*, off Utah Beach, was near-missed at 1955 by a shell that exploded in way of her forward engine room, perforating her hull plating with shell fragments and causing some casualties.[†] *Harding* (DD625) received minor damage when she grounded while support US Army Rangers off Pointe du Hoc. Mines continued to take a toll, sinking the minesweeper *Tide* (AM125), the transport *Susan B. Anthony* (AP72) and three LCTs. *Anthony* was carrying a full load of troops towards Omaha Beach when she struck a mine that flooded two holds and started fires in her engineering spaces. She sank in two hours; amazingly, no one was killed and only 45 wounded from among her passengers and crew. S-boat attacks that night claim the sinking of *LCI(L)105* and an LCT. (*LCI(L)105* was a Lend-Lease craft in Royal Navy service.)

The next day, D+2 (8 June 1944), saw a spike in US Navy casualties as the German response intensified. Soon after midnight, the Germans attacked with glide-bombs. As seen from *Jeffers*, the action centered on the ships near Utah Beach:

> At about 0125, a guided missile was observed overhead, altitude approximately 5,000 feet, headed in general vicinity of UTAH beaches. At 0130 another guided missile passed about 1500 feet overhead and was seen to strike the water approximately 3000 yards from JEFFERS. At 0150 the ship fired . . . at a HE-177 passing overhead at altitude of approximately 2000 feet; apparently no damage to plane resulted. At 0201 MEREDITH, occupying position on DIXIE Line Screen about one mile north-west of JEFFERS, was hit by the third (and last) guided missile seen by this ship's personnel.[‡] Unmistakable transmissions by parent aircraft were heard on these three occasions, and the ARQ operators jammed each transmission.[§]

The AN/ARQ-8 jammer was a small transmitter intended for installation in aircraft and small ships. *Nevada* had the larger and more sophisticated CXGE, and recorded multiple Hs 293 control signals:

---

[*]   Whitley, *German Coastal Forces*, p. 72; Rohwer, *Chronology of the War at Sea 1939–1945*, p. 331.

[†]   BB36-1, Enc A, p 15; DD621, p. 3.

[‡]   The Dixie Line was a screen of destroyers and other escorts paralleling the shore outside of the transport areas, providing anti-submarine and anti-S-boat protection.

[§]   DD621, p. 4.

Another victim of German action, probably an Hs 293 glide bomb, was Meredith *(DD726), seen here in happier days, while working up in Massachusetts Bay, 31 March 1944. She was initially damaged on 8 June 1944 off Utah Beach. She broke in two and sank the next day after being near-missed by another bomb. (NARA)*

Guided Missile Counter Measures:

. . . nearly all of the enemy control signal interceptions occurred during the early morning hours, at times when visibility was very good with clear sky and a bright moon. Apparently no flares were used in connection with radio controlled bomb attacks on this or nearby ships.[*]

As seen from *Nevada*, it was obvious a major attack by German glide bombs was underway that night and *Meredith* (DD726) was not the only target:

0034-0227   Intercepted and jammed 17 guided missile control signals.

. . .

0210   Four small flashes followed by vapor trails observed.[†] Strong guided missile signals being jammed. Heavy bomb struck about 500 yards from HMS BLACK PRINCE and 1000 yards from NEVADA.

0211   MEREDITH reported struck by bomb and requiring assistance . . .[‡]

From up close, the devastation was immense:

---

[*]   BB36-1, Part V, p. 2.

[†]   These flashes and smoke/vapor trails were characteristic of the Hs 293, whose rocket booster fired for 10 seconds.

[‡]   BB36-1, Enc A, p. 17.

6. A violent explosion shook the ship, appeared to lift her up and throw her forward. A huge geyser of water drenched the entire forward part of the ship and falling debris rained upon the open bridge area . . . There was a total absence of any flash, smoke or flame from this explosion. As the cloud of water settled only steam rushing from the after stack area was evident and this subsided rapidly. The explosion appeared to have occurred deep down in the ship on the port side amidships. It vented itself upward and outward on the main deck and the ship's side over the After Fire room. All power and lighting was lost immediately; the ship stopped dead in the water, turning slowly to starboard . . .

. . .

8. At about 0220 the ship appeared to settle deeper in the water, the list increased to 12° and the starboard side of the main deck was awash. All hands were ordered to the main deck to stand by the life floats and nets. At about 0230 after having received a complete report of the damage sustained and reports of injured, I decided to transfer all personnel to nearby ships for their own safety. The ship was drifting towards the enemy shore and with the increased settling in the water this appeared to be the best decision. The major damage was . . . a gaping hole 65 feet wide on the port side, open to the sea . . .[*]

However, *Meredith*, badly damaged, did not appear to be sinking. *Jeffers*, along with *Bates* (DE68), were ordered to stand by the abandoned destroyer. As seen from *Jeffers*:

At 0445 MEREDITH had been carried by the tide to a point well within range of enemy coastal batteries at Cape Barfleur, and since she gave every indication of remaining afloat indefinitely, at 0500, . . . a salvage party was sent aboard MEREDITH to determine practicability of salvage. The report of this party being favorable, JEFFERS was put alongside, starboard side to port side of MEREDITH, the 15° list to starboard was reduced, by jettisoning topside weights, to 5–10 degrees, her rudder was set manually, and JEFFERS commenced towing her back to assault area, . . . At 0715, two salvage tugs . . . arrived, took MEREDITH in tow . . . and at 0730 JEFFERS cast off and returned to assigned position in Area Screen.[†]

Hardly had the threat to *Meredith* been addressed, than another arose nearby. *Glennon* was approaching her gunfire support position off Utah Beach, near where *Corry* had been lost, when, at 0803, an explosion shook the ship:

2. The effect was violent throughout the ship. All power was lost due to the

[*] DD726, pp. 3–4.
[†] DD261, p. 4.

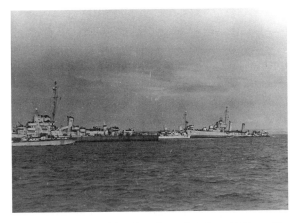

Glennon (DD620) struck a mine while off Utah Beach, 7 June 1944, and her stern settled to the point that she could not be towed away from shore battery gunfire. This view shows Glennon *to the right, with the minesweeper* Staff *(AM114) on her near bow. Nearer still is* Rich *(DE695) and a PT boat. Moments after this image was taken,* Rich *also struck a mine, broke in two and sank quickly.* Glennon *proved immovable and sank three days later under German shore bombardment. (NHHC)*

tripping of circuit breakers, but regained in about three minutes. The force of the explosion had been of such magnitude as to throw two men, who were standing on the fantail, 40 feet in the air, landing them in the water. One of these men was later recovered with both legs broken . . . A 600-pound depth charge was torn from the stern racks and thrown 50 feet, landing on the torpedo platform abreast #3, 5-inch gun mount. A 150-pound cement dan buoy anchor was thrown 125 feet from the fantail to the port 20 mm gun nest, torpedo platform. Water rose to a height of 25 feet about equally on the port and starboard quarters.[*]

Sixteen men who had been thrown into the water by the explosion were retrieved by the destroyer's whaleboat; unfortunately, a muster of the ship's company revealed 25 dead and another 38 wounded. Two minesweepers approached from ahead – *Staff* (AM114) on the port bow and *Threat* (AM124) to starboard. Although the ship was unable to move, her power plant was intact but both shafts were bent, she seemed in no immediate danger of sinking; *Staff* was passed a tow line and *Threat* was instructed to sweep a clear path to the transport area.

5. . . . While this was being undertaken, the USS RICH (DE) approached from eastward, asking by visual if assistance was required.[†] A visual reply

---

[*]   DD620, p. 8.

[†]   *Rich* was DE695 of the *Buckley* class.

was sent immediately, 'Negative, clear area cautiously due mines'. The RICH circled the stern and headed away at about 5 knots.*

This mass of ships must have been a tempting target for shore batteries; they attracted shellfire as *Rich* (DE695) was passing ahead of *Glennon*. Gunfire from *Tuscaloosa* and *Quincy* quickly silenced the German batteries, but not before *Rich* detonated a mine approximately 50 yards off her starboard beam, momentarily tripping her circuit breakers. This explosion was not seen from *Glennon*, so, her log picks up the story three minutes later:

> 6. About 0840, almost coincident with the end of enemy shellfire, when apparently in the swept channel headed eastward about 1,500 yards from the GLENNON, the RICH detonated a mine under her stern. The after 50 feet of the stern broke away, floating about 3 to 5 minutes before sinking. The forward section drifted away. Fifty to sixty seconds after the first detonation another mine exploded under the bow of the RICH. The ship broke across the forecastle just forward of the bridge structure and sank almost immediately. Fortunately there was an AM and many small craft, which were proceeding away from the GLENNON, quite close to the RICH, and survivors, who must have been very badly injured, were picked up almost immediately.†

In fact, the carnage was horrific. After *Rich*'s midships section sank a few minutes later, 62 of her crew were never found, 27 dead were recovered and another 73 were wounded, many of them seriously. Only 53 were rescued uninjured.

All attempts by *Staff* to tow *Glennon* to safety failed, because her hull had collapsed at the point of the explosion, just forward of her aftermost main battery mount, and her starboard screw was firmly embedded in the sand. At 0900, it was decided to take off all wounded and the half of her crew not engaged in repair work or manning guns. *Staff* took off 32 wounded and 167 other officers and men. These were safely landed at Portland the next day.‡

The large salvage tug *Kiowa* (ATF72) began attempting to free *Glennon* at 1130, but, despite the shifting of weight forward and the crew sallying ship, the attempt failed. Then an attempt was made to break off the sagging fantail by towing her bow athwartships, but, despite turning her in two complete circles, that was no more successful at freeing the ship. At 1630, the order arrived to take off the remaining crew after anchoring the ship forward so that, if the aft section broke free during the night, the bow would not drift onto an enemy-held shore. Unwilling to totally abandon the ship, because he still hoped to salvage the ship, Commander Clifford A. Johnson, *Glennon*'s CO, left his XO, the Engineering

---

* DD620, p. 9.
† Ibid.
‡ Ibid., pp. 10–1.

236

Officer and eight men, all volunteers, aboard to keep one boiler and the pumps functioning.

Johnson was able to persuade Rear-Admiral Don P. Moon commanding the Utah Beach forces that another attempt should be made to tow *Glennon* in the morning, and the skeleton crew was ordered to remain aboard and a salvage crew of five officers and 50 men was selected to return at first light. Johnson was ordered to return to *Glennon* immediately with a radar officer to retrieve all secret components in the ship's electronics, but darkness had set in by the time transport was arranged and this was delayed until morning.[*]

At dawn on 9 June, *Glennon*'s condition appeared unchanged, and plans were made to cut the starboard propeller shaft and, by that means, to free the ship. The day was spent gathering the equipment necessary to perform the desired salvage work and returning most of the crew not already in England back to the ship. By 2300, eight officers and 61 men were back aboard.

Meredith had not been as fortunate. Most of her crew was taken off during the day on 8 June and late in the day, she was towed by *Bannock* (ATF81) further offshore, to a position midway between Utah and Omaha Beaches. Her starboard midships 40 mm mount and two 20 mm mounts were removed to help lessen her list. The ship appeared stable the following morning, despite having been near-missed by a 2,000-lb bomb during the night that 'dropped about 800 yards off the port bow and shook the ship considerably; the stern moved and whipped sideways appreciably'.[†]

A dawn inspection by *Bannock*'s Salvage Officer found *Meredith* stable and the plan was to continue removing topside weights as soon as an LCT came alongside *Bannock* and she was able to offload the gun mounts that had been removed from *Meredith* the previous day.

> 19.   At 1010, 9 June without any preliminary warning the MEREDITH broke in two and went down amidships. The BANNOCK cut her lines to clear the side and stood off to render assistance. All Officers and men of the Security Watch on board jumped or lowered themselves clear of the ship and were picked up by the BANNOCK and passing boats.[‡]

Meredith suffered eight dead, 37 missing and 26 wounded.[§]

---

[*]   Ibid., pp. 12–4.

[†]   DD726, p. 10.

[‡]   Ibid..

[§]   The official version of the loss of *Meredith* states that it was due to 'what is believed to be a submerged contact mine' (DD726, p. 3), but all eyewitness accounts this author has seen agree that Hs 293 glide bombs were seen in the vicinity at the time of her damage, and it would be difficult to distinguish the effect of an Hs 293 detonating underwater next to a ship's hull from a the effect of striking a mine. It is noteworthy that both *Corry*'s and *Meredith*'s official reports give mines as the cause while earlier accounts did not. Some see this as a concerted effort by the US Navy to blame mines for losses caused by shelling and bombing. If this was indeed an attempt to cover up the real causes of these losses, it was, in this author's opinion, utterly pointless.

When dawn broke on 10 June, the work of attempting to free *Glennon* was well underway, but the Germans intervened, shelling the ship with impressive accuracy.

> 22.   At 0655, a 4 gun splash landed about 200 yards on the port quarter, apparently coming from the enemy shore battery in the Quineville area . . . The second salvo straddled with one or two hits aft, one entering the after engineroom. The third salvo straddled with a hit on the forecastle deck and a near miss on the starboard side which wounded two men, one seriously. All power was lost as a result of the first hits . . . The word was given to abandon ship. As the commanding officer reached the bottom of the inside ladder leading from the superstructure deck to the bridge he noted a terrific explosion in the vicinity of the bridge.[*]

Fortunately, only three men had been wounded and none killed in the shelling, but three men remained unaccounted for. Commander Johnson flagged down a passing PT boat, and headed back to *Glennon* to retrieve them. Later in the day, the XO and a small party came aboard to seal all watertight doors and make sure all classified papers and electronics had been destroyed. He reported there had been at least 11 separate direct hits by large caliber shells and uncountable near-misses for damage. Nevertheless, there was no fire aboard and the ship seemed stable.

> 26.   At 2145, 10 June 1944, the USS GLENNON commenced to list heavily and sank shortly thereafter. Whether there had been additional shelling or whether the ship had sufficient underwater fragmentation to cause her to sink is not known. At 2300, the remainder of the survivors sailed in the USS LST 381 for U.K.[†]

In total, *Glennon* lost 25 men and suffered another 38 wounded.

— —

The sinking of *Glennon* was the last major warship loss of Operation NEPTUNE. However, that should not be taken to indicate the battle for the waters off the Normandy beaches was over. Attacks by the S-boats at Cherbourg continued nightly against the Dixie Line and cross-Channel convoys with occasional success. On 9 June, *LST314* and *LST376* were sunk out of a convoy guarded by HMS *Beagle* (H30). At 0105 on 13 June, the destroyer *Nelson* (DD623) lost her stern to a torpedo from *S138* while on Dixie Line patrol, but survived. The remaining operational S-boats from Cherbourg transferred that night to Le Havre and the Germans began the systematic destruction of Cherbourg the next day. A successful RAF night bombing raid on Le Havre on the night of

---

[*]   DD620, p. 16.

[†]   Ibid., p. 19.

14/15 June sank 14 S-boats. On 19 June, a major storm swept down the Channel, destroying the MULBERRY harbor off Omaha Beach.

Dönitz had been preparing for the Allied invasion, holding back a significant number of U-boats in the French Atlantic ports. On 6 June, once confirmation of the invasion had been received, he ordered seven boats equipped with snorkel ventilation tubes based at Brest – Gruppe Landwirt (Group Farmer) – to make for the English Channel immediately, along with one additional snorkel boat from La Pallice.* These boats, which could recharge batteries while submerged, would at least have a chance of penetrating the anti-submarine screens around the fleet. Nine non-snorkel boats from Brest were ordered to the Western Channel to attack convoy traffic coming from the Irish Sea, despite knowing full well that they would likely be decimated by anti-submarine patrols. The hope was that by sacrificing the non-snorkel boats, the remainder would have a better chance of success. Four snorkel-equipped U-boats that had recently departed Norwegian bases for the North Atlantic were redirected to the Channel, bringing the total of snorkel-equipped boats converging on the invasion fleet to 12. An additional 19 non-snorkel boats from St-Nazaire, Lorient and La Pallice were to form a patrol across the Bay of Biscay in case the Allies were planning an additional invasion.†

The results of this operation was nothing short of disastrous for the Ubootwaffe. The 12 snorkel-equipped U-boats sent against the Normandy invasion fleet managed to sink two warships (possibly a third) and one merchant ship (with two more possible), damage one warship and three merchantmen beyond repair, and inflict minor damage on one warship and one cargo vessel, for the loss of five U-boats; 213 U-boatmen died. Incredibly, Dönitz thought this was an acceptable exchange rate and continued to send U-boats into the Channel for another month, with dwindling results.‡ He did, however, accept the futility of operating non-snorkel boats even in the Bay of Biscay. On 12 June, he noted as follows:

All boats without schnorchel in the Bay of Biscay ordered to put in to bases. Reason: Heavy enemy air activity will lead in the long run to high losses and

---

* Blair, *Hitler's U-Boat War: The Hunted*, pp. 579–89. The snorkel was a rigid tube that extended from a submerged U-boat to the surface, allowing its diesels to run while submerged, but the latest airborne radar used by RAF Coastal Command, the ASV MkIII, could sometimes detect the head of a snorkel, which could also be detected visually because it left a prominent wake. A U-boat operating totally submerged needed to use its snorkel a minimum of four hours to charge its batteries enough to run on electric motors for the next 20 hours. A U-boat operating in this manner could expect to cover no more than 100 nm/day under ideal conditions. (Snorkel is spelled many different ways; I have opted for the common American spelling. The most common German spelling is *Schnorchel*. The word 'snorkel' was often shortened to 'snort'.)

† [Hessler] *The U-boat War in the Atlantic 1939–1945*, vol. 3, pp. 67–8; Tarrant, *The Last Year of the Kriegsmarine*, pp. 71–80.

‡ [Hessler] *The U-boat War in the Atlantic 1939–1945*, vol. 3, pp. 71–6.

After the Normandy beachheads had expanded past the range of naval gunfire, there remained one more task for the fire support ships off the French Atlantic coast. Nevada *can be seen from* Quincy *approaching Cherbourg, 25 June 1944. (NARA)*

heavy wear and tear, which would only be bearable if an immediate enemy landing was expected along the Biscay coast. This is not an acute danger at present. Submarines to remain at readiness under bunkers.[*]

On 18 June, US Army troops pushing west from Utah Beach reached Barneville on the west coast of the Cotentin Peninsula, cutting off Cherbourg and two days later were in contact with the port's outer defenses. Also on 18 June, Operation NEPTUNE was concluded and the fire support groups returned to English ports to replenish, assembling at Portland on 21 June, now designated TF129 under the command of Rear-Admiral Deyo. On 25 June, TF129 was called on to support the land assault on Cherbourg on 25 June. The ships were divided into two fire support groups: Group 1 comprising *Nevada, Tuscaloosa, Quincy, Glasgow, Enterprise* and six destroyers; and Group 2 comprising *Texas, Arkansas* and five destroyers. Deploying in an east–west line 14,000 yards offshore at noon, the ships almost immediately began to receive accurate fire from shore defenses.[†]

Nevada began answering Call Fire requests from Army Shore Fire Control Parties at 1212 and continued that until 1327. The enemy fire was accurate enough to cause the minesweepers to be withdrawn at 1230. Destroyers and

---

[*]   *B.d.U. Op's WAR LOG,* 12.6.44.

[†]   BB36-2, Part 1, pp. 2–3.

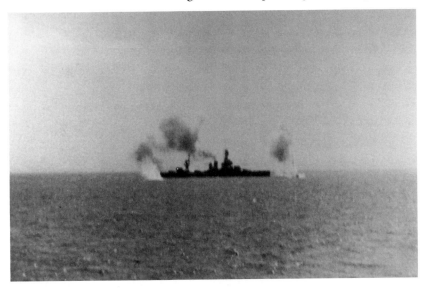

The Germans fought back, defending Cherbourg with several well-positioned shore batteries. This view shows Texas *straddled by large caliber shell splashes, 25 June 1944. (NHHC)*

MTBs laid a smoke screen that was sufficient to diminish, but not eliminate, the threat of the shore batteries. One particularly persistent battery, marked as No. 308 on the charts, near the western entrance to the outer harbor, managed to hit *Glasgow* with a 150 mm shell at 1251 and again at 1255. This battery of four guns drew the attention of one battleship, four cruisers and several destroyers intermittently until TF129 retired, and even then, managed to lob a few shells at the departing column.[*]

> During the period from 1206 until retirement at 1529, NEVADA was continuously under fire from enemy shore batteries. Multi-gun enemy salvos straddled the ship on 23 occasions in which large caliber shells missed from 25 feet to 300 yards . . . On two occasions large caliber shells passed through the superstructure and landed so close on the unengaged side that it is difficult to see how they missed hitting the ship. These and other near misses covered the decks with water and shrapnel.[†]

East of the port, *Texas*, *Arkansas* and their escorting destroyers, took on Batterie Hamburg, four old 240 mm/40 guns that had previously seen service on Austro-Hungarian armored cruisers. These guns had a longer range than the ships taking them on, so the Americans had to operate under the menace of

---

[*] Morison, *History,* vol. XI, pp. 201–4.

[†] BB36-2, Part 1, p. 3.

One of the prizes captured when Cherbourg fell to Allied land assault on 26 June 1944 was this reinforced concrete pen for S-boats. (NARA)

accurate fire from the shore.* Batterie Hamburg initially targeted the destroyers and minesweepers leading the battleships into position. In short order, *Barton* (DD722) was hit by a shot that fell short but ricocheted into her hull and *Laffey* (DD724) was hit near her bow anchor. Fortunately, the rounds being fired by Batterie Hamburg were possibly as old as the guns; neither exploded and no one was injured. At 1251, *O'Brien* (DD725) was hit in her CIC; this one did explode, killing 13 and wounding 19. At 1316, *Texas* was hit by a shell that glanced off the top of her conning tower, dislodging a periscope head, before exploding under her pilot house. One man, the helmsman, was killed and 11 others injured; the conn was transferred to the XO in the conning tower. Another 240 mm shell hit forward, coming to rest immediately below the wardroom; fortunately, it too was a dud. Against this, the two battleships fired 206 14-inch shells and 58 12-inch at Batterie Hamburg, while five destroyers fired 552 5-inch shells before they retired; one of the battery's four guns was knocked out. The fighting in Cherbourg continued for several more days; the main defensive position, the Arsenal, surrendered on 28 June. Some isolated pockets of German troops resisted until 1 July. TF129 was not involved after 25 June.

---

* *NavWeaps* (www.navweaps.com); Morison, *History,* vol. XI, p. 206. In shore battery mountings, the old German 240 mm/40 had a range of 26,600 m (29,090 yards), while neither *Texas* nor *Arkansas* could fire much further than 20,000 yards.

Two S-boats, one an older pre-1940 model with exposed torpedo tubes (left) and the other a newer model with faired-in tubes, are seen inside an S-boat bunker like the one at Cherbourg. (BAK)

The only one of the snorkel U-boats that operated against the Normandy beaches to have significant success was *U984* (Sieder). He managed to damage a destroyer escort and four Liberty ships, all but one of them to the point that they were written off as total losses. This level of success had become so exceptional at this stage of the war, Oberleutnant Heinz Sieder was awarded the Ritterkreuz for this one patrol. His other reward for this success was to be sent out again to attack the invasion shipping. He departed Brest on 26 July 1944. After a patrol with no success, *U984* was nearing Brest on 20 August when she was detected, hunted and killed by the Canadian 11th Escort Group. There were no survivors.[*]

After the action off Cherbourg, major US naval units saw no further action in support of the Normandy landings or the subsequent breakout towards the Seine and Rhine. The Atlantic or North Sea ports used by U-boats, S-boats and the K-Verbande (Kleinkampfverbande – Small Battle Units) were rapidly captured or isolated, and dealing with those naval units that could still operate in the area became largely the responsibility of the Royal Navy.[†]

---

[*]   Wynn, *U-Boat Operations*, vol. 2, p. 204; Niestlé, *German U-boat Losses*, p. 95.

[†]   The K-Verbande deployed a variety of unconventional weapons, such as Linsen radio-controlled motorboats and several varieties of midget submarines, including the Biber, Neger and Marder. They had some minor successes, sinking or damaging a few small ships, but proved mostly ineffective; cf. Tarrant, *The Last Year of the Kriegsmarine*, pp. 96–100.

The center of attention once again shifted to the Mediterranean where the Allies were preparing for Operation DRAGOON, the landings in southern France. As might have been expected, Churchill fought hard against this operation, hoping instead to use those forces to attack in Italy, with the intent of advancing through the Po valley and the 'Ljubljana Gap' towards Vienna or the Balkans, and tried hard to persuade Eisenhower to support his position.[*] Eisenhower's response was to maintain that he would do as ordered by the Allied political leaders, but that, from a military point of view, landings in Southern France and the capture of Toulon and Marseille were essential. The initial plan had been to land troops between Hyères and Cannes, east of Toulon, on the same day as the Normandy landings, but the decision to increase OVERLORD from three to five landings necessitated the use of landing craft intended for DRAGOON, which, in turn, meant DRAGOON could not take place until landing craft could be released from Normandy and transferred to the Mediterranean assembly ports that stretched from Oran to Brindisi. The date for DRAGOON was eventually set for mid-August.

— —

Of course, during and after and the extended support for the Anzio landings, the war in the Mediterranean had continued, with the Germans using what resources they had at hand. These included a shrinking number of U-boats and an increased number of S-boats, as captured Italian MAS (Motoscafo Armato Silurante – literally 'torpedo-armed motorboat') boats were taken over and put in service. The deployment of U-boats in the Mediterranean reached a maximum in January 1943, when there were 23 boats assigned to the 29th Flotilla operating out of La Spezia.[†] From then on, that number fluctuated, but generally shrank; a steady inflow of new boats failed to offset the increased rate of loss. The last new boat to pass the Straits of Gibraltar was *U960* (Heinrich), which entered the Mediterranean on 30 April 1944. The number of boats was 18 in March 1944, but after that the number declined steadily until the last three boats were lost in September. Altogether, 62 U-boats had entered the Mediterranean; every one of them was sunk or scuttled, including 11 lost in port to bomber attacks. Personnel losses came to 1893 dead and 930 captured.

This expenditure of boats and men was never matched by commensurate damage to Allied shipping, particularly after American forces entered the Mediterranean in force in 1943. By 1944, the shrinking number of U-boats achieved fewer and fewer successes to offset the steady rate of losses. Three U-boats operating from Toulon approached the inbound convoy UGS.37 soon after it passed the Straits of Gibraltar on 10 April escorted by five destroyers, seven destroyer escorts and the anti-aircraft cruiser HMS *Delhi* (D74). The numerous escort caused all three U-boats to abort their attacks and the convoy continued

[*] Eisenhower, *Crusade in Europe*, pp. 281–4.
[†] uboat.net; Blair, *Hitler's U-Boat War: The Hunted*, App. 7.

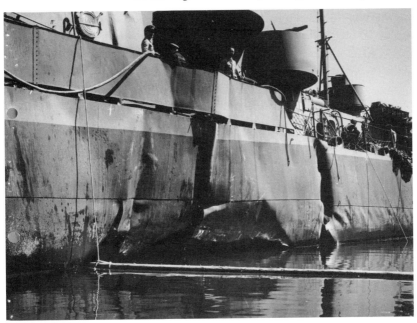

While escorting convoy UGS.37 from Hampton Roads into the Mediterranean, Holder *(DE401) fell victim to a torpedo dropped at close range by a Ju 88 east of Algiers, 12 April 1944. The destroyer escort proved tough and survived despite this damage to her midsection. In this condition, she was towed to New York. (NARA)*

eastward unmolested. The next night, a major air attack developed just east of Algiers near Cap Bengut with at least 25 Ju 88s carrying torpedoes and Do 217s carrying glide-bombs. The night was clear, the sea calm and a three-quarters moon lit the night. Two destroyer escorts leading the convoy were illuminated with flares at 2318 and the attack started soon after that. The escort commander ordered his ships to make smoke and that, along with effective radar-guided anti-aircraft fire and jamming by *Lansdale* (DD426), fitted with the improved XCJ-1, caused every attack on the merchantmen and LSTs to miss. *Holder* (DE401), one of the ships leading the convoy, was the only victim that night. A Ju 88 came in low and fast at 2339, dropping its torpedo less than 400 yards off *Holder's* port beam. There was little she could do; the order to increase speed and make a sharp left turn came too late. The torpedo took out her power plant and left her with a list and afire amidships, but *Holder* proved tough. By 0230, the fires and list were under control and she was under tow. Temporary repairs put her in condition to be towed to New York, where she arrived on 9 June. Sixteen of her crew had died and 12 more were seriously injured in the attack.[*]

UGS.37 arrived at Bizerte on 13 April, where it was officially dispersed, though

---

[*]   Roscoe, *United States Destroyer Operations*, pp. 366–7.

most of the ships remained together and continued to Augusta under British escort (two River-class frigates and four Flower-class corvettes). From there the few remaining ships of the convoy continued on towards Port Said. It was during this last leg that a German U-boat – *U407* (Korndörfer) operating out of Salamis – finally was able to score. Two Liberty ships – *Meyer London* and *Thomas G. Masaryk* – were torpedoed off Derna (Darnah), Libya at 1820 on 16 April. *London* sank in a little over an hour, but *Masaryk*, carrying drums of acetone, burnt a bright blue even after she had been towed near shore. There she was scuttled, extinguishing the flames. Remarkably, not a single life was lost on either ship. These were the only sinkings by a U-boat in the Mediterranean in April 1944.[*]

A day after the next convoy from America – UGS.38 – entered the Mediterranean, on 19 April, *Lansdale* again joined the escort. The next night, again near Cap Bengut, another air attack developed. This time, all the aircraft carried torpedoes. Nine Ju 88s came in from dead ahead at 2104 and obtained hits on two Liberty ships, *Paul Hamilton* and *Samite*. The former, loaded with ammunition and 504 troops, simply disintegrated in a spectacular explosion. Not a single man onboard survived; every one of the soldiers, the ship's crew of 48 officers and men and the 29 Armed Guards all perished. *Samite*, in British service, was torpedoed in the bow, but was able to limp into Algiers under her own power.

A second attack of perhaps seven Ju 88s followed directly on the heels of the first, and managed to torpedo two more merchantmen. SS *Royal Star* took a torpedo in the stern and sank slowly, taking with her one crew member and a valuable cargo of refrigerated meat; another Liberty ship, *Stephen F. Austin*, was hit in the bow and, like *Samite*, survived and reached safety.

A third wave of ten aircraft, five Ju 88s and five He 111s, came last, less than two minutes after the first attack, and concentrated on *Lansdale*. The Junkers attacked from starboard, two or three of them managing to put torpedoes in the water heading towards the destroyer. Two of the Heinkels on the port side launched torpedoes. Four of the five torpedoes spotted by *Lansdale*'s lookouts missed, but one hit her starboard side in way of her forward fire room. The explosion was massive, ripping out her bottom and venting upward through the superstructure deck just aft of the bridge. The damage was fatal. The ship drifted to a stop and her list increased steadily to 45°. At that point, at 2122, Lieutenant Commander D. M. Swift knew *Lansdale* could not be saved and he ordered the men overboard. Twenty minutes later, lying nearly on her beam ends, she broke in two and her after section sank immediately, followed by the bow a few minutes later. Two hundred and thirty-five men were pulled from the water, 137 of them by *Menges* (DE320); 47 were never found.[†]

---

[*]   Rohwer, *Axis Submarine Successes*, p. 256; uboat.net. *Masaryk* was eventually refloated and towed into Port Said, where she was declared a total loss.

[†]   Parkin, *Blood on the Sea*, pp. 206–7; Roscoe, *United States Destroyer Operations*, pp. 368–9; Wales, *Time Line of Attack*.

*Menges (DE320) was another destroyer escort damaged while escorting a convoy in the
Mediterranean. GUS.38 had departed Bizerte on 2 May 1944. Early the next morning,
Menges fell victim to a T5 acoustic torpedo fired by U371 (Fenski). While most of her
hull remained undamaged, the torpedo demolished her fantail, propellers and rudders,
requiring that she too be towed across the Atlantic for repairs. (NARA)*

The war with German air and sea forces reached a climax when the returning
convoy GUS.38 left Bizerte on 2 May with 81 ships in ballast.[*] The escort
comprised 13 ships – 12 destroyer escorts and the Secretary-class Coast Guard
cutter *Taney* (WPG37) – later supplemented by *Delhi*. Just after midnight, *Menges*,
patrolling 3,000 yards astern of the convoy, was watching out for enemy aircraft
as they were approaching Cap Bengut where the last two inbound convoys had
been attacked. However, the threat that night was a U-boat, *U371* (Fenski), on
the surface charging batteries. Oberleutnant Horst-Arno Fenski and most of
his crew had come over en masse from *U410*, which had been destroyed in a
bomb attack on Toulon on 11 March. Fenski was an experienced and successful
commander, who had been awarded the Ritterkreuz on 26 November 1943.

Heading west-north-west at cruising speed, *U371* was in fact overtaking
the convoy from behind. The U-boat showed up on *Menges*'s radar at 0025

---

[*]   DE320, p 1. Other sources give higher figures for the number of ships in GUS.38, but those
sources no doubt include ships that joined the convoy later from Algiers and Oran.

on 3 May.* After tracking the contact for 20 minutes, *Menges* was ordered to investigate. Ten minutes later, Fenski apparently noticed *Menges*, because the contact was seen to reverse course and increase speed to 14 knots. *Menges* increased speed to overtake, began zigzagging and streamed 'foxer' gear on the presumption the target was a U-boat.† At 0112, Fenski, aware that *Menges* was getting close, chose to dive. At the time, *U371* was directly ahead of *Menges* at a range of 3,200 yards. As he dove, Fenski fired the T5 acoustic torpedo kept in his stern tube for just this eventuality. Slowing and continuing to zigzag, *Menges* approached the point where the radar contact disappeared. At 0118, a massive explosion right aft demolished her fantail and carried away both propellers and rudders. The damage was substantial, but *Menges* was never in any danger of sinking; nevertheless, 31 men were killed in the explosion and 25 more injured. Two more were blown overboard, but were picked up by her motor whaleboat while she waited for a tug.

While *Menges* floated, unable to move, two of the convoy's escorts came back to assist. *Pride* (DE323) and *Joseph E. Campbell* (DE70) started searching for *U371* and quickly detected the U-boat. Seven depth charge attacks were delivered between 0255 and 0833, after which contact was lost. Earlier in the war, that might have ended the story, but this was 1944 and the resources existed to guard a convoy and pursue a submarine contact at the same time. Four additional escorts joined *Pride* and *Campbell* – including *L'Alcyon* – and a Swamp attack was begun. To carry out this form of ASW operation, devised by the combined Mediterranean naval staffs in late 1943, a force of escorts, aided by aircraft, was assigned the destruction of a U-boat and was expected to persist until that was achieved, no matter how much time that took.‡ (The underwater endurance of the U-boats involved in the Mediterranean in 1944 was limited to 36 to 48 hours at the most, after which time oxygen would have to be refreshed and batteries recharged, so there was a practical limit to the length of a Swamp operation.) *U371* had gone deep and was resting on the bottom, but time was not on Fenski's side. At 0315 on 4 May, approximately 26 hours after torpedoing *Menges*, he was forced to bring his boat to the surface. He managed to damage one more of his pursuers with a T5, after which he accepted the inevitable and ordered *U371* abandoned and scuttled. All but three of her crew were rescued.

Menges, meanwhile, had already been towed into Bougie to debark her casualties and then on to Oran, where temporary repairs were completed on 23 June. She was then towed to New York.

The story of the assault on GUS.38 was not yet over. One of Germany's most

---

* DD320-1, pp. 1–3; DD320-2, pp 4–5; Blair, *Hitler's U-Boat War: The Hunted*, pp. 522–3; Roscoe, *United States Destroyer Operations*, p. 370.
† 'Foxer' (or FXR) gear was a noise-making apparatus streamed in the wake of a ship to decoy an acoustic torpedo away from the ship's screws.
‡ Morison, *History*, vol. X, pp. 252–7.

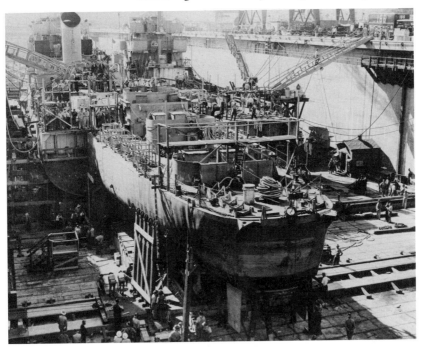

The still-intact aft end of Holder *was grafted to the undamaged forward two-thirds of* Menges *at New York Navy Yard to create a functioning destroyer escort that retained* Menges's *name and hull number. The resurrected* Menges *was back in action again on 15 November 1944. (NARA)*

decorated U-boat commanders, Kapitänleutnant Albrecht Brandi – he already wore the Eichenlaub (Oak Leaves) to the Ritterkreuz, only the 22nd to be so honored – was hunting the convoy. He was in *U967*, which had just arrived from the Atlantic at the end of March. This was Brandi's third Mediterranean command; the first two had been destroyed, one he ran aground on the coast of Spanish Morocco to prevent her sinking and the other had been bombed while at Toulon. At 0345 on 5 May, *Fechteler* (DE157) was hit amidships by a T5 near Isla de Alborán in the eastern approaches to the Straits of Gibraltar. It quickly became obvious the ship could not be saved; the crew was ordered off at 0415, not a moment too soon as *Fechteler* broke in two and her midsection sagged, leaving bow and stern pointing skyward. At 0500, there was a massive explosion, after which the wreck slid beneath the waves, taking 29 of her crew to the bottom. Brandi slipped away and, on returning to Toulon, received the Schwertern (Crossed Swords) to his Ritterkreuz, the fifth and last U-boatman to win this award.[*]

---

[*]   Morison, *History,* vol. X, p. 371. The other four to win the Schwertern – Kretschmer, Topp, Suhren and Lüth – were all significantly more successful than Brandi; it is difficult to understand why he was so honored, other than the fact that his comparatively meager

By this point, there were only a small handful of U-boats left active in the Mediterranean, and these faced a bleak future. The next westbound convoy, GUS.39, attracted *U616* (Koitscha), which, early on 14 May damaged two merchantmen with two torpedoes. Determined to catch the culprit, the escort commander ordered *Hilary P. Jones* and three destroyer escorts to remain behind and initiate another Swamp operation. Local naval authorities were contacted and an American ASW group based at Oran was dispatched to relieve the convoy escorts.[*] Seven veteran destroyers converged on the scene and, aided by RAF aircraft, hunted the U-boat relentlessly. One attack, by *Ellyson*, damaged one of the U-boat's oil tanks, causing her to trail a tell-tale oil slick. Held down by constant sonar search all day on 15 May, Koitscha finally had to surface that night to replenish air and batteries. Detected and attacked by Leigh Light Wellingtons, he dove, but soon had to resurface and was able to escape detection long enough charge his batteries and dive again. At dawn on 16 May, the destroyers found the oil slick, but were unable to locate the U-boat with sonar. That night, Koitscha surfaced and attempted a high-speed run to the north-east. Less than a hour later, at 2356, *U616* was found by a Wellington 30 nm away from the American destroyers. The bomber drove the U-boat under and marked the spot with light buoys. When Koitscha attempted to surface again an hour later, *U616* was detected with radar and illuminated by a searchlight. Koitcha dove yet again, but he would not escape this time. At 0800 a salvo of deep-set depth charges dropped by *Hambleton* brought *U616* to the surface, where Koitscha had no choice but to order the boat abandoned. All 53 of *U616*'s complement were rescued, most by *Ellyson*. Koitscha had been hunted for 76 hours; against this kind of persistence, no U-boat could succeed.

As if to punctuate this point, as *Ellyson* was entering Mers-el-Kébir that afternoon, she was missed by three torpedoes fired by *U960*, the last U-boat to enter the Mediterranean. Heinrich attempted to escape submerged to the north, but, in an immediate reprise of the just-completed Swamp operation, five fresh destroyers took off in pursuit, aided by two squadrons of Wellingtons and Venturas. This iteration of Swamp proved as effective as the previous. The five destroyers were arrayed along the presumed route of the U-boat, with two of them – *Ludlow* and *Niblack* – 20 nm ahead of the other three. Having been submerged for at least 35 hours, *U960* came to the surface at 2300 on 18 May, to ventilate and recharge batteries. So dense was the net, that a circling Wellington made radar contact within minutes, and *Niblack* and *Ludlow* went to investigate. Arriving at the contact location at 0054, the two destroyers began a slow radar and sonar sweep that produced no contacts. Heinrich had given the destroyers the slip, but, when he surfaced again after 0230, now desperate for air

---

successes came at a time when few U-boat commanders were having any success at all.
[*]   Blair, *Hitler's U-Boat War: The Hunted*, pp. 524–5; Roscoe, *United States Destroyer Operations*, pp. 371–3.

and battery charge, he was soon located by Ventura 'L for London' of No. 500 Squadron, 10 nm east of the two destroyers. By 0251, they had found the marker buoy dropped by the Ventura and had begun another sweep for *U960*.[*]

What followed must have been a nightmare for the U-boatmen. The two destroyers dropped 11 patterns of depth charges over a period of three-and-a-half hours starting at 0333. The last pattern of 11 charges set for very deep detonation dropped by *Niblack* at 0705 finally proved decisive.

0708   Submarine broke surface stern first. Opened fire with 5" and 40 mm batteries.

0712   Plane made an attack over submarine and dropped charges quite close to submarine. Luckily it was not hit by gunfire.

0714   Submarine sunk after several direct hits by NIBLACK and LUDLOW.

0717   NIBLACK dropped 10 charge pattern at medium setting over sinking submarine. Submarine was blown to the surface and sank with stern vertical.

0721   Lowered boat and picked up survivors – NIBLACK recovered 7 and LUDLOW 13.[†]

That same day, *U453* (Lührs) sank a British Liberty ship in the Ionian Sea. Three Royal Navy destroyers hunted the U-boat for a day-and-a-half, finally forcing *U453* to the surface after midnight on 21 May. Lührs's victim, *Fort Missanabie*, was the last ship to be sunk by a U-boat in the Mediterranean.

— · —

From a naval point of view, there were some similarities, but many more differences between the DRAGOON landings in southern France and the Normandy landings. The forces arrayed to support the landings were by far the most powerful deployed in the European theater. Five task forces, four of which directly supported landing operations at the four designated landing sites. From the west, they were:

TF86 – Sitka Force comprising *Augusta*, HMS *Dido* (C37), the old French battleship *Lorraine* and four destroyers, with *Omaha*, the equally old *Cincinnati* (CL6) and HMS *Sirius* (C82) in reserve;

TF84 – Alpha Force comprising HMS *Ramillies* (I07), *Quincy*, four Royal Navy light cruisers, the French light cruiser *Gloire* and six destroyers;

TF85 – Delta Force comprising *Texas*, *Nevada*, *Philadelphia*, the French light cruisers *Montcalm* and *Georges Leygues*, destroyer leaders *Le Fantasque*, *Le Terrible* and *Le Malin* (last seen at Casablanca), and seven destroyers;

---

[*]   DD424, Enc E, pp. 1–3.

[†]   Ibid., p. 3.

TF87 – Camel Force comprising *Arkansas, Tuscaloosa, Brooklyn, Marblehead* (CL12), HMS *Argonaut* (C61), the French light cruisers *Émile Bertin* and *Duguay Trouin*, and 11 destroyers; and, in more distant support, and, supporting these groups,

TF88 – Aircraft Carrier Force comprising two Task Groups; one with five Royal Navy escort carriers (all Lend-Lease), HMS *Royalist* (C89) and *Delhi*, and six Royal Navy and Greek destroyers; and one with *Tulagi* (CVE72), *Kasaan Bay* (CVE69), HMS *Hunter, Stalker* (D91), *Colombo, Caledon* (D53) and five American destroyers.

The aircraft carriers carried between them 96 Seafires, 72 Hellcats and 48 Wildcats. The aircraft were needed here because the closest airbases on Corsica and in North Africa were too distant to allow for continuous air coverage.

Mercifully, most of the fire support ships had very little to do on D-Day, 15 August. The skies were clear and seas calm and troops were put ashore with little difficulty and little in the way of enemy resistance. By the end of D+1, only those forces moving east and west along the shore had need of gunfire support. This was provided as needed, until Toulon and Marseille had been captured (28 August) and the Allies had established full control of the French coast up to the Italian border (9 September). Shore-based opposition to these activities was mostly minor. Only the St-Mandrier Peninsula south of Toulon possessed significant shore batteries, and these were engaged and largely neutralized between 19 and 26 August, when they were captured by ground troops.

The greatest excitement encountered by the naval forces supporting DRAGOON came in a series of sharp engagements in the dark of night between German small craft, mostly ex-Italian torpedo boats, corvettes, sloops and motor torpedo boats, and the ships screening the Allied fleets, mostly American destroyers.

The first of these encounters came in the pre-dawn dark before H-Hour, 15 August. The destroyer leader *Somers*, guarding the western flank of the Sitka Force, obtained a radar contact at 0347. Two ships were approaching from the west-south-west, heading straight towards the transport area. *Somers* was under strict orders not to open fire unless a target was positively identified as enemy and *Somers* herself had been sighted by the enemy. Also, Commander W. C. Hughes, *Somers*'s CO, knew that there were American PT boats operating to the west of his location, so the possibility that the two contacts were friendly could not be discounted.

Somers patiently tracked the contacts as the approached. Finally, at 0440, when the two ships were passing between *Somers* and HMS *Lookout* (G32), Hughes ordered the contacts challenged. When they failed to respond to two successive challenges and began to maneuver, Hughes gave the order to open fire. *Somers* was steaming south, while the two Germans appeared to be

Then, as now, American entertainers played for the 'boys' overseas. Here the Jack Haley Show appears on Texas, *at Taranto, August 1944. Jack Haley (right), who is now best known for his role as the Tin Man in the movie* The Wizard of Oz, *was a well-known stage and film singer and dancer. Rita Hayworth is to the left. In between was a very lucky sailor. (NARA)*

maneuvering in tight circles off her port side. She got off one salvo, of which one round hit the closer of the two. The targets then turned north, and *Somers* checked fire while she also turned north and increased speed. At this point, the larger and more distant of the two targets came into view, steaming north and making smoke. One salvo was fired at this ship, of which several rounds hit, 'causing a flash of flame the length of the target, immediately followed by numerous explosions forward and aft as ammunition began exploding.'*

Satisfied that this target was incapacitated, at 0450, *Somers* turned attention back to the original target, which was now seen to be heading south-east at 20 knots. Turning to follow, *Somers* sighted this target at 0505 and opened fire again at 0508. This ship returned fire with a medium-caliber machine gun, 20 mm or 40 mm, but obtained no hits. *Somers*, on the other hand, shot extremely well, and by 0520, this target had drifted to a stop. By 0532, the crew was seen to be abandoning ship, but Hughes opted to wait until first light, which meant that *Somers* started picking up survivors at 0620. As the target, now identified by survivors as *UJ6081*, the ex-Italian torpedo boat *Camoscio*, showed no signs of immediately sinking, Hughes ordered a boarding party away to attempt to save the ship.

---

*   DD381-3, p. 2.

Another kind of show was put on aboard US Navy ships at this time. Here, men on Philadelphia *are being briefed on the upcoming* DRAGOON *landings in Southern France, August 1944.* Philadelphia *was part of the gunfire support group for the* Delta *landings. (NARA)*

At 0703, *Somers* turned north to investigate the first target, only to find that this ship had already sunk. Survivors stated this ship was named '*Escabort*', but this was a miscommunication or maybe even an attempt at deception, because later examination proved she was *SG21*, the ex-French minesweeper/sloop *Amiral Sénès*. The two had departed Toulon around midnight, hoping to engage the invasion fleet. Unfortunately, their wish was granted. Ninety-nine survivors were picked up from the two ships, which had, between them, a nominal complement of 216.[*]

The boarding party had indeed boarded *Camoscio* at 0702 and found her to be beyond salvage, listing to starboard and settling aft. Working quickly, they gathered a number of useful charts and documents and departed the ship at 0716. It was not a moment too soon; *Camoscio* capsized at 0719 and sank three minutes later.[†]

— —

To keep the defenders off balance, the DRAGOON plan called for feints in the direction of La Ciotat about halfway between Marseille and Toulon. One such

---

[*]   DD381-3, pp. 2–3; O'Hara, *Struggle for the Middle Sea*, pp. 247–8; Morison, *History,* vol. XI, p. 252; Roscoe, *United States Destroyer Operations*, pp. 275–7.

[†]   DD381-3, Enc C, pp. 1–2. This is an attached report by the Boarding Officer, Lieutenant J. C. Hamblen.

Quincy was part of the gunfire support for Alpha Force, one of the few American units in this otherwise British sector, 15 August 1944. (NARA)

was underway early on 17 August. The diversion was created by gunfire from *Endicott* (DD495), HMS *Aphis* (T57) and *Scarab* (T59), accompanied by PT boats and numerous small craft. (*Aphis* and *Scarab* were under the command of Lieutenant Commander Douglas Fairbanks, Jr.) The shore bombardment had been successfully completed and the force was retiring south when, at 0545, *Endicott* received a call for assistance from *ARB21*, a small air rescue boat, trailing behind along with the two gunboats. The rescue boat reported that the gunboats were under attack by a pair of German corvettes. They were *UJ6073*, the former *Nimet Allah*, once the Khedival yacht of the Ottoman ruler of Egypt; and the smaller *UJ6082*, the ex-Italian *Antilope*, a sister to *Camoscio*. They had departed Toulon shortly before, heading for Marseille. Both were faster than the gunboats and carried guns that outranged their old 6-inch weapons. Nevertheless, it was only after ten minutes passed that *Endicott* turned north-west and rang up 35 knots.[*]

Twenty-five minutes later, at 0620, the destroyer came under fire from the German ships, which were hidden from *Endicott* by an early morning haze.

---

[*]   DD495, p. 2; Morison, *History*, vol. XI, p. 282; O'Hara, *Struggle for the Middle Sea*, pp. 248–9; Roscoe, *United States Destroyer Operations*, pp. 377–8. The delay in responding is not explained in this report, but was most likely due to the main battery issues described below.

French naval units played a significant role in supporting the DRAGOON *landings. Here, the light cruiser* Émile Bertin, *one of the ships that had so absorbed Allied attention when she was at Martinique earlier in the war, is seen from* Augusta. *She was originally part of the Camel Force fire support group, August 1944. (NARA)*

A German mine is detonated in the background as an LST unloads troops and supplies across a barge ramp for Operation DRAGOON, *17 August 1944. (NARA)*

Altogether the best-managed Allied landing, both because of the experience gained from earlier mistakes and because the resistance was almost non-existent, these vehicles drive off LST906 *over a barge ramp on to beaches made drivable by wire matting, 15 August 1944. A DUKW leads a squad of four M8 Greyhound light armored cars. (NARA)*

Because of the distance from friendly airfields, the DRAGOON *landing enjoyed significant Allied carrier support. Seven Royal Navy escort carriers (all Lend-Lease) and two from the US Navy provided continuous fighter coverage of the fleet and troops until airfields ashore could be secured. Here, an F6F-5 Hellcat of VF-74 warms up with a wingload of 5-inch artillery rockets on* Kasaan Bay *(CVE69). (NARA)*

The German UJ6082, *formerly the Italian corvette* Antilope, *ran afoul of* Endicott *(DD495) early on 17 August 1944 off La Ciotat, west of the* DRAGOON *landing beaches. As can be seen here,* Antilope, *mis-identified in initial reports as* Capaiulo, *got the worse of the exchange. (NARA)*

Only gradually, as the pre-dawn light increased and the range decreased, did the situation become clear. The gunboats were fleeing south at their best speed and pouring out a smokescreen that initially led Lieutenant Commander John D. Bulkeley, *Endicott's* CO, to believe one of them was afire. The Germans followed cautiously, apparently afraid of what might lie on the other side of the smokescreen. Not only were *Scarab* and *Aphis* outgunned by the Germans, but both were low on main battery ammunition due to the lengthy bombardment they had just completed. While in no danger of running out of 5-inch rounds, *Endicott* suffered from her own problems relating to the recent bombardment.

> 0646 Sighted two corvettes almost dead ahead . . . Commenced firing immediately at the larger of the two ships, the KEMID ALLAH.* . . At this time 5"/38 Gun #3 was the only main battery gun able to fire due to jammed breech blocks on the other three guns from over-heating due

---

* *Endicott's* report got wrong the names of both ships she engaged that morning. The other ship was originally called *Capaiulo* in the report, later 'corrected' to *Capriolo*, which was the name of a sister ship of *Antilope* and *Camoscio*.

to heavy shore bombardment in a short period of time shortly before the surface engagement. As each 5"/38 gun was able to fire, it was brought into action, although at no time was it possible to fire a full four-gun salvo. Heavy return fire was encountered from the main and machine gun batteries of the two enemy vessels. Numerous straddles were observed but high speed maintained by this vessel and frequent changes of course reduced the effectiveness of enemy fire.[*]

What followed was a half-hour-long brawl between *Endicott* and the two Germans at ranges as close as 1,500 yards. *Nimet Allah* was hit twice almost immediately in her engine room, which caused her to slow to a crawl.

0648   The larger target, KEMID ALLAH, was set on fire and began to list to port and explode. At about the same time the CAPAIULO was seen to fire two torpedoes at this vessel. This vessel was maneuvering radically and it is not known where the torpedoes passed.[†]

Two PT boats which were accompanying *Endicott* attempted to close *Antilope*, but were driven off and fired torpedoes that missed. *Endicott* got off a couple of torpedoes that came close enough that *Antilope* avoided being hit only by turning head on towards the destroyer and masked her main battery.

0702   ... USS ENDICOTT closed the CAPAIULO to 1,500 yards and fired all available main battery guns, 40 MM guns and 20 MM batteries. It was observed that the 40 MM's fire was particularly destructive and ... was the main factor in forcing them to temporarily cease fire . . . One prisoner of war stated that he took one look at his gun crew during the 40 MM fire and found the majority dead. He immediately jumped overboard . . . The CAPAIULO returned fire heavily for a few minutes until direct hits . . . caused her to explode the vicinity of the bridge and stack . . . HMS SCARAB and HMS APHIS opened fire at the same time and shots fell wide of the targets endangering the USS ENDICOTT . . . Accordingly, it was necessary for the ENDICOTT to direct the two gun boats to cease fire.

0709   The KEMID ALLAH sank.

0710   USS ENDICOTT continued firing all batteries at CAPAIULO, making many direct hits that resulted in successive explosions.

0717   Action completed. Ceased firing. CAPAIULO listed to port and commenced exploding from stem to stern. USS ENDICOTT commenced picking up survivors.

---

[*]   DD495, p. 2.

[†]   Ibid., p. 3.

0830   CAPAIULO sank.

0912   USS ENDICOTT, HMS SCARAB and HMS APHIS proceeded to Delta Assault Area, having recovered 169 prisoners on board the USS ENDICOTT and 41 prisoners between the two gun boats.[*]

It is not known how many crewmen in the two ships died. *Endicott*, on the other hand, got off lightly. She was hit forward at the waterline by a single medium-caliber shell, probably a 100 mm round from *Antilope*; the hole was plugged and several small fires extinguished. She suffered one minor injury.

The following night, the action shifted to the eastern screen, protecting the invasion fleet from intrusion from Italian ports. The closest Italian base to the east of the landings was Porto Maurizio, the harbor for the larger city of Imperia. From there, five motor torpedo boats sailed at 2120 on 17 August under the command of Kapitänleutnant Walther Grundelach. All five boats were former Italian MAS. They were *SA12* (ex-*MAS549*), *SA13* (ex-*MAS551*), *SA15* (ex-*MAS558*), *SA17* (ex-*MAS424(II)*) and *SA18* (ex-*MAS437*). Their task was to attack the invasion fleet.

The action started when at 2314, *Harding*, which was on the southward leg of a 10 nm-long north–south patrol line east of the landing beaches, made a radar contact due east of her position.[†] The contact's course was determined to be north-west at 8 knots. *Harding*'s CO, Commander G. G. Palmer, radioed his boss, CTU80.6.10 (Commander Beachhead Screen) in *Frankford* (DD497) for permission to investigate. This was obtained at 2324, and *Harding* turned to the north-east and raised her speed to 25 knots. She held this course for just eight minutes, because at 2331, a second radar contact was made, this one closer and moving much faster. The new target was just 4 nm to the south-east, heading just east of south at 24 knots. *Harding* turned to follow. When challenged by signal lamp, the contact failed to respond correctly. Salvos of starshells fired, starting at 2340, showed two or three small, fast boats, described as being 'very suspicious and did not appear to have a mast as friendly MTB or PT boats have'.[‡]

At 2344, the group of MAS split, with one group, identified as comprising two boats, heading east and the other, also with two boats, continuing to the south-west and then, at 2345, opened fire with a light-caliber machine gun, aiming at *Harding*'s searchlight. *Harding* followed this group and returned

---

[*]   DD495, pp. 3–4.

[†]   DD625, p. 1. *Harding* was the sole occupant of the 'Item Line', the easternmost patrol line protecting the landing beaches. The parallel 'Easy Line' of four destroyers patrolled the eastern side of the inner screen to the west of *Harding*; the five destroyers of the 'Charlie Line' protected the southern boundary. Of the ships later engaged this night, *Frankford* was in the middle of the 'Charlie Line', *Carmick* at its eastern end and *Satterlee* at the south end of the 'Easy Line'.

[‡]   DD625, p. 1. All US PT boats and RN MTBs had radar at this stage of the war, which required a noticeable mast; German small craft were not fitted with radar.

That night, 17 August 1944, Harding *(DD625) and* Frankford *(DD497 – seen here on 26 January 1944) intercepted a force of five German-manned MAS boats, Italian-built fast motor torpedo boats, engaging and sinking three of them. (NARA)*

fire. Now on the destroyer's starboard bow, this group turned left, to the south-south-east; *Harding*, wanting to stay between the enemy and the fleet, turned less sharply so that she passed across the MAS's wake at about 2349. *Harding* maneuvered carefully to stay as much as possible directly behind the MAS, so as not to present a good target for their torpedoes.

The group that *Harding* was following originally comprised three boats – *SA13*, *SA17* and *SA18* – but *SA18* had been damaged by *Harding*'s second salvo, which immobilized her and, unseen from the destroyer, she dropped behind and temporarily out of the action. Chasing the remaining two boats, the destroyer scored again, this time it was seen from *Harding*:

> At 2356B a sure hit was observed on one of these boats bearing 142 T and a large flash was observed in the direction of the engaged target and almost simultaneously one of the two pips disappeared from the radar screen.[*] This was reported to the Bridge by CIC and all effort was now concentrated on the one remaining boat of the right hand group.[†]

This was *SA13*. Survivors picked up later referred to *SA13* as the 'Eisenboot'; MAS551 was constructed of steel, very unusual for a MAS, which were normally

---

[*]   The 'B' at the end of '2356B' refers to the local time zone; the 'B' zone is two hours ahead of GMT (aka 'Z').

[†]   DD625, p. 1.

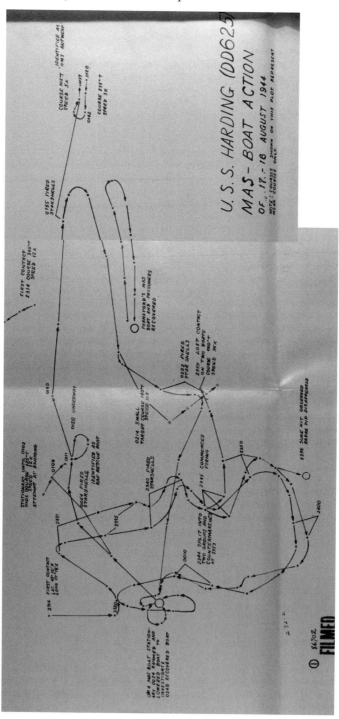

This chart, part of Harding's report of the action on 17/18 August 1944, shows the confused action that night in remarkably accurate detail. Harding's course starts in the upper left, at the point marked '2314', continues east, north-east and then south towards the small circle, marked '2356', which indicates where SA13 sank. The track then swings west and north to the second circle, where she rammed SA17 and lowered her whaleboat. Harding then went north-east and east, encountering an RAF rescue boat ('0111') and then HMS Antwerp (L4074) before returning to retrieve her whaleboat at the second small circle. Meanwhile, Frankford had encountered and sunk SA18 at the third small circle in the center of this chart. (NARA)

of wooden construction. They also stated that part of the reason why *Harding* had been able to keep up with the two MAS was that *SA13* had a maximum speed of 35 knots, a full 5 knots slower than the top speed of the wooden *SA17*. But, even after the loss of *SA13*, *SA17* could not escape from *Harding* because, soon after *SA18* was immobilized, she was hit by shrapnel that damaged the fuel feed to one engine and left her able to make a maximum of 31 knots. What followed was a predictable stern chase, with *Harding* following *SA17* as she swung first west and then north. The effectiveness of *Harding*'s gunfire was reduced by a brief failure of her FD radar about this time, but it was brought back on line at 0010 and, at 0014, *SA17* was damaged to the extent that she began to lose way. *Harding*, now with all boilers on line, was making 35 knots and rapidly overshot the slowing *SA17*. Looping back to the south, she rammed the MAS aft at 0024. *SA17* proved tough; she was now immobile and her crew was going overboard, but she showed no sign of sinking. Palmer brought *Harding* to a stop and put a boat into the water with orders to board the MAS and search for useful material.

A new participant entered the fray at this time. *Frankford* had left her patrol position at 2354 and, at 0030, approached *Harding*, which was stopped by the slowly settling MAS. At 0037, while slowly circling the two stopped vessels, *Frankford*'s radar picked up a contact 10,000 yards to the north-north-east. Turning to investigate, she rapidly approached *SA18* and opened fire.[*] The MAS got underway towards the north-east, but soon again slowed to a stop. *Frankford* ceased fire at 0048 when the range had dropped to 2,000 yards. *SA18* may have been immobilized again, but she was still full of fight. At 0050, *Frankford* turned on her searchlight, but the Germans fired at the light, and, at 0054, the destroyer opened fire again for three minutes.

At 0049, *Frankford*'s radar had detected a new target just west of due north at 9,000 yards. *Harding* was ordered to investigate and was vectored toward the target until her radar acquired it at 0051.[†] The target was rapidly approached as it was dead in the water. It was challenged three times by signal light without response, leading Palmer to assume she was hostile. At 0054 and again at 0055, the target was illuminated by starshells, showing a small boat about the size of a MAS. Still, the target did not respond. Finally at 0102, it was noticed that the target started moving east-south-east at 12 knots. Palmer ordered a course laid for ramming, as the range was now too short for main battery gunfire.

The *Harding* proceeded on a ramming course and 0111B as a final precaution turned 24-inch searchlight on in order to illuminate the target to provide a

---

[*]   Some sources, particularly Cernuschi and O'Hara, *MAS Contro Destroyers*, state that *Frankford* was engaged with *SA17* at this time, not *SA18*, and that it was only at approximately 0210 that *Frankford* first encountered *SA18* while looking for *SA17*. In this author's opinion, the evidence in favor of *SA18* being the boat encountered by *Frankford* both before and after the 0130–0210 excursion to the east far outweighs the evidence against.

[†]   DD625, p. 3; DD497, p. 2.

point of aim for the helmsman, since the target was not inside radar range and underway. Under illumination it was seen that the crew were all on deck with their hands raised as a signal of surrender, a British aircraft insignia was also noticed on the bow at this time, and the numeral 1246. At the last second the ship missed ramming by inches. The *Harding* circled and approached the craft bow on, illuminating it with the 24 inch searchlight. The Officer of the Deck, who still believed the boat to be German, hailed the boat in German and told the crew to jump in the water and swim to the ship. Someone on the boat shouted that they were English and that they surrendered.*

Not totally convinced, Palmer approached cautiously, but when it was found that the entire crew spoke English and the captain explained that it was an air-sea rescue boat, one of two operating with HMS *Antwerp* (L4074), a landing ship specializing in fighter direction (LSF), and that he had not responded to *Harding's* challenges for fear she was German, everyone agreed it had been a close-run thing, and, at 0128, the boat was allowed to proceed.

While this farce was playing out, the tactical picture only got more complicated. At 0059, *Frankford* again illuminated *SA18*, which was now afire aft. At 0102, *Frankford's* sonar man reported torpedo sounds, and, almost immediately after, a sharp jolt was felt forward. The first thought was she had been hit, but examination revealed no damage other than frayed nerves and a minor leak in the main steam line. Apparently, *SA18* managed to launch a torpedo, but it failed to run properly and exploded after hitting the seabed. A second torpedo was heard by sonar and a wake was seen passing 200 yards ahead of the ship. Obviously, *SA18* was far from dead, and *Frankford* opened fire again at 0113 with her 40 mm and 20 mm battery. At this time 11 of the MAS's crew abandoned ship without orders, leaving only the CO and three men.

Before any attempt could be made to rescue the men in the water, another contact was made 15,000 yards to the east-north-east. *Frankford* turned to investigate and ordered *Harding* to parallel her course to the north. At 0128, *Harding* was underway to the north-east, turning eastward nine minutes later. At 0151, both destroyers fired starshells, illuminating a ship 6,000 yards ahead; this time a prompt response showed that this was HMS *Antwerp*. Satisfied, the destroyers turned back at 0157.

Frankford found *SA18* still afloat, though taking on water steadily. Fourteen survivors were rescued, while a boarding party with a handy-billy attempted to save the boat. A towline was rigged and *Frankford* towed *SA18* for some distance, but, by 0410, it was obvious the boat could not be saved, and the boarding party was taken off. *SA18* was cut loose and sank ten minutes later.

On her way back to recover her whaleboat, left with *SA17*, *Harding* made yet another radar contact at 0214 some 6,000 yards south-west of *Frankford's*

---

* DD625, pp. 3–4.

position. This was challenged at 0221 and illuminated by starshell a minute later. This contact responded immediately and proved to be the second RAF boat operating with HMS *Antwerp*. *Harding* then set course back to the point where her whaleboat and *SA17* had been left. At 0232, she found her whaleboat with the boarding party and 12 survivors from *SA17*, which had in the meanwhile sunk. At 0338, *Harding* was back patrolling the eastern picket line.

After dawn, *Harding* requested and was given permission to look for survivors of the first boat sunk that night, *SA13*. None were found, but a few items were found floating at the scene, including a personal kit bag belonging to a seaman, Herwarth Kalus. By sheer coincidence, soon after leaving the scene of *SA18*'s sinking, *Frankford* came upon and rescued a single man in the water, who turned out to be the sole survivor of *SA13*, Herwarth Kalus.

While all this had been going on east of the landing beaches, there was action to the south, involving the two MAS last seen by *Harding* disappearing to the east at 2355, *SA12* and *SA15*. These boats had not fled the scene; they simply made a quick loop to the south and approached the point south-east of the landing beaches where the main southern and eastern patrol lines met. At 0020, the destroyer *Carmick* (DD493) and, two minutes later, the adjacent *Satterlee* (DD626) picked up a radar contact to the south-east, approaching at high speed.* *Carmick* fired starshells at 0025 and again at 0027 without sighting anything. Radar had by now resolved the contact into two distinct targets.

Satterlee opened fire at 0030. Almost immediately, *SA15* was hit and dropped out of the action, unseen by any of the participants and sinking some time later with no survivors. At the same time, a near-miss caused a torpedo on *SA12* to fall overboard and then explode. The same near-miss damaged the fire control of the other torpedo. With no working torpedoes, *SA12*'s CO turned the boat away to the south. Rapid work by his crew managed to repair the firing mechanism for the one remaining torpedo, and *SA12* turned back to the north at 0039. However, at 0047, just as the boat was preparing to launch the remaining torpedo, *Satterlee* scored a direct hit, and *SA12* drifted to a stop. *Carmick* opened fire on the now-stopped boat at 0052 and scored an immediate hit. *Carmick* ceased fire at 0056 and *Satterlee* three minutes later. *Carmick* moved off after an unidentified additional contact further south; *Satterlee* finished off *SA12* with 40 mm gunfire, continuing until the boat sank at 0115. Eleven survivors, many of them wounded, were picked up. With the sinking of *SA12*, all five of the MAS that sortied from Porto Maurizio on 17 August had been accounted for.

— —

The end of the U-boat campaign in the Mediterranean came unceremoniously.

---

* DD493, pp. 1–2; DD626, pp. 1–3; Cernuschi and O'Hara, *MAS Contro Destroyers*, pp. 24–5.

The last operational boat of the 29.U-flot was *U230* (Eberbach).[*] They departed Toulon on 17 August with orders to attack the invasion fleet, but lacking a snorkel and with a scratch crew of U-boatmen stranded in port, Eberbach had no chance. He claims to have fired four torpedoes at *Augusta* on 20 August, all of which missed because the cruiser, at that exact same moment, was near-missed by a shore battery and quickly began to maneuver. Regardless, *U230* ran aground the next night east of Toulon while attempting to recharge her batteries and was blown up by the crew.

In a final irony, Eberbach, plus three other officers and 46 men, attempted to flee Toulon in a fishing boat heading for Spain on the night of 27 August. They were stopped and taken prisoner by three American destroyers, including *Hambleton*.

Between this point and the end of the war, the Germans retained the Ligurian coast from the old border with France as far south as La Spezia, and from there and Porto Maurizio, they continued to operate a dwindling number of small craft, which the Allies countered with regular patrols by destroyers and PT boats. They also operated various craft of the K-Verbände. Typical encounters included *PT552* sinking four Linsen explosive motorboats off Toulon on 27 August, four Marder miniature submarines sunk by *Le Malin* and *Ludlow* off Cap Ferrat on 5 September and one more Linsen dispatched by *Hilary P. Jones* on 7/8 September. On 10 September, *Jones* and *Madison*, along with PT boats, sank three Marders soon after they departed Ventimiglia; one was sunk while submerged by *Jones*'s gunfire directed by a shore fire control party.[†] Later that day, the two destroyers and *Lorraine* shelled Ventimiglia and destroyed the remaining Marders. Shore bombardment became the most frequent activity of the destroyers that remained in the Mediterranean. Probably the last such was when *McLanahan* shelled San Remo on the Italian Riviera on 11 February 1945. She was slightly damaged by a large caliber near-miss by a shore battery as she was withdrawing. Sadly, one man was killed and eight more seriously wounded by shrapnel.

Nevertheless, sporadic German naval activity continued along the Ligurian coast until the surrender of German forces in Italy on 29 April 1945.

[*]   Morison, *History,* vol. XI, p. 284.
[†]   DD427, pp. 1–3.

8

Finishing the Job in the Atlantic
November 1943–May 1945

The demise of the U-boat force in Mediterranean, and the containment of the remaining German surface units, left the Atlantic as the last battleground in the long war to defeat the Kriegsmarine. 'Black May' in 1943 had blunted the U-boat threat against the North Atlantic convoys, but in no way marked the end of the struggle. The Kriegsmarine would never again threaten the lifeline that connected American industry and agriculture to the growing US military presence and the civilian workforce in the British Isles, but that did not mean that there would not be incidents of high drama as they fought against increasingly formidable odds. Nor did it mean that the Germans gave up trying to slip blockade-runners, surface ships and submarines (not all of them German), through the tightening noose of Allied warships and aircraft.

One of those moments of drama came on 1 November 1943, when the flush-decker *Borie* (DD215), while guarding the escort carrier *Card* (now designated CVE11) 700 nm north of the Azores, became entangled, literally, with *U405* (Hopmann).[*] *Borie* had been ordered to hunt for a single U-boat spotted by *Card*'s aircraft. When contact was made soon after dark, radar revealed not one but two U-boats on the surface, probably believing they were safe because of the rapidly rising seas. *Borie* attacked the closer of the two contacts, forcing the boat to dive. Several well-aimed depth charge attacks were followed by an underwater explosion and a large oil slick which in turn led to the assumption that the U-boat was dead. *U256* (Brauel), one of four U-boats converted to mount extra Flak weapons, was damaged, but it survived the attack and returned safely to Brest.

That left the other U-boat. At 0145, *Borie*'s radar screen registered a target that proved to be *U405*. As *Borie* charged, Hopmann took his boat deep, but another well-aimed pattern of depth charges forced *U405* to the surface, damaged to the point that she could no longer submerge. Intent on ramming the U-boat, *Borie* turned towards *U405*, but the U-boat had a tighter turning circle and managed

---

* Parkin, *Blood on the Sea*, pp. 178–84; Wynn, *U-Boat Operations*, vol. 1, p. 268; Morison, *History*, vol. X, pp. 162–8.

to elude the destroyer while they exchanged ineffective gunfire. It took nearly a half-hour before either damaged the other. *Borie* took two hits, one of which destroyed her radio shack. The U-boat's main gun was disabled by a direct hit.

While Hopmann was dealing with this damage, *Borie* turned to ram and rode up atop *U405*'s foredeck. Over the next ten minutes the two were locked together. The crews fired every weapon near to hand. Many of *U405*'s crew were killed in that time, but the boat itself seemed little worse for the experience. *Borie*, on the other hand, developed serious leaks as the two vessels wrenched against each other. By the time a large wave pulled them apart, *Borie* had only one working engine. The two boats continued to maneuver for advantage in close proximity until *Borie* found herself broadside to the U-boat's bow and fired a barrage of depth charges from her starboard throwers. This finally doomed the U-boat. At 0257, *U405* raised her bow nearly vertically and submerged for the final time.

This left *Borie* wallowing in the high seas. Her bottom was torn in so many places that water filled compartment after compartment. All power was lost shortly after 0900. As the day passed, her situation did not improve; the flooding was slowed but not stopped. At the end of the day, with forecasts of even worse weather on the way, and concerns about lurking U-boats, *Borie* was abandoned. The destroyer stubbornly remained afloat through the night, only to be scuttled the next morning. Amazingly, only three officers and 24 men were lost.

— —

In late 1942, realizing that the war would not be won anytime soon, the Germans looked outward for supplies of light metals and rubber, all of which existed in relative abundance in the territories of their Axis partner Japan. Between 27 September and 12 October, no fewer than nine blockade-runners slipped out of French Atlantic ports headed for Japanese-held territory. Of these, two were damaged while still in the Bay of Biscay and turned back. A third, *Anneliese Essberger*, was intercepted in the South Atlantic on 21 November by *Cincinnati*, *Milwaukee* (CL5) and *Somers*, and scuttled herself rather than be captured. The other six (along with others that later sailed individually) reached the Far East and the last of them were returning at the end of 1943, only to be intercepted by the US Navy's South Atlantic patrols (aided immeasurably by ULTRA decrypts) over a period of three days in January 1944.

The sequence started when ULTRA intercepts indicated that, from 2 January, U-boats operating in the South Atlantic were ordered to make no attacks on single ships south of 14°N because the blockade-runner *Weserland* was approaching.* *Weserland* was sighted by a Liberator of VB-107 out of Ascension Island at 1200 on 1 January approximately midway between Recife and Ascension. Approaching too close, the Liberator was damaged by accurate anti-aircraft fire from the ship, but managed to return to base safely. The closest naval

---

* *B.d.U. Op.'s WAR LOG,* 1.1.44.

Survivors from the German blockade-runner Weserland *are picked up by the destroyer* Somers *(DD381) on 3 January 1944, the morning after she was sunk after over a half-hour of near-continuous shelling from the destroyer's 5-inch guns. One hundred thirty-three survivors were pulled from seven lifeboats and a large raft. (NARA)*

vessel was *Somers*, approximately 225 nm north-north-west of the German's last reported position.* The destroyer turned towards the target and increased speed to 20 knots at 1512.

Somers continued steering generally south until, at 1325 the next afternoon, her radar detected a ship to the south-east at 34,250 yards. Six minutes later, a merchant ship was in sight heading south-west. *Somers* maneuvered to close the ship, which, when challenged, reported her identity as *Wascana Park* of British registry bound for Salvador da Bahia, a likely enough response given her position and course, but Commander Hughes was unable to find that ship in his ONI-209.† He ordered the ship to stop, emphasizing the point with a shot across the bow at 1601. A boarding party was sent across, reporting back at 1512 that the ship appeared to indeed be a British merchantman.

While this was going on, a radio message was received, reporting that another ship, some 60 miles to the east, was firing on another VB-107 Liberator, forcing that aircraft to head back to Ascension.‡ The ship had been initially identified as the British *Glenbank*, but after firing on the Liberator, it became clear that this was *Weserland*. *Somers* set course for the German as soon as her boarding party was recovered at 1540. The sun had set by the time radar contact was made at 1928. A second Liberator was circling *Weserland* and, at Hughes' request, dropped a flare and signaled for the ship to heave to. The ship not only did not comply, but began to steer an evasive course generally east of south at 12 knots. Using the destroyer's superior speed, Hughes maneuvered *Somers* so that she was 'up moon' from the ship about 7,000 yards to the east-south-east. Satisfied that the ship must be enemy, fire was opened at 2102. The first salvo hit the ship's bridge, killing four men, but *Weserland* continued to steam an evasive course before drifting to a stop after absorbing at least 50 hits from *Somers's* 5-inch main battery. Halting only long enough to determine that *Weserland* was not yet obviously sinking, Hughes resumed fire for another 15 salvos, finally stopping at 2136. Despite this pounding, it took almost an hour after this for *Weserland* to sink.§ After sunrise, *Somers* picked up 133 survivors from seven lifeboats and one large raft.

Anxious for the cargoes carried by these blockade-runners – *Weserland* had been loaded with rubber, tin and tungsten, all scarce in Germany – Dönitz ordered the two remaining blockade-runners following *Weserland* to enter the Atlantic at two-day intervals. Right on schedule, the next one encountered the

---

* DD381-2, pp. 1–7.

† Ibid., p. 3. ONI-209 was a publication of the Office of Naval Intelligence entitled *A Manual of Merchant Ships*. It was the US Navy's standard reference for identifying merchant ships.

‡ Roscoe, *United States Destroyer Operations*, p. 296. That aircraft was forced to ditch 70 nm short of Ascension; its ten-man crew was never found.

§ DD381-2, pp. 6–7. Hughes blamed the relative ineffectiveness of *Somers*' gunfire – even after an estimated 100 direct hits, it took over an hour for the 6528GRT *Weserland* to sink – on her main battery rounds being old and overdue for replacement.

barrier patrols on 4 January. *Omaha*, accompanied by *Jouett*, was on patrol out of Recife. Despite having a pair of floatplanes scouting either side of her course and working radar, it was a lookout on her foretop who first spotted *Rio Grande* at 0825 approximately 15 nm to the south-east.[*] The German crew set off scuttling charges and began abandoning ship even as *Omaha* was approaching. In what had now become standard practice, the American ships opened fire, aiming at a point ahead of the enemy lifeboats, in an attempt to drive them back towards their ship. After three salvos ahead of the lifeboats, it had become obvious that *Rio Grande* was sinking rapidly, and the fourth (and final) salvo from *Omaha* was at the ship. *Rio Grande* sank at 0925. Four lifeboats were seen in the water, but the ships were ordered to leave the scene immediately without picking up survivors. The order came from CTF41, Rear-Admiral Oliver. M. Read, in *Omaha*.[†]

Omaha and *Jouett* returned to the site of the sinking at 1046 the next day, 5 January. They found enough debris to confirm *Rio Grande*'s identity and numerous bales of raw rubber floating in the vicinity, but no trace of the four lifeboats. While occupied with this investigation, a radio message was received at 1246 reporting another suspicious ship approaching from the east. The two ships departed the scene to investigate this new contact and did not return.

Less than four hours later, the unidentified ship was in sight, now heading just north of west, 31,700 yards south-west of the approaching Americans.[‡] *Jouett* was ordered ahead at best speed to cut off the fleeing *Burgenland*, while *Omaha* worked up to 25 knots. The effort was pointless, because the Germans stopped as ordered and then, at 1732, set off scuttling charges that caused noticeable plumes of black smoke to rise from the ship's midsection. *Jouett* was ordered to open fire on the ship, which she did two minutes later. *Omaha* joined in at 1739. Ceasefire was ordered at 1742; by now, *Burgenland* was obviously sinking. As before, the American ships immediately cleared the area, despite seeing one raft and two lifeboats in the water with survivors. One lifeboat was seen to have been hit and sunk by gunfire.[§]

Aerial reconnaissance the next day revealed yet more floating bales of rubber, but, again, no sign of the survivors. Over the next several days, Brazilian and American coasters were able to recover almost 2,000 of the 245 kg bales of rubber.[¶] On 7 January, *Davis* found 21 survivors from *Burgenland*. The next day, in separate rescues, *Marblehead* found 72 survivors from *Rio Grande*, and *Winslow* (DD359) found another 35 from *Burgenland*. On 11 January, one lifeboat

[*]   CL4-3, pp. 1–3.

[†]   Ibid., p 2. While the author has been unable to find a specific reason for Read's order, it was undoubtedly related to the fact that *Rio Grande* was able to get off a radio report of her scuttling with precise location information before the charges were detonated.

[‡]   CL4-4, pp. 1–4; DD396, pp. 1–2.

[§]   DD396, p. 2.

[¶]   Morison, *History*, vol. X, p. 228.

Japanese submarine I-8, seen here arriving at Brest on 31 August 1943, was the only Yanagi boat to complete a round-trip from and back to Japan. (Ed Rumpf)

with 22 survivors from *Rio Grande* reached the Brazilian coast. Two days later, another 34 survivors were picked up by the Brazilian minelayer *Camocim*, the last of the crew of the three blockade-runners to be found alive.

On 13 May 1944, the U-boat hunters of the US Navy's escort-carrier based hunter-killer groups, which now numbered eight, found themselves chasing an unexpected quarry. The story started in June 1942, when the large Japanese submarine *I-30* was detached from a group operating in the Indian Ocean and ordered to proceed to France on the first of what were to be known as Yanagi (Willow) missions. Off Madagascar on a combat patrol, *I-30* was met by a supply ship and loaded a small token cargo of mica and shellac for the Germans. Early in July, she entered the Atlantic, arriving at Lorient on 5 August.* *I-30* departed again on 22 August, carrying German torpedoes, various other weapons, the blueprints for the Würzburg air-search radar, industrial diamonds and 50 Enigma coding machines. The submarine reached Penang on 8 October and then proceeded to Singapore, where ten of the Enigma machines were landed. On 13 October, when leaving Singapore, *I-30* struck a British mine and sank immediately. Most of the crew was rescued, but almost all of the materiel was lost.

---

*   All of *I-30*'s Type 95 oxygen torpedoes were removed before she set off for France. This was one secret weapon the Japanese were unwilling to share at that stage of the war.

It was another year before the idea was raised again, this time with the emphasis shifted to the carriage of strategic materials to Germany from the Far East where they were relatively plentiful. Submarine *I-8* departed Kure on 1 June 1943 with a double crew, because the Germans had agreed to turn over one of their new long-range Type IXC/40 U-boats to the Japanese. At Penang, *I-8* took on a cargo of quinine, tin and rubber, landing her scout aircraft to compensate for the added weight. On 20 August, *I-8* rendezvoused with *U161* (Achilles), which transferred an officer and two petty officers along with a Metox radar detector to help the Japanese navigate the increasingly treacherous approaches to France. (This turned out to be a stroke of luck for the three Germans because *U161* was lost with all hands weeks later off Brazil after an attack by a VP-74 Mariner.)

I-8 arrived at Brest on 31 August, unloaded her cargo and spare crew, added a 20 mm Flakvierling on her after deck, loaded a cargo of various weapons and electronics, plus some penicillin, and departed on 5 October. She arrived at Kure on 21 December, the only Japanese submarine to complete a round-trip Yanagi mission.

Of more interest to this story is the fate of the spare crew brought to Brest in *I-8*. Under the command of Lieutenant Commander Norita Sadatoshi, the crew of 48 officers and men trained for six months at German facilities on the Baltic before taking over *U1224* at Kiel on 15 February 1944. She was commissioned into the Imperial Japanese Navy as *RO-501* 13 days later. Training in the Baltic continued until 30 March when she departed Kiel with a cargo of mercury, lead, steel, optical glass and aluminum, along with drawings for a Type IXC/40 U-boat and an Me 163 Komet rocket fighter. Topping up fuel at Kristiansund, Norway, on 16 April, she departed for Japan, taking the long route around the British Isles. It is possible she refueled from *U488* (Studt) off the Azores later in the month, shortly before the latter was sunk by destroyer escorts accompanying *Croatan* (CVE25) on 26 April. On 6 May, Norita sent a coded message stating he had been forced to dive by aircraft. The source of the signal was pinpointed by Allied HF/DF. Seven days later, *Francis M. Robinson* (DE220), escorting *Bogue*, made a sonar contact west of the Cape Verde Islands. A Hedgehog barrage followed by a pattern of Mk 8 magnetic-influence depth charges led to a massive underwater explosion.

RO-501 was only the first of two Japanese submarines sunk by the US Navy in the Atlantic. The other also was sunk by *Bogue*'s group. *I-52* had departed Singapore in April with a cargo of tin, rubber and quinine. On 22 June, she rendezvoused with *U530* (Lange) west of the Cape Verde Islands. The next night, running on the surface in bad weather, *I-52* was detected by a TBM of VC-69 off *Bogue*.[*] The pilot, Lieutenant Commander Jesse D. Taylor, dropped a pattern of sonobuoys and then a flare that revealed the submarine on the

---

[*]   *U-boat Archive* (www.uboatarchive.net).

The only instance in which a U-boat successfully challenged the domination of the US Navy's escort carrier hunter-killer groups was when U549 (Krankenhagen) torpedoed Block Island (CVE21), 29 May 1944. The U-boat was able to put three torpedoes into the escort carrier before being detected and attacked. (NARA)

surface. He attacked first with two depth bombs, one of which exploded close aboard, and, then, after *I-52* submerged, with a Fido homing torpedo. Propeller noises heard with the sonobuoys disappeared after the Fido exploded, and Taylor heard breaking-up noises. However, a second Avenger on the scene heard faint propeller sounds almost an hour later and dropped another Fido near the sonobuoy with the loudest signal. A violent explosion 18 minutes later ended the noises and produced a large debris field with blocks of raw rubber floating in an oil slick.

The US Navy's escort-carrier groups dominated the waters along the Central Atlantic convoy routes, drastically reducing the effectiveness of those U-boats that survived the increasingly difficult passage across the Bay of Biscay into the open ocean. Yet Germany's U-boats still had the power to strike back if conditions were right. Conditions indeed were right for *U549* (Krankenhagen) for one brief moment on 29 May 1944. *Block Island* (CVE21) had departed Casablanca on 23 May, screened by the four destroyer escorts of CortDiv60. The only change to the group since it had been formed in April was the replacement of *Buckley* (DE51) with *Robert I. Paine* (DE578), because *Buckley* had been

One of the escorts attacking U549 was Barr *(DE576). Krankenhagen managed to fire a T5 acoustic torpedo which operated as designed; attracted to the propeller sounds of the destroyer escort, it exploded under her fantail, causing the damage seen here, 29 May 1944.* Barr *survived, but lost 16 of her crew. U549 was sunk with all hands by two of* Block Island's *remaining escorts. Note that* Barr, *despite being a very new ship – she had been in commission barely three months – carries a quad 1.1-inch AA mount aft, a weapon that had long since been superseded by the 40 mm Bofors on larger ships. (NARA)*

damaged in a surface battle with *U66* (Seehausen) on 6 May reminiscent of that between *Borie* and *U405*, and was on her way Stateside for repairs. The assigned hunting ground was in the waters west of Madeira and the Canaries. *U549* was sighted on the surface just after midnight on 28 May by a VC-55 Avenger and then detected and attacked at dawn by *Ahrens* (DE575) and *Paine*, but the attack failed and contact was lost.

U549 was found again the next night and attacked by a pair of Avengers, but once again submerged safely. The group continued the hunt throughout the day on 29 May without finding the U-boat. Apparently, Krankenhagen had maneuvered around to the left of the group and from a position inside the screen fired two electric torpedoes at 2013 that hit *Block Island* in the bow and right aft under the after elevator. The first hit blew a hole through the bow and twisted the port forward corner of the flight deck upward, but did not seriously endanger the ship. The hit aft was a different matter; the single propeller shaft was sheared through and a significant amount of flooding occurred. The shaft tunnel flooded and caused leakage into the engine room. *Block Island* drifted to a stop.

If that had been all the damage *Block Island* received, she might have survived, but Krankenhagen launched a third torpedo that hit just forward of the second.

The slow flooding of the machinery spaces now became fast, and when an 18-inch gap appeared across the flight deck, it became obvious that the aft end of the ship was sagging and might break off. At 2040, Captain Francis M. Hughes gave the order to abandon ship. She slid stern-first beneath the waves at 2155. Only 13 men died from her crew and the embarked squadron; 951 were rescued. Four of the six Wildcats aloft at the time of the attack failed to reach La Palma, Canary Islands, the closest land; their pilots were never found.

TG21.11 was not finished with Krankenhagen, nor he with them. Even before the third torpedo hit, *Eugene E. Elmore* (DE686) spotted *U549*'s periscope and attacked with depth charges. Krankenhagen responded with a T5 which exploded under the fantail of *Barr* (DE576) at 2033, killing four, wounding 14 and leaving another dozen unaccounted for. The destroyer escort's hull aft of the after engine room was a twisted mass, but she was never in danger of sinking. She would be towed to Casablanca and eventually rebuilt as a high-speed transport, APD39. *Paine* was left to look after *Barr*, while *Elmore* and *Ahrens* hunted *U549*. Krankenhagen fired one more torpedo; this one missed *Elmore*. Then the two destroyer escorts attacked. *Ahrens* made sonar contact and *Elmore* launched three salvoes of Hedgehogs in rapid succession. At least one of them hit. Breaking-up noises were followed by a spreading field of debris and oil. Fifty-eight men died in *U549* that evening.

The story of the capture of *U505* (Lange) near the African coast on 4 June 1944 by men from *Pillsbury* (DE133), part of a task group based on *Guadalcanal* (CVE60), has been told frequently enough that it need not be recounted here. Suffice it to say that through a combination of planning and luck, the Americans were able to prevent the U-boat's sinking and tow her across the ocean to Bermuda. By this point in the war, the intelligence value of this capture was not great and the risk that word might get back to Germany and lead to a change in encryption techniques sufficiently serious that Captain Daniel V. Gallery's feat was not greeted with universal acclaim by the Navy establishment.

— —

In the spring of 1945, the Americans became convinced on the basis of very flimsy intelligence that the Germans intended to send V1-equipped U-boats to the American coast to bombard New York and other coastal targets.* In fact, Dönitz had planned one last defiant gesture. A group of seven long-range Type IXs equipped with snorkels were to depart Norwegian ports and make the long submerged passage across the Atlantic. One of those boats was delayed due to problems with its snorkel. The other six made up Gruppe Seewolf, tasked with sweeping along the North Atlantic convoy routes, attacking targets of

---

* Blair, *Hitler's U-Boat War: The Hunted*, pp. 683–4; Morison, *History*, vol. X, pp. 344–56. The V1, the first of Hitler's retaliation (*Vergeltungs*) weapons, was a pulse-jet-propelled unmanned flying bomb.

opportunity and then raiding the dense traffic along the American East Coast, much of it once again sailing independently.

Due to ULTRA intercepts, the Allies were well aware of Seewolf and routed all convoys well to the south, which brought the added advantage that they missed a series of storms and fog banks that made life on the North Atlantic miserable for sailors in April and often made snorkeling impossible for the Seewolf boats. There were plenty of American sailors on the North Atlantic in April because the US Navy reacted to the rumors of a flying bomb attack on the East Coast with an extravagant concentration of ASW assets, codenamed Operation TEARDROP. The initial deployment was two escort carriers, each with a screen of four destroyer escorts, plus 12 more destroyer escorts sweeping ahead. These sank two of the Seewolf boats on the night of 15/16 April and a third one five nights later.

At this point, the first TEARDROP groups were replaced by another pair of escort carriers and a total of 22 destroyer escorts. On 24 April, one of *Bogue*'s escorts, *Frederick C. Davis*, last seen off Anzio, detected a U-boat stalking the escort carrier. Just as *Davis* turned to attack the contact, she was struck amidships by a T5 from her intended victim. The effect of this single torpedo was devastating; *Davis* broke in two and sank in less than ten minutes. Only 66 out of her crew of 192 officers and men survived.

As might be expected, this set off a determined hunt for the U-boat. *U546* (Just) was hunted aggressively for ten hours until a Hedgehog salvo from *Flaherty* (DE135) brought her to the surface at 1836, where she was smothered by gunfire from at least four other destroyer escorts. Thirty-three of her crew of 59 were rescued. They might have wished otherwise, since a number were rather harshly interrogated, first at Argentia and then at Washington in an attempt to determine whether they were attempting a missile attack on the US. It was only after the war with Germany was over that the Americans finally realized that the supposed V1 attack had never been real.

Two of the Seewolf boats evaded the TEARDROP barriers and survived long enough to surrender off the East Coast on 14 May 1945.

On 23 February 1945, *U853* (Frömsdorf) left Stavanger and began the slow snorkel across the Atlantic. The passage was uneventful, until, on 23 April, off Portland, ME, the old patrol boat *Eagle No. 56* exploded, broke in two and sank while towing a target float for Navy bombers. It is probable that she was sunk by *U853*. Forty-nine officers and men died in the sinking. *Selfridge* (DD357) rescued the 13 survivors and depth charged a sonar contact, without result.

Twelve days later, in the late afternoon on 5 May, the collier *Black Point* was torpedoed off Narragansett, RI. The explosion took off most of her stern and the ship quickly settled to the bottom with her bow still above water. Thirty-four men were rescued; 12 died. This time there was no doubt that the sinking was by U-boat torpedo, and a scratch group of two destroyer escorts and a patrol

The last US merchantman lost in the Atlantic was sunk off Rhode Island by U853 (Frömsdorf) on 5 May 1945. That night the U-boat was detected and attacked repeatedly then and again in the morning. This image shows a Hedgehog pattern fired by Moberly *(PF63) on 6 May. By this point, the U-boat had already been destroyed and her crew of 56 was already dead. (NHHC)*

frigate starting hunting for *U853*. Less than two hours after the torpedoing of *Black Point*, *Atherton* (DE169) had a solid sonar contact on an immobile object lying on the shallow seabed, although in those waters, it could have just as easily been a wreck as a live U-boat. After several attacks with depth charges and Hedgehogs, contact was lost, but was then regained at 2337. *Atherton* then delivered a Hedgehog attack that probably finished off *U853*. Daylight revealed debris and an oil slick, but that was not considered conclusive and the attacks by *Atherton* and *Moberly* (PF63) continued intermittently until noon on 6 May, when Frömsdorf's cap and part of *U853*'s chart table were recovered. Fifty-six men died in the U-boat.

Black Point was the last American merchantman to be lost in the Battle of the Atlantic and the last sinking in American waters. *U853* was not the last U-boat sunk by the US Navy in that long battle. That sad distinction went to *U881* (Frischke). Originally supposed to be one of the Seewolf boats, but delayed due to mechanical problems, *U881* was detected by *Farquhar* (DE139), screening

The final act of the US Navy in the War in Europe was to accept the surrender of the small number of surviving U-boats near the American East Coast. Here, U858 (Bode), one of the Seewolf boats, is seen surrendering on 10 May 1945 south of Cape Race. She was escorted south to Lewes, DE, where her formal surrender took place four days later. (NARA)

Mission Bay (CVE59), sweeping south-east from Argentia to supplement the two escort carrier groups still assigned to TEARDROP. *Farquhar* detected the U-boat approaching *Mission Bay* before dawn on 6 May and launched a single depth charge attack, after which contact was lost. It was only post-war that the sinking of *U881* at that time and place, and the death of all 53 of her crew, was confirmed.

— —

The Germans were, in fact, developing advanced new U-boat types with dramatically improved underwater characteristics, weaponry and sensor systems. These boats, which had been under active development since early in 1943, were being built in large numbers and the first were ready for combat operations in February 1945. However, the very small number available before the German surrender in May 1945 prevented them having any serious impact on the war's outcome.

Postscript

Crossing the Rhine (March 1945)

Although the US Navy's presence off the Atlantic coast of France was reduced after the capture of Cherbourg, there remained a small contingent at that port to protect against raids from the Channel Islands and the Biscay ports that remained in German hands. Vice-Admiral Kirk was put in command of these forces, establishing the Command, US Naval Forces, France, on 12 September 1944. It was to Kirk's headquarters, set up at Lucienne outside Paris, that engineers from Lieutenant General Bradley's Twelfth Army Group came seeking landing craft to help cross the Rhine.[*]

Operation DELAWARE, under the command of Commander William J. Whiteside, covered the activities of TG122.5, which was formed in early 1945 to provide landing craft support for US Army units as they approached the Rhine.[†] The initial plan was to provide each of Bradley's three armies with 24 LCVPs, which were to be transported across France from Le Havre on tank recovery trailers. When it was pointed out that LCVPs were too small to carry an M4 Sherman tank, an additional 45 LCMs were assigned to support Bradley. From Antwerp, they went by water down the Albert Canal as far as the Meuse River south of Maastricht, but from there, they too were mounted on Army trailers and trucked on narrow roads already crowded with military traffic across the Eiffel Mountains to positions behind the assault forces.[‡]

There were three Task Units in TG122.5. The first to be called into action was TU122.5.1, which was alerted on 7 March to be ready to support crossings in the 1st Army sector above Bonn. That same afternoon, soldiers of the US 9th AD captured the railroad bridge at Remagen intact and began pushing troops across the Rhine to establish a secure bridgehead. Because the bridge was narrow and had sustained damage in the initial German demolition attempts, the landing craft were needed to supplement the slow trickle of troops and vehicles crossing

---

[*]   Kirk, *Oral History*, p. 266.

[†]   Ibid.

[‡]   Morison, *History*, vol. IX, p. 318. An LCM weighed 70 t when loaded on an M25 Tank Transporter and was more than 77 ft long.

the river.* The first boats were afloat on the Ahr River at Bad Neuenahr, a tributary of the Rhine, on 11 March. They were put to work immediately ferrying troops across the Rhine along a 35-mile stretch of the river either side of Remagen. They also assisted Army engineers building pontoon bridges and even served as picket boats, dropping depth charges on suspected enemy frogmen. By 27 March, TU122.5.1 had ferried approximately 14,000 troops and 400 vehicles across the river.[†]

TU122.5.2 was put to work on Patton's Third Army front on 22 March at Oppenheim above Mainz. This was just the first of four crossings in the 3rd Army sector, including one on 28 March by the 80th ID at Mainz against heavy opposition. In all cases, Patton's plan called for the first crossings to be made before dawn with no advance artillery barrage in order to achieve maximum tactical surprise. The crossings were made with minimal planning; local commanders were expected to use their initiative in determining when and where to cross.

In the Ninth Army sector further north, crossings were made by TU122.5.3 on either side of Rheinberg, near Duisburg, starting late on 23 March. As this army was now part of Montgomery's 21st Army Group, the landings were much more methodical. A lavish two-hour artillery barrage preceded the first crossings, which were supported by the largest airborne operation of the war. In typical Montgomery fashion, the whole plan was carefully orchestrated down to the smallest detail. The next day, Eisenhower met with Churchill, Sir Alan Brooke – Chief of the Imperial General Staff – and Montgomery at the latter's headquarters to review the progress of the operation. After Ike departed around noon, Churchill persuaded Montgomery to commandeer an LCM and crossed to the eastern bank of the Rhine, accompanied by Montgomery, Brooke and US Lieutenant General William Simpson – Commander of the Ninth Army – and several photographers. Eisenhower was reportedly furious when he heard about this stunt, though in his post-war memoirs, he simply stated 'had I been present he would never have been permitted to cross the Rhine that day.'[‡]

By the end of March, the participation of TG122.5 in combat operations was concluded. It is entirely fitting that one of the final acts in the US Navy's participation in the conquest of the European Axis should include carrying the armies of the victorious Allies across the Rhine, historically the final barrier to the conquest of Germany.

---

* The bridge finally collapsed on 17 March.
† Morison, *History,* vol. XI, p. 319.
‡ Eisenhower, *Crusade in Europe*, p. 390.

Appendix A

Reverse Lend-Lease

The Lend-Lease Act of 11 March 1941 unleashed a flood of war material of all types, everything from food and fuel to bombs and bombers. It included a good number of warships, most notably 38 escort aircraft carriers and 78 destroyer escorts. However, the flow of ships was not entirely one way. In particular, during the bleak months in early 1942 when the U-boats were playing havoc along the American East Coast, the Royal Navy sent ten Flower-class corvettes and 24 ASW trawlers to assist the US Navy implement coastal convoys and the other measures necessary to protect the vital movement of goods, particularly oil, between ports in the Caribbean and the Gulf of Mexico and American industrial centers in the north-east.

The ten corvettes, offered on 10 February 1942, were true 'Reverse Lend-Lease', in that the ships were commissioned into the US Navy classed as gunboats and manned by US Navy crews for the duration of the war. On the other hand, the 24 anti-submarine trawlers offered at the same time were deployed to US East Coast ports and acted under the orders of Admiral Andrews' Eastern Sea Frontier, but remained in the Royal Navy with Royal Navy crews.

Flower-class Corvettes

Temptress (PG62):   former HMS *Veronica* (K37), launched at Smith's Dock Co. Ltd, Middlesboro, on 17 October 1940. Transferred to US Navy on 16 February 1942. Commissioned on 21 March 1942. Departed Londonderry on 11 April 1942 to join escort of ON.85. Returned to Royal Navy on 26 August 1945.

Surprise (PG63):   former HMS *Heliotrope* (K03), launched at John Crown & Sons Ltd, Sunderland, transferred to US Navy and commissioned at Hull on 24 March 1942. Departed Londonderry on 24 April 1942 to join escort of ON.89. Returned to Royal Navy on 26 August 1945.

Spry (PG64):   former HMS *Hibiscus* (K24), launched at Harland and Wolff, Ltd, Belfast, on 6 April 1940. Transferred to US Navy and commissioned at Leith on 2 May 1942. Departed Londonderry on 30 May 1942 to join escort of ON.99. Returned to Royal Navy on 26 August 1945.

Saucy (PG65): former HMS *Arabis* (K73), launched at Harland and Wolff Ltd, Belfast, on 14 February 1940. Transferred to US Navy and commissioned at Belfast on 30 April 1942. Departed Londonderry on 16 May 1942 to join escort of ON.95. Returned to Royal Navy on 26 August 1945.

Restless (PG66): former HMS *Periwinkle* (K55), launched at Harland and Wolff Ltd, Belfast, on 21 February 1940. Transferred to US Navy and commissioned on 15 March 1942. Departed Londonderry on 11 April 1942 to join escort of ON.85. Returned to Royal Navy on 26 August 1945.

Ready (PG67): former HMS *Calendula* (K28), launched at Harland and Wolff Ltd, Belfast, in 1940. Transferred to US Navy and commissioned at Tilburg on 12 March 1942. Departed Londonderry on 15 April 1942 to join escort of ON.86. Returned to Royal Navy on 23 August 1945.

Impulse (PG68): former HMS *Begonia* (K66), launched at Cook, Welton, and Gemmell Ltd, Hull, on 18 September 1940. Transferred to US Navy and commissioned at London on 16 March 1942. Departed Londonderry on 15 April 1942 to join escort of ON.86. Returned to Royal Navy in August 1945.

Fury (PG69): former HMS *Larkspur* (K82), launched at Fleming and Ferguson Ltd, Paisley, in 1941. Transferred to US Navy and commissioned on 17 March 1942. Departed Londonderry on 11 April 1942 to join escort of ON.85. Returned to Royal Navy on 22 August 1945.

Courage (PG70): former HMS *Heartsease* (K15), launched at Harland and Wolff Ltd, Belfast, in 1939. Transferred to US Navy on 18 March 1942 and commissioned on 3 April 1942. Departed Londonderry on 24 April 1942 to join escort of ON.89. Returned to Royal Navy on 23 August 1945.

Tenacity (PG71): former HMS *Candytuft* (K09), launched at Grangemouth Dry Dock Co. Ltd, Grangemouth, on 8 July 1940. Transferred to US Navy on 4 March 1942 and commissioned at New York on 11 June 1942. Returned to Royal Navy on 26 August 1945.

Technically also Reverse Lend-Lease, 15 Modified Flower-class corvettes were ordered in Canada for the Royal Navy under the Lend-Lease program, but eight were transferred to the US Navy before completion: *Action* (PG86), *Alacrity* (PG87), *Brisk* (PG89), *Haste* (PG92), *Intensity* (PG93), *Might* (PG94), *Pert* (PG95) and *Prudent* (PG96). Most were manned by Coast Guard crews. All saw service in the Eastern Sea Frontier and were transferred to the US Maritime Commission in 1946–7 for disposal. The remaining seven (PG88, PG90-91 and PG97-100) were delivered to the Royal Navy as originally planned. (One of these seven had an interesting time of it. The hull ordered as PG88 was transferred to the Royal Navy as planned on 31 January 1943 and named HMS *Dittany* (K279), but she was transferred back to the US Navy on 7 March and given the name *Beacon* (PG88). On 31 May, however, she was re-re-transferred to the Royal Navy and fought out the war as HMS *Dittany* before being returned to the US Navy for disposal in June 1946.)

River-class Frigates

The US Navy ordered ten of the Royal Navy's River-class frigates, considerably bigger than the Flower-class corvettes, from the Canadian Vickers yard. These were ships designed to be built to commercial rather than naval standards, meaning the construction was much lighter than in the similarly sized destroyer escorts. The advantages of commercial-standard construction were that the ships could be built more quickly in yards not accustomed to naval construction. In the event, only the first two were delivered to the US Navy, classed as patrol frigates: *Asheville* (PF1) and *Natchez* (PF2). The remaining eight frigates in the Canadian order were transferred to the Royal Navy as Lend-Lease. All were returned to the US for disposal in 1946. Meanwhile, the US Maritime Commission, using modified plans, ordered 100 more patrol frigates from American commercial yards, starting with *Tacoma* (PF3). Of this number, four were cancelled, and 21 were transferred to the Royal Navy which classed them as 'Colony'-class frigates. The remaining 77 patrol frigates were manned by US Coast Guard crews.

ASW Trawlers

The offer of 24 anti-submarine trawlers was also made on 10 February 1942. By this time, it was obvious that German attack on the shipping off the US East Coast was not going to slow, and the British were pressing Admiral King to institute coastal convoys. Unlike the Flower-class corvettes, the trawlers were available immediately. Also, since they were manned throughout by their original Royal Navy Patrol Service crews, there was no delay bringing them into service, other than the difficulties experienced finding the correct grade of coal for their boilers (all but two were coal-fired) and maintaining ships with unfamiliar equipment at US Navy shipyards. The trawlers operated from ports along the length of the US eastern seaboard.

One of the 24 – HMT *Northern Princess* (406) – was lost to U-boat attack while crossing the Atlantic to begin operating with the Americans, being sunk by *U587* (Borcherdt) near Grand Banks on 8 March 1942.* None of the crew of 38 officers and men were recovered. Of the remaining 23 trawlers, an additional

---

* uboat.net. This attribution for the loss of HMT *Northern Princess* is somewhat speculative, due in part because *U587* was herself lost on this patrol, purportedly the first U-boat to be sunk after location by HF/DF. However, current opinion is that the prior attributions for her loss are incorrect. For example, Rohwer, *Axis Submarine Successes*, p. 83, credits her sinking to *U94* (Ites). Contemporary sources listed her loss as due to unknown causes in bad weather, implying that she foundered in a storm.

five were lost while serving along the US East Coast. These were:

HMT *St. Cathan* (FY234):   Sank after colliding with the Dutch merchantman *Hebe* on 11 April 1942 near Little River, SC.

HMT *Senateur Duhamel* (FY327):   Sank off Cape Lookout, NC, on 6 May 1942 after colliding with the US Navy auxiliary *Semmes* (AG24).

HMT *Bedfordshire* (FY141):   Torpedoed by *U558* (Krech) on 12 May 1942 off Cape Lookout, NC. One crewman survived because he missed the ship's sailing that morning.

HMT *Kingston Ceylonite* (FY214):   Mined off Virginia Beach, VA, while escorting convoy KN.109 on 15 June 1942. (The KN convoys were coastal convoys between Key West, FL, and Hampton Roads, VA.) The minefield was laid by *U701* (Degen) on 12 June.

HMT *Pentland Firth* (FY108):   Sank off Sandy Hook, NJ, in the outer harbor of New York City after colliding with the US Navy minesweeper *Chaffinch* (AM81) on 19 September 1942.

The remaining 18 trawlers were returned to Royal Navy control in October 1942.

Appendix B

Landing Craft Designations

The Americans built and employed a large number of different types of landing craft in the Second World War. They also were supported by a number of unique types developed by the Royal Navy. The only things they had in common was that they had all been originally designed to be used in amphibious operations and the all had hull type designators starting with the letter 'L'. In virtually every case, these craft were not given names, nor were the smaller ones even given hull numbers. The following is a list of the landing craft types mentioned in this book, with a brief description of each type. It is not a complete listing of all landing craft types used by the Americans in the Second World War. Several types were used only in the Pacific theater and do not appear in this account.

> LCA – Landing Craft, Assault – A small (13½ t) landing craft for personnel, built by the Royal Navy, but sometimes used to transport American troops. Capable of carrying 35 troops over short distances, it had a narrow bow ramp and an armored bulkhead to protect the troops from small arms fire as they approached a beach. Similar in size and purpose to the American LCP(R).
>
> LCF(L) – Landing Craft, Flak (Large) – This was a British-built LCT Mk 3 or 4, larger than the American-built LCT Mk 5, converted to mount one of several anti-aircraft fits that generally included a number of 2-pounder (40 mm) pom-poms and 20 mm Oerlikons. Generally 12 guns were mounted, four of one type and eight of the other, all in single mounts. They were used to provide anti-aircraft support for landing craft close to shore.
>
> LCG(L) – Landing Craft, Gun (Large) – Converted from LCT Mk 3s or 4s, these generally carried a pair of 4.7-inch single mounts and as many as seven 20 mm Oerlikon mounts. They were used to provide gunfire support for landing craft close to shore.
>
> LCI – Landing Craft, Infantry – Officially, the base type was designated LCI(L), standing for Landing Craft, Infantry (Large). Developed in the

US to a Royal Navy requirement, they were designed to carry up to 200 troops, landing them directly on a beach over a pair of bow ramps. They were 158 ft long and displaced 234 t when empty. Because they were too large to transport across the Atlantic even as deck cargo, they were given sufficient endurance to cross the ocean on their own. 923 were built, of which 211 were provided to the Royal Navy. They were popular, in part, because they were fast for a landing craft, capable of a top speed of 15.5 knots, which allowed them to survive where a slower craft, such as an LST, might fall prey to enemy fire. Several variants were built (or field-modified) to perform specialized tasks, including: LCI(R) fitted with six 5-inch rocket launchers; LCI(G) gunboats fitted with two single 40 mm Bofors mounts plus an assortment of lighter weapons and rocket launchers; LC(FF) fitted with additional deckhouses and communication equipment to act as flotilla flagships: and LCI(M) which mounted a 4.2-inch mortar.

LCM – Landing Craft, Mechanized – A small landing craft for vehicles or personnel built during the Second World War in at least six different versions in both the US and Great Britain. They ranged between 44 ft (13.6 m) and 73 ft (22.5 m) in length and displaced between 26 and 62 t. They were intended for short-range operation only, lacking any enclosed compartments beyond a rudimentary pilot house on some of the larger variants. They were carried to the landing zone by attack transports (APAs).

LCP – Landing Craft, Personnel – The smallest of the widely used landing craft, they were 36 ft in length and displaced 5.8 t empty. They could carry up to 36 troops or 4 t of cargo. Short-ranged, they were intended only for carrying troops and materiel from ship to shore. There were two main types: the LCP(R), which had a narrow ramp at the bow to facilitate off-loading, and the LCP(L) or Eureka boat, which did not. Sometimes called a Higgins Boat. These were not given individual hull numbers. These had a pair of machine gun positions on either side of the bow. The narrowness of the bow ramp of the LCP(R) made exiting over the ramp a slow process.

LCT – Landing Craft, Tank – This, the smallest of landing craft made for the US Navy to receive individual numbers, originated in an Admiralty requirement for a cross-Channel landing craft. The request was for a landing craft capable of short-range transport and landing of six medium tanks or heavy trucks. They displaced 286 t empty and had a length of 117 ft. The Mk 5 version had a bow ramp; the Mk 6 version was slightly bigger and had ramps forward and aft, which allowed them to be linked as a floating causeway. This was an extremely useful craft, and it was built in large numbers, nearly 1,500 being built for the US and Royal Navies.

LCVP – Landing Craft, Vehicle, Personnel - At 9 t empty, this was similar in size and purpose to an LCP(R), from which it was developed, except that it had a broader ramp at the bow, so it could carry a Jeep or a small truck. The broader ramp was achieved by moving the machine gun positions aft of the cargo well.

LST – Landing Ship, Tank – Developed in response to an Admiralty request for a ship capable of carrying tanks and other heavy land vehicles across the Atlantic and of landing them directly on a beach, a total of 1,152 LSTs were built for the Royal Navy and the US Navy. They amply fulfilled their purpose, being capable of landing 500 t of wheeled or tracked vehicles over a bow ramp. They were built in several series, averaging an empty displacement of 1,625 t, a length of 316 ft and a cruising speed of 9 knots. They were ubiquitous throughout the amphibious campaigns of the Second World War, where the designation LST was commonly understood to stand for 'Large Slow Target'. As their numbers increased during the war, some were converted to repair ships, tenders, store ships and barracks ships.

Sources

It should be noted that, given the research resources available at the beginning of the twenty-first century, some sources I have used are available in cyberspace. (A small percentage of these are available only online.) In these cases, I have given the hyperlink to the source rather than the more traditional publisher information. It is characteristic of such sources that they are more ephemeral than paper-and-ink sources. When the site that serves the pages is changed or ceases to exist, the effect can be as if every copy of a particular book was instantly vaporized. All links listed here were active and available at the time this manuscript was written. (In cases when an internet source is used only once and no author is credited, I have sometimes opted to list the link in a footnote to the text.)

All primary sources not otherwise identified as to origin are from the US National Archives and Records Administration (NARA), which holds the US Navy's WWII-era records at the Archives II site in College Park, MD.

Primary Sources – Action/Damage Reports

A few of these sources are shown as being undated. That simply means that the cover page of the report, which often was the only page displaying the submission date, has become separated from the report and is no longer filed with it. Typically, action reports were submitted anywhere from a few days to a few weeks after the action described. They are ordered here by hull number or, in the case of aircraft, pilot's name. The abbreviations in the left-hand column are those used in the footnotes.

ACV11   *Report of Air Operations of U.S.S. CARD during the period May 15 through July 2, 1943*, ACV11-A4, Serial 025, 3 July 1943.

ACV13-1 *Report of Antisubmarine Action by Aircraft*, VC-13 Report No. 1(a), 13 July 1943.

ACV13-2 *Report of Antisubmarine Action by Aircraft*, VC-13 Report No. 2, 14 July 1943.

AP22   *U.S.S. WAKEFIELD BOMB DAMAGE, January 30, 1942, Singapore*, undated. (While undated, this report cites a conference letter dated 29 April 1942.)

Sources

AP23-1   *Report of Task Force Fourteen from detachment Commander Task Force 14.1 on December 23, 1941, to departure of Task Force 14.2 from Bombay on January 10, 1942*, AP23/A4-3/(01), 10 January 1942.

AP23-2   *Report of Movements of U.S.S. WEST POINT and U.S.S. WAKEFIELD from January 10, 1942, to February 16, 1942*, AP23/A4-3, Serial 06, 15 February 1942.

AP25   *Report of Operations, October 24, 1942 to November 30, 1942*, AP25/, Serial 2141, 11 December 1942.

BB36-1   *Action Report – U.S.S. NEVADA (BB36) participation in Operation [redacted] period 3-17 June 1944*, BB36/A16-3/A9, Serial 0060, 23 June 1944. (The operation name was blacked out in the file copy; it would most likely have been *Neptune*.)

BB36-2   *Action Report – U.S.S. NEVADA (BB36) participation in Bombardment of Cherbourg, 25 June 1944*, BB36/A16-3/A9, Serial 0064, 30 June 1944.

BB56   *Report of Damage Sustained as a Result of Depth Charge Explosions*, BB56/A16-3, Serial 056, 8 May 1942.

BB59   *Report of engagement with JEAN BART, shore batteries, and vessels of the French fleet on November 8, 1942 off Casa Blanca, French Morocco*, BB59/A16, Serial 007, 13 November 1942. (Enclosure A is a chronological log of *Massachusetts'* actions.)

CA31   *Action Report – U.S.S. AUGUSTA – Casablanca-Fedala Area, French Morocco, 8-10 November, 1942*, CA31/A16-3, Serial 00110, 29 November 1942. (Enclosure A is a chronological log of *Augusta's* actions; Enclosure D attempts to account for each of the French vessels involved.)

CL4-1   *German Motor Ship ODENWALD Disguised as S.S. WILLMOTO, United States Registry – Seizure of*, CL4/A16-3(S1)(GCJ), 12 November 1941. (This report and that of *Somers* was found at www.uboatarchive.net/Odenwald.htm)

CL4-2   *Report of Salvage of German Motor Ship Odenwald Flying United States Ensign and Bearing Name "WILLMOTO"*, no serial, 11 November 1941. (This report by Lt George K. Carmichael, who commanded the boarding party and later the prize crew, was an enclosure with *CL4-1*.)

CL4-3   *Unidentified blockade runner, sinking of, on 4 January 1944*, CL4/A8, Serial 03, 7 January 1944.

CL4-4   *German blockade runner, BURGENLAND, Sinking of, on 5 January 1944*, CL4/A8, Serial 04, 8 January 1944.

CL41-1   *Action Report and Report of Operations*, CL41/A16-3, Serial 053, 20 July 1943.

CL41-2   *Damage to U.S.S. PHILADELPHIA from collision with U.S.S LAUB*, CL41/L11-1, Serial 0012, 30 May 1944.

CL42-1   *Report of Action – Interception and scuttling of German Blockade Runner believed to be the 'KOTA TJANDI' ('KARIN') March 10, 1943*, 10 March 1943.

CL42-2   *Report of damage to U.S.S. SAVANNAH from bomb hit on 11 September, 1943*, CL42/L11-1, Serial 009, 14 October 1943.

CL42-3   *U.S.S. SAVANNAH (CL42) BOMB DAMAGE, Gulf of Salerno, Italy, 11 September, 1943*, War Damage Report No. 44, NavShips 44 (424), 15 June, 1944.

CV4   *Operation "LEADER" – Report of*, CV4/A16-3, Serial 0201, 9 October 1943.

CVE13-3   *Report of Antisubmarine Action by Aircraft*, VC-13 Report No. 3, 16 July 1943. (This was part of same sequence of reports as *ACV13-1* and *ACV13-2*, but the ship's hull number was changed from *ACV13* to *CVE13* the day before.)

DD147   *Destruction of German Submarine – Report of*, A9/DD147, Serial 014, 15 April 1942.

DD150   *U.S.S. BLAKELEY – WAR DAMAGE REPORT*, DD150/L11-1, Serial 028, 4 June 1942.

DD381-1 *Capture of German Ship ODENWALD*, 0476, 10 November 1941.

DD381-2 *Action Report, Pursuit and Sinking by Gunfire of German Blockade Runner MS WESERLAND, 1-3 January 1944*, A16-3/DD381, Serial 07, 4 January 1944.

DD381-3 *Action Report, Sinking by Gunfire of Two German Ships - German Corvette COMASCIO and second ship identified as German Corvette ESCABORT*, DD381/A16-3(1)/dct, Serial 00223, 28 August 1944.

DD396   *Action Report – Interception and Sinking of S.S. BURGENLAND, German Blockade Runner*, DD396/A16-3/Mf, Serial 04, 6 January 1944.

DD402-1 *Report of Activities on November 8, 1942*, Enclosure (G)(6), 11 November 1942.

DD402-2 *Report of Action on July 26, 1943*, DD402/A16, Serial 055, 23 August 1943.

DD405   *Report of action with enemy "E" Boats and subsequent sinking of U.S.S. ROWAN (DD405)*, DD405/A16-3, 13 September 1943.

DD424   *Report of Submarine Search and Ultimate Destruction of German Submarine*, DD424/A16-3, Serial 0011, 20 May 1944.

DD427   *Destruction of German Explosive Boat (Drone) and Human Torpedoes – Report of*, DD427/A16-3/A9/he, Serial 41, 12 September 1944.

DD432   *Engagement with submarine while escorting British convoy SC48 at 0010 on October 17, 1941 -report on*, no serial, 20 October 1941.

DD438   *Action Report of U.S.S. LUDLOW during Operation ANZIO*, DD438/A5-1, Serial 0636, 11 February 1944.

DD455   *U.S.S. HAMBLETON Report of Torpedo Damage, November 11, 1942*, DD455/L11-2, Serial 057, 29 November 1942.

DD463   *Action Report and Report of Loss of ship; Submission of, 19 June 1944.*

DD493   *Action Report – 18 August 1944*, DD493/A16/(087), 19 August 1944.

DD495   *Report of Action with Enemy Surface Vessels on 17 August 1944*, 23 August 1944.

DD497   *Action Against MAS Boats – Report of*, DD497/A16/ Serial 008, 19 August 1944.

DD620   *Combined Action and Loss of USS GLENNON in Operation "Neptune" - report on*, DD620/A16/A9, Serial 0008, 23 June 1944.

DD621   *Narrative Action Report of U.S.S. JEFFERS (DD621) for Operation [redacted]*, DD621/A9/A16-3, Serial 00106, 30 June 1944.

DD625   *MAS Boat Action – Report of*, Serial 0026, 22 August 1944.

DD626   *Report of Action, 18 August 1944*, DD626/A16-3, Serial 031, 18 August 1944.

DD640   *Action Report – forwarding of*, 12 November 1943. (This includes the DesRon 15 CO's endorsement letter, dated 30 November 1943.)

DD641   *Action with enemy aircraft, Evening of 6 November, 1943 – Report of*, DD641/A16-3, Serial 045, 15 November 1943.

DD726   *Report of Loss of U.S.S. Meredith (DD726) – Submittal of*, DD726/A16/A9, 20 June 1944.

DE320   *Action Report of U.S.S. MENGES on 3 May, 1944 (against enemy submarine)*, A16-3/CO320, Serial 360-C, 9 May 1944.

Smith   *Report of Scouting and Search of PBY-5 No. AH545 "Catalina" for Bismarck 26 May, 1941*, www.history.navy.mil/faqs/faq118-3.htm.

Sources

Primary Sources – Other (author known)

Cherpak, Evelyn M., Ed., *The Memoirs of Admiral H. Kent Hewitt*, Naval War
  College Press, Newport RI, 2004. (Available online at www.ibiblio.org/anrs/
  docs/1004hewitt_memoirs.pdf.)
Churchill, Winston S., *The Second World War: The Gathering Storm*, Houghton Mifflin
  Company, Boston, MA, 1948.
Churchill, Winston S., *The Second World War: Their Finest Hour*, Houghton Mifflin
  Company, Boston, MA, 1949.
Churchill, Winston S., *The Second World War: The Grand Alliance*, Houghton Mifflin
  Company, Boston, MA, 1950.
Churchill, Winston S., *The Second World War: The Hinge of Fate*, Houghton Mifflin
  Company, Boston, MA, 1950.
Churchill, Winston S., *The Second World War: Closing the Ring*, Houghton Mifflin
  Company, Boston, MA, 1951.
Crapanzano, Angelo, *World War II Oral History*, www.slapton.org/indextiger.htm. (An
  excellent eyewitness account of Exercise TIGER.)
Dönitz, Grand Admiral Karl, *Memoirs: Ten Years and Twenty Days*, Greenhill Books,
  London, 1990.
Eisenhower, General Dwight D., *Crusade in Europe*, Doubleday & Co., Inc., Garden
  City, NY, 1948.
Kirk, Vice-Admiral Alan G., *Oral History – World War II Rhine River Crossing*, 1945,
  www.history.navy.mil/library/online/rhine_kirk.htm
Map Room File, Franklin Delano Roosevelt Library and Museum. (This file contains
  most, but not all, of the correspondence between FDR and WSC during the war.)
Stark, Adm. Harold R., *Memorandum for the Secretary*, 12 November 1940,
  docs.fdrlibrary.marist.edu/psf/box4/a48b01.html. (Popularly known as the
  Plan Dog Memo.)

Primary Sources – Other (author unknown/uncredited)

B.d.U. Op.'s WAR LOG, National Archives & Records Administration, Washington, DC.
Fuehrer Conferences on Naval Affairs, 1939–1945, Greenhill Books, London, 1990.
[Hessler, Günther] *The U-boat War in the Atlantic 1939–1945*, Her Majesty's Stationery
  Office, London, 1989.
OEG Report No. 51, ASW in World War II, Office of CNO. (Available at
  www.ibiblio.org/hyperwar/USN/rep/ASW-51/index.html#contents)
U85-Kriegstagebuch-3rd Patrol.
U156-Kriegstagebuch-3rd Patrol.
U.S. Navy Active Ship Force Levels, 1917–Present, www.history.navy.mil/branches/org9-4.
  htm#1938.
War Diary, North Atlantic Naval Coastal Frontier, December 1941, www.uboatarchive.
  net/ESFWarDiaryDec41.htm.
War Diary, North Atlantic Naval Coastal Frontier, February 1942, www.uboatarchive.
  net/ESFWarDiaryFeb42.htm.
War Diary, North Atlantic Naval Coastal Frontier, March 1942.
War Diary, Eastern Sea Frontier, April 1942.

Secondary Sources (author/editor known)

Abbazia, Patrick, *Mr. Roosevelt's Navy: The Private War of the U.S. Atlantic Fleet, 1939–1942*, Naval Institute Press, Annapolis, MD, 1975.

Angelini, Richard, *Troop Convoy AT-20: August 21, 1942*, http://webspace.webring.com/people/ju/um_10869/at20.html.

Atkinson, Rick, *The Day of Battle: The War in Sicily and Italy, 1943–1944*, Macmillan, New York, 2008.

Bailey, Thomas A., and Paul B. Ryan, *Hitler vs. Roosevelt: The Undeclared Naval War*, The Free Press, New York, 1979.

Blair, Clay, *Hitler's U-Boat War: The Hunters, 1939–1942*, Random House, New York, 1996.

Blair, Clay, *Hitler's U-Boat War: The Hunted, 1942–1945*, Random House, New York, 1998.

Breyer, Siegfried, *Battleships and Battle Cruisers: 1905–1970*, Doubleday & Co., Inc., Garden City, NY, 1973.

Brown, Louis, *Technical and Military Imperatives: A Radar History of World War II*, Taylor & Francis Group, New York, 1999.

Browning, Dr Robert M. Jr, *Coast Guard Makes the First Capture of WWII*, http://www.uscg.mil/history/articles/Northland.asp.

Cernuschi, Enrico and Vincent P. O'Hara, *MAS Contro Destroyers*, in *Storia Militare*, no. 213, June 2011, pp 16–26.

Cressman, Robert J., *The Official Chronology of the U.S. Navy in World War II*, Naval Institute Press, Annapolis, MD, 2000. (The basic reference for the day-to-day activities of the USN.)

Cressman, Robert J., *USS Ranger: The Navy's First Flattop from Keel to Mast, 1934–46*, Potomac Books, Inc., Washington, DC. 2003.

Clifford, Lieutenant Colonel Kenneth J., USMCR, Editor, *The United States Marines in Iceland, 1941–1942*, Historical Div., HQ U.S. Marine Corps, Washington, DC, 1970. (This pamphlet was extracted from a larger work: *History of the United States Marine Corps Operations in World War II*, vol. I.)

Dailey, Franklyn E., Jr, *No 'Abandon Ship' for Ingraham, DD-444: USS Philadelphia, Buck, Bristol Logs, and USS Chemung Court of Inquiry Fill Convoy AT-20 Records Gap*, www.daileyint.com/seawar/apejtwas.htm.

Dixon, Mark E., *The Great Marcus Hook Swindle*, www.mainlinetoday.com/Main-Line-Today/November-2009/The-Great-Marcus-Hook-Swindle/index.php?cparticle=1&siarticle=0#artanc.

Farago, Ladislas, *The Tenth Fleet*, Richardson & Steirman, New York, 1986.

Fisher, Robert C., ' "We'll Get Our Own": Canada and the Oil Shipping Crisis of 1942', in *The Northern Mariner*, vol. III, no. 2, April 1993. (This journal is published by The Canadian Nautical Research Society.)

Friedman, Norman, *U.S. Aircraft Carriers: An Illustrated Design History*, Naval Institute Press, Annapolis, MD, 1983.

Friedman, Norman, *U.S. Destroyers: An Illustrated Design History*, Naval Institute Press, Annapolis, MD, 1982.

Gannon, Michael, *Operation Drumbeat*, HarperCollins Publishers, New York, NY, 1990.

Gibson, Charles Dana, *Ships and Men of the Army Transport Service (ATS)*, http://www.usmm.org/atshistory.html, 1999.

Sources

Hague, Lieutenant Commander Arnold, RNR, *The Supply of Malta 1940–1942*, www.naval-history.net/xAH-MaltaSupply01.htm.

Hansen, Kenneth P., 'King, Canada, and the Convoys: A Reappraisal of Adm. Ernest King's Role in Operation Drumbeat', in Maochun Miles Yu (ed.), *New Interpretations in Naval History: Selected Papers from the Fifteenth Naval History Symposium*, Naval Institute Press, Annapolis, MD, 2009.

Hickam, Homer H., Jr, *Torpedo Junction*, Naval Institute Press, Annapolis, MD, 1989.

Jordan, Winston, *Man Overboard!*, Proceedings of the US Naval Institute, Annapolis, MD, Dec. 1987. (This article was found reproduced at the excellent USS *Washington* website at http://usswashington.com/moverbrd.htm.)

Kemp, Paul, *U-Boats Destroyed: German Submarine Losses in the World Wars*, Arms & Armour Press, London, 1997.

Kolbicz, Rainer, *U-boat attacks on convoy SC-48 and the mysterious loss of HMS GLADIOLUS during the night of 16/17 October 1941*, http://www.uboat.net/articles/73.html, 23 May 2010.

Kolkman, Donald, 'US Rationing during WWII', *International Journal of Rationing*, vol. 1, no. 1, 2009.

Lavelle, Jim, *U.S.S. GUNNEL SS-253: First War Patrol October 19, 1942–December 7, 1942*, http://www.jmlavelle.com/gunnel/patrol1.htm.

Layton, Rear-Admiral Edwin T., USN, *And I Was There: Pearl Harbor and Midway - Breaking the Secrets*, Naval Institute Press, Annapolis, MD, 2006.

Medoff, Rafael, 'Megillat Hitler,' FDR, and the Jews, in *Jerusalem Post*, 25 March 2011, www.wymaninstitute.org/articles/2011-3-megillat-hitler.php.

Miller, Kieth, *How Important Was Oil in World War II?*, 11 October 2001, hnn.us/articles/339.html.

Mordal, Jacques, *La Bataille Navale de Casablanca*, in *La Revue*, no. 18, 15 September 1950, pp. 227–53 and no. 19, 1 October 1950, pp. 434–60.

Morison, Samuel E., *History of United States Naval Operations in World War II*, vol. I: *The Battle of the Atlantic September 1939-May 1943*, Little, Brown and Co., Boston, 1947.

Morison, Samuel E., *History of United States Naval Operations in World War II*, vol. II: *Operations in North African Waters October 1942–June 1943*, Little, Brown and Co., Boston, 1947.

Morison, Samuel E., *History of United States Naval Operations in World War II*, vol. IX: *Sicily–Salerno–Anzio January 1943-June 1944*, Little, Brown and Co., Boston, 1954.

Morison, *History of United States Naval Operations in World War II*, vol. X: *The Atlantic Battle Won May 1943–May 1945*, Little, Brown and Co., Boston, 1956.

Morison, Samuel E., *History of United States Naval Operations in World War II*, vol. XI: *The Invasion of France and Germany 1944-1945*, Little, Brown and Co., Boston, 1957.

Niestlé, Axel, *German U-boat Losses during World War II: Details of Destruction*, Naval Institute Press, Annapolis, MD, 1998.

O'Connor, Jerome M., 'FDR's Undeclared War', *Naval History*, vol. 18, no. 1, US Naval Institute, Annapolis, MD, February 2004.

O'Hara, Vincent P., *The U.S. Navy against the Axis: Surface Combat 1941–1945*, Naval Institute Press, Annapolis, MD, 2007.

O'Hara, Vincent P., *Struggle for the Middle Sea: The Great Navies at War in the Mediterranean Theater, 1940–1945*, Naval Institute Press, Annapolis, MD, 2009.

O'Hara, Vincent P., *The Battle of Casablanca: The Marine Nationale versus the U.S. Navy*, in *Warship 2011*, John Jordan (ed.), Naval Institute Press, Annapolis, MD, 2011.

Olson, Lynne, *Citizens of London*, Random House, New York, NY, 2010.

Parkin, Robert Sinclair, *Blood on the Sea: American Destroyers Lost in World War II*, Da Capo Press, Cambridge, MA, 2001.

Paterson, Lawrence, *Hitler's Grey Wolves: U-Boats in the Indian Ocean*, Greenhill Books, London, 2004.

Petrie, Captain John N., USN, *American Neutrality in the 20th Century: The Impossible Dream*, McNair Paper 33, Institute for National Strategic Studies, National Defense University, Washington DC, January 1995.

Rohwer, Jürgen, *Axis Submarine Successes 1939–1945*, Naval Institute Press, Annapolis, MD, 1983.

Rohwer, Jürgen, *Chronology of the War at Sea 1939–1945: The Naval History of World War Two*, Naval Institute Press, Annapolis, MD, 2005.

Roscoe, Theodore, *United States Destroyer Operations in World War II*, Naval Institute Press, Annapolis, MD, 1953.

Rössler, Eberhard, *The U-boat: The Evolution and Technical History of German Submarines*, Naval Institute Press, Annapolis, MD, 1989.

Sage, Henry J., *Background to World War II: American Foreign Policy 1920–1941*, http://www.academicamerican.com/worldwar2/topics/1920WWII1940.htm, 3 November 2006.

Scarborough, Captain William E., USN (Ret.), 'The Neutrality Patrol: To Keep Us Out of World War II?', *Naval Aviation News*, March–April 1990.

Sebag-Montefiore, Hugh, *Enigma: The Battle for the Code*, John Wiley & Sons, Inc., Hoboken, NJ, 2000.

Smith, Gordon, *World War I at Sea: United States Navy*, http://www.naval-history.net/WW1NavyUS.htm, 9 January 2009.

Svonavec, Stephen, *Fleet Organization Web Site*, http://www.fleetorganization.com/index.html, 2009.

Tarrant, V. E., *The U-Boat Offensive 1914–1945*, Arms & Armour Press, London, 1989.

— *The Last Year of the Kriegsmarine: May 1944–May 1945*, Arms & Armour Press, London, 1994.

Taylor, Theodore, *Fire on the Beaches*, W. W. Norton & Co., New York, 1958.

Thomas, Martin, 'After Mers-el-Kébir: The Armed Neutrality of the Vichy French Navy, 1940–43', *The English Historical Review*, vol. 112, no. 447, Oxford University Press, Oxford, June 1997.

Tilley, John A., *The Coast Guard & the Greenland Patrol*, http://www.uscg-iip.org/cms/index.php?option=com_content&view=article&id=83&Itemid=68. (Despite the '.org' tag, this is an official US Coast Guard site, supporting the International Ice Patrol.)

Wales, Charles C., *Time Line of Attack on Convoy UGS 38 and Sinking of USS Lansdale DD426 – 20 April 1944*, 10 January 2011, http://home.roadrunner.com/~cwales/Time%20Line%20html.html.

Whitley, M. J., *German Coastal Forces of World War Two*, Arms & Armour Press, London, 1992.

Widner, James F., *The Bombing of Pearl Harbor*, http://www.otr.com/r-a-i-new_pearl.shtml, 29 July 2010.

Winton, John, ULTRA *at Sea*, William Morrow & Co., New York, 1988.

Wynn, Kenneth, *U-Boat Operations of the Second World War*, vol. 1: *Career Histories, U1–U510*, Caxton Editions, 2003.

Sources

Wynn, Kenneth, *U-Boat Operations of the Second World War,* vol. 2: *Career Histories, U511–UIT25,* Caxton Editions, 2003.

Secondary Sources (author unknown/uncredited)

Harry Hopkins: President Franklin D Roosevelt's Deputy President,
 http://www.historynet.com/harry-hopkins-president-franklin-d-roosevelts-deputy-president.htm.
Q-Ships (Anti-submarine vesels disguised as merchant vessels),
 http://www.history.navy.mil/docs/wwii/q-ships.htm.
Ten Minutes to Abandon Ship! SS Washington in Stand-Off With U-Boat!,
 http://www.usmm.org/washington.html.
The Exercise Tiger National Foundation,
 http://www.exercisetiger.org/.

Indispensable Sites

These are sites I referenced constantly during the writing of this and many other books.

Arnold Hague Convoy Database, www.convoyweb.org.uk/hague/index.html.
 (Very nearly complete coverage of Atlantic convoys.)
Destroyer History Foundation, www.destroyerhistory.org/destroyers/index.html.
 (Comprehensive coverage of USN destroyers, particularly those that fought in WWII.)
Dictionary of American Naval Fighting Ships, www.history.navy.mil/danfs/index.html.
 (The entries in this immense effort vary considerably in detail and completeness. For the most part, though, it's an excellent first reference for any USN ship.)
Naval-History.Net, www.naval-history.net/xGM-aContents.htm.
 (An invaluable resource for RN ships' histories.)
NavWeaps: Naval Weapons, Naval Technology and Naval Reunions, www.navweaps.com/.
 (This site covers, in magnificent detail, very nearly all the weapons used by the world's navies in the twentieth century, excepting aviation ordnance.)
Ships in Atlantic Convoys, www.warsailors.com/convoys/index.html.
uboat.net: 1995-2010, uboat.net/index.html.
 (Covers not only U-boats, but also their victims. Highly recommended.)
U-boat Archive, www.uboatarchive.net.
 (Extremely useful site run by Captain Jerry Mason, USN (Ret) and his wife. It contains many original reports related to the Battle of the Atlantic.)
Cutters, Craft & Coast Guard-manned Army & Navy Vessels, www.uscg.mil/history/webcutters/CUTTERLIST.asp.
American Merchant Marine at War, www.usmm.org.
The Second World War – A Day by Day Account, homepage.ntlworld.com/andrew.etherington/index.html.
 (This useful chronology of the war combines a number of sources.)

Index

Merchant ships are identified as to nationality with ISO two-letter nation codes in parentheses (cf. http//:www.worldatlas.com/aatlas/ctycodes.htm). Places in the US and Canada are identified by standard two-letter state or province designators. US warship names are followed by hull number; all other warship names and all class names are followed by a navy designator and a hull type designator in parentheses. Besides USN and RN, navy designators used below are: RAN – Australia, RCN – Canada, KM – Germany, MN – France, IJN – Japan, RM – Italy, RNeN – Netherlands and RNoN – Norway. Naval personnel are identified as to service with the same navy designators. (Note: I have made no effort to distinguish reserve from regular naval personnel.) Page references to captions are in **bold** face.